EVERYTHIN

CLOSE TO THE MOTORWAY

IMPROVE YOUR JOURNEY AND SAVE MONEY

2004 Edition

Published by Milcot Publishing

First Edition- Published by Milcot Publishing Limited in 2003

Wellesley House
7 Clarence Parade
Cheltenham
Gloucestershire
GL50 3NY

www.closetothemotorway.co.uk

NOTICE OF LIABILITY

The information in this book is believed to be correct at time of press, but no liability can be accepted for any loss or damage arising from the contents. Some of the information in this book, in particular prices, must be assumed to be only a rough guide. Prices, especially for fuel and hotels, can change on a daily basis. Also, hotels quote prices in a way that does not always allow easy comparison, and have prices which are open to negotiation.

ACKNOWLEDGEMENTS

Thanks to Margaret Adams, Steve Evans, Alan Pool, Steve Dalby, Viv Marsh and Terry Vernon from BGP Printers, Simon Buck at Clowes, Mick Boulter and John Rout of Essex Ambulance Service, Diane Roodt of Corus Hotels and Claire Hall from Webb's of Wychbold.

COVER DESIGN

Many thanks to Colin Nightingale at Lunatrix

Printed by Clowes of Beccles

FEEDBACK

We welcome your feedback and suggestions on this book or notification of any corrections needed. Please send an e-mail to feedback@closetothemotorway.co.uk or write to us at the address above.

ISBN 0-9546085-0-X

Contents

Introduction

Britain's motorways can be great for getting places in a hurry, but often you need to take a break. For instance, have you ever experienced any of the following?:-

- Wanted to eat somewhere other than a motorway service area?
- Wanted to buy petrol but discovered the next service area is miles away?
- Wanted to know if there were any things to see en-route?
- Wanted to get off the motorway for a short stroll?
- Wanted to get medicine whilst travelling?
- Wanted to avoid paying motorway prices for fuel?
- Wanted to phone a nearby Tourist Information Centre?
- Wanted to get off the motorway for a while to let the traffic subside?
- Needed to buy a new tyre or an exhaust whilst on the motorway?
- Been tired and wanted to find a hotel 3-4 junctions away?
- Planned a business trip and needed to select a hotel en-route?
- Wanted to know what services were available at a motorway service area?
- Been stuck in a snowstorm and wished you could find a hotel?
- Needed to find a hospital whilst travelling on the motorway?
- Wanted a hotel near the motorway where you can hold a meeting?
- Wanted to know where you can find shopping facilities close to the motorway?
- Wanted to find an telephone number for a car rescue company or a hotel chain?
- Wanted to know what information to collect in the event of an accident?
- Wanted somewhere handy to record tyre pressures and other car details?

If you can answer yes to any of these questions Close to the Motorway is just the thing you need. It's small enough to store in your car, and its layout makes it easy to find the facility you are after. Best of all it's great value, so don't worry about writing your own notes in the book to make it even more useful.

We trust you find this an essential tool that makes your motorway driving much more enjoyable and productive.

Understanding the Guide

HOW FAR DO WE STRAY FROM JUNCTIONS?

We assume that people using this guide do not have the time to explore far from the motorway, so generally we cover up to 1 mile from a junction. In very built-up areas, the range may be restricted to less than a mile, as travelling times are longer. On occasions we cover a range of up to 2 miles from a junction, if we think it is particularly worthwhile.

MAPS

Most junctions have maps to show directions to the facilities mentioned. The maps use the conventions shown on the right. Where necessary, additional directions are given in the text.

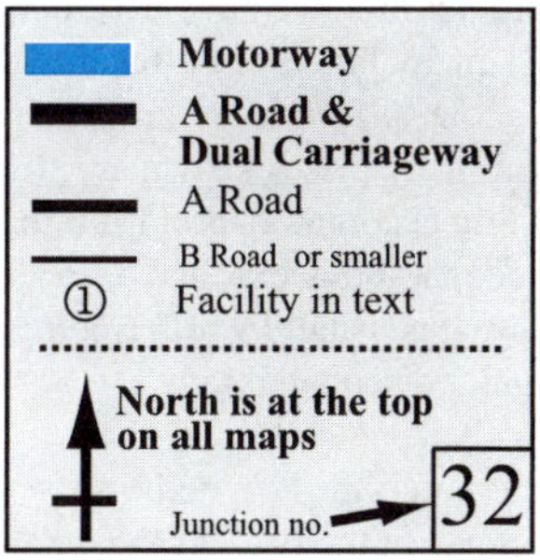

PRICES AND PRICE INDICATORS

Fuel Prices:-The competitiveness of filling stations relative to motorway service stations is indicated by the following symbols:- **SAVE** ££££. The more ££s the better up to our maximum of 4.
Most filling stations try to maintain their relative competiteveness over the long term so the price guide should give a good indication of prices on the day you visit.

Food Prices:-The prices given for food are rough guidelines for the price of a main course meal. Where lunch and dinner are offered, the higher price of the two is generally quoted. Prices do not include drinks and service charges.

Hotel Prices:- The prices given for hotels are typical prices for a double room during midweek, and are rounded up to the nearest pound. Where breakfast is included this is mentioned in the text. See the section on hotels for more information.

PUBS

Please note that some pubs are omitted from the guide, usually because they concentrate mainly on providing drinks, rather than food. For more information see 'Restaurants'.

RESTAURANTS

Restaurant & pub opening times show the times at which food is available. In many cases the facility in question may well open longer hours for drinks.
We have not commented on which facilities provide vegetarian food, as all outlets provide at least one option for vegetarians.
Please note that some facilities are omitted from this guide in order to make it more readable and concise. This includes pubs that provide little or no food, some very small outlets such as fish and chip shops, and some other facilities at junctions where a good range of food outlets have already been described. In this latter event motorists will be able to drive around in the knowledge that there is plenty of choice at hand. We also omit some hotel restaurants from the food sections in order to keep the guide concise, but this is no reflection on their quality. Most hotel restaurants will be open every day for breakfasts and dinners, and on most days for lunch.

Where restaurants are marked by a ☞ symbol please consult the 'Restaurant, Hotel & Meeting Directory' at the back of the guide for more information.

We have not classified restaurants & pubs in terms of quality but our experience is that you get what you pay for. In this respect, our price indicators are very useful to help you select where to eat. For more information, please see under Prices.

HOTELS

Prices given for hotels are typical prices for a double room during midweek, and are rounded up to the nearest pound. Where breakfast is included this is mentioned in the text.

Where possible we have tried to quote 'typical midweek rates' for a double room. Unfortunately many hotels are often unwilling to quote a 'typical' price for a room. Instead, some will quote 'prices from' and others will quote 'rack rates' or maximum rates. For this reason many prices shown are 'from' prices or 'rack rates'. Please bear this in mind when selecting accommodation from the guide, as some hotels may well offer a large discount on a price that looks expensive, especially if occupancy is low or if there is a competing hotel nearby. It is usually worth ringing a few of the more expensive looking hotels to see if you can get a discounted rate.

Where hotels are denoted by a ☞ symbol please consult the 'Restaurant, Hotel & Meeting Directory' at the back of the guide for more information, or for a central reservations number.

In the case of hotel chains we give the 'hotel location'. This is the location you cite when you phone the Central Reservations to make a booking.

THINGS TO DO

This guide concentrates on things to do which are very close to the motorway. In general we assume people will just be looking for a quick break from their journey. In exceptional cases we will mention facilities and towns further away, if we consider they offer lots of facilities or are of particular interest to travellers.

TOP SPOTS

In the summary of each motorway we give a brief overview of the facilities near each junction. Those junctions with shading are 'top spots' for stopping, and they will have relatively good facilities or perhaps a good range. In the case of fuel they will offer larger discounts than at other junctions.

TOURIST INFORMATION CENTRES

Tourist Information Centres can provide a wealth of information and cover a wide area. For this reason we add entries for Tourist Information Centres even though they are often quite a distance from a junction. You probably won't want to drive to these and so no addresses are given. Call these Information Centres if you want to book accommodation in nearby towns or cities, or to ask about tourist information in general.

HOSPITALS

We give details of hospitals where they provide Accident and Emergency or Minor Injury Departments. Generally we will include hospitals if they are within about 10 miles of a junction. At the start and end of motorways, however, the nearest hospital may be in excess of 10 miles away.

SYMBOLS

Please note we deliberately avoids the use of symbols to make the guide easier to use.

YOUR FEEDBACK

We welcome any feedback on this guide and how to make it more useful and accurate. If you have any comments please send them to us by one of the following methods.

E-Mail- www.closetothemotorway.co.uk
Letters- Customer Service Dept, Milcot Publishing, Welleseley House, 7 Clarence Parade, Cheltenham, Gloucestershire, GL50 3NY

M1-London to Leeds

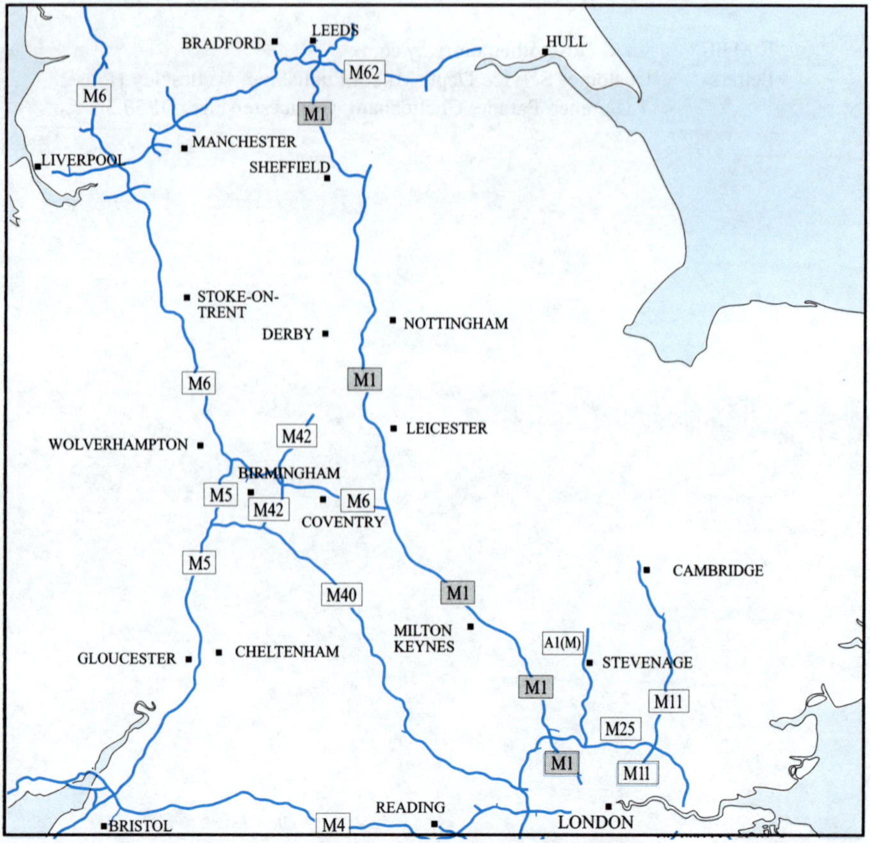

M1-Summary of Junctions

Radio stations & frequencies		Junction	Fuel	Food	Hotels	Essentials	Things to do
Capital 95.8 Magic 105.4	LBC 97.3 Heart 106.2	1	24hr	✓	✓	A&E TIC	✓
Capital 95.8 KISS 100	LBC 97.3 Magic 105.4	2				A&E Svc	
Capital 95.8 KISS 100	LBC 97.3 Magic 105.4	S	24hr	✓	✓		
Capital 95.8 Magic 105.4	LBC 97.3 Heart 106.2	4	24hr	✓		A&E	✓
Mercury 96.6 3CR 103.8	Chiltern 97.6 Magic 105.8	5	24hr	✓	✓	A&E Pharmacy	✓
Mercury 96.6 BBC 3CR 103.8	LBC 97.3 Magic 105.8	6	24hr	✓	✓	A&E	✓
Mercury 96.6 BBC 3CR 103.8	LBC 97.3 Magic 105.8	6A					✓
Mercury 96.6 BBC 3CR 103.8	LBC 97.3 Magic 105.8	7					
Mercury 96.6 BBC 3CR 103.8	Magic 105.8 Hertbeat 106.9	8	24hr	✓	✓	A&E, TIC Pharmacy	
KISS 100 BBC 3CR 103.8	Chiltern 97.6	9	24hr	✓	✓		
XFM 104.9 BBC 3CR 103.8	KISS 100 Chiltern 97.6	10		✓	✓	Svc	✓
BBC 3CR 103.8	Horizon 103.3	11	24hr	✓	✓	A&E Svc TIC	
BBC 3CR 103.8	Chiltern 97.6	S	24hr	✓	✓		
BBC 3CR 103.8	Chiltern 97.6	12	✓	✓		Svcs, Pharmacy	
BBC 3CR 104.5	Horizon 103.3	13	24hr	✓		A&E Svcs	✓
BBC 3CR 103.8	Horizon 103.3	14	24hr	✓	✓	A&E TIC	
3CR 103.8	Horizon 103.3	S	24hr	✓	✓		
Nthmptn 104.2 Northants 96.0	Horizon 103.3 3CR 104.5	15	24hr	✓	✓	A&E TIC	
Nthmptn 104.2 Northants 96.0	Horizon103.3	15a S	24hr	✓	✓	A&E	

Top Stops are highlighted

Radio stations & frequencies		Junction	Fuel	Food	Hotels	Essentials	Things to do
Nthmptn 104.2	Northants 96.0	16	✓	✓	✓	A&E TIC	
Nthmptn 104.2	Northants 96.0	S	24hr	✓	✓		
Heart FM 100.7 BBC WM 95.6	Mercia 97.0 Saga 105.7	17					
Rugby 107.1 Heart FM 100.7	Lstr Snd 105.4 Century 106.0	18		✓	✓	A&E	
BBC WM 95.6 BBC 3CR 103.8	Lstr Snd 105.4 Rugby 107.1	19					
Mercia 97.0 Fosseway 107.9	Leicstr 104.9 Lstr Snd 105.4	20	24hr	✓	✓	Pharmacy	✓
Century 106.0 Takeover 103.2	Saga 106.6 Leicstr 104.9	21	24hr	✓	✓	A&E TIC	✓
Mercia 97 Takeover 103.2	Century 106.0 Lstr Snd 105.4	S	24hr	✓	✓	Pharmacy	
Takeover 103.2 Century 106.0	Leicstr 104.9 WM 104.9	21a				TIC	
Mercia 97 Takeover 103.2	WM 104.9 Leicstr 104.9	22 S	24hr	✓	✓	TIC	
Saga 106.6 Century 106.0	Leicstr 107.6 Leicstr 104.9	23	24 Hr (Diesel)	✓	✓		
Notts 104.9 Century 106.0	Lstr Snd 105.4 Saga 106.6	23a S	24hr	✓	✓		✓
Oak 107 Saga 106.6	Notts 104.9 Century 106.0	24			✓		
Oak 107 Saga 106.6	Notts 104.9 Century 106.0	24a			✓	A&E	
Oak 107 Saga 106.6	Century 106 Notts 104.9	25	✓	✓	✓	A&E TIC	
Notts 104.9 Saga 106.6	Oak 107.0 Century 106	S	24hr	✓	✓		
Notts 104.9 Saga 106.6	Oak 107.0 Century 106	26	24hr	✓	✓	A&E TIC	
Saga 106.6 Leics Snd 105.4	Notts 104.9 Real 106.2	27					
Derby 95.5 Century 106	2-Ten 102.8 Notts 104.9	28	24hr	✓	✓	A&E	✓
Saga 101.4 Century 106	2-Ten 102.8 Notts 104.9	S	24hr	✓	✓		
Peak 107.4 Real 106.2	Notts 95.5 Saga 105.7	29	✓	✓	✓	A&E	

Radio stations & frequencies		Junction	Fuel	Food	Hotels	Essentials	Things to do
Peak 107.4 Sheff 94.7	Notts 95.5 Real 106.2	30	✓	✓	✓	A&E TIC	✓
Real 107.7 Saga 106.6	Sheff 94.7 Galaxy 105.1	S	24hr	✓	✓	TIC	
Real 107.7 Saga 106.6	Sheff 94.7 Galaxy 105.1	31	24hr		✓	Svc	
Real 107.7 Saga 106.6	Sheff 94.7 Galaxy 105.1	32					
Real 106.2 Galaxy 105.6	Sheff 104.1	33	24hr		✓	A&E TIC	
BBC RFM 89.3	Real 106.2	34	24hr	✓	✓	A&E, TIC	✓
Real 106.2 Hallam 102.9	Sheff 88.6 Leeds 92.4	35	24hr	✓		A&E TIC	
Real 106.2 Hallam 102.9	Sheff 88.6 Leeds 92.4	35a	24hr	✓	✓		
Real 106.2 Sheff 104.1	Hallam 102.9 Galaxy 105.1	36	24hr	✓	✓	Svc Pharmacy	
BBC Leeds 92.4 Sheff 104.1	Hallam 102.9 Galaxy 105.1	37	24hr	✓	✓	A&E TIC	
Real 106.2 Minster 104.7	York 103.7 Galaxy 105.1	38					✓
Real 106.2 Minster 104.7	York 103.7 Galaxy 105.1	S	24hr	✓	✓		
Leeds 92.4 Rad Aire 96.3	Pulse! 102.5 Galaxy 105.1	39	✓	✓	✓	A&E Svc	✓
Ridings 106.8 Galaxy 105.6	Leeds 92.4 Real 106.2	40	24hr	✓	✓	A&E Svc, TIC	
Ridings 106.8 Galaxy 105.6	Leeds 92.4 Real 106.2	41	24hr	✓		A&E	
Ridings 106.8 Galaxy 105.6	Leeds 92.4 Real 106.2	42					
Ridings 106.8 Galaxy 105.6	Leeds 92.4 Real 106.2	43				A&E TIC	
Minster 104.7 Galaxy 105.6	Leeds 92.4 Real 106.2	44		✓		A&E Svc, TIC	
Ridings 106.8 Galaxy 105.6	Leeds 92.4 Real 106.2	45					
Humb 95.9 Pulse! 102.5	Rad Aire 96.3 Leeds 92.4	46	24hr	✓	✓	A&E TIC	
Viking 96.9 York 103.7	Century 106.0	47	✓	✓		Svc	
Viking 96.9 York 103.7	Century 106.0	48	Motorway Ends			TIC	

M1 Junction Details

M1 Junction 1
Wembley

FUEL

Tesco SAVE £££ 0.5m ①
Open- *Daily 24 hours*
Info- *Carwash. WC at store.*
Tel- *0845 677 9073*

FOOD

Tesco Cafe☞ £3.50 0.5m ①
Open- *M-W 0800-1800, Th-Sa 0800-2000, Sun 1100-1700*
Info- *Cash machine at store*
Tel- *0208 219 7700*

Others 0.3m ③
Open- *M-F 1000-1730, Sat 0900-1830, Sun 1100-1630*
Info- *Several cafes at Brent Cross.*
Tel- *0208 202 8095*

ACCOMMODATION

Holiday Inn☞ £160 0.4m ②
Info- *Restaurant & bar. Brent Cross location*
Tel- *0208 201 8686*

ESSENTIALS

Royal Free Hospital 5.2m
Dir'n- *From M1 go east along the North Circular and then right down Golders Green Road (A502). Drive past Hampstead tube station, then turn left down Rosslyn Hill. Turn left on Pond Street and the Royal Free is on the right.*
Tel- *0207 794 0500*

Islington Tourist Information Centre
Tel- *0207 278 8787*

THINGS TO DO

Brent Cross Shopping Centre 0.3m ③
Open- *M-F 1000-1800, Sat 0900-1900, Sun 1100-1700*
Info- *North London's major shopping centre.*
Tel- *0208 202 8095*

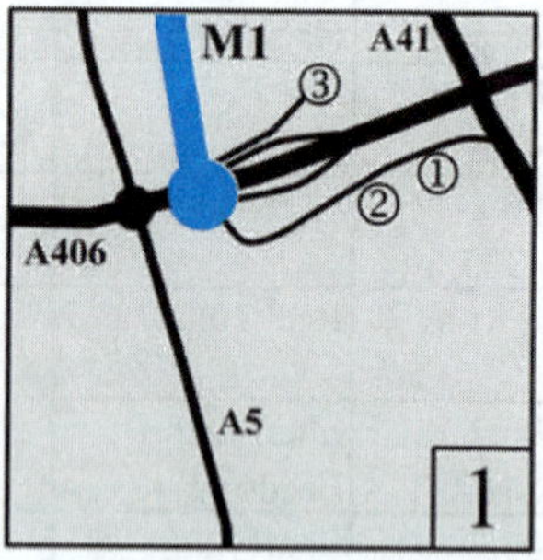

M1 Junction 2
Restricted

Exit only from the southbound direction, and enter only to the southbound direction.

ESSENTIALS

Barnet Hospital 5.5m
Dir'n- *From exit take the A1 northbound. Turn right along A411, then hospital is on the right in Wellhouse Lane.*
Tel- *0208 216 4000*

Northway Tyres 0.9m ①
Open- *Daily 0830-1800*
Info- *Tyres, exhausts, brakes, shocks, etc*
Tel- *0208 203 5292*

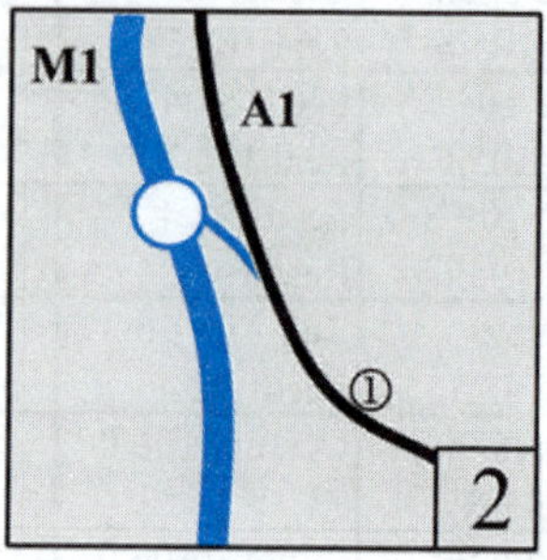

M1 Junction 3
Non-existent

London Gateway Services

This services has a roadbridge & footbridge.

FUEL SHELL

Cash machines, carwash, HGV fuelling

FOOD WELCOME BREAK

The Granary, Burger King, bakery

Info- *Cash machine*

ACCOMMODATION

Days Inn☞ £69

Info- *Restaurant & bar. London Gateway location*

Tel- *0208 906 0611*

M1 Junction 4
Restricted

Exit only to the southbound direction, and entrance only to the northbound direction.

FUEL

Esso SAVE £££ 1m ①

Open- *Daily 24 hours*

Info- *Carwash, cash machines, WC*

Tel- *0208 958 8166*

FOOD

McDonald's☞ £3.50 1m ①

Open- *M-W 0800-1800, Th-Sat 0800-2000, Sun 1100-1700*

Tel- *0208 958 3482*

ESSENTIALS

Barnet Hospital 5m

Dir'n- *From exit follow A41 south, then A1 north. Turn right along A411, then hospital is on the right in Wellhouse Lane.*

Tel- *0208 216 4000*

THINGS TO DO

RAF Museum Free 4m

Open- *Daily 1000-1800*

Info- *National air museum.*

Dir'n- *Drive south on the A41 and follow signs.*

Tel- *0208 205 2266*

Aldenham Country Park Free 3.5m ②

Open- *Daily 0900-1700*

Info- *Park & nature reserve.*

Dir'n- *From exit follow signs to A5183 north, Left on A411, then right to entrance on Aldenham road.*

Tel- *0208 953 9602*

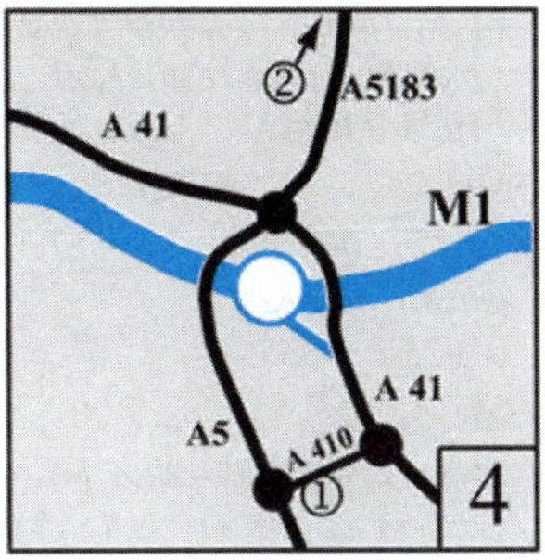

M1 Junction 5
Watford

FUEL

Total SAVE ££££ 0.7m ①

Open- *Daily 24 hours.*

Info- *Car wash*

Tel- *01923 699560*

Asda SAVE ££££ 1.5m ②

Open- *Between Mon 0800 to Sat 1000, Sun 1000-1600*

Dir'n- *Exit A41 before the roundabout.*

Tel- *01923 250380*

Shell SAVE ££££ 1.5m ③

Open- *Daily 24 hours*

Info- *LPG, carwash, WC*

Tel- *01923 800920*

BP SAVE ££££ 1.5m ③

Open- *Daily 24 hours*

Info- *WC*

Tel- *01923 672129*

Sainsbury Exp. SAVE ££££ 1.5m ③

Open- *Daily 24 hours*

Info- *LPG, cash machine, carwash.*

Tel- *01923 681984*

Tesco SAVE ££££ 1.5m ④

Open- *Daily 24 hours*

Info- *WC, carwash, cash machines at store.*

Tel- *01923 486445*

FOOD

Toby Inn☞ £7.00 0.6m ⑤

Open- *Daily 1200-2200*

Tel- *01923 225826*

Quincey's Bar/Grill £9.00 0.6m ⑥

Open- *M-Sa 1200-2300, Sun 1200-1030*

Info- *American style restaurant*

Tel- *01923 229137*

Pizza Hut☞ £6.70 1.5m ③

Open- *Su-Th1200-2200, F-Sa 1200-2300*

Info- *Cash machine*

Tel- *01923 680055*

Asda Cafe☞ £3.00 1.5m ②

Open- *M-Sat 0800-2000, Sun 1000-1500*

Info- *Cash machines at the store. This store is very large and supplies a wide range of goods.*

Tel- *01923 250 380*

Tesco Cafe☞ £3.50 1.5m ④

Open- *M-Sat 0800-2000, Sun 0930-1600*

Info- *Cash machines at the store*

Tel- *0845 677 9702*

ACCOMMODATION

Hilton Hotel☞ £99 0.7m ⑦

Info- *Restaurant & bar. Watford location*

Tel- *01923 235881*

Premier Lodge☞ £55 1.6m ⑧

Info- *Watford location*

Tel - *0870 9906620*

Dir'n- *Approach by turning left just after reaching the Harlequin Centre roundabout.*

ESSENTIALS

Watford General Hospital 2.3m

Tel- *01923 244366*

Dir'n- *Drive towards Premier Lodge but go around the Harlequin Centre roundabout. Turn onto Vicarage Road on west side of roundabout. Hospital is on Vicarage Road on left hand side.*

Asda Instore Pharmacy 1.5m ②

Open- *M-F 0930-1730, Sat 0930-1700, Sun 1000-1600*

Tel- *01923 219060*

THINGS TO DO

Watford Junction Station 1.4m

Info- *4 trains an hour to London Euston. Journey about 20 minutes, £10 standard return*

Dir'n- *Station is signposted as you head towards Premier Lodge.*

Tel - *0845 722 5444*

Harlequin Centre 1.6m ⑨

Open- *M-Sa 0900-1800, Sun 1100-1700*

Info- *A wide range of shops and restaurants all close to the motorway. Use the car parks, which are well signposted.*

Tel- *01923 250292*

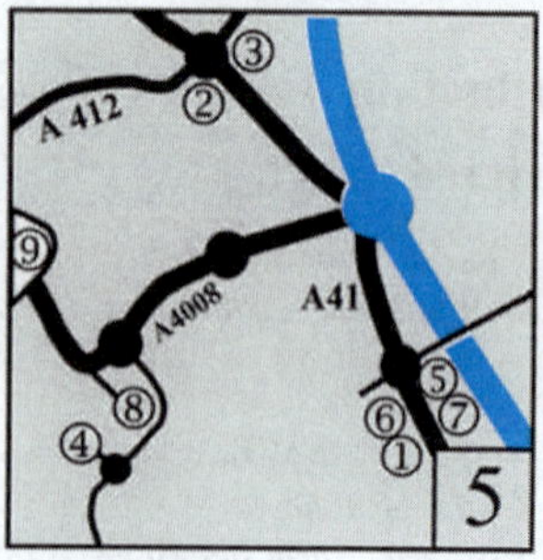

M1 Junction 6
Abbots Langley

FUEL

Shell SAVE £££ 0.8m ①

Open- *Daily 24 hours*

Info- *WC, carwash*

Tel- *01923 819900*

Total SAVE ££££ 0.7m ②

Open- *Daily 24 hours*

Info- *WC, carwash*

Tel- *01923 680024*

Esso SAVE ££££ 2m ③

Open- *Daily 24 hours*

Info- *WC*

Tel- *01923 663915*

FOOD

Little Chef☞ £6.50 0.1m ④
Open- *Daily 0700-2200*
Tel- *01923 661842*

Harvester☞ £6.50 0.9m ⑤
Open- *Su-F 1200-2130, Sat 1200-2200*
Tel- *01923 672061*

TGIF☞ £11 1.1m ⑥
Open- *Daily 1200-2300*
Tel- *01923 672310*
Dir'n- *Enter via A412, just before the parade of shops on the left hand side.*

Chiquito☞ £8.50 1.7m ⑦
Open- *M-Sat 1200-2300, Sun 1200-2130*
Tel- *01923 682321*

Frankie & Benny's☞ £8.50 1.7m ⑦
Open- *M-F 1200-2300, Sat 1400-2230*
Tel- *01923 662690*

Others
Info- *The arcade just beyond TGIF has a fish & chip shop, sandwich bar, and a Chinese takeaway.*

ACCOMMODATION

Thistle Hotel☞ £113 0.8m ⑧
Info- *On-site restaurant & bar. St Albans location*
Tel- *0870 333 9144*

Travel Inn☞ £55 1.1m ⑥
Info- *Watford location. Next to TGIF.*
Dir'n- *Enter via A412, before the parade of shops on the left hand side.*
Tel- *0870 197 7261*

ESSENTIALS

Watford General 4.5m
Dir'n- *Head to Watford on A405, and the hospital is well signposted.*
Tel- *01923 244366*

St Albans Tourist Information Centre
Tel- *01727 864511*

THINGS TO DO

St Albans City Centre 3.5m
Info- *If heading northbound visit the historic town of St Albans, which has a cathedral, remains of a Roman settlement, and a pleasant shopping area. Traffic can be heavy at peak times.*

M1 Junction 6A
M1/M25 interchange

M1 Junction 7
M1/M10 interchange

St Albans Tourist Information Centre
Tel- *01727 864511*

THINGS TO DO

St Albans City Centre
Info- *If heading southbound visit the historic town of St Albans, which has a cathedral, remains of a Roman settlement, and a pleasant shopping area. Traffic can be heavy at peak times.*

M1 Junction 8
Hemel Hempstead

FUEL

BP SAVE ££ 0.2m ①
Open- *Daily 24 hours*
Info- *LPG, WC*
Tel- *01442 269003*

Shell SAVE ££ 0.8m ②
Open- *Daily 24 hours*
Info- *HGVs, WC, carwash, cash machine*
Tel- *01442 275010*

Tesco SAVE ££ 1.8m ③
Open- *Daily 24 hours*
Info- *WC at store.*
Tel- *01442 420445*

FOOD

Tesco Cafe☞ £3.50 1.8m ③
Open- *M-F 0800-1800, Sun 1000-1600*
Info- *Cash machine*
Tel- *0845 677 9349*

Leather Bottle £7.00 0.9m ④
Open- *Daily 1200-2100*
Info- *Village pub with varied hot & cold meals.*
Tel- *01442 253463*

ACCOMMODATION

Holiday Inn☞ £135 0.3m ⑤
Info- *Bar & restaurant. Hemel Hempstead location*
Tel- *0870 400 9041*

ESSENTIALS

Hemel General 3m
Dir'n- *Follow signs to Hemel Hempstead, and the A&E is well signposted.*
Tel- *01442 213141*

Village Pharmacy 0.9m ④
Open- *M-Sat 0900-1700*
Tel- *01442 252316*

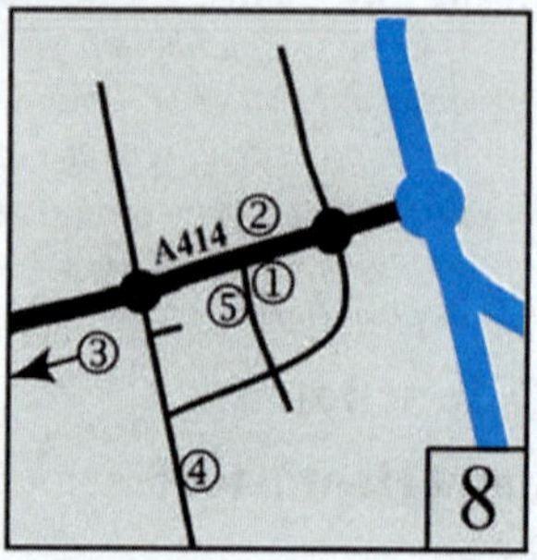

M1 Junction 9
Redbourne

FUEL

Shell SAVE ££ 0.4m ①
Open- *Daily 24 hours*
Info- *WC*
Tel- *01582 842098*

Shell Truck Stop SAVE ££ 0.4m ②
Open- *M-F 0600-2200, Sat 0700-1400*
Info- *Truck washing, LNG*
Tel - *01582 840215*

FOOD

Harvester Restaurant☞ £7.00 0.1m ③
Open- *Daily 1000-2200*
Tel- *01582 842800*

Watling Street Cafe £4.00 0.4m ②
Open- *M-F 0600-1000, Sat 0700-1300*
Info- *Transport cafe.*
Tel- *01582 840270*

Mela Indian Rest. £7.00 0.9m ④
Open- *Sat-Th 1200-2300, Fri 1700-2300*
Info- *Indian restaurant & takeaway*
Tel- *01582 842664*

ACCOMMODATION

Express by Hldy Inn☞ £63 0.1m ⑤
Info- *Cont. breakfast included. Luton-Hemel location*
Tel- *0800 897121*

Hertf'dshire Moat Hs☞ £135 1.1m ⑥
Info- *On site restaurant & health club. St Albans location*
Tel- *01582 449933*

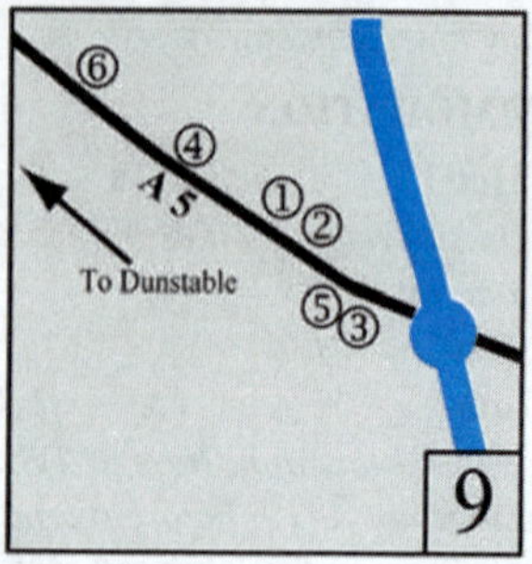

M1 Junction 10
Luton Airport

ACCOMMODATION

Travel Inn☞ £55 2.0m ①
Info- *Beefeater restaurant adjacent. Luton Airport location*
Tel- *01582 417654*

Ibis Hotel☞ £63 2.5m ①
Info- *Bar & restaurant. Luton Airport location*
Dir'n- *The hotel is on the left as you approach the airport.*
Tel- *01582 424488*

ESSENTIALS

Halfords 1.8m ②
Open- *M-F 0800-2000, Sat 0900-1700, Sun 1000-1600*
Info- *Large store for spare parts*
Tel- *01582 422525*

AA Service Centre 1.8m ②
Info- *Car servicing & repair, inside the Halfords store.*
Tel- *01582 442505*

THINGS TO DO

Luton Airpt Pkwy Station 1.9m ③
Info- *Frequent trains to London St Pancras, journey time approx 35 mins, standard return £18.70.*
Tel- *0845 7484950*

Stockwood Collection Free 1.4m ④
Open- *Apr-Oct 1000-1700 (not Mondays). Winter Sat-Sun 1000-1600*
Info- *Craft/Horse Drawn Vehicle museum*
Tel- *01582 738714*

Airport spectators 2.3m ⑤
Open- *Summer Wed to Sun 1000-1700*
Dir'n- *Follow signs to airport, park in short term car park. Follow yellow markings to the spectators' centre.*
Tel- *01582 405100*

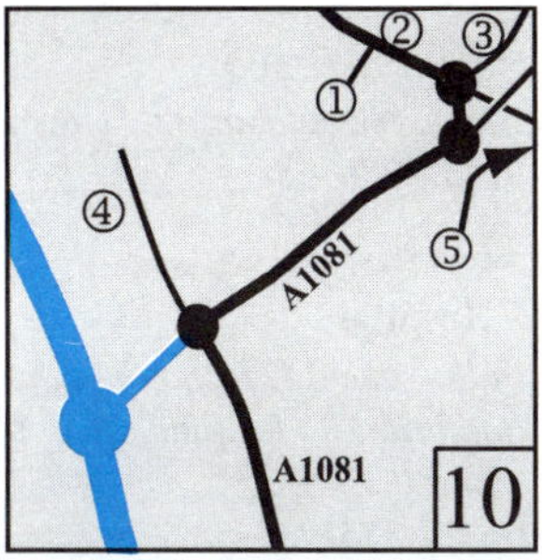

M1 Junction 11
Luton

FUEL

Jet SAVE ££ 0.1m ①
Open- *Daily 0700-2200*
Info- *No facilities*
Tel- *01582 574366*

Esso SAVE ££ 1.0m ②
Open- *Daily 24 hours*
Info- *WC, cash machine*
Tel- *01582 593886*

Tesco SAVE ££ 0.9m ③
Open- *Daily 24 hours*
Info- *WC, cash machine at store.*
Tel- *01582 687545*

FOOD

Tesco Cafe☞ £3.00 0.9m ③
Open- *M-Sa 0800-1800, Su 0930-1600*
Info- *Cash machine at store*
Tel- *0845 677 9226*

Harvester pub/rest.☞ £7.00 0.5m ④
Open- *M-F 1200-1430, 1700-2130, Sat/Sun 1200-2100*
Tel- *01582 572718*

ACCOMMODATION

Travelodge☞ £60 0.9m ①
Tel- *0870 191 1696*

The Chiltern Hotel £85 0.9m ⑤
Info- *On-site restaurant. Regal Hotels.*☞
Tel- *01582 575911*

ESSENTIALS

Luton & Dunstable Hospital 0.3m ⑦
Dir'n- *Head towards Dunstable, and the hospital is well signposted*
Tel- *01582 491122*

Luton Tourist Information Centre
Tel- *01582 401579*

Supertyres 0.4m ⑥
Info- *Tyre & exhaust centre*
Tel- *01582 561133*

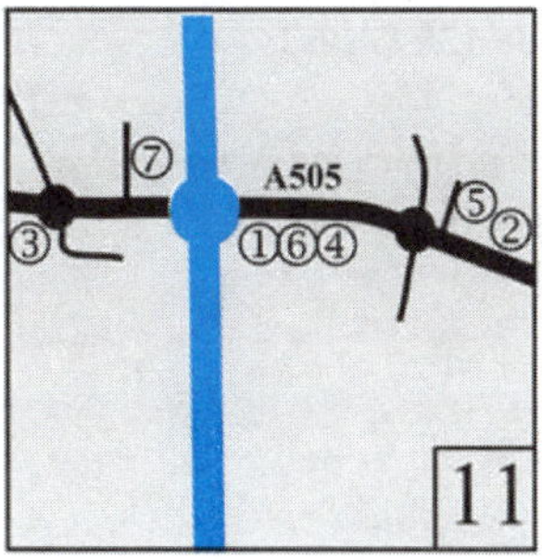

Toddington Services

This services has a roadbridge but no footbridge.

FUEL BP

Cash machine, HGV fuelling, car wash (northbound only). Free parking for 2 hours then £6 per 24 hours. Lorry park

FOOD MOTO

freshexpress, Burger King, Little Chef, Harry Ramsden's, Upper Crust.
Info- *Cash machine*

ACCOMMODATION

Travelodge☞ £60
Info- *Toddington location.*
Tel- *0870 191 1713*

M1 Junction 12 Toddington

FUEL

BP SAVE ££ 1.4m ①
Open- *Daily 0700-2200*
Info- *WC, carwash & jetwash, cash machine.*
Tel- *01525 875034*

FOOD

There are several small shops, pubs and restaurants in Toddington about 1 mile from the junction.

ESSENTIALS

Tuda Pharmacy 0.9m ②
Open- *0900-1700 M-Sat*
Tel- *01525 872093*

A J Autos 1.0m ③
Info- *Car servicing & repair*
Tel- *01525 872630*

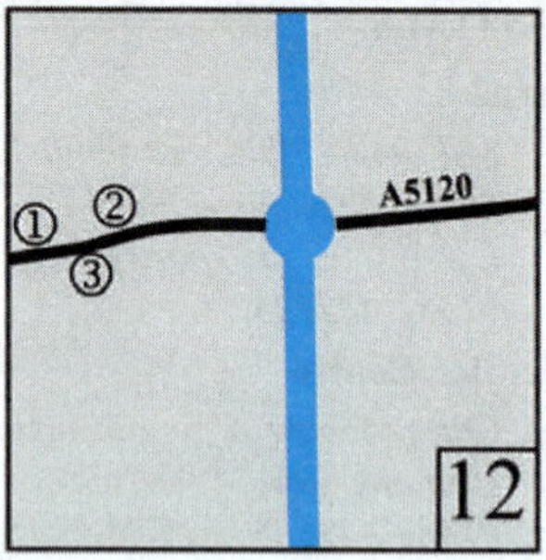

M1 Junction 13 Milton Keynes South

FUEL

Keyfuels SAVE £ 0.2m ①
Open- *Daily 24 hours*
Info- *This is a truck stop. WC, carwash, showers, cafe (not 24 hours). HGV parking*
Tel- *01908 281084*

FOOD

Val's Cafe £2.50 0.7m ②
Open- *M-F 0600-1700, Sat 0600-1300*
Info- *Small takeaway with limited range of sandwiches & drinks.*
Tel- *01525 280436*

Saigon City £5.00 0.7m ②
Open- *Daily 1700-2300*
Info- *Chinese/Vietnamese takeaway food.*
Tel- *01525 280368*

ESSENTIALS

Bedford Hospital 9.5m
Dir'n- *Follow the A421 and then the A6 to Bedford. The hospital is signposted along the A6.*
Tel- *01234 355122*

Guise Motor Repairs 0.2m ③
Open- *Daily 24 hours*
Info- *24 hour recovery service & Avis car rental.*
Tel- *01908 588777*

THINGS TO DO

Woburn Safari Park £9 2.1m ④
Open- *1000-1700 (summer daily, winter Sat/Sun)*

Info- *Extensive wildlife park in the grounds of Woburn House.*
Tel- *01525 290407*
Dir'n- *Follow signs for A4012 (Woburn). The Safari Park is well signposted.*

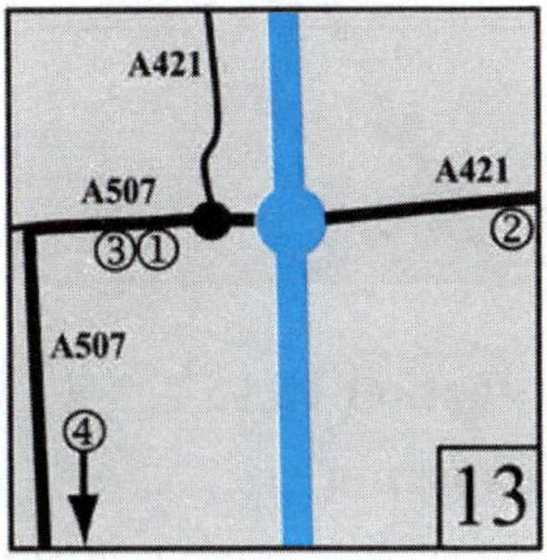

M1 Junction 14
Milton Keynes

FUEL

Total SAVE £ 0.9m ①
Open- *Daily 24 hours*
Info- *WC, carwash, cash machine.*
Tel- *01908 559340*

FOOD

Harvester Restaurant☞ £7.00 0.9m ②
Open- *Daily 1200-2130*
Tel- *01908 395144*

ACCOMMODATION

Express by Hldy Inn☞ £75 0.9m ②
Info- *Cont. breakfast included. Milton Keynes location.*
Harvester pub/restaurant adjacent.
Tel- *0800 434040*

C'tyard by Marriot☞ £106 0.5m ③
Info- *On-site restaurant.*
Tel- *01908 613688*

ESSENTIALS

MK General Hospital 4m
Dir'n- *Head towards ⑤ on map. Hospital is just off A421 after 4 miles.*
Tel- *01908 660033*

Milton Keynes Tourist Info. Centre
Tel- *01908 558300*

THINGS TO DO

NCP Coachway £8.50 0.2m ④
Info- *About 25 coaches a day to London. Journey approx 105 mins. Free car parking (closes at 2030). Costs £8.50 for London day return.*
Tel- *0870 580 8080*

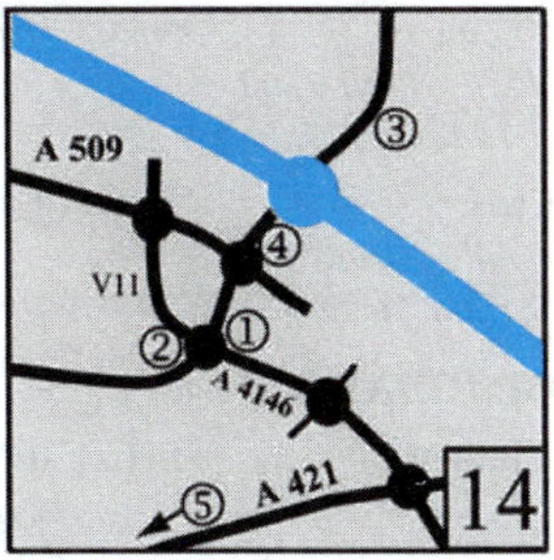

Newport Pagnell Services

This services has a footbridge & roadbridge.

FUEL SHELL

Cash machine, HGV fuelling (northbound & southbound). Free parking for 2 hours then £6 per day. HGV parking.

FOOD WELCOME BREAK

foodconnection, bakery, KFC, Burger King, Coffee Primo, The Granary Restaurant.
Info- *Cash machine.*

ACCOMMODATION

Welcome Lodge☞ £45
Info- *Newport Pagnell location. Hotel is on northbound side.*
Tel- *01908 610878*

M1 Junction 15
Northampton

FUEL

Shell SAVE £ 0.9m ①
Open- *Daily 24 hours*
Info- *LPG, HGV fuelling, WC, carwash, cash machine (no Maestro cards).*
Tel- *01604 664940*

FOOD

Toby Inn☞ £6.50 0.9m ②
Open- Daily 1200-2200
Tel- 01604 769676

Little Chef☞ £6.50 0.9m ③
Open- Daily 0700-2200
Tel- 01604 701078

Burger King☞ £4.00 0.9m ③
Open- Daily 1100-2100
Tel- 01604 701078

Little Chef☞ £6.50 1.0m ④
Open- Daily 0700-2200
Tel- 01604 705722

ACCOMMODATION

Hilton Hotel☞ £110 0.2m ⑤
Info- On-site restaurant & bar. Dogs by arrangement. Price is for B&B. Northampton location.
Tel- 01604 700666

Innkeeper's Lodge☞ £55 0.9m ②
Info- Cold buffet breakfast included. Northampton South location.
Tel- 0870 243 0500

Premier Lodge☞ £47 2m ⑥
Info- Northampton East location. Homespreads pub/rest. on-site.
Dir'n- Drive towards Northampton and take the first slip road. At the roundabout take last turn off before the return to the A508/M1. Hotel is on right after about 100 yards.
Tel- 0870 700 1522

ESSENTIALS

Northampton General Hosp. 4m
Dir'n- Follow A508 to Northampton, then follow the A428 signs to town centre. The hospital is signposted along this road.
Tel- 01604 634700

Northampton Tourist Info. Centre
Tel- 01604 622677

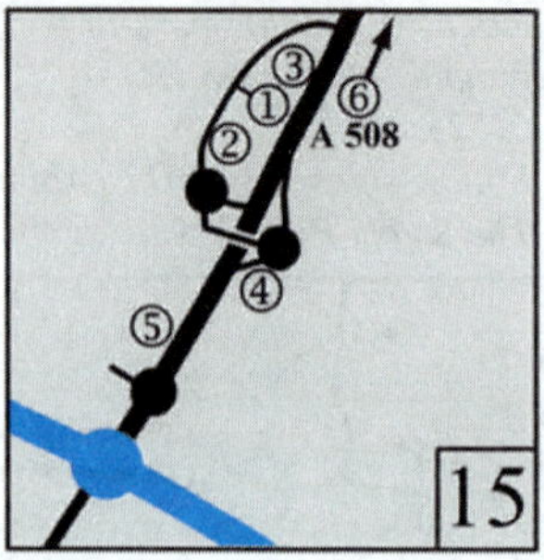

M1 Junction 15A Northampton

The A508 from this junction in the direction towards Oxford does not allow a rapid return to the junction. There are no facilities close to this junction apart from the services.

ESSENTIALS

Northampton General Hosp. 4.7m
Dir'n- Follow A43 signs to Northampton and then follow city centre signs. The hospital is well signposted on this route.
Tel- 01604 634700

Junction 15A Services

There is no connection between northbound and southbound services.

FUEL BP

LPG, cash machine, HGV fuelling and parking. Free car parking for 2 hours then £6 per day.

FOOD ROADCHEF

'on route' rest., Wimpy Bar, Costa Coffee (northbound), The Granary Restaurant (southbound).

Info- Cash machine

M1 Junction 16
Northampton

FUEL

Total SAVE ££ 1.9m ①
Open- M-F 0630-2200, Sat-Sun 0800-2200
Info- WC
Tel- 01604 833892

FOOD

Red Lion Truckstop £4.00 0.6m ②
Open- Mon-Fri 0600-2130
Info- Truckers' cafe & pub, showers.
Tel- 01604 831914

Beefeater☞ £7.00 1.5m ③
Open- M-F 1200-1400, 1700-2130, Sat 1200-2230, Sun 1200-2100
Info- 'The Turnpike', next to Travel Inn.
Tel- 01604 830565

ACCOMMODATION

C'tyard by Marriot☞ £80 1.4m ④
Info- Bar & restaurant. Daventry location.
Tel- 01327 349022

Travel Inn☞ £43 1.5m ③
Info- Northampton location.
Tel- 01604 832340

ESSENTIALS

Northampton General Hosp. 5m
Dir'n- Follow A45 to Northampton, then follow the A4500 to the town centre. The hospital is signposted along this road.
Tel- 01604 634700

Northampton Tourist Info. Centre
Tel- 01604 622677

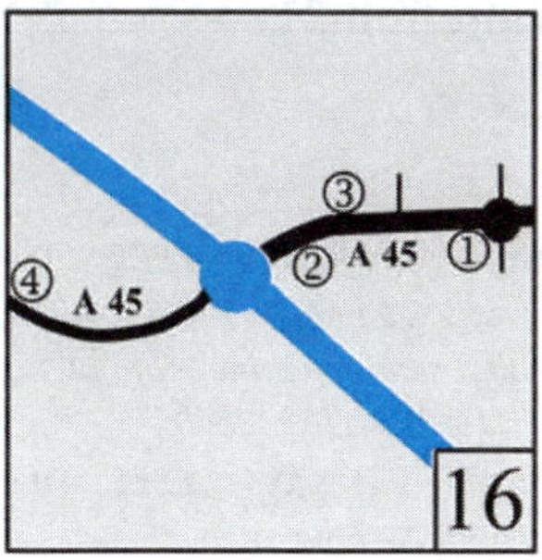

Watford Gap Services

There are a footbridge and roadbridge available at this services.

FUEL SHELL
Cash machine, HGV fuelling & parking.
Free parking for 2 hours then £6 per day.

FOOD ROADCHEF
onroute restaurant, Costa Coffee, Wimpy
Info- Cash machine.

ACCOMMODATION

Travel Inn £43 0.1m
Info- Daventry (Watford Gap) location. Nearby Stag Inn is available for meals to hotel guests.
Tel- 01327 871333

M1 Junction 17
M1/ M45 interchange

There is no access to local services at this junction.

M1 Junction 18
Rugby North

FOOD

The Red Lion £4.00 1.1m ①
Open- M-F 1200-1400, 1900-2100, Sat 1900-2130
Tel- 01788 822384

ACCOMMODATION

Ibis Hotel☞ £43 0.4m ②
Info- On-site restaurant. Dogs by arrangement. Rugby East location.
Tel- 01788 824331

Holiday Inn☞ £105 0.5m ③
Info- On-site restaurant & health club. Daventry/Rugby location.
Tel- 0870 400 9059

ESSENTIALS

Hospital of St Cross 6m
Dir'n- Follow A428 into Rugby, then the hospital is signposted.
Tel- 01788 572831

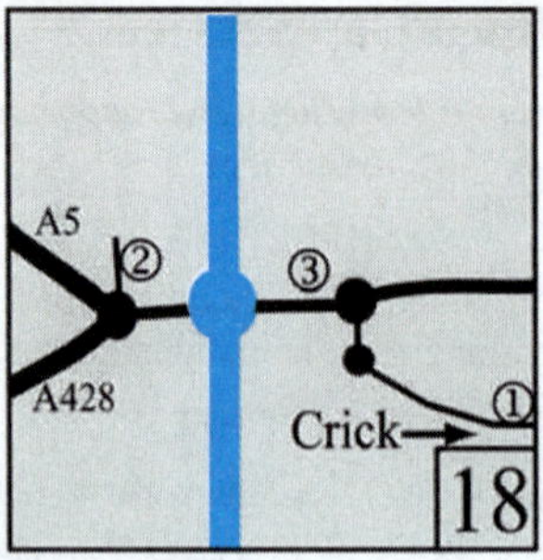

M1 Junction 19
M1/M6 interchange

M1 Junction 20
Lutterworth

The town of Lutterworth is less than a mile away and provides a fair short break from the motorway. It has a range of small shops, and a few food and accommodation options in addition to those mentioned here. Cash machines also available in the town.

FUEL

Texaco SAVE £ 0.8m ①
Open- *Daily 24 hours*
Info- *WC, jetwash.*
Tel- *01455 200560*

Total SAVE £ 1.0m ②
Open- *Daily 24 hours*
Info- *WC*
Tel- *01455 556888*

Texaco SAVE ££ 1.4m ③
Open- *Daily 0700-2200*
Info- *WC, jetwash.*
Tel- *01455 553911*

FOOD

The Greyhound Hotel £6 0.6m ⑥
Open- *M-Sat 1200-1400, 1900-2145, Sundays 1900-2145.*
Info- *Bar & restaurant.*
Tel- *01455 553307*

The Shambles £5 0.6m ⑤
Open- *M-F 1200-1900, Sat-Sun 1200-1500*
Info- *Pub serving varied hot & cold meals.*
Tel- *01455 552620*

New Sunar Gow £7 0.6m ⑦
Open- *Su-Th 1730-2400, F-Sa 1730- 0100*
Info- *Balti & Tandoori rest. & takeaway.*
Tel- *01455 552686*

Roseanne's Tearooms £4.00 0.7m ④
Open- *M-F 0900-1500, Sat 0900-1600*
Info- *Hot and cold meals and snacks.*
Tel- *01455 552212*

Safeways Cafe☞ £3.50 0.8m ⑧
Open- *M-Sa 0800-1800, Sun 0900-1500*
Tel- *01455 550223*

ACCOMMODATION

Denbigh Arms Hotel £43 0.8m ⑥
Info- *Bar and restaurant.*
Tel- *01455 553537*

The Greyhound Hotel £52 0.8m ⑥
Info- *Price is for B&B.*
Tel- *01455 553307*

ESSENTIALS

Fortnums Chemists 1m ⑨
Open- *M-F 0900-1800, Sat 0900-1700*
Info- *There is also a Lloyds Chemists in the High Street.*
Tel- *01455 552692*

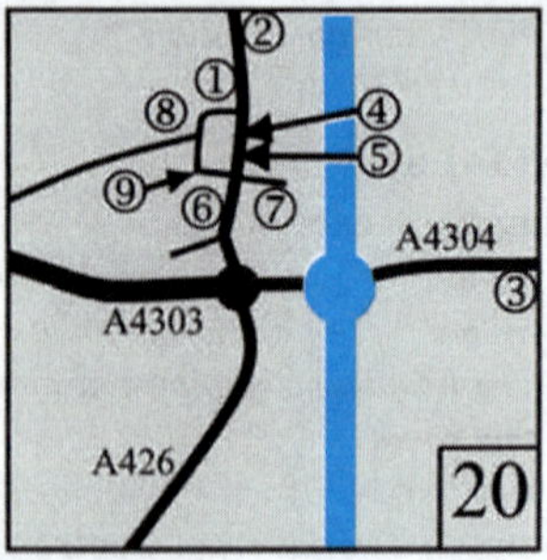

M1 Junction 21
Leicester

FUEL

Sainsbury SAVE ££££ 0.9m ①
Open- *Daily 24 hours*
Info- *WC, cash machine, cafe at store.*
Tel- *0116 263 1152*

Asda SAVE ££££ 0.9m ②
Open- *Daily 24 hours*

Info- *Jetwash. WC, cash machine, cafe at store.*
Tel- *0116 282 5346*

FOOD

Pizza Hut☞ £6.00 0.9m ①
Open- *Daily 1130-2300*
Tel- *0116 289 2990*

Sainsbury Cafe☞ £3.50 0.9m ①
Open- *M-Sat 0800-2030, Sun 1000-1530*
Tel- *0116 263 1153*

Starbucks Cafe☞ £3.50 0.9m ①
Open- *M-Sat 0900-2030, Sun 1100-1630*
Dir'n- *Inside Borders bookstore.*

McDonald's☞ £3.50 0.9m ②
Open- *Daily 0700-2300*
Tel- *0116 263 0563*

ACCOMMODATION

Hilton Hotel☞ £150 0.8m ③
Info- *On-site bar, rest., health club, pool. Leicester location*
Tel- *0116 263 0066*

ESSENTIALS

Leicester Royal Infirmary 4m
Dir'n-Follow signs for A5460 (Leicester). Turn right on Upperton Road to the hospital which is well signposted.
Tel- *0116 254 1414*

Leicester Tourist Information Centre
Tel- *0906 294 1113*

THINGS TO DO

Fosse Shopping Park 0.8m ④
Open- *M-Sat 0930-2000, Sun.1045-1700*
Info- *Many shops and food outlets.*
Tel- *0116 263 0603*

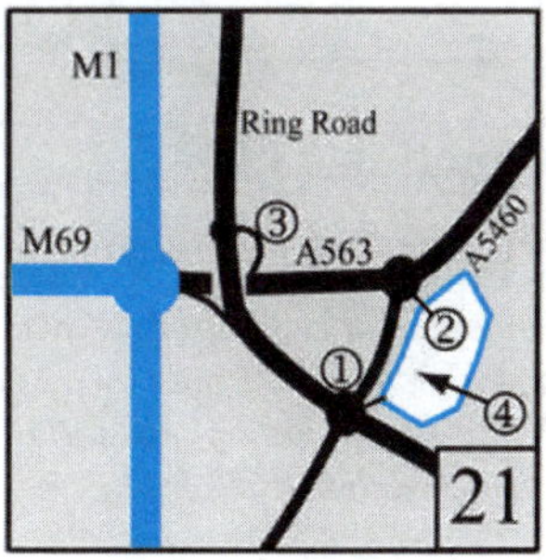

Leicester Forest Services

There is a footbridge at this services.

FUEL BP

LPG, HGV fuelling & parking. Cash machine. Free parking for 2 hours then £6 per day.

FOOD WELCOME BREAK

foodconnection restaurant, Coffee Primo, Burger King, KFC
Info- *Cash machines.*

ACCOMMODATION

Days Inn☞ £45 0.1m
Info- *Leicester location.*
Tel- *0116 239 0534*

M1 Junction 21A Restricted

This is a restricted junction, allowing exit northbound and entrance southbound.

ESSENTIALS

Leicester Tourist Information Centre
Tel- *0906 294 1113*

Junction 22 Services

The services are just off the motorway at Junction 22.

FUEL BP

LPG, HGV fuelling, carwash.

FOOD

Little Chef (Daily 0700-2200), Burger King (Daily 1100-2100)
Info- *Cash machine for Link, Plus and Diners club .*

ACCOMMODATION

Travelodge☞ £50
Info- *Leicester Markfield location.*
Tel- *0870 191 1583*

M1 Junction 22
Leicester North

FUEL

BP SAVE ££ 0.7m ①

Open- *M-F 0600-2200, Sun 0700-2200*
Info- *WC, jetwash.*
Dir'n- *After fuelling re-enter towards roundabout, not dual carriageway.*
Tel - *01530 242222*

FOOD

Flying Horse £4.50 0.7m ②

Open- *Daily 1200-1400, 1730-2330*
Info- *Cantonese restaurant & takeaway.*
Tel- *01530 245610*

Coach & Horses £4.50 1.2m ③

Open- *M-F 1200-1400, 1800-2030, Sun 1200-1500*
Info- *Hot & cold meals & daily specials.*
Tel- *01530 242312*

ACCOMMODATION

Field Head Hotel £84 1.2m ④

Info- *Bar, restaurant. Active Htl Group.*
Tel- *01530 245454*

ESSENTIALS

Leicester Tourist Info. Centre

Tel- *0906 294 1113*

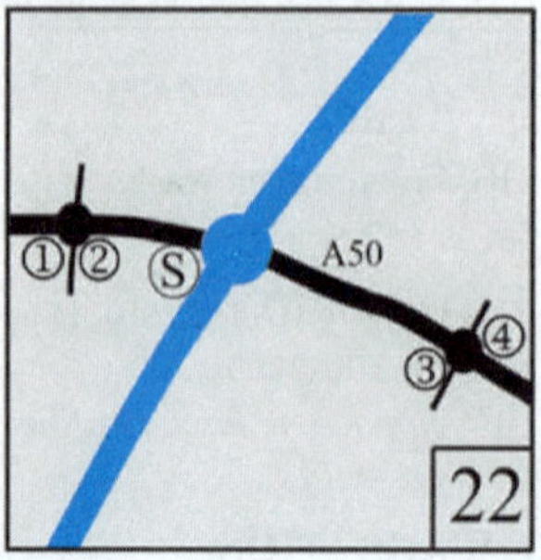

M1 Junction 23
Loughborough

FUEL

Keyfuels SAVE ££ 0.4m ①

Open- *Daily 24 hours*
Info- *WC, showers. Cafe., HGV parking.*
Tel- *01509 507480*

Texaco SAVE ££ 0.7m ②

Open- *M-F 0600-2200, Sat-Sun 0800-2100*
Info- *WC, carwash. Dual carriageway extends return journey by approx 0.5 miles.*
Tel- *01509 643770*

BP SAVE ££ 1.6m ③

Open- *Daily 24 hours*
Info- *HGV fuelling. Cash machine (not Maestro). Dual carriageway extends distance.*
Tel- *01509 238530*

FOOD

Truckstop cafe/rest. £4.00 0.4m ①

Open- *M-F 0600-2100, Sat 0600-2300*
Info- *Transport cafe & restaurant.*
Tel- *01509 507480*

Harvester☞ £7.00 1.4m ④

Open- *Daily 1200-2200*
Tel- *01509 214165*

ACCOMMODATION

Quality Htl & Suites☞ £80 1.4m ⑤

Info- *Bar, restaurant & health club. Price includes breakfast. ETB commended. Loughborough location.*
Tel- *01509 211800*

M1 Junction 23A
Restricted

No northbound entry, but this is available via Junction 24, about 1 mile away. No map is needed for this junction, just follow signs to the airport & hotel.

ACCOMMODATION

Express by Hldy Inn☞ £70 0.7m

Info- *Bar, restaurant. East Midlands Airport location. Price includes continental breakfast.*

Dir'n- *The hotel is signposted as you head towards East Midlands Airport.*

Tel- *01509 678000*

THINGS TO DO

East Midlands Airport 0.4m

Info- *This is within 2 miles of this junction. Just behind the Holiday Inn provides an easily accessible free viewing location.*

Junction 23A Services

Entry to services is from northbound M1 only, and entry to M1 J23A is southbound only. Additional accesses are via Junction 24 about 2 miles away.

FUEL BP

HGV fuelling, car wash, LPG. Free parking for 2 hours then £6 per 24 hours. Lorry park.

FOOD MOTO

Burger King, Little Chef, Harry Ramsden's, freshexpress.

Info- *Cash machine.*

ACCOMMODATION

Travelodge £45 0.5m

Info- *Donnington Park location.*

Tel- *0870 191 1573*

M1 Junction 24A
Kegworth

The small town of Kegworth is less than a mile away and offers a range of general facilities.

ACCOMMODATION

Hilton Hotel☞ £125 0.4m ①

Info- *On-site restaurant & bar. Well behaved dogs by arrangement. East Midlands Aiport location.*

Tel- *01509 674000*

ESSENTIALS

Derbyshire Royal Infirmary 9m

Dir'n- *Follow A50 and then the A6 into Derby town centre. The hospital is on the left close to the town centre.*

Tel- *01332 347141*

Derbyshire Children's Hosp. 10m

Dir'n- *Follow A50/A6 into Derby town centre, then turn west onto the A5111 ring road. Next take the A516 south (Uttoxeter Road). The Children's Hospital is on the site of the City General Hospital.*

Tel- *01332 340131*

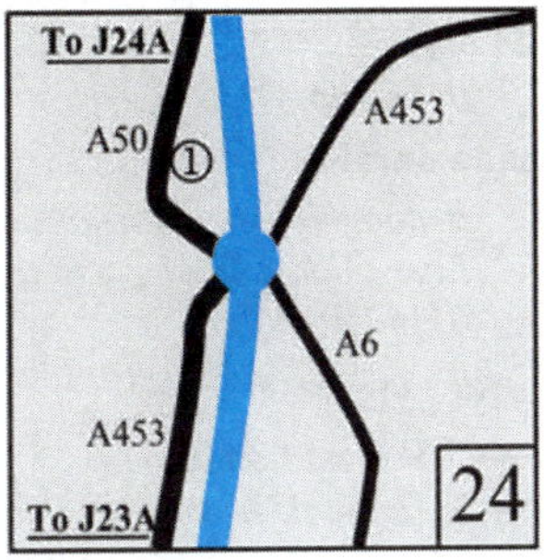

M1 Junction 24a
Restricted

This junction only allows exit from the M1 southbound, and entrance to the M1 northbound.

HOTELS

Hilton Hotel☞ £125 1m ①

Info- *See entry for hotel at Junction 24.*

Dir'n- *See map forJunction 24.*

M1 Junction 25
Derby

Make sure not to take the A52 west direction, as the return journey is very long.

FUEL

Texaco SAVE ££ 1.2m ①

Open- *M-Sat 0730-2100, Sun 0900-2100*

Info- *WC*

Tel- *0115 949 1398*

FOOD

Branaghan's restrnt. £10 0.6m ②
Open- *M-F 1130-1430, 1700-2200, Sat/ Sun 1130-2200*
Info- *American style restaurant.*
Tel- *0115 946 2000*

ACCOMMODATION

Holiday Inn☞ £94 0.4m ③
Info- *On-site restaurant & bar. Derby/ Nottingham location.*
Tel- *0870 400 9062*

Novotel☞ £65 0.5m ④
Info- *On-site restaurant. Dogs at £5 charge each. Nottingham/Derby location.*
Tel- *0115 946 5111*

Ramada Jarvis☞ £125 0.6m ②
Info- *Branaghan's restaurant adjacent. East Midlands Airport location*
Tel- *0115 946 0000*

ESSENTIALS

Queens Medical Centre 6m
Dir'n- *Take the A52 to Nottingham. As you pass the University on your right hand side you will come to a large traffic island with QMC on the right.*
Tel- *0115 924 9924*

Derby Tourist Information Centre
Tel- *01332 255802*

Nottingham Tourist Information Centre
Tel- *0115 915 5330*

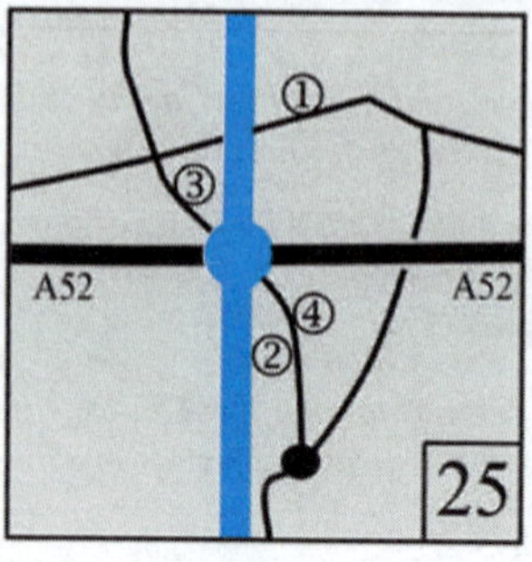

Trowell Services

This services has a footbridge between carriageways.

FUEL ESSO
HGV fuelling & parking. Cash machine, Free parking for 2 hours then £6 per day.

FOOD MOTO
foodexpress restaurant, Little Chef, Burger King, Harry Ramsden's.
Info- *Cash machine.*

ACCOMMODATION

Travelodge☞ £50
Info- *Nottingham Trowell location.*
Tel- *0870 191 1593*

M1 Junction 26
Nottingham North

FUEL

Texaco **SAVE** ££ 1.1m ①
Open- *Daily 24 hours*
Info- *WC, carwash.*
Tel- *0115 975 8890*

BP **SAVE** ££ 1.5m ②
Open- *Daily 24 hours*
Info- *WC, LPG, cash machine.*
Tel- *0115 927 2707*

FOOD

Brewsters☞ £6.50 1.0m ③
Open- *M-Sat 1130-2200, Sun 1200-2200*
Tel- *0115 976 2200*

Beefeater☞ £7.00 1.5m ④
Open- *Daily 1200-2230*
Info- *The 'Miller's Barn'.*
Tel- *0115 951 9971*

Broxtowe Inn £7.00 1.6m ⑤
Open- *M-Sat 1200-2130, Sun 1200-2030*
Info- *Varied pub menu.*
Dir'n- *Enter via road that runs at the back of the BP garage.*
Tel- *0115 927 8210*

ACCOMMODATION

Travel Inn☞ £43 1.5m ④

Dir'n- *Next to Beefeater. Nottingham West location.*

Tel- *0115 951 9971*

ESSENTIALS

Queens Medical Centre 7m

Dir'n- *Take the A610 to Nottingham, and then go south on the A6514 to the A52 where you will see QMC signposted.*

Tel- *0115 924 9924*

Nottingham Tourist Information Centre

Tel- 0115 915 5330

M1 Junction 27
Hucknall

There are no facilities near this junction.

M1 Junction 28
Alfreton

There are several pubs and a fish and chip shop in nearby South Normanton.

FUEL

BP SAVE ££ 0.8m ①

Open- *M-Sat 0600-2200, Sun 0800-2200*

Tel- *01773 811268*

BP SAVE ££ 1.2m ②

Open- *Daily 24 hours*

Info- *Carwash.*

Tel- *01773 811251*

FOOD

Brewsters☞ £6.50 0.3m ③

Open- *M-Sat 11130-2200, Sun 1200-2200*

Tel- *01773 862899*

Many Others 0.8m ⑤

Open- *M/Tu/W/F 1000-1800, Th 1000-2000 Sat 0900-1800, Sun 1100-1700*

Info- *At the outlet mall:- Arkwright's Fish and Chips, Burger King, Madison's Coffee Shop, Bitz n Pizza, Bradwells Kiosk, Spud-U-Like.*

Tel- *01773 545000*

ACCOMMODATION

Renaissance Hotel £99 0.2m ④

Info- *Bar, restaurant. Derby/Nottingham location. Dogs welcome.*

Tel- *01773 812000*

Travel Inn☞ £43 0.3m ③

Info- *Located next to Brewsters. Mansfield (Tibshelf) location.*

Tel- *01773 591010*

ESSENTIALS

Kings Mill Hospital 4.5m

Dir'n- *Take the A38 towards Mansfield, and the hospital is very close to the junction of the A38 and the A6075.*

Tel- *01623 622515*

Touchbase Mtg Centre☞ 0.3m ③

Info- *A range of meeting facilities. Mansfield location.*

Tel- *0870 243 3113*

THINGS TO DO

McArthur Glen Outlet Mall 0.8m ⑤

Open- *M-F 1000-2000, Sat 0900-1800, Sun 1100-1700.*

Info- *Wide range of food and gift outlets.*

Tel- *01773 545000*

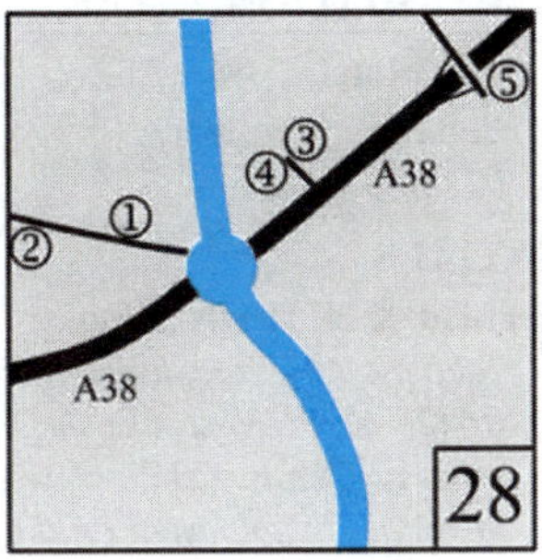

Tibshelf Services

There are a footbridge and roadbridge at this services.

FUEL TEXACO

HGV fuelling & parking. Free parking for 2 hours then £6 per day. Facilities same both carriageways.

FOOD ROADCHEF

'Food Fayre'restaurant, Wimpy, Wimpy Chicken, Costa Coffee.

Info- *Cash machine*

ACCOMMODATION

Travel Inn☞ £43 0.2m

Info- *Mansfield (Tibshelf) location.*

Tel- *01773 591010*

Chesterfield Tourist Information Centre

Tel- *01246 345777*

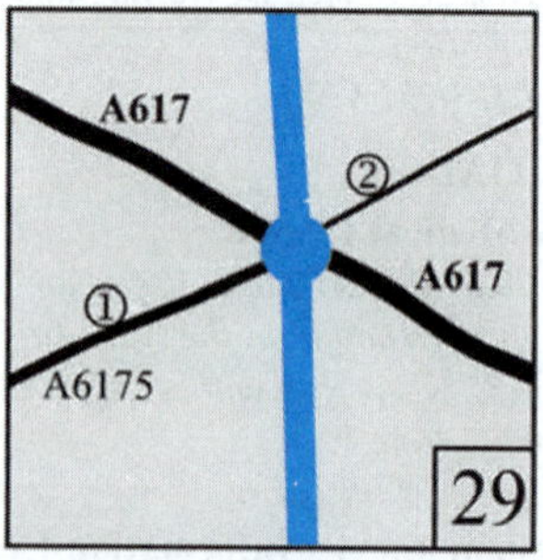

M1 Junction 29
Chesterfield

FUEL

Shell SAVE ££ 1m ①

Open- *M-F 0600-2130, Sat-Sun 0800-2000*

Info- *WC, jetwash.*

Tel- *01246 850329*

FOOD

Twin Oaks rest. £10 0.4m ②

Open- *M-F 0700-0900, 1200-1400, 1900-2130, Sat-Sun 0800-0930, 1200-1400, 1900-2130*

Info- *Extensive menu at Motel restaurant. Vegan meals available.*

Tel- *01246 855455*

ACCOMMODATION

Twin Oaks Motel £42 0.4m ②

Info- *Bar & restaurant.*

Tel- *01246 855455*

ESSENTIALS

Chesterfield & N. Derby Hosp. 7m

Dir'n- *Take the A617 to Chesterfield, then B6425 north. Next take the A632 towards Chesterfield, where the hospital is signposted on the right.*

Tel- *01246 277271*

M1 Junction 30
Barlborough

The village of Barlborough is less than 0.5 miles away and offers a range of pubs, most of which provide food.

FUEL

Total SAVE £££ 0.2 ①

Open- *M-Sat 0700-2100, Sun 0900-2000*

Info- *WC*

Tel- *01246 810600*

Q8 SAVE £££ 1.2m ②

Open- *M-Sat 0700-1900, Sun 0800-1800*

Info- *LPG, WC*

FOOD

Treble Bob☞ £6.60 0.5m ③

Open- *M-Sat 1200-2200, Sun 1200-2130*

Info- *Tom Cobleigh chain. Extensive range of food.*

Tel- *01246 813005*

McDonald's☞ £3.50 0.5m ③

Open- *Daily 0730-2300*

Tel- *01246 819520*

Mulan Chinese rest. £8.00 1m ②

Open- *M-Sat 1800-2400, Sun 1800-2200*

Info- *Chinese restaurant & takeaway.*

Tel- *01246 433337*

Sitwell Arms £6.00 1.4m ②

Open- *M-Sat 1200-1500, 1730-2130, Sundays 1200-1500, 1900-2100*

Info- *Village pub, wide range of meals.*

Tel- *01246 435226*

ACCOMMODATION

Ibis Hotel☞ £40 0.5m ③

Info- *Restaurant. South Barlborough location. Dogs by arrangement.*

Tel- *01246 813222*

The Sitwell Arms £60 1.4m ②

Info- *Pub and restaurant.*

Tel- *01246 435226*

ESSENTIALS

Chesterfield & N. Derby Hospital 7m

Dir'n- *Take the A619 towards Chesterfield, then the A61 south. Next take the A632 towards Bolsover, where the hospital is signposted on the left after a short distance.*

Tel- *01246 277271*

Chesterfield Tourist Information Centre

Tel- *01246 345777*

THINGS TO DO

Renishaw Hall £6 2.7m

Open- *April-Sep, Th-Sun 1030-1630*

Info- *Garden, museum, cafe & craft shop.*

Dir'n- *Beyond ② on the map.*

Tel- *01246 432310*

Woodall Services

There is a footbridge between northbound & southbound services, and a road link for access to the Days Inn for northbound users.

FUEL SHELL

HGV fuelling & parking. Free parking for 2 hours then £6 per day.

Services continued in next column

Services continued

FOOD WELCOME BREAK

'The Granary', McDonald's, KFC (northbound), 'The Granary', Burger King, KFC, Coffee Primo (southbound).

Info- *Cash machines.*

ACCOMMODATION

Days Inn☞ £45

Tel- *0114 248 7992*

ESSENTIALS

Chesterfield Tourist Info. Centre

Tel- *01246 345777*

M1 Junction 31
Aston

FUEL

Jet SAVE ££ 0.8m ①

Open- *Daily 24 hours*

Info- *WC, carwash, post box.*

Tel- *0114 287 4167*

ACCOMMODATION

Aston Hall Hotel £90 0.6m ②

Info- *On site restaurant. Country house hotel. Rate includes breakfast.*

Tel- *0114 287 2309*

ESSENTIALS

Accident Repair Centre 0.2m ③

Open- *Daily 24 hours*

Info- *24 hour recovery service.*

Tel- *0114 287 2296*

M1 Junction 32
M1/M18 interchange

M1 Junction 33
Rotherham

FUEL

Total SAVE ££ 1.2m ①
Open- *Daily 24 hours*
Info- *WC, carwash.*
Tel- *01709 726900*

ACCOMMODATION

C'tyard by Marriott☞ £102 0.9m ②
Info- *Bar, restaurant. Rotherham location.*
Tel- *01709 830630*

ESSENTIALS

Rotherham Hospital 2m
Dir'n- *Follow A630 towards Rotherham and the hospital is signposted.*
Tel- *01709 820000*

Rotherham Tourist Information Centre
Tel- *01709 835904*

Sheffield Tourist Information Centre
Tel- *0114 221 1900*

M1 Junction 34
Meadowhall

The large Meadowhall shopping complex contains a wide variety of shops and restaurants. There are more facilities in this area in addition to those mentioned here.

FUEL

Jet SAVE ££ 0.5m ①
Open- *Daily 24 hours*
Info- *LPG, carwash.*
Tel- *0114 256 2343*

Sainsbury SAVE ££ 0.6m ②
Open- *M-Sat 0700-2100, Sun1000-1800*
Dir'n- *At entrance to the Meadowhall complex.*
Tel- *0114 261 1979*

Sainsbury # 2 SAVE ££ 0.3m ③
Open- *M-Sat 0700-2200, Sun 1000-1800*
Info- *Carwash, jetwash. WC & cash machines at store.*
Tel- *0114 261 1087*

FOOD

TGIF☞ £10 0.4m ④
Open- *M-Sat 1200-2330, Sun 1200-2300*
Tel- *0114 2334486*

Sainsbury Cafe☞ £3.50 1m ⑤
Open- *M-Sat 0900-1830, Sun 1100-1700*
Info- *Cash machines at supermarket.*
Dir'n- *At Meadowhall follow signs to Hypermarket.*
Tel- *0114 256 8684*

Pizza Hut☞ £6.00 1m ⑥
Open- *Sun-Th 1200-2200, F-Sa 1200-2300*
Dir'n- *In Tinsley Retail Park. McDonald's next door.*
Tel- *0114 256 2211*

Brewsters☞ £6.50 1.6m ⑦
Open- *M-Sat 1100-2200, Sun 1200-2200*
Dir'n- *Opposite the Hallam Arena.*
Tel- *0114 243 2320*

ACCOMMODATION

Premier Lodge☞ £47 0.4m ④
Info- *TGIF adjacent.*
Sheffield Meadowhall location.
Tel- *0870 700 1540*

Travel Inn☞ £43 1.6m ⑧
Info- *Restaurant.*
Sheffield Attercliffe location.
Tel- *0870 238 3316*

ESSENTIALS

Northern General Hospital 3m

Dir'n- *Follow signs to Sheffield city centre, then turn right at A6102. The hospital is on the right just after passing the A6135.*

Tel- *0114 243 4343*

Rotherham Tourist Information Centre

Tel- *01709 835904*

Sheffield Tourist Information Centre

Tel- *0114 221 1900*

THINGS TO DO

Magna £8.00 0.4m

Open- *Daily 1000-1700*

Info- *Impressive Science & Technology Museum.*

Dir'n- *This is well signposted on the A6178 to Rotherham.*

Tel- *01709 720002*

Meadowhall £Free 1m ⑤

Open- *M-F 1000-2100, Sat 0900-1900, Sun 1100-1700*

Info- *Very large shopping complex.*

Tel- *0845 600 6800*

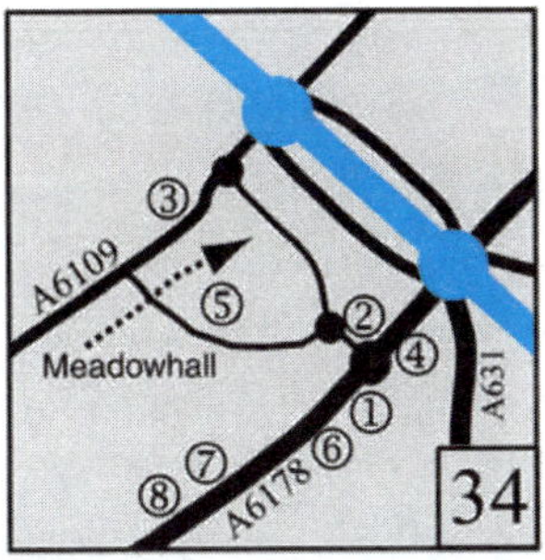

M1 Junction 35
Chapeltown

FUEL

Texaco SAVE ££ 0.6m ①

Open- *Daily 24 hours*

Info- *Carwash. Fish & chip shop opposite.*

Tel- *0114 257 4400*

FOOD

The Sportsman £4.00 0.9m ②

Open- *Daily 1200-1400, 1730-2030*

Info- *Varied hot & cold meals. Children's play area.*

Tel- *0114 240 1824*

ESSENTIALS

Northern General Hospital 7m

Dir'n- *Follow signs to Chapeltown, then take the A6135 to Sheffield. The hospital is on the left just before reaching the A6102.*

Tel- *01142 434343*

Sheffield Tourist Information Centre

Tel- *0114 221 1900*

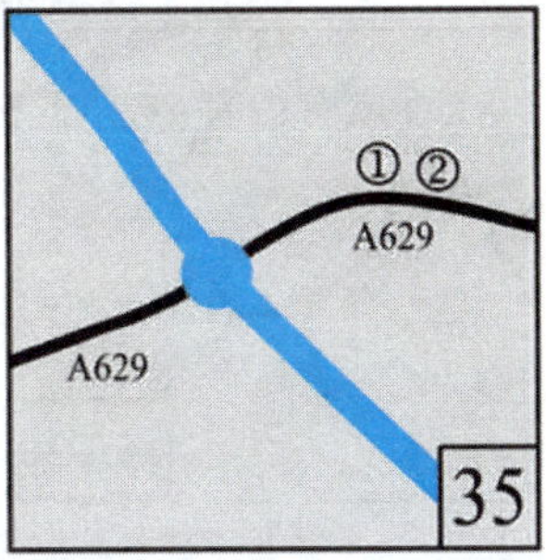

M1 Junction 35A
Restricted

This only allows merging with traffic to/from the A616. Following the A616 allows easy connection to Junction 36 a few miles north (and passes by various facilities- see ④ & ⑤ at J36). There is a WW2 tank on display as you drive towards the Miners Arms!

FOOD

Miners Arms £5.00 0.5m ①

Open- *Daily 1200-2030*

Info- *Family pub/restaurant.*

Tel- *0114 257 0092*

Thorncliffe Arms £5.00 0.5m ①

Open- *Daily 1200-1430, 1700-2030*

Info- *Family pub/restaurant.*

Tel- *0114 245 8942*

Shell SAVE ££ 1m ③

Open- *Daily 24 hours*

Info- *WC, jetwash, carwash, HGV fuelling.*

Tel- *01226 350479*

FOOD

Brewsters☞ £6.50 1m ③
Open- *M-Sat 1130-2200, Sun 1200-2200*
Tel- *01226 350035*

McDonald's☞ £3.50 1m ③
Open- *Daily 0700-2400*
Tel- *01226 740025*

ACCOMMODATION

Travel Inn☞ £43 1m ③
Info- *Sheffield/Barnsley location.*
Tel- *01226 350035*

M1 Junction 36
Hoyland

See map for junction 35A

FUEL

Jet **SAVE** £££ 0.4m ②
Open- *M-F 0600-2200, Sat-Sun 0800-2200*
Tel- *01226 743331*

Shell **SAVE** ££ 1m ③
Open- *Daily 24 hours*
Info- *WC, jetwash, carwash, HGV fuelling.*
Tel- *01226 350479*

FOOD

Brewsters☞ £6.50 1m ③
Open- *M-Sat 1130-2200, Sun 1200-2200*
Tel- *01226 350035*

McDonald's☞ £3.50 1m ③
Open- *Daily 0700-2400*
Tel- *01226 740025*

Tankersley Manor Bar £7.00 0.5m ④
Open- *M-Sat 1200-1430, 1800-2130, Sun 1200-1600 and 1800-2130.*
Info- *Pleasant bar within the hotel, which serves a wide range of food.*
Tel- *01226 744700*

ACCOMMODATION

Tankersley Manor Hotel £139 0.5m ④
Info- *Restaurant and bar attached to this pleasant hotel.*
Tel- *01226 744700*

Travel Inn☞ £43 1m ③
Info- *Sheffield/Barnsley location.*
Tel- *01226 350035*

ESSENTIALS

Numark Pharmacy 0.6m ⑤
Open- *M-F 0900-1230, 1330-1800*
Dir'n- *Turn left at the first set of lights heading towards ③.*
Tel- *01226 743156*

Tyre & Exhaust Centre 1m ⑥
Info- *Challenger tyre & exhaust centre.*
Tel- *01226 360000*

M1 Junction 37
Barnsley

FUEL

Shell **SAVE** £££ 0.5m ①
Open- *Daily 24 hours.*
Info- *WC, jetwash.*
Tel- *01226 737100*

FOOD

The Gate Inn £4.00 0.2m ②
Open- *M-Sat 1200-1400, 1700-1900, Sun-1200-1600*
Info- *Pub food.*
Tel- *01226 282705*

Brooklands Rest £13 0.4m ③
Open- *M-Sat 0700-0930, 1200-1400,1900-2100 (no lunch Sat.), Sun 0800-1000, 1200-1445,1900-2100*
Info- *Refined dining in hotel restaurant.*
Tel- *01226 299571*

ACCOMMODATION

Brooklands Hotel £115 0.4m ③
Info- *On-site restaurant, bar, pool, health club. ETC 4 star. Price is B&B.*
Tel- *01226 299571*

ESSENTIALS

Barnsley General Hospital 2m

Dir'n- Follow signs to Barnsley/A628, and the hospital is signposted.

Tel- 01226 730000

Barnsley Tourist Information Centre

Tel- 01226 206757

Ford Dealer 0.7m ④

Dir'n- Just beyond the Shell garage.

M1 Junction 38
Wooley

THINGS TO DO

Bretton Country Park £nil 0.3m ①

Open- Daylight hours

Info- Large country park with trails & Henry Moore statues.

Yorkshire Sculpture Pk £nil 1.0m ②

Open- Summer 1000-1800, Winter 1000-1700

Info- Many Henry Moore statues in park setting. Car parking £1.50 per car.

Tel- 01924 830302

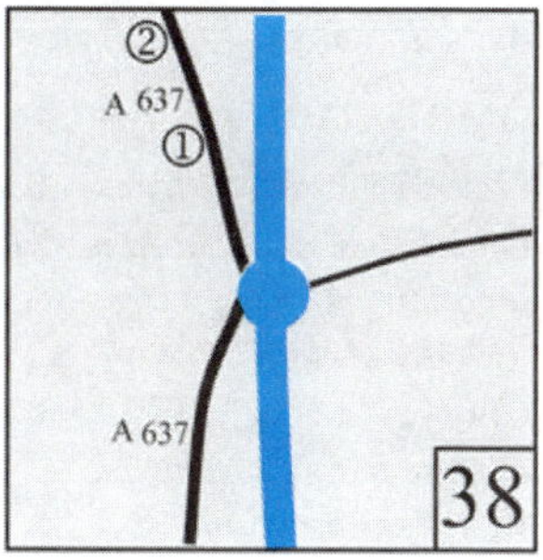

Wooley Services

There are a footbridge & roadbridge at this services.

FUEL ESSO

HGV fuelling & parking. Free parking for 2 hours then £6 per day.

FOOD MOTO

Burger King, Harry Ramsden's, Ritazza.

Info- Cash machine.

ACCOMMODATION

Travelodge☞ £45

Info- Wakefield Wooley Edge location.

Tel- 0870 191 1678

M1 Junction 39
Crigglestone

FUEL

Total **SAVE** £ 0.5m ①

Open- M-F 0700-1900. Sat 0800-1800, Sun 0900-1700

Info- Next to small car repair centre.

Tel- 01924 274756

Esso **SAVE** ££ 0.7m ②

Open- M-Sat 0700-2200, Sun 0800-2200

Info- WC, carwash, jetwash.

Tel- 01924 371209

FOOD

Cedar Court Rest. £14 0.2m ③

Open- M-F 0700-1030, 1200-1400, 1800-2200, Sat 0730-1030, 1800-2130, Sun 0800-1030, 1200-1400, 1800-2100

Info- Refined dining at hotel restaurant.

Tel- 01924 276310

The Red Kite £7.00 04m ④

Open- M-Sat 1200-2200, Sun 1200-2130

Info- Extensive menu. Part of M&B grp.

Tel- 01924 259044

Kingfisher Restaurant £5.50 0.5m ⑤

Open- Daily 1130-2200

Info- Fish meals, burgers etc.

Tel- 01924 274994

The Navigation Inn £5.00 0.7m ⑥

Open- *Daily 1200-2000*
Info- *Varied hot & cold meals. Quiet canalside location.*
Tel- *01924 274361*

ACCOMMODATION

Cedar Court Hotel £120 0.2m ③

Info- *On-site bar, restaurant, health club. A Best Western hotel.*
Tel- *01924 276310*

Express by Hldy Inn☞ £55 0.4m ④

Info- *Next to The Red Kite pub-restaurant.*
Tel- *01924 259044*

ESSENTIALS

Pinderfield Hospital 3m

Dir'n- *Follow signs to Wakefield/A636, and then to the A642 north of Wakefield, where the hospital is signposted.*
Tel- *01924 201688*

Knight Servicing 0.5m ①

Open- *M-F 0800-1800*
Info- *Small garage for repairs.*
Tel- *01924 274756*

Car Dealers 0.7m ⑦

Info- *Nissan & Renault.*
Dir'n- *Just beyond the Red Kite.*

THINGS TO DO

Canalside Walk 0.7m ⑥

Info- *Nice canalside walks next to pub.*
Dir'n- *Park near the Navigation Inn.*

Pugney Country Park Free 0.7m ⑧

Open- *Daylight hours.*
Info- *Pleasant country park, lake, and boats to hire. WCs.*

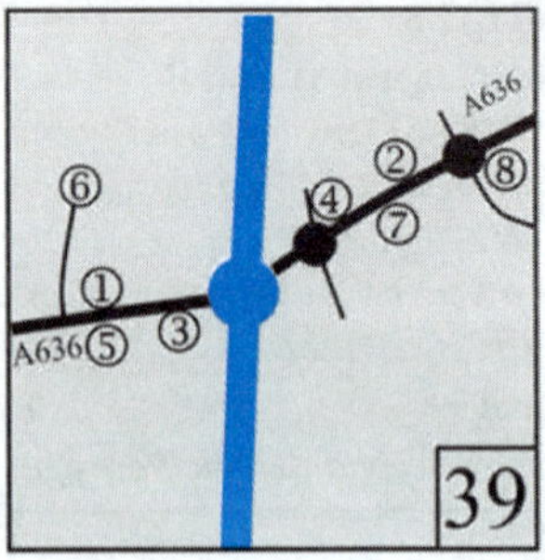

M1 Junction 40
Dewsbury

FUEL

Shell **SAVE** £££ 0.4m ①

Open- *Daily 24 hours*
Info- *WC, jetwash.*
Tel- *01924 282570*

BP **SAVE** £££ 0.5m ②

Open- *Daily 24 hours*
Info- *WC, carwash, jetwash, cash machine (Cirrus, Visa, Link, Plus).*
Tel- *01924 265947*

FOOD

Abdul's Restaurant £6.50 0.5m ③

Open- *Daily 1700-2330*
Info- *Indian restaurant and takeaway. Next to sandwich/fish & chip shops.*
Tel- *01924 200570*

Traders Restaurant £11 0.4m ④

Open- *Daily 1200-1400, 1700-2200, M-F 0630-1000, Sat/Sun 0730-1100*
Info- *Dine at the Holiday Inn restaurant.*
Tel- *0870 400 9082*

ACCOMMODATION

Days Hotel☞ £50 0.2m ⑤

Info- *On-site bar & restaurant. Wakefield location.*
Tel- *01924 274200*

Holiday Inn☞ £98 0.4m ④

Info- *On-site bar & restaurant. Wakefield location.*
Tel- *0870 400 9082*

ESSENTIALS

Pinderfield Hospital 3m

Dir'n- *Follow signs to Wakefield/A638, and then to the A642 north of Wakefield, where the hospital is signposted.*

Tel- *01924 201688*

Wakefield Tourist Information Centre

Tel- *01924 305000*

Bridge Recovery/Garage 0.6m ⑥

Open- *M-F 0900-1800 for repairs.*

Info- *24 hour recovery and car repairs.*

Tel- *01924 273368*

THINGS TO DO

Ossett 1.3m

Info- *The small town of Ossett has a fair range of facilities, and is quite pleasant for a short stop.*

M1 Junction 41
Wakefield North

FUEL

BP SAVE £££ 0.3m ①

Open- *Daily 24 hours*

Info- *WC, carwash, cash machine (Cirrus, Visa, Link, Plus).*

Tel- *01924 822260*

Esso SAVE £££ 0.5m ②

Open- *Daily 0500-2300*

Info- *WC, carwash & cash machine.*

Tel- *01924 823192*

FOOD

The Bay Horse Inn £5.50 0.3m ③

Open- *Daily 1200-2000*

Info- *Varied menu. Satellite TV.*

Tel- *01924 825926*

China Express £5.00 0.4m ④

Open- *Daily 1700-2330*

Info- *Indian & Thai takeaway meals.*

Tel- *01924 823888*

ESSENTIALS

Pinderfield Hospital 3.5m

Dir'n- *Follow signs to Wakefield/A650. and then to the A642 north of Wakefield where the hospital is located.*

Tel- *01924 201688*

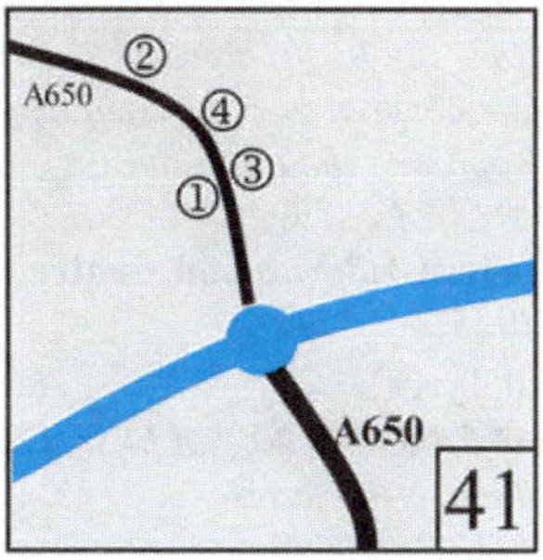

M1 Junction 42
M1/M62 interchange

M1 Junction 43
Restricted

This allows traffic from the M1 northbound to join the M621 for Leeds centre, and traffic from the M621 southbound to join the M1 southbound.

ESSENTIALS

Leeds General Infirmary 4m

Dir'n- *Take the M621 towards Leeds, and then Junction 4 turn off. The hospital is signposted as you head to the city centre.*

Tel- *0113 243 2799*

Leeds Tourist Information Centre

Tel- *0113 242 5242*

M1 Junction 44
Rothwell

FOOD

John 'O' Gaunts £8.00 0.6m ①
Open- *Tu-F 1130-1430, Tu-Sat 1730-2200, Sun 1130-2130*
Info- *Extensive bar & restaurant menu.*
Tel- *0113 282 2243*

ESSENTIALS

Leeds General Infirmary 4m
Dir'n- *Take the B6481 towards Leeds, and the hospital is signposted as you approach the city centre.*
Tel- *0113 243 2799*

Leeds Tourist Information Centre
Tel- *0113 242 5242*

Rothwell Tyres 0.6m ②
Open- *M-F 0830-1800, Sat 0830-1700*
Info- *Tyres & batteries.*
Tel- *0113 288 0099*

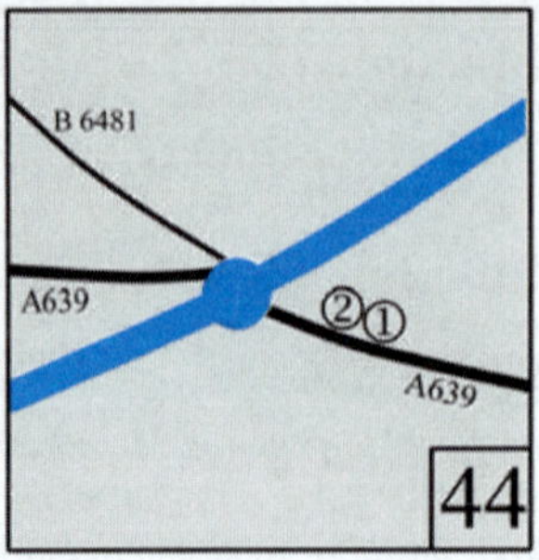

M1 Junction 45
Under construction

M1 Junction 46
Leeds East

FUEL

Texaco **SAVE** £££ 0.3m ①
Open- *Daily 24 hours*
Info- *Carwash. WC, cafe, cash machine.*
Tel- *0113 284 0100*

Sainsbury **SAVE** £££ 0.3m ②
Open- *Daily 24 hours*
Info- *Carwash, WC, cafe, cash machines at store.*
Tel- *0113 232 8154*

FOOD

Sainsbury Cafe☞ £3.50 0.3m ②
Open- *M-F 0730-1930, Sat 0730-1830, Sun 1100-1500*
Info- *Cash machine at store.*
Tel- *0113 232 8151*

Beefeater Restaurant☞ £7.00 1.0m ③
Open- *Daily 1200-2200*
Tel- *0113 286 2100*

Hilton Restaurant £15 1.2m ④
Open- *Daily 0700-0930, 1200-1400, 1900-2130*
Info- *Refined dining at the Hilton Hotel.*
Tel- *0113 286 6556*

ACCOMMODATION

Hilton Hotel☞ £100 1.2m ④
Info- *Bar, restaurant, health club. Leeds Garforth location.*
Tel- *0113 286 6556*

ESSENTIALS

St James Univ. Hospital 4.5m
Dir'n- *Take the A6120, then the A63, and then the A64 to Leeds. Turn off the A64 just before the A64(M) & head north onto Burmontoffs St. The hospital is on the left.*
Tel- *0113 243 3144*

Leeds Tourist Information Centre
Tel- *0113 242 5242*

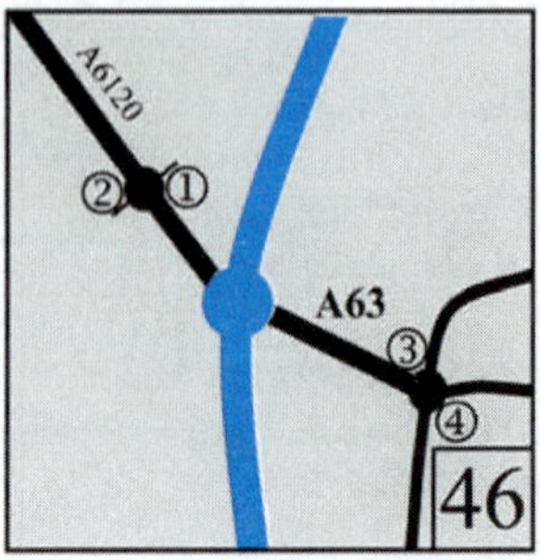

M1 Junction 47
Garforth

FUEL

Keyfuels SAVE £nil 0.9m ①
Open- *M-F 0800-1800, Sat 0900-1200*
Tel- *0113 286 2926*

Safeway SAVE £££ 1.0m ②
Open- *0600-2300*
Info- *Cafe, WC at store.*
Tel- *0113 287 5227*

FOOD

Aagrar Indian Rest. £8.50 0.5m ③
Open- *Sun-Th 1730-2330, F/Sa 1800-2330*
Info- *Indian restaurant with takeaway.*
Tel- *0113 287 6606*

Safeway Cafe☞ £3.50 0.5m ②
Open- *Sa/M/Tu 0800-1900, W/Th/F 0800-2000, Sun 1000-1530*
Tel- *0113 287 3145*

ESSENTIALS

Toll Bar Garage 0.9m ①
Open- *M-F 0800-1800, Sat 0900-1200*
Info- *Small garage for repairs.*
Tel- *0113 286 2926*

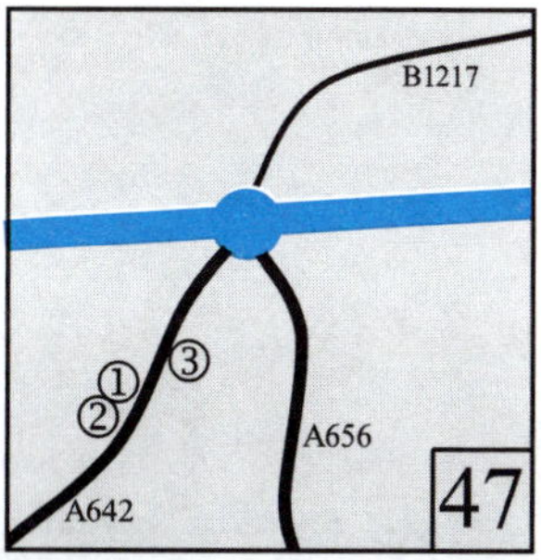

M1 Junction 48
Motorway merges with A1(M)

ESSENTIALS

York Tourist Information Centre
Tel- *01904 621756*

M2-Rochester to Faversham

M2 Summary of Junctions

Radio stations & frequencies		Junction	Fuel	Food	Hotels	Essentials	Things to do
Invicta 103.1 Magic 105.4	Essex 95.3 Kent 96.7	1					
Invicta 103.1 KM FM 100.4	Essex 95.3 Kent 96.7	2	24hr	✓		TIC	✓
Heart 106.2 LBC 97.3	Invicta 103.1 KM FM 100.4	3		✓	✓	A&E Svc	
KM FM 107.9 Heart 106.2	Essex 95.3 Kent 96.7	4	✓	✓		A&E	
KM FM 107.9 Heart 106.2	Essex 95.3 Kent 96.7	S	24hr	✓	✓		
Invicta 103.1 BBC Essx 95.3	Essex 95.3 Kent 96.7	5		✓			
Kingsfry 106.6 BBC Essx 95.3	Essex 95.3 Kent 96.7	6	✓	✓		TIC Svc	✓
Kingsfry 106.6 BBC Essx 95.3	Essex 95.3 Kent 96.7	7	✓	✓	✓	A&E TIC	✓

Top Stops are highlighted

M2 Junction Details

M2 Junction 1
Rochester/Motorway starts

This junction is an intersection with the A2, and there are no local facilities accessible.

M2 Junction 2
Rochester/Chatham

FUEL

Spur SAVE £ nil 1.0m ①
Open- *M-F 0600-2000, Sat 0700-2000, Sun 0900-1600*
Info- *Small independent garage.*
Tel- *01634 717987*

Esso SAVE ££ 1.1m ②
Open- *Daily 24 hours*
Info- *WC, carwash.*
Tel- *01634 719286*

FOOD

The White Hart £7.50 1m ③
Open- *M-Sat 1200-1500, 1900-2100, Sun 1200-1500*
Info- *Local pub with extensive menu & real ales.*
Tel- *01634 711857*

McDonald's☞ £8.50 1.2m ④
Open- *Su-Th 1000-2300, F/Sa 1000-2400*
Tel- *01634 719122*

Chiquito's☞ £6.00 1.2m ④
Open- *M-Sat 1200-1430, 1830-2100, Sun 1200-1800*
Tel- *01634 713816*

Frankie & Benny's☞ £8.50 1.2m ④
Open- *Su-Th 1200-2200, F/Sa 1200-2300*
Tel- *01634 712209*

Exchange Bar & Grill £8.50 1.2m ④
Open- *M-Sat 1200-2230, Sun 1200-2300*
Info- *Mexican meals & burgers. Real ales.*
Tel- *01634 719306*

ESSENTIALS

Rochester Tourist Information Centre
Tel- *01634 843666*

Ford Dealer 1.1m ②
Dir'n- *Next to the Esso filling station.*

THINGS TO DO

Diggerland £2.50 1.1m ⑤
Open- *Weekends & bank holidays 1000-1700*
Info- *Have fun driving and watching a large variety of diggers. Price just includes entry & rides are extra.*
Tel- *08700 344437*

Rochester 1.3m
Info- *A historic town with an attractive centre that is well worth a quick visit. Rochester has a castle, an impressive naval museum, and is well equipped with restaurants & small shops.*

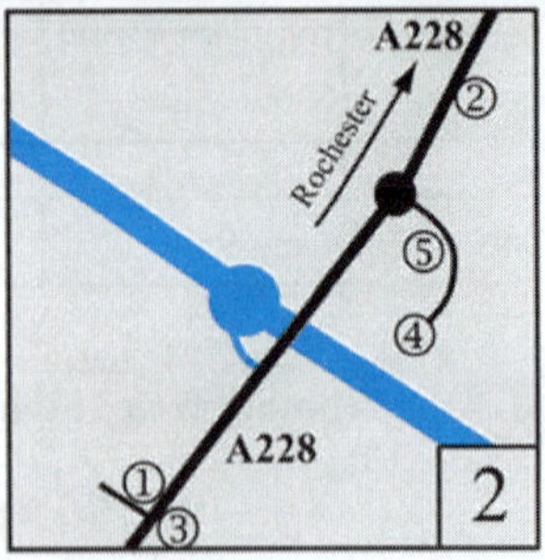

M2 Junction 3
M20 Link Road

FOOD

Squires restaurant £20 1m ①
Open- *Daily 0730-0930, 1230-1430, 1900-2200*
Info- *Refined dining at the Bridgewater Manor hotel.*
Tel- *01634 201333*

Rotisserie restaurant £10 1m ②

Open- *M-F 0630-1000, Sa/Sun 0730-1100*
M-F 1230-1430, Daily 1800-2200

Info- *Extensive menu at the Holiday Inn.*

Tel- *0870 400 9069*

ACCOMMODATION

Bridgewater Manor £130 1m ①

Info- *Bar, restaurant, leisure club, tennis court & pool. A Marston Hotel.*

Tel- *01634 201333*

Holiday Inn☞ £130 1m ②

Info- *Bar, restaurant, health club & pool. Rochester-Chatham location.*

Tel- *0870 400 9069*

ESSENTIALS

Medway Maritime Hospital 4.5m

Dir'n- *Take the A229 north towards Chatham and the hospital is signposted.*

Tel- *01634 830000*

Formula One Autocentre 1.4m ②

Open- *M-F 0830-1730, Sat 0900-1700, Sun 1000-1600*

Info- *Car servicing and tyres.*

Dir'n- *At the first roundabout past the Holiday Inn*

Tel- *01634 671100*

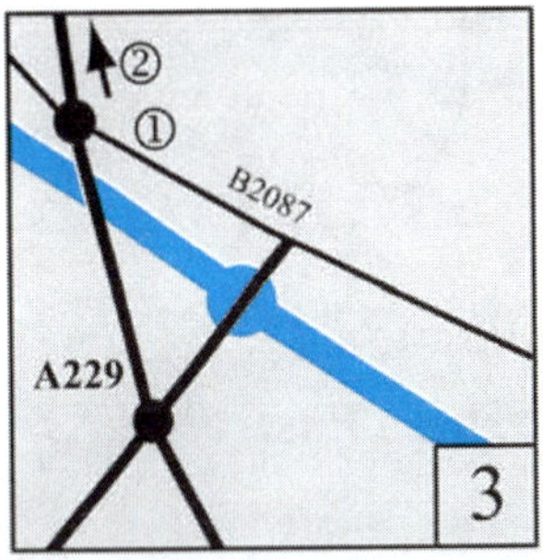

M2 Junction 4
Gillingham

FUEL

Asda SAVE ££ 1.1m ①

Open- *M-Sat 0630-2130, Sun 0830-1700*

Info- *WC, cash machine at store.*

Tel- *01634 671100*

FOOD

McDonald's☞ £7.50 1m ①

Open- *Daily 0800-2200*

Tel- *01634 268814*

ESSENTIALS

Medway Maritime Hospital 4.5m

Dir'n- *Take the A278 north towards Gillingham, and then the A2 west towards Chatham. The hospital is signposted from the A2.*

Tel- *01634 830000*

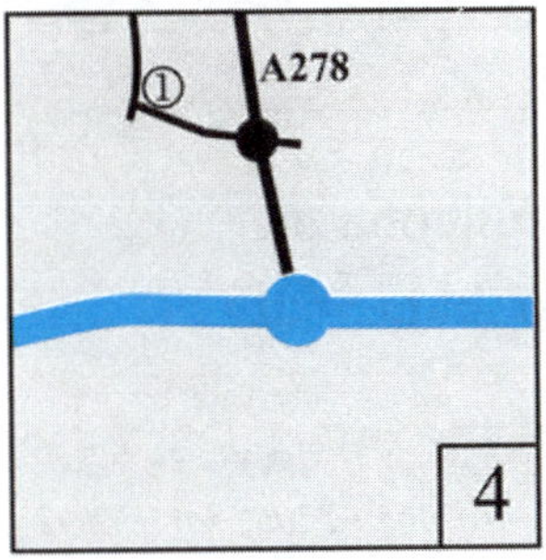

Medway Services

There are a footbridge and roadbridge at this services.

FUEL BP

HGV fuelling & parking. Free parking for 2 hours then £6 per day.

FOOD MOTO

Burger King, Little Chef, Upper Crust

Info- *Cash machines.*

ACCOMMODATION

Travelodge☞ £50

Info- *Medway location.*

Tel- *0870 191 1697*

M2 Junction 5
Sittingbourne

FOOD

The Harrow £8.00 1m ①

Open- *M-Sat 1200-1400, 1900-2030, Sun 1200-1500*

Info- *Extensive hot & cold menu.*

Dir'n- *Take the first right exit off the dual carriageway, and then turn right at the T junction.*
Tel- *01795 842546*

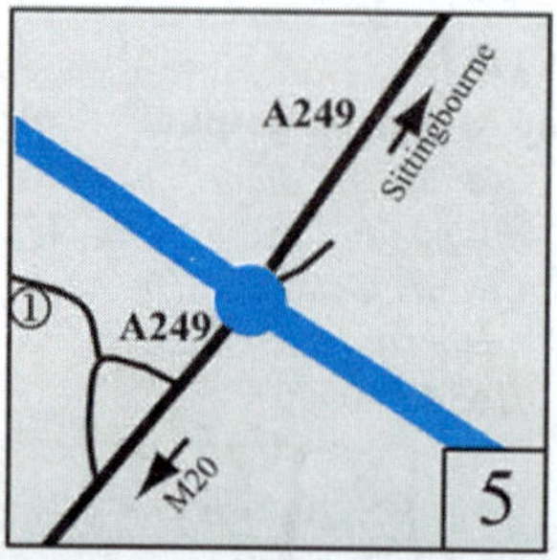

M2 Junction 6
Faversham South

FUEL

Jet SAVE ££ 1m ①
Open- *M-F 0630-2200, Sat 0700-2200, Sun 0800-2100*
Info- *WC.*
Dir'n- *This is in Stone Street in the centre of Faversham.*
Tel- *01795 265661*

Shell SAVE ££ 1m ②
Open- *M-Sat 0600-2200, Sun 0700-2100*
Info- *WC, LPG.*
Tel- *01795 542910*

FOOD

The Elephant £7.50 0.5m ③
Open- *Ownership change at time of press.*
Info- *Thai food and standard favourites. Real ales.*
Tel- *01795 531999*

The Windmill £4.50 0.8m ④
Open- *Daily 1200-1400, 1830-2100*
Info- *Varied menu at village pub.*
Tel- *01795 536505*

The Ship £4.50 1.1m ⑤
Open- *Daily 1200-1400, 1900-2100*
Info- *Varied menu at village pub.*
Tel- *01795 532408*

ESSENTIALS

Faversham Tourist Infomation Centre
Tel- *01795 534542*

Autocheck 1m ①
Info- *Car servicing & tyres*
Dir'n- *Next to the Jet Garage in Stone Street in Faversham.*
Tel- *01227 751441*

THINGS TO DO

Faversham 1.7m
Info- *Faversham is a pleasant small town with numerous historic buildings,*

Shepherd Neame Brewery
Open- *Shop M-F 0900-1700*
Info- *Brewery tours by arrangement.*
Tel- *01795 532206*

Brogdale Fruit Collection 1.7m ⑥
Open- *Daily 1000-1700*
Info- *National Fruit Collection. Free entry to large orchards, shop, cafe & plant centre.*
Dir'n- *As you drive towards Faversham, take the A2 towards Sittingbourne and Brogdale is well signposted.*
Tel- *01795 535286*

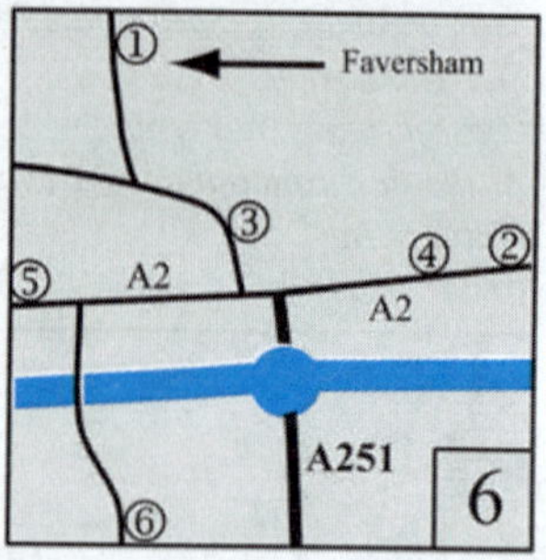

M2 Junction 7
Faversham East

FUEL

Shell SAVE ££ 0.9m ①
Open- *M-Sat 0600-2200, Sun 0700-2100*
Info- *WC, LPG.*
Tel- *01795 542910*

FOOD

The Windmill £4.50 1.1m ②
Open- *Daily 1200-1400, 1830-2100*
Info- *Varied menu at village pub.*
Tel- *01795 536505*

White Horse Inn £10 1m ③

Open- *Daily 1200-1500, 1815-2130*

Info- *Extensive menu at this local inn.*

Dir'n- *At the motorway roundabout take the turn-off before the A299, and at the T junction at the end turn left.*

Tel- *01227 751343*

Garden Hotel rest. £10 1m ④

Open- *Daily 1200-1500, 1815-2130*

Info- *Extensive menu at the Garden Hotel.*

Dir'n- *See the White Horse Inn directions above.*

Tel- *01227 751411*

Others 1.1m

Info- *Faversham has a fair range of pubs and restaurants.*

ACCOMMODATION

White Horse Inn £75 1m ③

Info- *13 bedrooms in this local inn. Price is B&B.*

Dir'n- *See the White Horse Inn directions above.*

Tel- *01227 751343*

The Garden Hotel £70 1m ④

Info- *Restaurant on-site, pets welcome. Price is B&B.*

Dir'n- *See the White Horse Inn directions above.*

Tel- *01227 751411*

ESSENTIALS

Kent & Canterbury Hospital 1.7m

Dir'n- *Take the A2 towards Canterbury, where the hospital is signposted.*

Tel- *01227 766877*

Faversham Tourist Infomation Centre

Tel- *01795 534542*

Canterbury Tourist Infomation Centre

Tel- *01227 766567*

Whitstable Tourist Infomation Centre

Tel- *01227 275482*

THINGS TO DO

Faversham 1.7m

Info- *Faversham is a pleasant small town with numerous historic buildings, and the Shepherd Neame brewery to visit. See Jn 6 for more details.*

Canterbury 6m

Info- *This renowned city has a historic centre and Cathedral, and a wide range of other tourist facilities.*

Whitstable 6m

Info- *This is a pretty and cosmopolitan seaside town with pleasant walks, pubs and restaurants.*

Brogdale Fruit Collection 1.7m ⑥

Open- *Daily 1000-1700*

Info- *National Fruit Collection with free entry to large orchards, shop, cafe & plant centre.*
Special events in Sept & October.

Dir'n- *Take the A2 towards Sittingbourne and Brogdale is well signposted.*

Tel- *01795 535286*

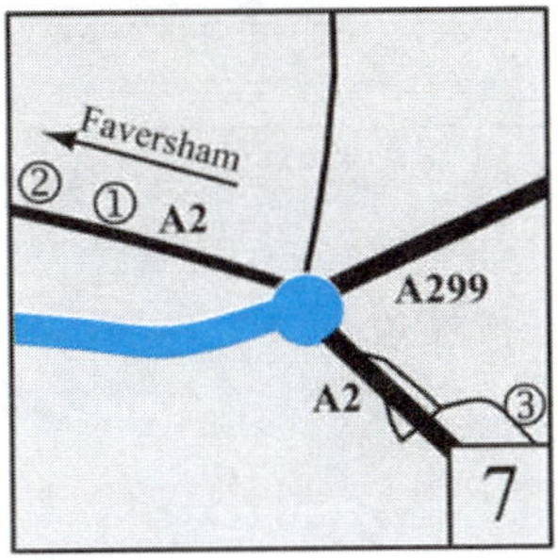

M3-London to Southampton

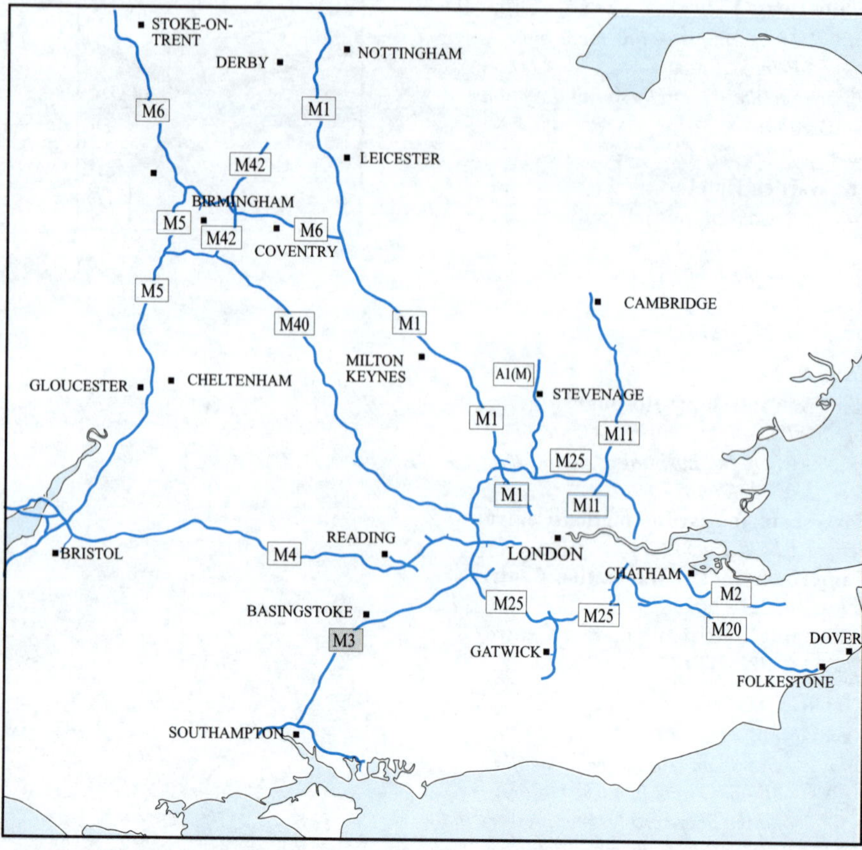

M3 Summary of Junctions

Radio stations & frequencies		Junction	Fuel	Food	Hotels	Essentials	Things to do
Capital 95.8 Magic 105.4	LBC 97.3 Heart 106.2	1	Motorway starts			A&E	
Capital 95.8 KISS 100	LBC 97.3 Magic 105.4	2				A&E	
Capital 95.8 KISS 100.0	Heart 106.2 Eagle 96.4	3	24hr	✓	✓	Pharmacy Svc	✓
BBC LDN 94.9 Virgin 105.8	Eagle 96.4 SCR 104.6	4	24hr	✓	✓	A&E,TIC Pharmacy	
BBC LDN 94.9 2-Ten 102.9	Virgin 105.8 Eagle 96.4	4a	✓	✓	✓	TIC	
BBC LDN 94.9 2-Ten 102.9	Virgin 105.8 Eagle 96.4	S	24hr	✓	✓		
2-Ten 102.9 Eagle 96.4	LDN 94.9 SCR 104.6	5	24hr	✓	✓	Pharmacy	
2-Ten 102.9 BBC SCR 104.6	Delta 102.0 Berks 104.1	6			✓	A&E TIC	✓
Kestrel 107.6 RDG 107.0	Win FM 107.2 Wave 105.2	7		✓			
Kestrel 107.6 RDG 107.0	Win FM 107.2 Wave 105.2	8					
Win FM 107.2 Wave 105.2	Berks 104.1 2-Ten 102.9	S	24hr	✓	✓		
Win FM 107.2 Wave 105.2	Berks 104.1 2-Ten 102.9	9	24hr	✓		TIC A&E	✓
Berks 104.1 2-Ten FM 102.9	Win FM 107.2 Wave 105.2	10				TIC A&E	
BBc Slnt 96.1 Wave 105 105.2	Ocean 96.7 Power 102.9	11				A&E TIC	
BBC Slnt 96.1 Wave 105 105.2	Ocean 96.7 Power 102.9	12	✓	✓	✓	Svc	
BBc Slnt 96.1 Wave 105 105.2	Ocean 96.7 Power 102.9	13	✓	✓	✓	Svc	
BBc Slnt 96.1 Wave 105 105.2	Ocean 96.7 Power 102.9	14	Motorway ends			A&E TIC	

Top Stops are highlighted

M3 Junction Details

M3 Junction 1
Motorway starts

ESSENTIALS

West Middlesex Hospital 4.5m
Dir'n- *Take the A316 to London, and then the A310 to Brentford. The hospital is on the right, off the A310.*
Tel- *0208 560 2121*

M3 Junction 2
M3/M25 interchange

ESSENTIALS

St Peter's Hospital 3m
Dir'n- *Take the M25 south to Junction 11, and then the A320 west, where the hospital is signposted.*
Tel- *01932 872000*

M3 Junction 3
Bagshot

FUEL

BP SAVE £ 1.4m ①
Open- *Daily 24 hours*
Info- *WC & cash machines.*
Tel- *01276 476469*

Total SAVE £ 1.4m ②
Open- *M-Sat 0700-2100, Sun 0800-2100*
Info- *Carwash.*
Tel- *01276 473881*

FOOD

Dirbar Tandoori £8.00 0.6m ③
Open- *M-Fri 1700-2300, Sa/Su 1700-2330*
Info- *Indian meals to take away.*
Tel- *01276 476579*

Hardy's TexMex £10 0.7m ④
Open- *M-Sat 1800-2200, Sun 1700-2100*
Info- *Texan and Mexican style food.*
Tel- *01276 477477*

Herbie's Pizza £8.00 0.7m ④
Open- *Su-Th 1200-2300, Fr/Sa 1130-2400*
Info- *Takeaway pizza and pasta.*
Tel- *01276 476777*

Hungry Horse Pub☞ £3.00 0.7m ⑤
Open- *Daily 1200-2130*
Info- *Extensive hot & cold menu. Satellite TV.*
Tel- *01276 473812*

Bredwyn S'dwich Shop £2.00 0.7m ④
Open- *M-F 0830-1430, Sat/Sun closed.*
Info- *Takeaway sandwiches to order & hot and cold drinks.*
Tel- *01276 473578*

New China Takeaway £6.00 0.7m ⑤
Open- *Daily 1730-2330*
Info- *Chinese meals to take away.*
Tel- *01276 473284*

Bel Vedere £13 0.7m ⑥
Open- *M-F 1200-1430, 1900-2230, Sat 1900-2300*
Info- *Refined Italian dining.*
Tel- *01276 475583*

Brewers Fayre☞ £7.00 0.9m ⑦
Open- *M-Sat 1130-2300, Sun 1200-2230*
Tel- *01276 479942*

Old Barn Restaurant £6.50 1.0m ⑧
Open- *Daily 1100-2300*
Info- *Varied bar & restaurant menu.*
Tel- *01276 476673*

Jacks £5.00 1.0m ①
Open- *Daily 0700-2230*
Info- *Breakfasts & fried dinners.*
Tel- *01276 473193*

Out & Out Pub☞ £13 1.2m ⑨
Open- *Daily 1100-2300*
Tel- *01276 473196*

ACCOMMODATION

Fighting Cocks £50 0.8m ⑥
Info- *Independent pub with rooms. Prices are for room only.*
Tel- *01276 473160*

Travel Inn☞ £45 1.2m ⑨
Info- *Bagshot location.*
Tel- *0870 197 7021*

ESSENTIALS

Roadwheel Tyre & Exhaust 0.6m ③
Open- *M-F 0830-1700, Sat 0830-1300*
Info- *Tyre & exhaust centre.*
Tel- *01276 476579*

Lloyds Pharmacy 0.8m ⑤
Open- *M-F 0900-1830, Sat 0900-1730*
Tel- *01276 473211*

THINGS TO DO

Lightwater Country Park 0.7m ⑩
Open- *Daylight hours*
Info- *300 hectare park with lake, woods and heathland.*

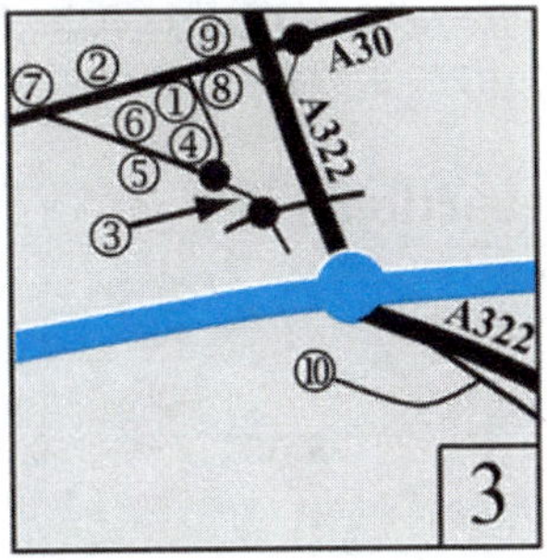

M3 Junction 4
Frimley

The road layout at this junction is complex. Follow signs to Frimley town centre for restaurants, and for Farnborough town centre for the BP filling station. Follow signs to the A331/Camberley/Bracknell for the Sainsbury store.

FUEL

Sainsbury SAVE £ 0.9m ①
Open- *Daily 24 hours*
Info- *Carwash. WC & cash machine at store.*
Tel- *01276 676829*

BP SAVE £ 1.4m ②
Open- *Daily 24 hours*
Info- *WC , carwash & cash machines.*
Tel- *01252 524457*

FOOD

Sainsbury Cafe☞ £3.50 0.9m ①
Open- *M-Sat 0800-1900, Sun 0900-1500*
Tel- *01276 676829*

Gallant restaurant £10 1.0m ③
Open- *M-Sat 1200-1400, 1800-2300*
Info- *Peking & Cantonese meals*
Tel- *01276 64484*

The Ancient Raj £10 1.0m ④
Open- *M-Sa 1200-1430, 1800-2300, Sun 1200-1430, 1800-2200*
Info- *Indian meals. Dine in & take away.*
Tel- *01276 26042*

Frimley Tandoori £8 1.1m ⑤
Open- *Daily 1200-1400, 1800-2300*
Info- *Indian meals to take away.*
Tel- *01276 685537*

Yum Yum £7.50 1.2m ⑥
Open- *Daily 1800-2330*
Info- *Chinese meals to take away.*
Tel- *01276 63280*

Bensons Coffee Shop £6.50 1.2m ⑥
Open- *M-F 0800-1530, Sat 0900-1500*
Info- *Varied light meals & snacks.*
Tel- *07798 723228*

Villa Bianca £10 1.1m ⑦
Open- *Daily 1230-1400, 1830-2230*
Info- *Italian restaurant with extensive menu.*
Tel- *01276 62879*

ACCOMMODATION

Innkeeper's Lodge☞ £50 1.2m ⑧
Info- *Frimley location.*
Tel- *01276 691939*

ESSENTIALS

Frimley Park Hospital 0.7m ③
Dir'n- *Hospital is signposted as you head towards Frimley.*
Tel- *01276 604604*

Moss Pharmacy 1.1m ④
Open- *M-Sat 0900-1730*
Tel- *01276 63636*

Farnborough Tourist Information Centre
Tel- *01252 320968*

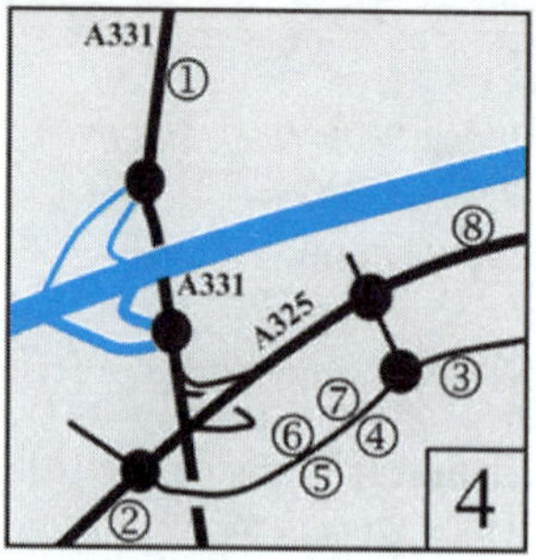

M3 Junction 4a
Farnborough

FUEL

Total SAVE ££ 1.2m ①
Open- Daily 0600-2300
Info- Carwash, cash machine.
Tel- 01252 772630

FOOD

Harvester £7.00 1.2m ①
Open- M-Sat 1200-2200, Sun 1200-2130
Tel- 01252 816655

ACCOMMODATION

Innkeeper's Lodge☞ £60 0.9m ①
Info- Fleet location.
Tel- 01252 774600

ESSENTIALS

Farnborough Tourist Information Centre
Tel- 01252 320968

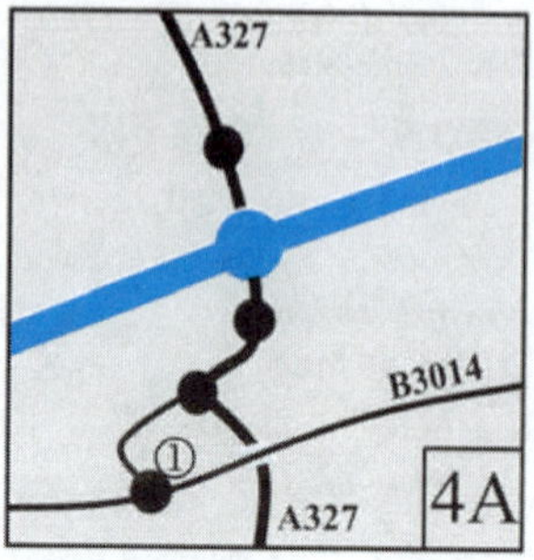

Fleet Services

There is a footbridge at this services.

FUEL SHELL

LPG, HGV fuelling. Free parking for 2 hours then £6 per 24 hours. Lorry park.

FOOD WELCOME BREAK

foodconnection, Burger King, Coffee Express, McDonald's.
Info- Cash machines (no Maestro or Cirrus)

ACCOMMODATION

Days Inn ☞ (Westbound) £55
Info- Basingstoke East location
Tel- 01252 815587

M3 Junction 5
Hook

FUEL

Q8 SAVE £ 0.9m ①
Open- Daily 24 hours
Info- WC, carwash.
Tel- 01256 701620

Texaco SAVE £ 1.1m ②
Open- M-Sat 0500-2200, Sun 0630-2200
Info- Carwash, WC.
Tel- 01256 740660

Total SAVE £ 1.1m ③
Open- Daily 0700-2200
Info- Jetwash.
Tel- 01256 743772

FOOD

Dorchester Arms £7.00 0.8m ④
Open- M-Th 1130-1430,Fr-Sat 1130-1430, 1830-2130 , Sun 1200-1500
Info- Varied hot & cold meals.
Tel- 01256 762690

The Gate of India £8.00 0.8m ⑤
Open- Daily 1230-1430, 1800-2330
Info- Indian restaurant & takeaway.
Tel- 01256 761216

Tesco Cafe☞ £3.50 0.6m ⑥
Open- M/Tu/W/Sat 0800-1800, Th/F 0800-1900, Sun 1000-1600

Info- *Cash machine at store.*
Tel- *0845 677 9352*

Raven Pub/Restaurant £7.00 0.8m ⑦
Open- *M-Sat 1200-1430, 1800-2230,*
Sun 1200-1430, 1900-2130
Info- *Extensive hot & cold menu*
Tel- *01256 762541*

Hook Tandoori £9.00 0.8m ⑧
Open- *Daily 1200-1430, 1800-2330*
Info *Indian restaurant & takeaway.*
Tel- *01256 764844*

Taste of Little India £8.50 0.9m ⑨
Open- *Daily 1730-2300*
Info *Indian restaurant with takeaway.*
Tel- *01256 767474*

The White Hart £7.00 1.0m ②
Open- *M-Sat 1100-2200, Sun 1200-2130*
Info- *Extensive hot & cold menu.*
Tel- *01256 762462*

The Old White Hart £4.50 1.0m ⑨
Open- *Daily 1200-1430, Tu-Th 1800-2100*
Info *Varied bar meals. Satellite TV.*
Children allowed up to 6pm.
Tel- *01256 762560*

Others
Info- *There are several other pleasant restaurants en-route to the Q8 filling station.*

ACCOMMODATION

Raven Hotel £88 0.8m ⑦
Info- *A Greene King Hotel. Price is B&B.*
Tel- *01256 762541*

Oaklea Guest House £60 1.0m ⑨
Info- *Private guest house with bar.*
AA/ETB 3◆.
Tel- *01256 762673*

ESSENTIALS

Moss Pharmacy 0.9m ②
Open- *M-F 0900-1800, Sat 0900-1600*
Tel- *01256 762497*

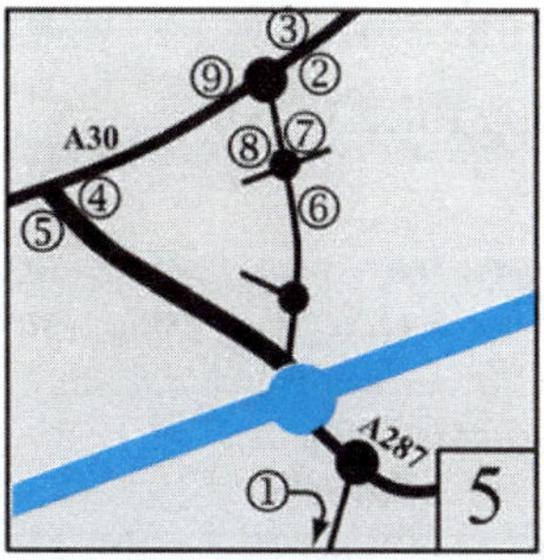

M3 Junction 6
Basingstoke

ACCOMMODATION

Hilton Hotel £150 1.4m ①
Info- *Bar, restaurant, pool & gym.*
Basingstoke location.
Dir'n- *Well signposted from the A30.*
Tel- *01870 240 6562*

ESSENTIALS

North Hampshire Hospital 3.5m
Dir'n- *This is well signposted as you drive towards Basingstoke.*
Tel- *01256 473202*

ESSENTIALS

Basingstoke Tourist Information Centre
Tel- *01256 817618*

THINGS TO DO

Crabtree Plantation 1.3m ②
Open- *Daylight hours.*
Info- *Public wood & ponds.*

M3 Junction 7
Basingstoke West

FOOD

The Queen Inn £10 0.4m ①

Open- *Daily 1200-1430, 1800-2130*
Info- *Extensive hot & cold menu. Children welcome before 7pm.*
Tel- *01256 397367*

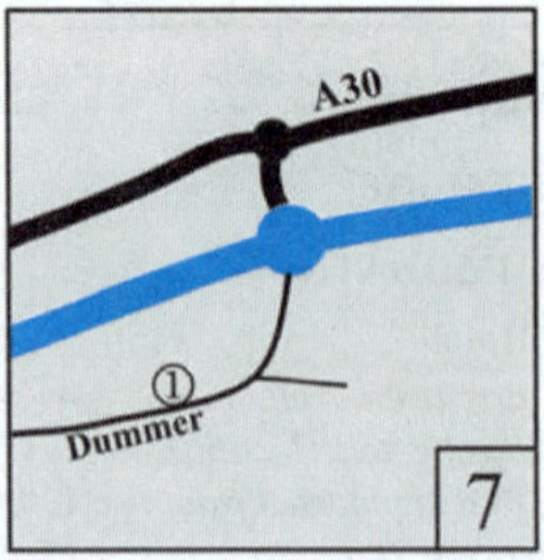

M3 Junction 8
Restricted

This junction only allows entry to the M3 east, and exit from the M3 west.

Winchester Services

There are no footbridge or roadbridge at this services.

FUEL TEXACO

HGV fuelling. Free parking for 2 hours then £6 per 24 hours. Lorry park. Cash machine.

FOOD ROADCHEF

Food from onroute, Dr Beak's Kitchen, Costa Coffee, Wimpy.
Info- *Cash machine.*

ACCOMMODATION

Travel Inn £45
Info- *Winchester location.*
Tel- *0870 197 7272*

M3 Junction 9
Winchester

FUEL

Tesco SAVE ££ 0.3m ①
Open- *Daily 24 hours*
Info- *Jetwash, carwash. WC and cash machine at store.*
Tel- *0845 677 9723*

Shell SAVE ££ 0.3m ②
Open- *Daily 24 hours*
Info- *LPG, carwash, WC, cash machine.*
Tel- *01962 876810*

FOOD

Tesco Cafe☞ £3.50 0.3m ①
Open- *M--W 0800-1800, Sun 1000-1500, Th/F/Sat 0700-2000*
Info- *Cash machine at store.*
Tel- *0845 677 9723*

ESSENTIALS

Royal Hampshire Hospital 3m
Dir'n- *Follow signposts to Winchester city centre, and from the centre to the B3040/A3090. The hospital is signposted within a mile of the centre.*
Tel- *01962 863535*

Winchester Tourist Info. Centre
Tel- *01962 840500*

Car dealers
Info- *Nissan, MG and Rover dealers.*
Dir'n- *Next to the Shell filling station.*

THINGS TO DO

Winchester 2m
Info- *The historic city of Winchester provides a good break from the motorway.*

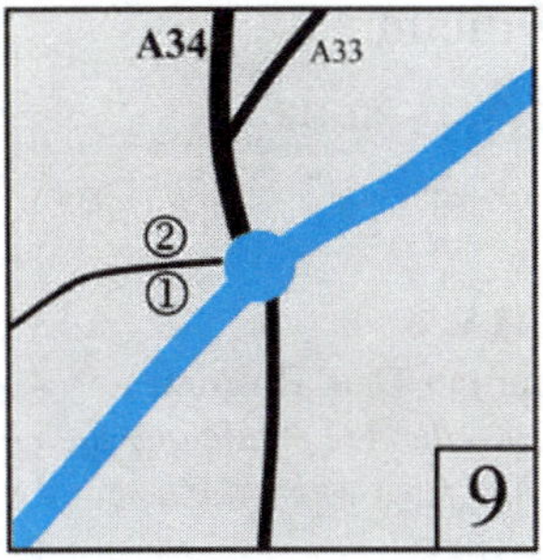

M3 Junction 10
Restricted

This junction only allows entry to the motorway going westwards, or exit coming from the west.

ESSENTIALS

Royal Hampshire Hospital 2.5m

Dir'n- *Follow signposts to Winchester city centre, and from the centre to the B3040/A3090. The hospital is signposted within a mile of the centre.*

Tel- *01962 863535*

Winchester Tourist Information Centre

Tel- *01962 840500*

M3 Junction 11
Twyford

ESSENTIALS

Royal Hampshire Hospital 3m ①

Dir'n- *This is well signposted as you head towards Winchester/St Cross on the B3335.*

Tel- *01962 863535*

Winchester Tourist Information Centre

Tel- *01962 840500*

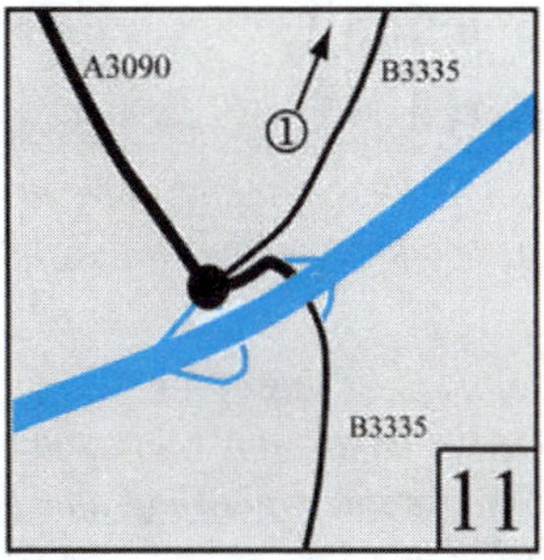

M3 Junction 12
Chandlers Ford

FUEL

Shell SAVE ££ 1.0m ①

Open- *Daily 0600-2300*

Info- *WC, jetwash.*

Tel- *023 8025 9990*

FOOD

Harvester £7.00 0.9m ②

Open- *Daily 1200-2130*

Info- *Family pub/restaurant chain.*

Tel- *023 8061 9181*

ACCOMMODATION

Travelodge☞ £45 0.9m ②

Info- *Southampton Eastleigh location. Located next to Harvester.*

Tel- *0870 191 1514*

ESSENTIALS

Kwik Fit 1.0m ①

Open- *M-F 0800-1800, Sat 0800-1700, Sun 1000-1600*

Tel- *023 8025 9990*

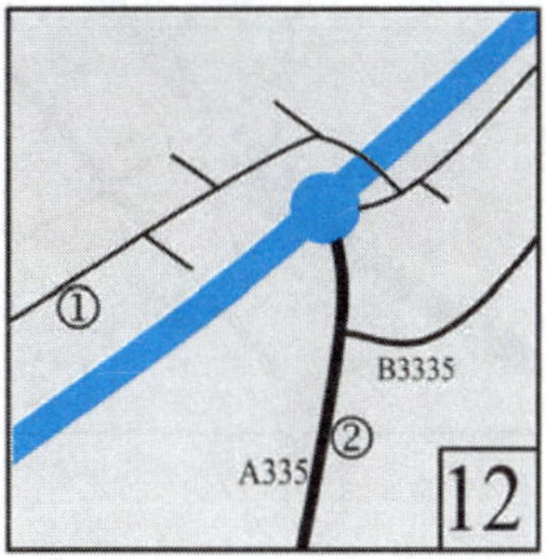

M3 Junction 13
Restricted

This junction does not allow entry to the motorway heading eastwards.

FUEL

Total SAVE ££ 0.5m ①
Open- *M-Sat 0630-2300, Sun 0700-2200*
Info- *Alldays late night shop attached.*
Tel- *023 8064 1722*

FOOD

Brewers Fayre☞ £7.00 0.2m ②
Open- *Daily 0800-1000, 1200-2200*
Tel- *023 8065 0541*

The Leigh £5.00 0.2m ③
Open- *M-F 1200-1430, 1700-1900, Sat 1900-2100, Sun 1230-1530*
Info- *Pub food. Satellite TV.*
Tel- *023 8061 2174*

ACCOMMODATION

Travel Inn☞ £45 0.2m ②
Info- *Southampton Eastleigh location. Located next to Brewers Fayre.*
Tel- *0870 197 7090*

Holiday Inn☞ £125 0.2m ④
Info- *Restaurant/health club. Eastleigh location.*
Tel- *0870 400 9075*

ESSENTIALS

HiQ Autocentre 0.4m ⑤
Info- *Tyre & exhaust centre*
Tel- *023 8061 4566*

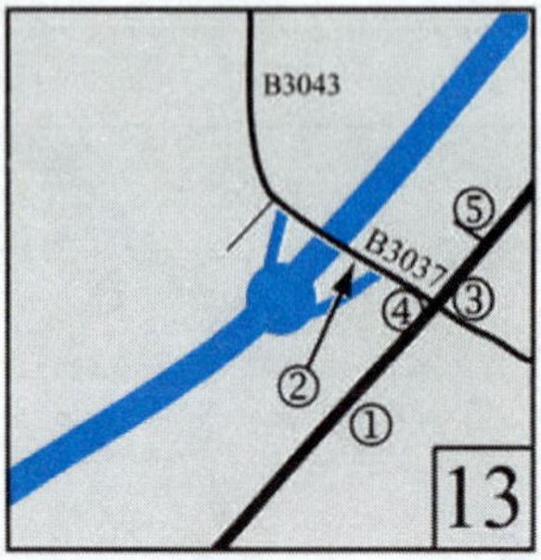

M3 Junction 14
Motorway ends

The motorway ends here and merges with the M27.

ESSENTIALS

Southampton Gen. Hospital 4.5m
Dir'n- *Take the A33 south, and then the A35 from where the hospital is signposted.*
Tel- *023 8077 7222*

Southampton Tourist Information Centre
Tel- *023 8083 3333*

M4-London to Swansea

M4 Summary of Junctions

Radio stations & frequencies		Junction	Fuel	Food	Hotels	Essentials	Things to do
Capital 95.8 Magic 105.4	LBC 97.3 Heart 106.2	1	24hr			A&E	
Capital 95.8 KISS 100	LBC 97.3 Magic 105.4	2				A&E	
Capital 95.8 LBC 97.3	964 Eagle 96.4 KISS 100.0	S	24hr	✓	✓		
Capital 95.8 LBC 97.3	964 Eagle 96.4 KISS 100.0	3	24hr	✓		A&E, TIC	
Capital 95.8 964 Eagle 96.4	LDN 94.9 LBC 97.3	4	24hr	✓	✓	A&E Pharmacy	
Capital 95.8 964 Eagle 96.4	LDN 94.9 LBC 97.3	4a					
BBC LDN 94.9 LBC 97.3	Capital 95.8 KISS 100.0	5	24hr	✓	✓	A&E Svc	
2-Ten 102.9 Star 1066 106.6	Heart 106.2 Shake FM 89.3	6	24hr	✓	✓	A&E	
2-Ten 102.9 Star 1066 106.6	Heart 106.2 Shake FM 89.3	7	24hr	✓		Pharmacy	
2-Ten FM 102.9 Star 1066 106.6	Heart 106.2 Shake FM 89.3	8/9	24hr	✓			
2-Ten FM 97.0 RDG 107.0	BBC Berks 104.1 Kestrel	10				A&E TIC	
2-Ten FM 97.0 RDG 107.0	Berks 104.1 Kestrel 107.6	11	✓	✓	✓	TIC A&E	
2-Ten FM 97.0 RDG 107.0	Berks 104.1 Kestrel 107.6	S	24hr	✓	✓		
2-Ten FM 97.0 RDG 107.0	Berks 104.1 Kestrel 107.6	12	24hr	✓	✓	A&E, TIC Pharmacy	
Oxford 95.2 Berks 104.1	2-10 FM 102.9 Kick FM 105.6	13 S	24hr	✓		TIC	
Kick FM 105.6 2-Ten FM 102.9	Berks 104.1	14		✓			
Kick FM 105.6 2-Ten FM 102.9	Berks 104.1	S	24hr	✓	✓		
Swindon 103.6 GWR 97.2	Fox FM 102.6 BBC Oxford	15	24hr	✓	✓	A&E TIC	

Top Stops are highlighted

Radio stations & frequencies		Junction	Fuel	Food	Hotels	Essentials	Things to do
Oxford 95.2 BBC Glos 95.8	Bristol 95.5 GWR 97.2	16		✓	✓	TIC	
BBC Brstl 95.5 Swindon 103.6	GWR Sw 97.2 GWR W 102.2	17	24hr	✓		TIC	
BBC Brstl 95.5 BBC Swin 103.6	GWR Sw 97.2 GWR W 102.2	S	24hr	✓	✓		
BBC Brstl 95.5 BBC Swin 103.6	GWR W 102.2 BBC W 104.3	18		✓	✓	TIC	
BBC Brstl 95.5 BBC Swin 103.6	GWR W 102.2 BBC W 104.3	19				A&E TIC	
BBC Brstl 95.5 BBC Swin 103.6	GWR W 102.2 BBC W 104.3	20				TIC	
BBC Brstl 95.5 BBC Swin 103.6	GWR W 102.2 BBC W 104.3	21					
BBC Wales 95.9 Redragon 97.4	BBC Bstl 95.5	22					
BBC Brstl 95.5 BBC Swin 103.6	GWR W 102.2 BBC W 104.3	19					
BBC Brstl 95.5 BBC Swin 103.6	GWR W 102.2 BBC W 104.3	23 S	24hr	✓	✓	Svc	
BBC Wales 95.9 Redragon 97.4	BBC Bstl 95.5	24	24hr	✓	✓	TIC	
BBC Bstl 95.5 Redragon 97.4	Wales 95.9	25	✓	✓		Pharmacy TIC	
BBC Bstl 95.5 Redragon 97.4	Wales 95.9	25a				A&E	
BBC Bstl 95.5 Redragon 97.4	Wales 95.9	26	24hr	✓		A&E TIC Pharmacy	
BBC Bstl 95.5 Redragon 97.4	Wales 95.9	27	24hr	✓	✓	TIC	✓
Redragon 103.2 BBC Bstl 85.5	Real 105.4 GWR B 106.9	28	✓			A&E TIC	
Redragon 103.2 BBC Bstl 85.5	Real 105.4 GWR B 106.9	29				A&E TIC	
Redragon 103.2 BBC Bstl 85.5	Real 105.4 GWR B 106.9	30 S	24hr	✓	✓	A&E, TIC Pharmacy	
			Junction 31 is non-existent				
Redragon 103.2 BBC Bstl 85.5	Real 105.4 GWR B 106.9	32	24hr	✓	✓	A&E TIC	
Vibe 101 101.0 GTFM 106.9	Orchard 102.6 Wales 103.9	33 S	24hr	✓	✓		

Radio stations & frequencies		Junction	Fuel	Food	Hotels	Essentials	Things to do
Vibe 101 101.0 GTFM 106.9	Orchard 102.6 Wales 103.9	34	24hr	✓	✓	A&E	
Bridge 106.3 Wales 94.6	Real 105.4 BBCymru 95.0	35	24hr	✓	✓	Pharmacy TIC	
Bridge 106.3 Wales 94.6	Real 105.4 BBCymru 95.0	36	24hr	✓	✓	A&E, TIC Svc	✓
The Wave 96.4	BBCymru 96.8	37	24hr	✓	✓		
The Wave 96.4	BBCymru 96.8	38		✓		A&E	
The Wave 96.4	BBCymru 96.8	39		✓		A&E	
The Wave 96.4	BBCymru 96.8	40	24hr	✓	✓	Svc	
The Wave 96.4	BBCymru 96.8	41	24hr	✓	✓	A&E Svc	
The Wave 96.4	BBCymru 96.8	41a		✓	✓	A&E	
R Pembs 102.5 Wales 93.9	Cymru 104.2	42	24hr	✓		A&E	
R Pembs 102.5 Wales 93.9	Cymru 104.2	43	✓	✓	✓		✓
BBCymru 93.7	Wales 93.9	44	24hr	✓		TIC Svc	
BBCymru 93.7	Wales 93.9	45	24hr	✓	✓	A&E Svc, TIC	
R Pembs 93.7 Wales 93.9	The Wave 96.4 Real 105.2	46		✓	✓	A&E TIC	
R Pembs 93.7 Wales 93.9	The Wave 96.4 Real 105.2	47 S	24hr	✓	✓	A&E TIC	✓
R Pembs 93.7 Wales 93.9	The Wave 96.4 Real 105.2	48	24hr	✓		Pharmacy Svc	
R Pembs 93.7 Wales 93.9	The Wave 96.4 Real 105.2	49	24hr	✓	✓	A&E	

M4 Junction Details

M4 Junction 1
Motorway starts

This is a restricted junction. There is no exit going east. Entry westbound is along the slip road to Junction 2.

FUEL

Esso **SAVE** ££ 0.1m ①
Open- *Daily 24 hours*
Info- *WC*
Tel- *0208 994 1119*

ESSENTIALS

Charing Cross Hospital 4m
Dir'n- *Take the A4 east and turn right across Hammersmith Bridge. The hospital is signposted on Fulham Palace Road.*
Tel- *0208 846 1234*

M4 Junction 2
Restricted Access

This is a restricted junction. Exit is allowed eastbound, and entry westbound is from the slip road from Junction 1.

ESSENTIALS

West Middlesex Hospital 3m
Dir'n- *Take the A4 west, and then the A310/B454 to Twickenham. The hospital is just before the A3004 junction.*
Tel- *0208 560 2121*

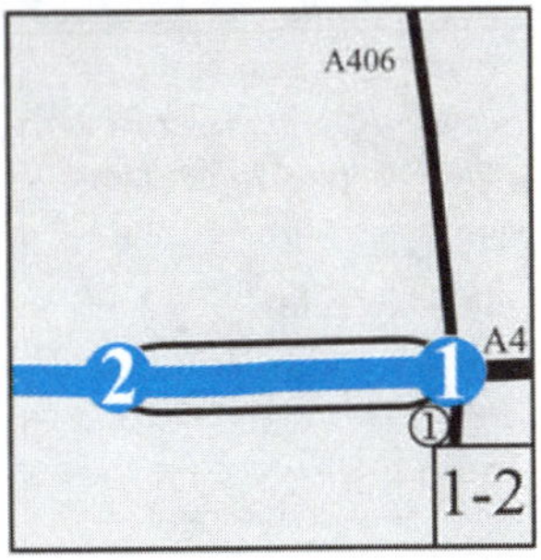

London Heston Services

There is no footbridge or roadbridge at this services.

FUEL BP
LPG (westbound), HGV fuelling, cash machine. Car parking £6 per 24 hours after first 2 hours.

FOOD MOTO
Little Chef, Burger King (eastbound), freshexpress, Burger King, Harry Ramsden's (westbound).
Info- Cash machine.

ACCOMMODATION

Travelodge☞ £69
Info- *Heathrow/Heston location. Hotel situated by both carriageways..*
Tel- *0870 191 1537*

OTHER

Business Centre
Info- *Meeting & office services. Heston Service Area location. Westbound direction only*
Tel- *0208 571 5721*

M4 Junction 3
Southall

FUEL

Tesco **SAVE** £ 0.5m ①
Open- *Daily 24 hours*
Info- *WC, carwash. Cafe, cash machine at store.*
Tel- *0208 210 7145*

Murco **SAVE** ££ 0.5m ②
Open- *Daily 24 hours*
Info- *Carwash, jetwash.*
Tel- *0208 573 7427*

Esso **SAVE** £ 0.9m ③
Open- *Daily 24 hours*
Info- *WC, carwash*
Tel- *0208 573 6912*

FOOD

Tesco Cafe☞ £3.50 0.6m ①
Open- *M-Sat 0800-2000, Sun 1200-1800*
Info- *Cash machine at store.*
Tel- *0845 677 9338*

The Crane £3.50 0.5m ④
Open- *M-F 1100-2130, Sat/Sun 1100-2000*
Info- *Inexpensive pub meals.*
Tel- *0208 5732103*

Pizza Delicia £8.00 0.5m ④
Open- *Daily 1130-2300*
Info- *Takeaway pizzas.*
Tel- *0800 783 8134*

Hayes Tandoori £8.00 0.5m ④
Open- *Daily 1200-1430, 1800-2230*
Info- *Indian meals to eat in or take away.*
Tel- *0208 7561234*

ESSENTIALS

Ealing Hospital 4m
Dir'n- *Take the A312 north, and then the A4020 east. The hospital is off the A4020.*
Tel- *0208 967 5000*

Hounslow Tourist Information Centre
Tel- *0208 583 2929*

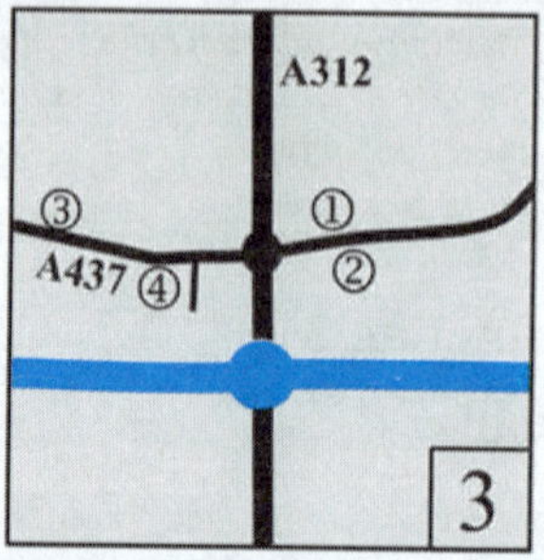

M4 Junction 4
Heathrow

FUEL

Esso SAVE £ 0.6m ①
Open- *Daily 24 hours*
Info- *WC*
Tel- *01895 448826*

Total SAVE £ 1.1m ②
Open- *Daily 24 hours*
Info- *WC, jetwash. HGV fuelling.*
Tel- *0208 7500982*

FOOD

Rotisserie restaurant £10 0.7m ③
Open- *Daily 0630-1030, 1230-1430, 1830-2230*
Info- *Refined eating in Holiday Inn restaurant*
Tel- *0208 990 0000*

The Plough £6.00 0.8m ④
Open- *M-Sat 1200-1400, 1830-2100, Sundays 1200-1800*
Info- *Varied hot & cold meals.*
Tel- *0208 759 1938*

Other restaurants
Info- *At the Novotel, Crowne Plaza, and Comfort Inn.*

ACCOMMODATION

Novotel☞ £135 0.2m ⑤
Info- *On-site restaurant, bar, health club. London Heathrow location.*
Tel- *01895 431431*

Crowne Plaza☞ £192 0.2m ⑥
Info- *On-site restaurant, bar, health club. London Heathrow location.*
Tel- *01895 445555*

Holiday Inn☞ £120 0.7m ③
Info- *On-site restaurant, bar & mini gym. London Heathrow location.*
Tel- *0208 990 0000*

Comfort Inn☞ £89 1.1m ⑦
Info- *On-site restaurant & bar. Heathrow location.*
Tel- *0208 573 6162*

Shepiston Guest House £60 1.2m ⑦
Info- *Private guest house. Price is B&B.*
Tel- *0208 573 0266*

Others
Info- *There are several other airport hotels on the A4 about 1-1.5 miles away.*
Dir'n- *Just follow signs to Heathrow and then to the A4 east/London-bound.*

ESSENTIALS

Hillingdon Hospital 2.5m
Dir'n- *This is signposted as you head north on the A408.*
Tel- *01895 238282*

Medics Pharmacy 1.3m ⑧
Open- *M-F 0900-1900, Sat 0900-1800*
Tel- *0208 573 1799*

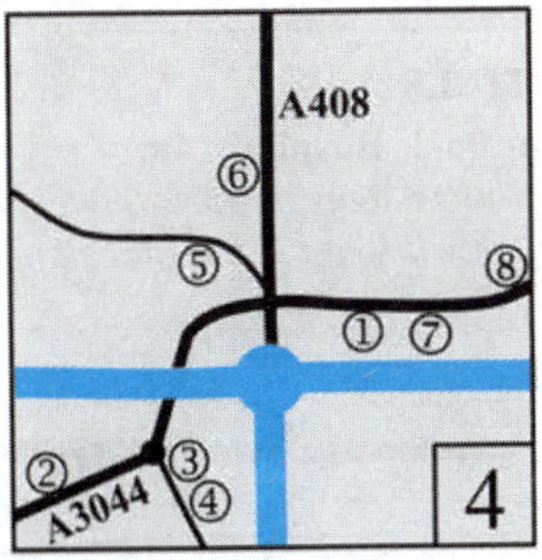

M4 Junction 4A
M4/M25 interchange

M4 Junction 5
Langley

FUEL

BP SAVE ££ 0.2m ①
Open- *Daily 24 hours*
Info- *WC, LPG.*
Tel- *01753 545531*

BP # 2 SAVE ££ 1.0m ②
Open- *Daily 24 hours*
Info- *Cash machine.*
Tel- *01753 681417*

Esso SAVE ££ 1.5m ③
Open- *Daily 0600-2400*
Info- *WC, cash machine. Small Tesco freshexpress store.*
Tel- *01753 227600*

Total SAVE ££ 1.5m ④
Open- *Daily 0600-2300*
Info- *WC, carwash, jetwash.*
Tel- *01753 218342*

FOOD

Marriott Hotel rest. £10 0.3m ⑤
Open- *M-F 0630-1030, 1230-1400, 1830-2200, Sat 0630-1100, 1830-2200*
Info- *Extensive menu at the hotel.*
Tel- *0870 400 7244*

Toby Inn☞ £7 0.3m ⑥
Open- *M-F 1200-1400, 1700-2200, Sat-Sun 1200-2200*
Info- *Varied hot & cold menu.*
Tel- *01753 591212*

Harvester☞ £7.00 0.6m ⑦
Open- *Sun-Th 1200-2200, F-Sa 1200-2200*
Tel- *01753 543009*

Quality Inn restaurant £10 0.4m ⑥
Open- *Daily 0600-2230*
Info- *Extensive menu in hotel restaurant.*
Tel- *01753 684001*

ACCOMMODATION

Marriott Hotel☞ £129 0.3m ⑤
Info- *Restaurant, pool, health club. Slough/Windsor location.*
Tel- *0870 400 7244*

Innkeeper's Lodge☞ £80 0.3m ⑥
Info- *Includes cont. breakfast. Toby Inn adjacent. Slough/Windsor location.*
Tel- *01753 591212*

Quality Suites Hotel☞ £125 0.4m ⑧
Info- *On-site restaurant & bar. Heathrow location.*
Tel- *01753 684001*

Airport Guest House £P 0.5m ⑧
Info- *Price is for B&B.*
Tel- *01753 686770*

ESSENTIALS

Wexham Park Hospital 3m
Dir'n- *Take the A4 towards Slough and turn right onto the A412, from where the hospital is signposted.*
Tel- *01753 633000*

Colnbrook Garage 0.5m ⑨
Open- *M-F 0800-2000, Sat 0800-1700*
Info- *Small garage for repairs.*
Tel- *01753 682003*

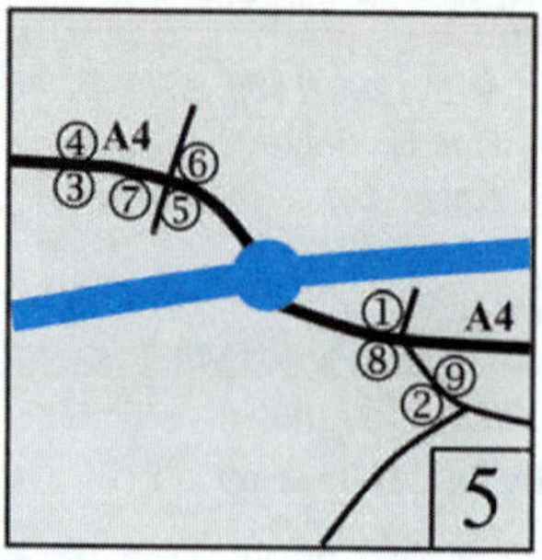

M4 Junction 6
Windsor/Slough

FUEL

Murco SAVE ££ 0.5m ①
Open- *Daily 24 hours*
Info- *WC*
Tel- *01753 532587*

Esso SAVE £ 1.5m ②
Open- *Daily 24 hours*
Info- *WC, carwash.*
Tel- *01753 853164*

FOOD

Courtyard Brasserie £10 0.5m ④
Open- *Daily 0800-2300*
Info- *Extensive menu in hotel brasserie.*
Tel- *01753 551551*

Domino's Pizza☞ £8.50 0.6m ⑥
Open- *M-Sat 1130-2330, Sun 1230-2330*
Info- *Takeaway pizzas.*
Tel- *01753 552525*

Three Tuns Pub £3 0.6m ⑦
Open- *Daily 1200-2000*
Info- *Varied hot & cold bar meals.*
Tel- *01753 521911*

ACCOMMODATION

C'tyard by Marriott☞ £113 0.5m ③
Info- *On-site brasserie & fitness room. Slough-Windsor location.*
Tel- *01753 551551*

Royal Windsor Motel £70 1.5m ④
Info- *Small independent motel. Breakfast not available.*
Tel- *01753 855819*

Copthorne Hotel☞ £150 0.5m ⑤
Info- *Restaurant, bar, health club. Slough-Windsor location.*
Tel- *01753 516222*

ESSENTIALS

Wexham Park Hospital 4m
Dir'n- *Follow signs towards Slough, and you will see the hopsital signposted.*
Tel- *01753 633000*

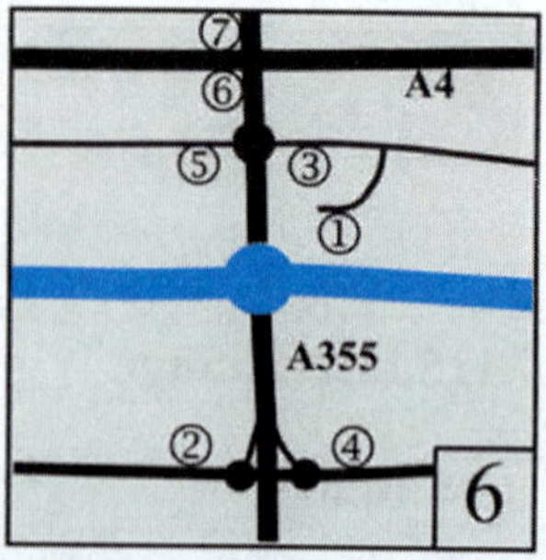

M4 Junction 7
Slough West

FUEL

Esso SAVE ££ 0.8m ①
Open- *Daily 24 hours*
Info- *WC, cash machine.*
Tel- *01628 666877*

FOOD

Kai Leung £7.00 0.6m ②
Open- *Daily 1800-2300, M-F 1200-1400*
Info- *Peking/Cantonese rest. & takeaway.*
Tel- *01628 666411*

Al Jamil Balti £5.00 0.8m ③
Open- *Sun-Th 1700-2330, Fr-Sa 1700-0030*
Info- *Kashmiri restaurant & takeaway.*
Tel- *01628 733033*

KFC☞ £4.00 0.7m ④
Open- *M-Th 1130-2400, Fr–Sat 1130-0100, Sun 1130-2300*
Tel- *01628 603020*

Starbucks Cafe☞ £4.00 0.8m ⑤
Open- *M-F 0800-1930, Sat 0730-1700*
Info- *Sandwiches and drinks. Cash machine.*

Dir'n- *Inside Sainsbury store.*
Tel- *01628 661529*

ESSENTIALS

Consell Pharmacy 0.7m ④
Open- *M-F 0900-1800, Sat 0900-1730*

Sainsbury Pharmacy 0.8m ⑤
Open- *M-Sat 0800-2200, Sun 1000-1600*
Info- *Pharmacy inside Sainsbury store.*
Tel- *01628 661529*

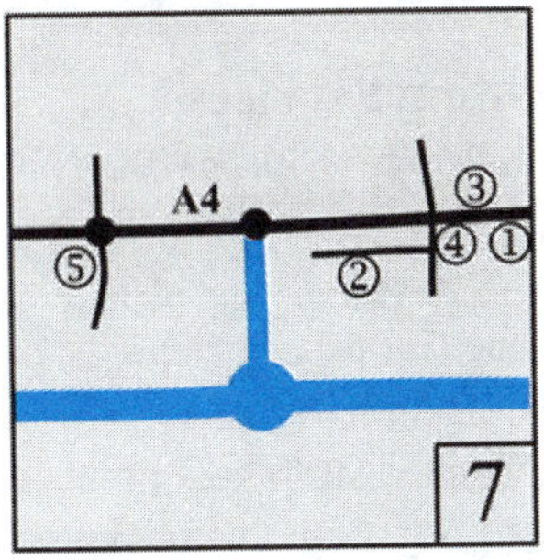

M4 Junction 8/9
Maidenhead/A404M

FUEL

Esso SAVE ££ 1.6m ①
Open- *Daily 24 hours*
Info- *WC, carwash, cash machine. Road layout extends distance.*
Tel- *01628 623315*

FOOD

The George £7.00 1.5m ②
Open- *M-Sat 1200-1430, 1800-2130*
Info- *Varied bar & restaurant menu.*
Tel- *01628 628317*

The Belgian Arms £7.00 1.5m ②
Open- *M-Sat 1200-1400, 1830-2100, Sundays 1200-1400*
Info- *Extensive menu & real ales.*
Dir'n- *In Holyport St, less than 200 metres from 'The George'.*
Tel- *01628 634468*

Emperor of India £9.00 1.6m ③
Open- *Daily 1200-1430, 1800-2300*
Info- *Indian restaurant with takeaway. Road layout extends distance.*
Tel- *01628 624100*

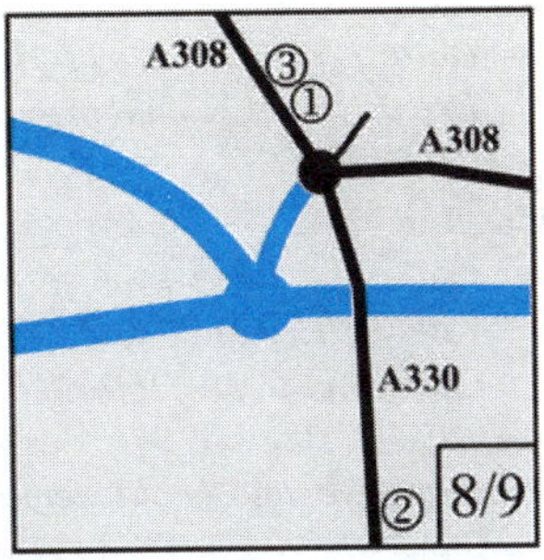

M4 Junction 10
M4/M329 interchange

ESSENTIALS

Royal Berkshire Hospital 5m
Dir'n- *Take the A329(M), and then the A3290 to Reading. At the A4 junction turn left and the hospital is signposted on the left.*
Tel- *0118 987 5111*

Reading Tourist Information Centre
Tel- *0118 956 6226*

M4 Junction 11
Reading South

FUEL

BP SAVE £££ 0.5m ①
Open- *M-Fri 0600-2200, Sa/Su 0700-2100*
Info- *WC*
Tel- *0118 931 0802*

BP#2 SAVE £££ 0.5m ②
Open- *M-Sat 0700-2200, Sun 0900-2100*
Info- *LPG.*
Tel- *0118 988 2334*

Shell SAVE ££££ 0.5m ③
Open- *M-Sat 0600-2200, Sun 0700-2200*
Info- *WC, cash machine.*
Tel- *0118 922 4500*

FOOD

Harry Ramsden's £4.00 0.5m ①
Open- *Daily 1130-2300*
Info- *Takeaway fish & chips etc.*
Tel- *0118 987 3255*

The Swan £7.50 0.5m ④
Open- *Daily 1200-1500, 1830-2130*
Info- *Extensive hot & cold menu.*
Tel- *0118 988 3674*

Holiday Inn rest. £10 0.5m ⑤
Open- *Daily M-F 0630-1000, 1230-1430, 1800-2200, Sat 0730-1100, 1800-2200, Sun 0730-1100,1200-1500, 1830-2130*
Info- *Extensive hot & cold menu.*
Tel- *0870 400 9067*

Pizza Hut☞ £6.00 1.2m ⑥
Open- *Sun-Th 1200-2200, Fr-Sa 1200-2300*
Tel- *0118 945 1100*

McDonald's☞ £3.50 1..2m ⑥
Open- *Daily 0700-2300*
Tel- *0118 975 2343*

Le Cafe £12 1..2m ⑦
Open- *Daily 1200-1400, 1830-2230*
Info- *Informal dining at Millennium Hotel.*
Tel- *0118 925 3500*

Cilentro Restaurant £25 1..2m ⑦
Open- *M-Sat 1900-2200*
Info- *Refined dining at Millennium Hotel.*
Tel- *0118 925 3500*

ACCOMMODATION

Millennium Hotel☞ £195 0.7m ⑦
Info- *On-site restaurant & bar. Health club & pool. Reading location.*
Tel- *0118 925 3500*

Holiday Inn☞ ⑤
Info- *On-site restaurant, bar, health club. Reading South location.*
Tel- *0870 400 9067*

ESSENTIALS

Royal Berkshire Hospital2.5m
Dir'n- *Take the A33 to Reading. At the A4 junction turn right, and the hospital is signposted on the right.*
Tel- *0118 987 5111*

Reading Tourist Information Centre
Tel- *0119 566226*

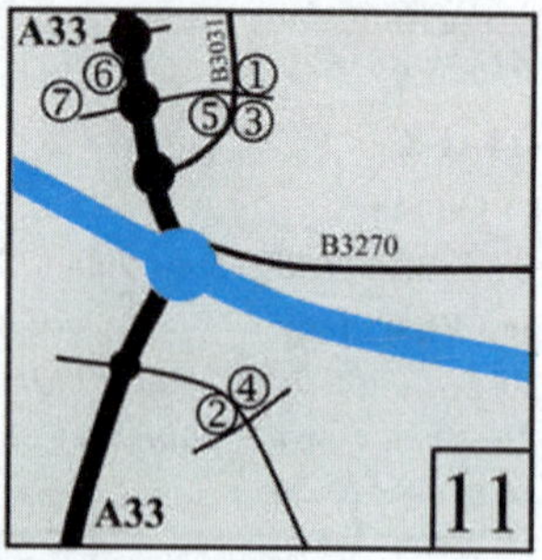

Reading Services

No footbridge or roadbridge.

FUEL BP
LPG, HGV fuelling and parking. Cash machine. Car parking £6 per 24 hours after first 2 hours.

FOOD MOTO
Upper Crust, freshexpress, Burger King, Harry Ramsden's, Ritazza.
Info- *Cash machines.*

ACCOMMODATION

Travelodge☞ £60
Info- *Reading M4 location. Located by both carriageways.*
Tel- *0870 191 1709*

M4 Junction 12
Reading West

FUEL

Sainsbury **SAVE** £££ 0.2m ①
Open- *Daily 24 hours*
Info- *Carwash. WC, cash machine at store.*
Tel- *0118 938 2200*

BP **SAVE** £ 0.6m ②
Open- *Daily 0600-2200*
Info- *WC, cash machine, postbox.*
Tel- *0118 942 7912*

FOOD

Starbucks☞ £3.50 0.2m ①
Open- *M-Th 0700-2000, Fr 0730-2130, Sat 0730-2100, Sun 1000-1600*
Info- *Inside Sainsbury store.*
Tel- *0118 938 2200*

The Bull £3.50 0.5m ③
Open- *M-F 1200-1400*
Info- *Pub food & real ales.*
Tel- *0118 930 3478*

King Wok £6.00 0.6m ④
Open- *M-F 1230-1430, 1800-2300*
Sat 1800-2330, Sun 1800-2230
Info- *Takeaway Chinese meals.*
Tel- *0118 930 3921*

Blue Cobra £10 0.6m ⑤
Open- *M-Sat 1200-1400, 1800-2300*
Info- *Indian & Thai rest. & takeaway.*
Tel- *0118 930 4040*

Cafe/Takeaway £3.00 0.6m ④
Open- *M-Sat 0800-1500*
Info- *Pizzas, burgers, chicken etc.*
Tel- *0118 932 3433*

The Crown £5.00 0.8m ④
Open- *M-F 1200-1400*
Info- *Pub food, real ales. No children.*
Tel- *0118 930 2310*

Silsilla £8.50 1.0m ⑥
Open- *Daily 1730-2330, M-F 1200-1400*
Info- *Indian takeaway & restaurant.*
Tel- *0118 941 7551*

Murdoch's Restaurant £10 1.0m ⑦
Open- *W-F 1200-1400, M-Sat 1745-2145,*
Sun 1200-1400, 1745-2100
Info- *Extensive international menu.*
Tel- *0118 945 1344*

ACCOMMODATION

Calcott Hotel 0.8m ⑧
Info- *Bar & restaurant (often with entertainment). Medium to large independent hotel.*
Tel- *0118 941 6423*

ESSENTIALS

Royal Berkshire Hospital 5m
Dir'n- *Take the A4 towards Reading. The hospital is signposted to the right off the A4.*
Tel- *0118 987 5111*

Sainsbury Pharmacy 0.2m ①
Open- *M-F 0830-2100, Sat 0800-2000,*
Sun 1000-1600
Info- *Inside Sainsbury store.*
Tel- *0118 938 2200*

Theale Pharmacy 0.6m ④
Open- *M-F 0900-1800, Sat 0900-1700*
Tel- *0118 930 2542*

Reading Tourist Information Centre
Tel- *0118 956 6226*

THINGS TO DO

Riverside Picnic Area 1.8m
Info- *Lovely riverside walk & picnic spot.*
Dir'n- *Go into Theale, and then follow signs to the station. Go past the station and this is on your left.*

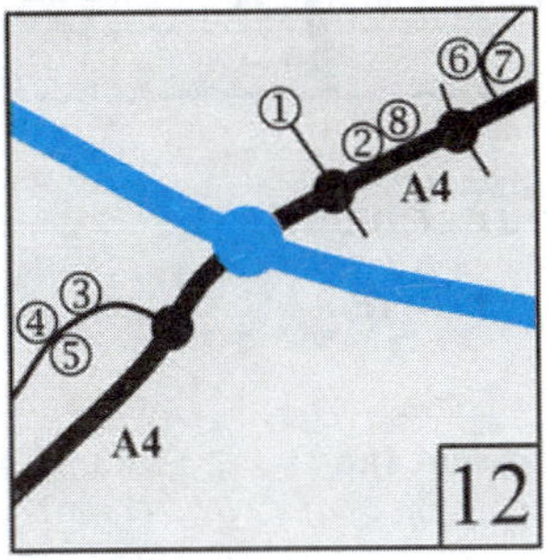

Chieveley Services

This services is located just off the motorway at Junction 13.

FUEL BP/SHELL (HGV)
HGV fuelling and parking. Cash machine. Car parking £6 per 24 hours after first 2 hours.

FOOD MOTO
Burger King, freshexpress, Harry Ramsden's, Upper Crust.
Info- *Cash machines.*

M4 Junction 13
Chieveley

There is a hotel opposite the motorway services but it involves a journey of over 2 miles due to the dual carriageway.

Ye Olde Red Lion £7.00 1.5m ②
Open- *M-Sat 1200-1400, 1800-2130,*
Sun 1200-1500
Info- *Varied bar menu.*
Tel- *01628 248379*

ESSENTIALS

Newbury Tourist Information Centre

Tel- *01635 30267*

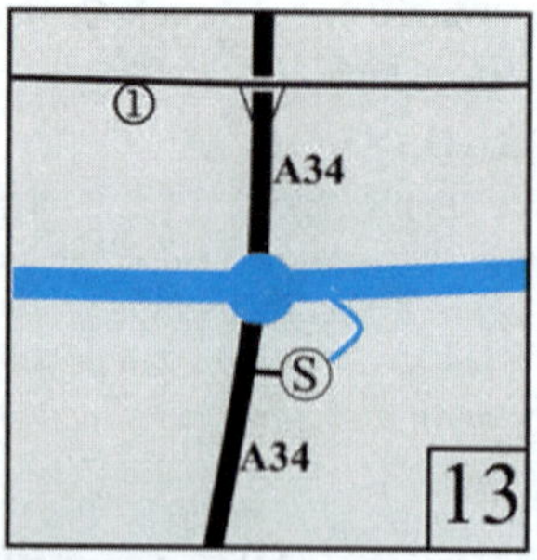

M4 Junction 14
Hungerford

FOOD

The Pheasant Inn £7.00 0.4m ①

Open- *Sun-Th 1230-1430, 1900-2100,*
Fr-Sat 1230-1430, 1930-2130

Info- *Extensive menu & real ales.*

Tel- *01488 648284*

The Tally Ho £8.50 1.6m ②

Open- *Daily 1200-1415, 1900-2115*

Info- *Extensive hot & cold menu.*

Tel- *01488 682312*

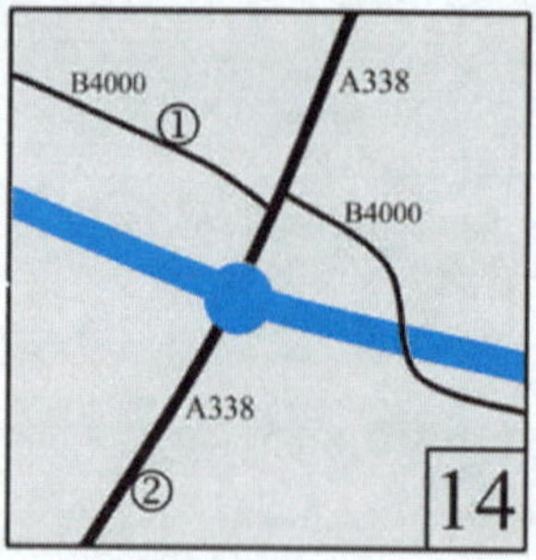

Membury Services

This services has a footbridge.

FUEL BP

HGV fuelling and parking.
Cash machine. Car parking £6 per 24 hours after first 2 hours.

FOOD WELCOME BREAK

Red Hen, 'Bakery', Burger King, Coffee Express, KFC.

Info- *Cash machines.*

ACCOMMODATION

Days Inn☞ £50

Info- *Swindon East location.*

Tel- *01488 72336*

M4 Junction 15
Swindon East

FUEL

Esso **SAVE** £££ 0.8m ①

Open- *Daily 24 hours*

Info- *WC, carwash.*

Tel- *01793 740251*

FOOD

The Plough Inn £8.50 0.2m ②

Open- *M-F 1200-1430, 1600-2100,*
Sat-Sun 1200-1400, 1900-2100

Info- *Extensive menu, real ales.*

Tel- *01793 740342*

The Baker's Arms £7.00 0.9m ③

Open- *M-Sat 1230-1430, 1830-2130,*
Sun 1230-1500, 1900-2130

Info- *Extensive hot & cold menu.*
Real ales.

Tel- *01793 740313*

Chiseldon House rest. £14 1.1m ④

Open- *Daily 1200-1430,1700-2130*

Info- *Refined dining in hotel rest.*

Tel- *01793 741010*

ACCOMMODATION

Chiseldon House Htl £100 1.1m ④

Info- *On-site restaurant, bar, pool. Price is for B&B. A Best Western Hotel.*☞ *Chiselden location.*

Tel- *01793 741010*

Landmark Hotel £88 1.3m ⑤
Info- *Bar, restaurant. Pets by arrangement. Independent hotel.*
Tel- *01793 740149*

ESSENTIALS

Gt Western Hospital 1.2m
Dir'n- *This is well signposted as you drive towards Swindon.*
Tel- *01793 604020*

Swindon Tourist Information Centre
Tel- *01793 530328*

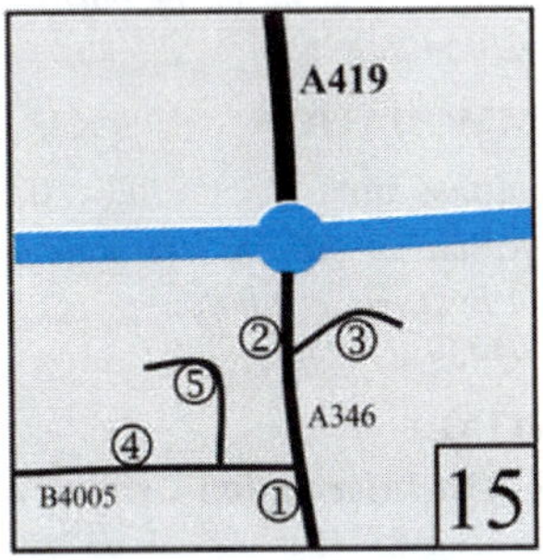

M4 Junction 16
Swindon West

FOOD

Beefeater☞ £7.00 0.2m ①
Open- *M-Th 0700-2200, Fr 0700-2230, Sat 0800-2300, Sun 0800-2100*
Tel- *01793 881490*

Hilton Hotel rest. £12 0.2m ②
Open- *M-F 0630-1000, 1230-1400, 1900-2200. Sat-Sun 0730-1030, 1230-1400 (not Sat), 1900-2200.*
Info- *Extensive menu.*
Tel- *01793 881777*

Sally Pussey's Inn £8.50 0.9m ③
Open- *Daily 0800-1100, 1200-2100*
Info- *Extensive menu, real ales. No breakfasts served Sundays.*
Tel- *01793 852430*

ACCOMMODATION

Hilton Hotel☞ £120 0.2m ②
Info- *On site restaurant, bar, healthclub. Swindon location.*
Tel- *01793 881777*

Travel Inn☞ £45 0.2m ①
Info- *Swindon location. Next to Beefeater.*
Tel- *0870 197 7247*

Express by Hol. Inn☞ £75 0.8m ④
Info- *Price incl. continental breakfast. Swindon West location.*
Tel- *01793 818800*

ESSENTIALS

Swindon Tourist Information Centre
Tel- *01793 530328*

Car Dealers
Info- *Citroen, Audi and VW dealers.*
Dir'n- *En route to Express by Hol. Inn.*

Touchbase Meeting Centre ①
Info- *Meeting facilities at Travel Inn.*
Tel- *0870 243 3113*

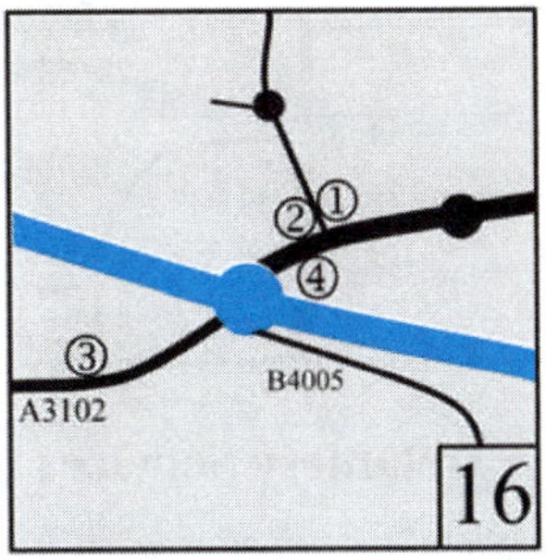

M4 Junction 17
Chippenham

FUEL

Keyfuels Diesel SAVE ££££ 0.6m ①
Open- *Daily 24 hours with HGV fuel cds.*
Info- *HGV diesel only. WC, showers, 24 hour cafe. HGV parking.*
Tel- *01249 750645*

Murco SAVE ££ 0.7m ②
Open- *Daily 24 hours.*
Info- *WC, jetwash.*
Tel- *01666 837161*

FOOD

Silvey Truckstop £4.0 0.6m ①
Open- *24 hrs between M 0630 & Sat 1400*
Info- *Transport cafe with showers.*
Tel- *01249 750645*

Stanton Manor Rest £15 1.0m ③
Open- *Daily 1200-1400, 1900-2130*
Info- *Refined dining in country hs hotel.*
Tel- *01666 837552*

ACCOMMODATION

Stanton Manor Hotel £100 1.0m ③
Info- *Country house hotel. On-site restaurant & bar.*
Tel- *01666 837552*

ESSENTIALS

Chippenham Tourist Information Centre
Tel- *01249 706333*

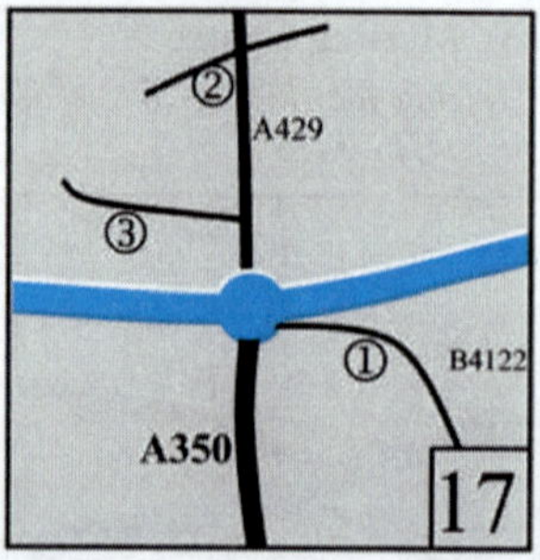

Leigh Delamere Services

This services has a footbridge.

FUEL ESSO

HGV fuelling and parking. Cash machine. Car parking £6 per 24 hours after first 2 hours.

FOOD MOTO

freshexpress, Burger King, Harry Ramsden's, Upper Crust, Ritazza Coffee.
Info- *Cash machines.*

ACCOMMODATION

Travelodge £50
Info- *Chippenham location. Hotel in both directions.*
Tel- *0870 191 1726*

OTHER

'Business Centre'.
Info- *Meeting facilities.*
Tel - *0208 571 5721*

M4 Junction 18
Chipping Sodbury

FOOD

The Compass Inn £8.00 0.5m ①
Open- *M-Sat 1000-2200, Sun 1200-2130*
Info- *Extensive menu in the hotel bar.*
Tel- *01454 218242*

The Portcullis Inn £7.50 0.5m ②
Open- *Daily 1200-1400, 1900-2100*
Info- *Extensive menu in the bar/bistro.*
Tel- *01454 218263*

ACCOMMODATION

The Compass Inn £90 0.5m ①
Info- *Restaurant & bar. Pets welcome. A Best Western hotel.* ☞
Tel- *01454 218242*

ESSENTIALS

Bath Tourist Information Centre
Tel- *01225 477101*

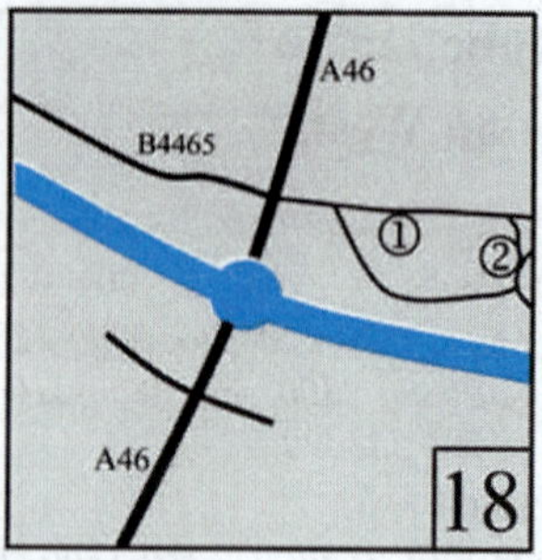

M4 Junction 19
M4/M32 interchange

ESSENTIALS

Frenchay Hospital 1m
Dir'n- *Take the M32 to Bristol and take the first exit. The hospital is signposted from the exit.*
Tel- *0117 970 1070*

Bristol Tourist Information Centre
Tel- *0117 926 0767*

M4 Junction 20
M4/M5 interchange

ESSENTIALS

Bristol Tourist Information Centre
Tel- *0117 926 0767*

M4 Junction 21
M4/M48 interchange

M4 Junction 22
M4/M49 interchange

J 23 (Magor) Services

This services is located just off the motorway.

FUEL ESSO

HGV fuelling and parking. Car parking £6 per 24 hours after first 2 hours.

FOOD FIRST

'First' restaurant, Burger King.
Info- Cash machines.

ACCOMMODATION

Travelodge☞ £45
Info- *Newport-Magor location.*
Tel- *01633 881896*

ESSENTIALS

Hillcroft Garage
Info- *Light & heavy recovery.*
Tel- *0500 002430*

M4 Junction 23
M4/M48 interchange

M4 Junction 23A
Magor

FUEL

Esso SAVE ££ 0.9m ①
Open- *M-F 0730-1930, Sat 0800-1800, Sun 1000-1400.*
Tel- *01633 800229*

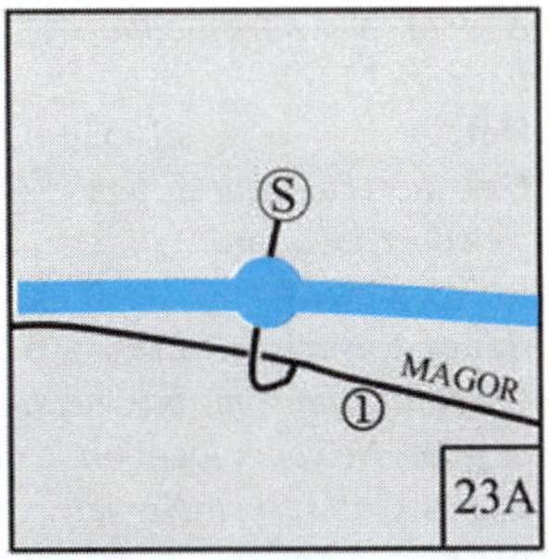

M4 Junction 24
Newport East

FUEL

Esso SAVE ££ 0.8m ①
Open- *Daily 24 hours*
Info- *WC, cash machine.*
Tel- *01633 281241*

FOOD

Holiday Inn Rest. £10 0.2m ②
Open- *Su-F 1230-1400, Daily 1900-2200*
Info- *Refined dining in the hotel rest.*
Tel- *01633 412777*

McDonald's☞ £3.50 0.3m ③
Open- *Daily 0730-2300*
Tel- *01633 412087*

Beefeater☞ £7.00 0.3m ③
Open- *M-Th 1200-2300, F/Sat 1200-2300, Sun 1200-2100*
Tel- *0870 197 7193*

Owen's Restaurant £13 0.5m ④
Open- *M-Sat 0700-2130*
Info- *Refined dining at the Celtic Manor.*
Tel- *01633 413000*

The Olive Tree £15 0.5m ④
Open- *Daily 0700-1030, 1230-1500, 1900-2230*
Info- *Refined dining at the Celtic Manor.*
Tel- *01633 413000*

Toby Inn☞ £7.00 0.7m ⑤
Open- *Daily 1200-2200*
Tel- *01633 282155*

ACCOMMODATION

Holiday Inn☞ £90 0.2m
Info- *On-site restaurant, bar, health club*

& pool. Newport location.
Tel- *01633 412777*

Hilton Hotel☞ £145 0.3m
Info- *On-site restaurant & bar. Newport location.*
Tel- *01633 413737*

Celtic Manor Resort £190 0.5m
Info- *On-site restaurant, bar, health club & pool. Newport location. Coldra Woods Golf resort. No pets.*
Tel- *01633 413000*

Travel Inn☞ £45 0.5m
Info- *Newport (South Wales) location.*
Tel- *0870 197 7193*

ESSENTIALS

Newport Tourist Information Centre
Tel- *01633 842962*

M4 Junction 25
Restricted

This junction combines with Junction 25A to give full motorway access. There is a wide range of cost-effective restaurants en route to Newport, but parking may be difficult.

FUEL

Esso **SAVE** ££ 0.8m ①
Open- *Daily 0700-2300*
Info- *Cash machine.*
Tel- *01633 266581*

FOOD

Spicy Aroma Rest. £6.00 0.2m ②
Open- *Daily 1700-2300*
Info- *Indian restaurant & takeaway.*
Tel- *01633 259393*

The China Kitchen £6.00 0.3m ②
Open- *M,W-Sa 1700-2300, Sun 1800-2300*
Info- *Takeaway Chinese meals.*
Tel- *01633 259956*

The Victoria Pub £4.00 0.4m ③
Open- *Daily 1200-1430, 1800-2100*
Info- *Bar food. Satellite TV.*
Tel- *01633 258252*

Copperfield's Cafe £4.00 0.4m ③
Open- *M-Sat 0900-1530, Sun 1100-1400*
Info- *Hot & cold meals & breakfasts.*
Tel- *01633 222323*

Polash Tandoori £7.00 0.5m ④
Open- *Daily 1800-2400*
Info- *Indian restaurant & takeaway.*
Tel- *01633 252891*

ESSENTIALS

Pharmacy £7.00 0.2m ②
Open- *M-F 0845-1815, Sat 0900-1300*
Tel- *01633 244757*

Newport Tourist Information Centre
Tel- *01633 842962*

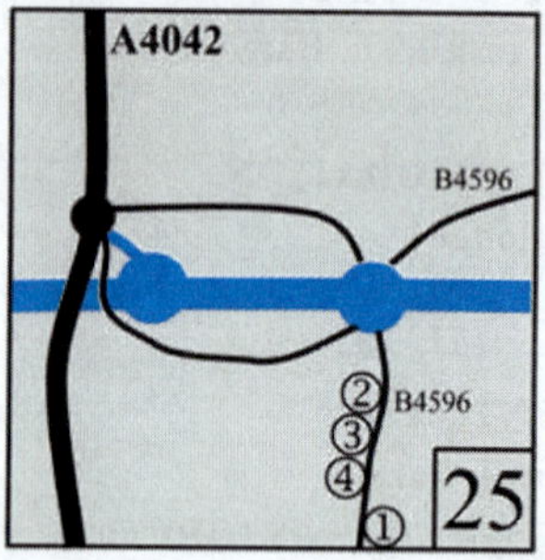

M4 Junction 25A
Restricted

This junction combines with Junction 25 to give full motorway access.

ESSENTIALS

Royal Gwent Hospital 1.7m
Dir'n- *Follow the A4042 towards Newport and the hospital is signposted near to the town centre.*
Tel- *01633 234234*

M4 Junction 26
Newport North

FUEL

Shell SAVE £££ 0.3m ①

Open- Daily 24 hours
Info- LPG, WC, cash machine.
Tel- 01633 820000

FOOD

Harvester☞ £7.00 0.5m ②

Open- Daily 1200-2200
Tel- 01633 858667

Shoboraj Rest. £7.00 0.3m ③

Open- Su-Th 1730-2400, F/Sat 1730-0100
Info- Indian restaurant & takeaway.
Tel- 01633 822822

Indian Cottage £6.50 0.3m ③

Open- Daily 1700-2400
Info- Indian takeaway.
Tel- 01633 852724

Modern Balti takeaway £5.00 0.3m ③

Open- Sun-Th 1700-2300, F/Sa 1700-2400
Info- Indian takeaway.
Tel- 01633 258000

Beijing House £5.00 0.6m ⑤

Open- M-Sat 1200-1400, 1730-2330
Info- Chinese takeaway.
Tel- 01633 857232

CJ's Fish Bar £7.00 0.6m ⑥

Open- M-W 1145-2230, Th-Sat 1145-2300
Info- Fish bar and small off licence.
Tel- 01633 665212

McDonald's☞ £3.50 0.6m

Open- Daily 0700-2300
Tel- 01633 253433

ESSENTIALS

Royal Gwent Hospital 1.5m

Dir'n- Follow signs towards Newport and the hospital is signposted near to the town centre.
Tel- 01633 234234

Malpas Pharmacy 0.5m ②

Open- M-F 0900-1830, Sat 0900-1300
Tel- 01633 654077

Newport Tourist Information Centre

Tel- 01633 842962

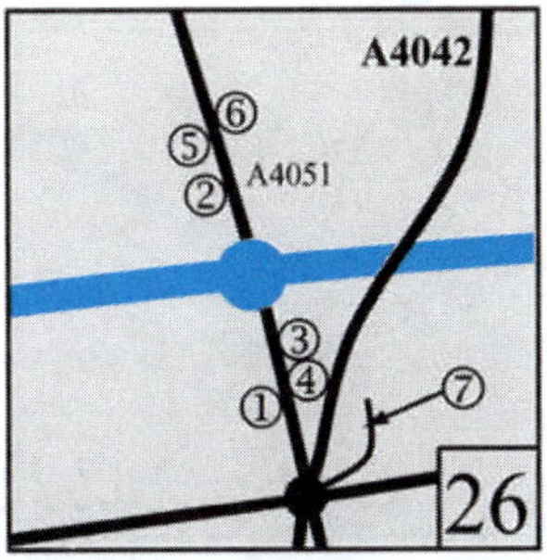

M4 Junction 27
Newport West

FUEL

Texaco SAVE ££ 0.3m ①

Open- Daily 0700-2300
Info- WC, carwash.
Tel- 01633 898400

Total SAVE ££ 0.6m ②

Open- Daily 24 hours
Info- Carwash.
Tel- 01633 894021

FOOD

The Rising Sun £7.50 0.7m ③

Open- M-Sat 1200-1415, 1800-2130, Sun 1200-1430
Info- 4 Q's rating at pub/restaurant.
Tel- 01633 895126

The Olde Oak £6.50 1m ④

Open- Daily 1200-1430, 1830-2130
Info- Varied meals at local pub. Real ales.
Tel- 01633 892883

ACCOMMODATION

The Rising Sun £50 0.7m ③

Info- B&B at bar/restaurant. AA 4◆
Tel- 01633 895126

ESSENTIALS

Newport Tourist Information Centre

Tel- 01633 842962

THINGS TO DO

Fourteen Locks Centre £nil 1m ⑤

Info- Canal side walks and a small visitor centre.

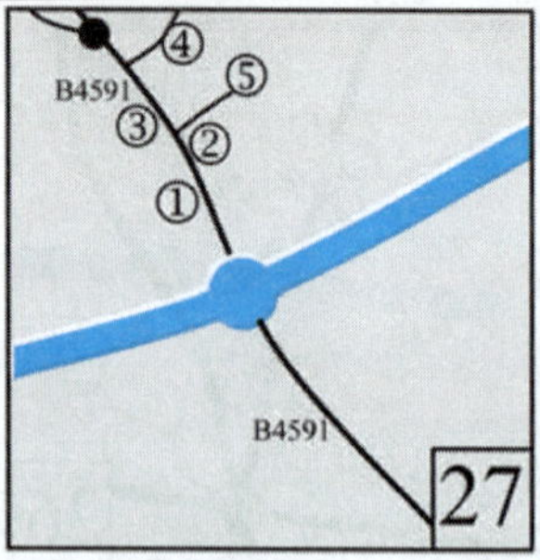

M4 Junction 28
Newport Southwest

FUEL

Asda SAVE £££ 0.8m ①

Open- *M-F 0830-2200, Sat 0800-2000, Sun 1000-1630*
Info- *WC, cash machine, cafe at store.*
Dir'n- *Follow superstore signs from junction.*
Tel- *01633 815571*

FOOD

Asda Cafe £3.00 0.8m ①

Open- *At time of press this was closed. It may re-open as a McDonald's*
Tel- *01633 816246*

ESSENTIALS

Royal Gwent Hospital 2m

Dir'n- *This is well signposted on the A48 into Newport.*
Tel- *01633 234234*

Newport Tourist Information Centre

Tel- *01633 842962*

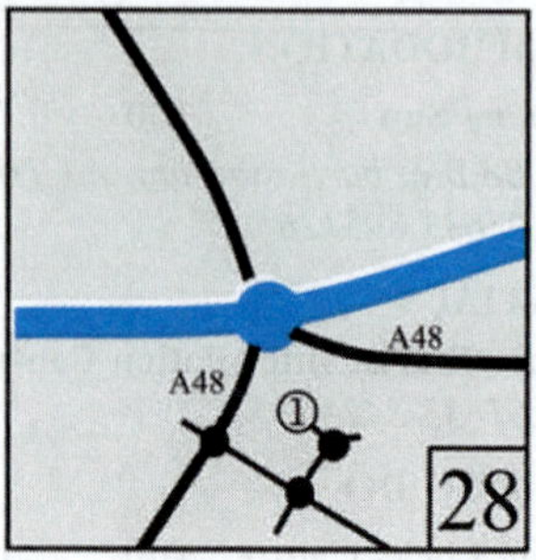

M4 Junction 29
M4/A48(M) interchange

This junction is restricted and no services are accessible. Traffic can only exit the motorway to head to and from Cardiff.

ESSENTIALS

University Hospital, Wales 7m

Dir'n- *Take the A48(M) towards Cardiff. Then take the A469 turn off, where the hospital will be signposted.*
Tel- *029 2074 7747*

ESSENTIALS

Cardiff Tourist Information Centre

Tel- *029 2022 7281*

J30 (Cardiff Gate) Services

This services is located just off the motorway.

FUEL TOTAL (SAVE ££)

LPG, HGV fuelling and parking. Car parking £6 per 24 hours after first 2 hours.
This services is cheaper than most.

FOOD

Burger King, Little Chef, Toby Carvery Pub.
Info- *Cash machines.*

ACCOMMODATION

Ibis Hotel☞ £41

Info- *Bar & nearby restaurant. Cardiff Gate location.*
Tel- *029 2073 3222*

M4 Junction 30
Cardiff East

FUEL

Asda SAVE £££ 0.8m ①

Open- *M-Sat 0700-2030, Sun 1030-1530*
Info- *WC, cash machines at store.*
Tel- *029 2034 0276*

FOOD

Asda Cafe £3.00 0.8m ①

Open- *M-Sat 0830-2030, Sat 0800-1930,*

Sun 1030-1530
Tel- *029 2034 0276*

McDonald's £3.50 0.8m ①
Open- *Daily 0700-2300*
Tel- *029 2073 3228*

Campanile Rest. £7.00 1.5m ②
Info- *Bar & bistro at the hotel.*
Tel- *029 2054 9044*

ACCOMMODATION

Hotel Campanile☞ £42 1.5m ②
Info- *Bar & bistro. Cardiff location. Dogs allowed by arrangement.*
Tel- *029 2054 9044*

ESSENTIALS

University Hospital, Wales 5m
Dir'n- *Take the A4232 and then the A48(M) towards Cardiff. Then take the A469 turn off, where the hospital is signposted.*
Tel- *029 2074 7747*

Cardiff Tourist Information Centre
Tel- *029 2022 7281*

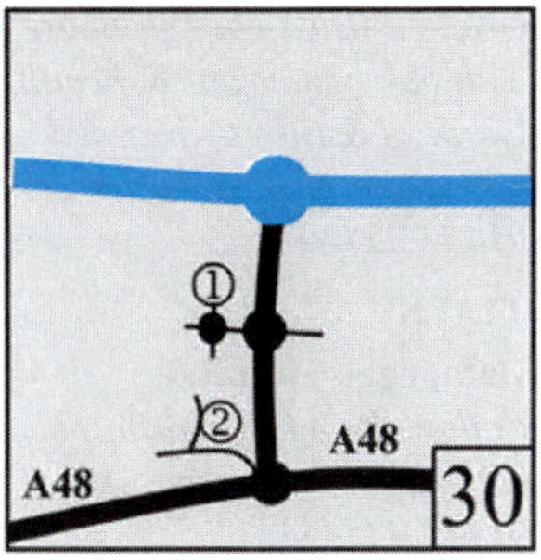

M4 Junction 31
Non-existent

M4 Junction 32
Cardiff

FUEL

Esso SAVE ££ 0.1m ①
Open- *Daily 24 hours*
Info- *HGV fuelling, carwash.*
Dir'n- *Follow signs to Superstore*
Tel- *029 2061 6044*

BP SAVE ££ 1.3m ②
Open- *Daily 0600-2300*
Info- *WC, carwash, jetwash.*
Tel- *029 2061 6141*

FOOD

McDonald's☞ £3.50 0.4m ③
Open- *Daily 0730-2300*
Info- *Asda store adjacent.*
Dir'n- *Follow signs to Superstore.*
Tel- *029 2069 1700*

Asda Cafe☞ £3.50 0.4m ③
Open- *Daily 0830-2000, Sat 0800-1800, Sun 1000-1600*
Info- *Asda store adjacent.*
Dir'n- *Follow signs to Superstore*
Tel- *029 2061 3213*

Salingers Restaurant £7.50 0.4m ④
Open- *Daily 1200-1400, 1700-2200*
Info- *Dining at the Village Hotel rest.*
Tel- *0870 606 3606*

The Holly Bush £7.50 0.4m ⑤
Open- *M-Sa 1200-1400, 1730-2100, Sun 1200-2100*
Info- *Extensive menu & carvery*
Tel- *029 2062 5037*

The Lewis Arms £4.00 0.9m ⑥
Open- *M-Sat 1200-1430, 1800-2030, Sun 1200-1430*
Info- *Bar meals at local pub.*
Tel- *029 2081 0330*

Toby Inn☞ £7.00 1.3m ⑦
Open- *Daily 1200-1500, 1700-2200*
Tel- *029 2069 2554*

Quality Hotel Rest☞ £9.00 0.3m ⑧
Open- *M-F 0700-0930, 1900-2130, Sat 0800-1000, 1230-1400, 1900-2130, Sun 0800-1000, 1900-2130*
Info- *Extensive menu in the hotel.*
Tel- *029 2052 9988*

ACCOMMODATION

Village Hotel☞ £109 0.2m ④
Info- *Bar, rest, leisure club & pool. No pets. Cardiff location.*
Tel- *0870 606 3606*

Quality Hotel☞ £108 0.3m ⑧
Info- *Bar & restaurant.*
Tel- *029 2052 9988*

Innkeeper's Lodge £45 1.3m ⑦
Info- *Toby Inn adjacent.*
Tel- *029 2069 2554*

ESSENTIALS

University Hospital, Wales 3m
Dir'n- *Take the A470 towards Cardiff, and the hospital is signposted just before the A48.*
Tel- *029 2074 7747*

Cardiff Tourist Information Centre
Tel- *029 2022 7281*

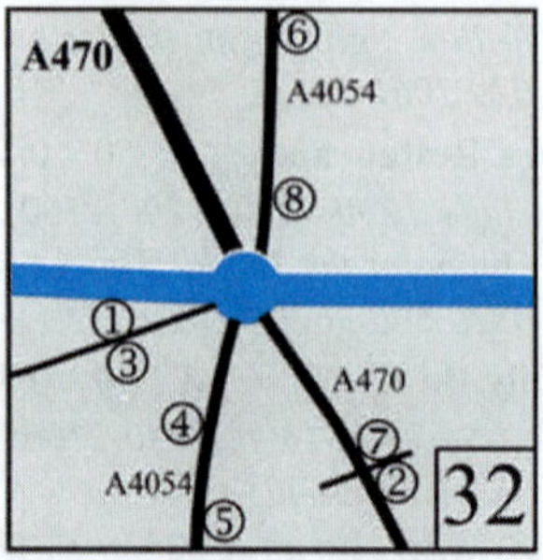

J33 (Cardiff West) Services

This services is located just off the motorway.

FUEL ESSO

HGV fuelling and parking. Car parking £6 per 24 hours after first 2 hours.
This services has cheaper fuel than most.

FOOD MOTO

Burger King, freshexpress.
Info- Cash machines.

ACCOMMODATION

Travelodge☞ £45
Info- *Cardiff West location.*
Tel- *0870 191 1725*

M4 Junction 33
Cardiff West

There are no services (apart from the Cardiff West Services) close to this junction.

M4 Junction 34
Llantrisant

FUEL

Texaco **SAVE** ££ 1m ①
Open- *Daily 24 hours*
Info- *WC.*
Tel- *01443 224115*

FOOD

Castell Mynach Pub £7.00 0.7m ②
Info- *A 'Six Continents' pub. Extensive hot & cold menu.*
Tel- *01443 220941*

ACCOMMODATION

Miskin Manor £126 1.5m ③
Info- *Grade 2 listed country house hotel with bar, restaurant & health club. Gardens & rosette awarded restaurant. A Best Western hotel.*☞
Tel- *01443 224204*

ESSENTIALS

Royal Glamorgan Hospital 4.5m
Info- *Follow the A4119 north. The hospital is well signposted.*
Tel- *01443 443443*

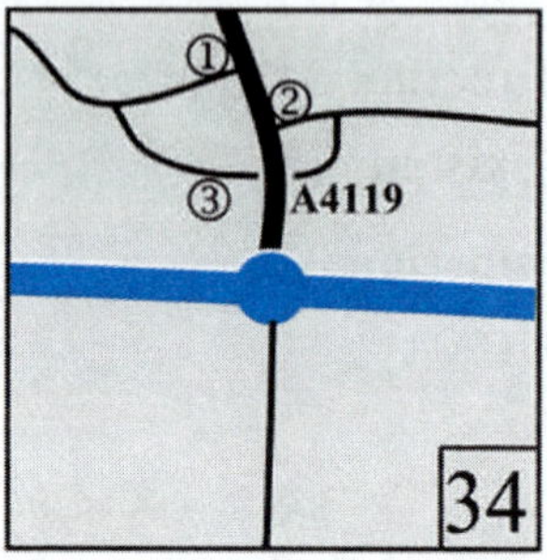

M4 Junction 35
Bridgend East

FUEL

Texaco SAVE £ 0.2m ①
Open- *Daily 24 hours*
Info- *LPG, WC, carwash.*
Tel- *01656 863686*

Murco SAVE ££ 0.2m ②
Open- *Daily 24 hours*
Info- *WC, carwash, cash machine.*
Tel- *01656 863855*

FOOD

McDonald's☞ £3.50 0.2m ①
Open- *Daily 0730-2300*
Tel- *01656 865484*

Brewsters☞ £6.50 0.2m ①
Open- *M-Sat 1130-2200, Sun 1200-2200*
Tel- *01656 860133*

Cafe Petite £7.50 0.8m ③
Open- *Daily 1800-2300*
Info- *Steak house with varied menu.*
Tel- *01656 862783*

Spice Land £7.50 0.9m ④
Open- *Daily 1800-2300, Sun 1200-1400*
Info- *Bangladeshi restaurant & takeaway.*
Tel- *01656 861678*

ACCOMMODATION

Travel Inn☞ £45 0.2m ①
Info- *Bridgend location. Brewsters nearby.*
Tel- *0870 197 7041*

ESSENTIALS

Pencoed Chemist 0.9m ④
Open- *M-F 0900-1300, 1400-1730, Sat 0930-1230.*
Tel- *01656 860292*

Bridgend Tourist Information Centre
Tel- *01656 654906*

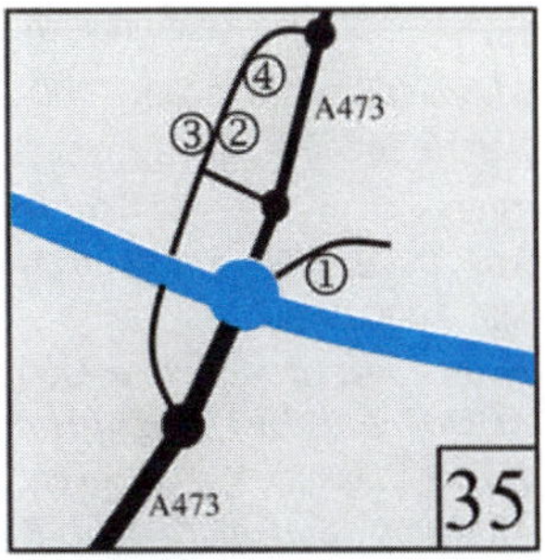

J36 (Sarn Park) Services

This services is located just off the motorway.

FUEL SHELL

HGV fuelling and parking. Car parking £6 per 24 hours after first 2 hours.
Info- *Fuel at this services is cheaper than most.*

FOOD WELCOME BREAK

Red Hen, The Granary restaurant.
Info- Cash machines.

ACCOMMODATION

Welcome Lodge☞ £40
Info- *Sarn Park location.*
Tel- *01656 659218*

ESSENTIALS

Civic Rescue & Repair
Info- *24 hour car rescue.*
Tel- *01792 700007*

M4 Junction 36
Bridgend

FUEL

Sainsbury SAVE ££ 0.2m ①
Open- *Daily 24 hours*
Info- *WC, cash machine at store.*
Tel- *01656 648951*

FOOD

Sainsbury Cafe☞ £3.50 0.2m ①
Open- *M-Sa 0700-2000, Sun 0930-1530*
Tel- *01656 648951*

Harvester☞ £7.00 0.2m ②
Open- *M-Sat 0700-2200, Sun 1200-2100*
Tel- *01656 768668*

Many others £3-£6 0.3m ①
Open- *M-F 0900-2000, Sat 0900-2100, Sun 1000-1800*
Info- *Food court at McArthur Glen Mall. McDonald's, KFC, Pizza Hut, Harry Ramsden's, Fatjackets, Madisons, Singapore Sam, Rollover Hot Dogs.*

Ty-Risha £7.00 0.6m ③
Open- *M-Sat 1200-2100, Sun 1200-1800*
Info- *Varied menu & real ales at local pub.*
Tel- *01656 725287*

The Masons Arms £8.00 1m ③
Open- *Daily 1200-1430, 1800-2130*
Info- *Extensive hot & cold menu.*
Tel- *01656 720253*

ACCOMMODATION

Express by Hol. Inn☞ £55 0.2m ②
Info- *Bridgend location.*
Tel- *01656 646200*

The Masons Arms Htl £58 1m ③
Info- *B&B at this pub/hotel.*
Tel- *01656 720253*

ESSENTIALS

Princess of Wales Hospital 2m
Dir'n- *This is signposted from motorway junction.*
Tel- *01656 752752*

Bridgend Tourist Information Centre
Tel- *01656 654906*

THINGS TO DO

McArthur Glen Outlet Centre 0.3m ①
Open- *M-F 1000-2000, Sat 1000-1800, Sun 1100-1700*
Info- *Wide range of shops & food.*
Tel- *01656 665700*

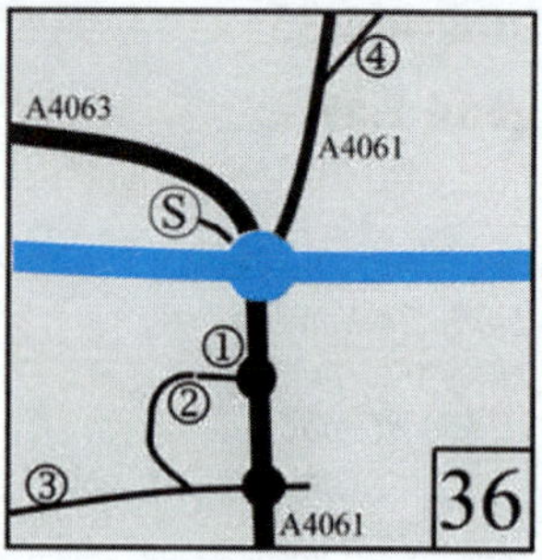

M4 Junction 37
Porthcawl

FUEL

Esso SAVE ££ 0.6m ①
Open- *Daily 24 hours*
Info- *HGV fuelling, jetwash.*
Tel- *01639 746658*

FOOD

Maundy's Fish Cafe £3.00 0.7m ②
Open- *M-F 0800-1400, 1700-2100*
Info- *Fried meals, pies, curries. Eat in and takeaway.*
Tel- *01656 745745*

Greenacre Pub £5.00 0.9m ③
Open- *Daily 1200-1400, 1800-2100*
Info- *Varied meals in local pub.*
Tel- *01656 744707*

The Three Horseshoes £4.50 0.5m ④
Open- *Daily 1200-1430, M-Sa 1830-2130, Sun 1830-2100*
Info- *Bar food in local pub.*
Tel- *01656 740037*

The Raj £7.50 0.6m ①
Open- *Daily 1800-2400, Sa-Su 1200-1430*
Info- *Indian restaurant & takeaway.*
Tel- *01656 741174*

ACCOMMODATION

Greenacre Motel £55 0.9m ③
Info- *17 bedroom motel attached to this local pub.*
Tel- *01656 743041*

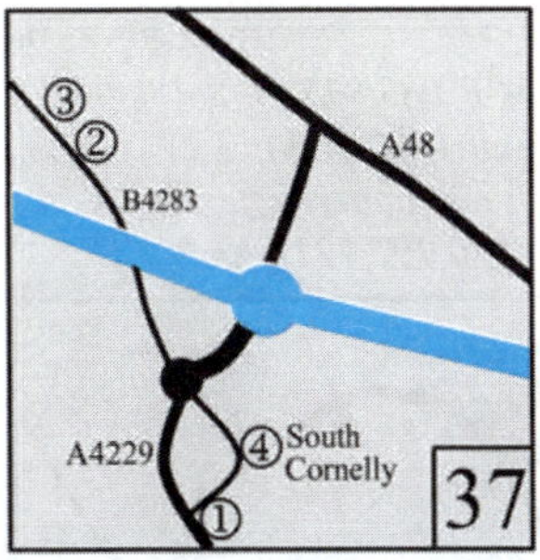

M4 Junction 38/39
Margam

Junction 39 has a missing westbound entry, but this is provided at Junction 38 about 1 mile away. Junction 38 has no exits.

FOOD

Margam Abbey Rest. £6.00 0.4m ①
Open- *Daily 1230-1600, Sat 1900-2130,*
Info- *Sandwiches & varied menu.*
Tel- *01639 871184*

The Twelve Knights £8.50 0.4m ②
Open- *Daily 0730-2130*
Info- *Extensive hot & cold menu.*
Tel- *01639 882381*

ESSENTIALS

Neath/Port Talbot Hospital 3.5m
Dir'n- *Signposted on A48 to Port Talbot.*
Tel- *01639 862000*

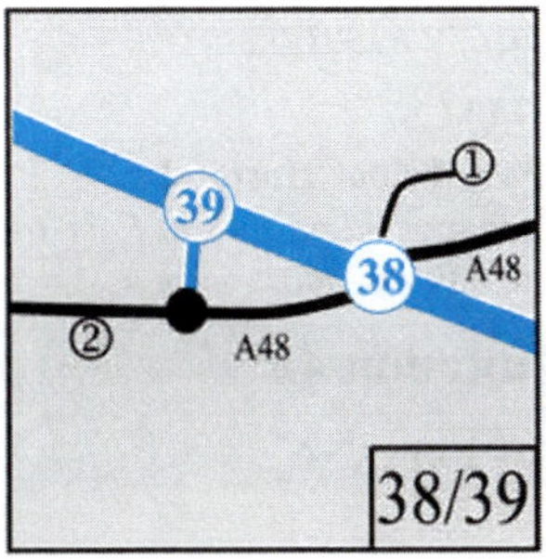

M4 Junction 40
Port Talbot East

FUEL

Texaco **SAVE** £££ 0.6m ①
Open- *Daily 24 hours*
Info- *WC, jetwash.*
Tel- *01639 883418*

FOOD

Grand Hotel £5 0.8m ②
Open- *Daily 1200-1330,1800-2100*
Info- *Pub meals in the bar of local hotel.*
Tel- *01639 891999*

Lord Caradon Pub £5.00 1m ③
Open- *M-Sat 1000-2200, Sun 1200-2130*
Info- *Varied menu at Wetherspoon's pub & real ales.*
Tel- *01639 896007*

Others 1m ③
Info- *Several inexpensive cafes, pubs and restaurants in Port Talbot town centre.*

ACCOMMODATION

Grand Hotel £45 0.8m ②
Info- *Small independent hotel. Price is for B&B. Bar & restaurant.*
Tel- *01639 891999*

ESSENTIALS

JR Motor Spares 0.6m ④
Open- *M-F 0830-1700, Sat 0900-1600*
Info- *Local car spares shop.*
Tel- *01639 884806*

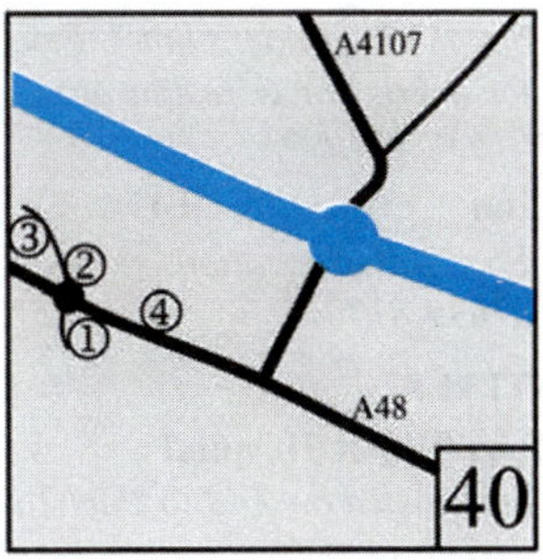

M4 Junction 41
Restricted

This junction is restricted, but Junction 41A (1.5 miles away) provides the missing accesses. Junction 40 is also 1.5 miles away and has full access to the motorway.

FUEL

Texaco SAVE £££ 0.8m ①
Open- *Daily 24 hours*
Info- *WC, jetwash.*
Tel- *01639 883418*

FOOD

McDonald's☞ £3.50 0.6m ②
Open- *Daily 0730-2300*
Tel- *01639 870593*

Grand Hotel £5 0.8m ③
Open- *Daily 1200-1330, 1800-2100*
Info- *Pub meals in the bar of local hotel.*
Tel- *01639 891999*

Lord Caradon Pub 0.8m ④
Open- *M-Sat 1000-2200, Sun 1200-2130*
Info- *Varied menu at Wetherspoon's pub & real ales.*
Tel- *01639 896007*

Others 0.8m ④
Info- *There are several inexpensive cafes, pubs and restaurants in Port Talbot.*

Beefeater☞ £7.00 1.2m ⑤
Open- *Sat-Sun 0800-1000, 1200-2130*
M-F 0800-1000, 1200-2130
Tel- *0870 197 7211*

ACCOMMODATION

Grand Hotel £45 0.8m ③
Info- *Small independent hotel. Price is for B&B. Bar & restaurant.*
Tel- *01639 891999*

Travel Inn☞ £45 1.2m ⑤
Info- *Port Talbot location.*
Tel- *01639 813017*

ESSENTIALS

Neath/Port Talbot Hospital 4.5m
Dir'n- *Signposted on A48 to Port Talbot.*
Tel- *01639 862000*

ATS £45 0.6m ②
Open- *M-F 0830-1730, Sat 0800-1700, Sun 1000-1600*
Info- *Tyres, batteries, exhausts.*
Tel- *0870 197 7211*

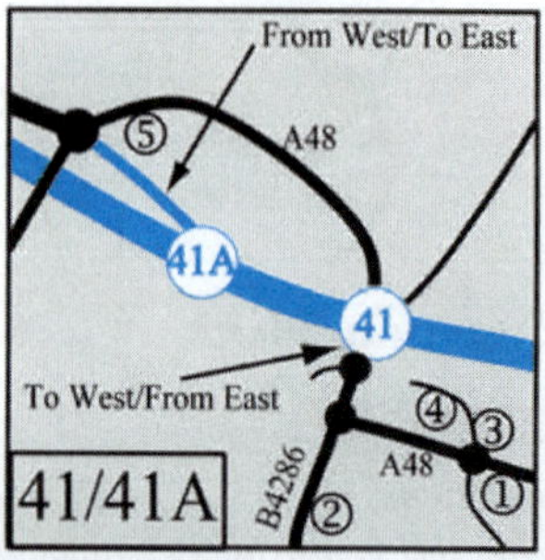

M4 Junction 41A
Restricted

This junction allows exit westbound and entry heading east. Junction 41 (1.5 miles away) provides the accesses that are missing from this junction.

FOOD

Beefeater☞ £7.00 1m ⑤
Open- *Sat/Sun 0800-1000, 1200-2130,*
M-F 0800-1000, 1200-2130
Tel- *0870 197 7211*

ACCOMMODATION

Travel Inn☞ £45 1m ⑤
Info- *Port Talbot location.*
Tel- *01639 813017*

ESSENTIALS

Neath/Port Talbot Hospital 2.5m
Dir'n- *Signposted on A48 to Port Talbot.*
Tel- *01639 862000*

M4 Junction 42
Briton Ferry

FUEL

Shell SAVE £££ 1.5m ①
Open- *Daily 24 hours*
Info- *LPG, WC.*
Tel- *01792 326900*

FOOD

McDonald's☞ £3.50 1.3m ②
Open- *Su-Th 0700-2300, F-Sat 0700-2400*
Tel- *01639 823612*

ESSENTIALS

Neath/Port Talbot Hospital 6m
Dir'n- *Signposted on A48 to Port Talbot.*
Tel- *01639 862000*

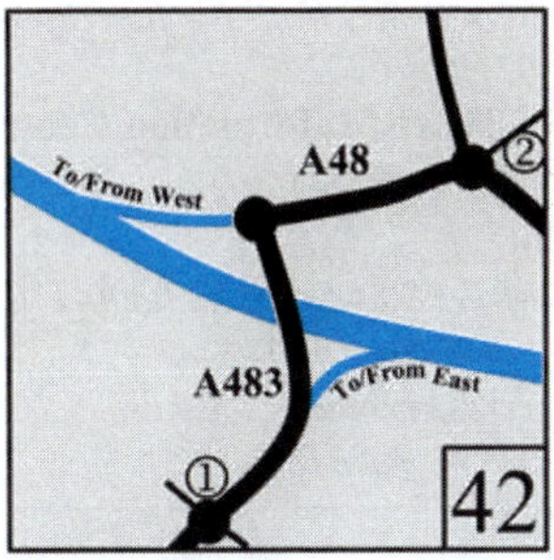

M4 Junction 43
Neath

FUEL

Total SAVE ££ 1.6m ①
Open- *Daily 0600-2300*
Info- *WC, carwash.*
Tel- *01792 326934*

FOOD

Harvester☞ £7.00 0.1m ②
Open- *Su-Th 1200-2100, F-Sa 1200-2200*
Tel- *01792 321384*

McDonald's☞ £3.50 1.6m ①
Open- *M-W 0730-2300, Th/Sun 0730-2400, Fr-Sat 0730-0300*
Info- *Cash machine nearby.*
Tel- *01792 817010*

ACCOMMODATION

Express by Hol. Inn☞ £55 0.1m ②
Info- *Swansea location.*
Tel- *0870 442 5560*

THINGS TO DO

Pant-y-Sais Fen £nil 1.6m ③
Info- *Boardwalk through a grassland fen.*
Open- *Daylight hours.*

M4 Junction 44
Swansea East

FUEL

Texaco SAVE £££ 0.5m ①
Open- *Daily 24 hours*
Info- *WC, carwash.*
Tel- *01792 817 505*

Total SAVE £££ 0.7m ②
Open- *M-F 0700-2200, Sa-Su 0800-2000*
Info- *WC*
Tel- *01792 701330*

FOOD

The Bowen Arms £4.50 0.2m ③
Open- *M-Sa 1200-1400, 1800-2100, Su 1200-1400*
Info- *Varied home cooked menu at local pub.*
Tel- *01792 812321*

ESSENTIALS

Swansea Tourist Information Centre
Tel- *01792 468 321*

Autofix 0.2m ③
Open- *M-F 0830-1700, Sat 0830-1200*
Info- *Tyres, MOT, brakes, batteries.*
Tel- *01792 816769*

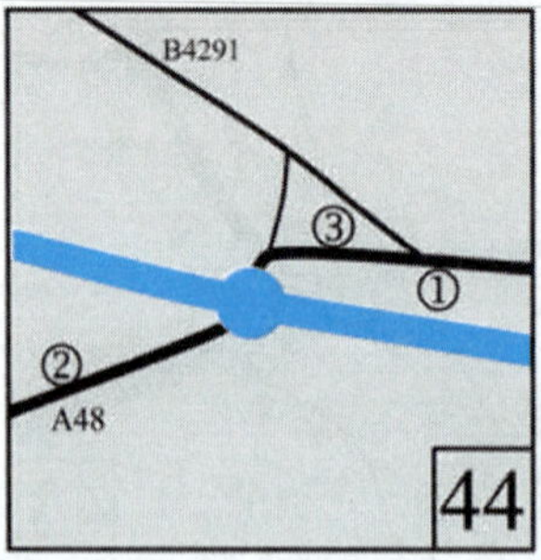

M4 Junction 45
Swansea North

For all facilities take the second slip road off the A4067.

FUEL

Esso SAVE ££ 1.2m ①
Open- *Daily 24 hours*
Info- *Carwash.*
Tel- *01792 701519*

ASDA SAVE £££ 1.2m ②
Open- *Daily 24 hours (with a credit card)*
Info- *WC, cash machine at store.*
Tel- *01792 791022*

Texaco SAVE ££ 1.3m ③
Open- *Daily 24 hours.*
Info- *WC, jetwash.*
Tel- *01792 700071*

FOOD

McDonald's☞ £3.50 0.9m ④
Open- *Sun-Th 0700-2300, F-Sat 0700-2400*
Tel- *01792 774295*

KFC☞ £4.00 1.1m ②
Open- *Daily 1100-2200*
Tel- *01792 700417*

Burger King☞ £4.00 1.1m ②
Open- *M-Sat 0830-2400, Sun 1000-2400*
Tel- *01792 781262*

Millers Kitchen☞ £6.50 1.1m ⑤
Open- *M-Sat 1200-2200, Sun 1200-2100*
Info- *Extensive menu.*
Look for 'The Dylan Thomas'.
Tel- *01792 701670*

Brewsters☞ £6.50 1.2m ②
Open- *M-Sat 1200-2200, Sun 1200-2100*
Tel- *01792 311920*

ACCOMMODATION

Travel Inn☞ £45 1.2m ②
Info- *Swansea location.*
Tel- *0870 197 7246*

ESSENTIALS

Morriston Hospital 1.5m
Dir'n- *Signposted from the junction.*
Tel- *01792 702222*

Swansea Tourist Information Centre
Tel- *01792 468321*

Kwik Fit 1.3m ⑥
Open- *M-F 0800-1800, Sa 0800-1700, Sun 1000-1600*
Info- *Tyres, exhausts, brakes.*
Tel- *01792 701018*

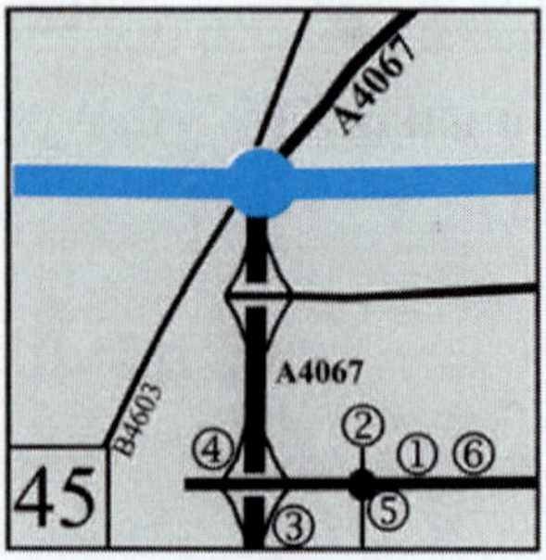

M4 Junction 46
Swansea North

FOOD

Plough & Harrow £5.50 0.2m ①
Open- *M-Sa 1200-1400, 1700-2100, Sun 1200-1400*
Info- *Varied hot & cold menu.*
Tel- *01792 771816*

ACCOMMODATION

Fairyglen Guest House £40 0.5m ②
Info- *Price is for B&B..*
Tel- *01792 790307*

ESSENTIALS

Morriston Hospital 1.5m
Dir'n- *Signposted from the junction.*
Tel- *01792 702222*

Swansea Tourist Information Centre
Tel- 01792 468321

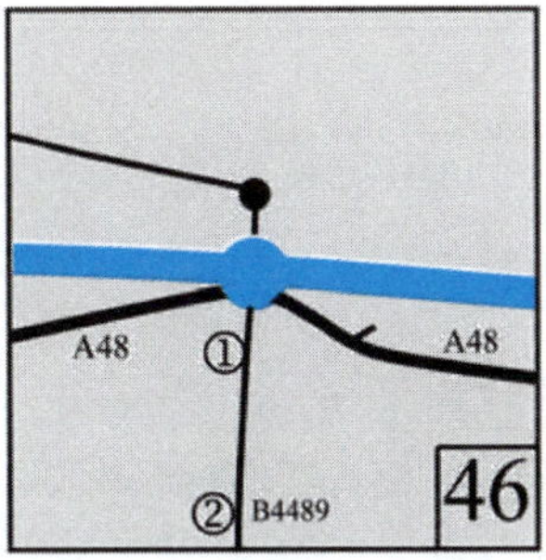

J47 Swansea West Services

This services is located just off the motorway at Junction 47.

FUEL BP
HGV fuelling and parking. Car parking £6 per 24 hours after first 2 hours.

FOOD MOTO
McDonald's, Little Chef, Burger King.
Info- Cash machine.

ACCOMMODATION

Travelodge☞ £50
Info- Swansea location.
Tel- 0870 191 1555

M4 Junction 47
Swansea West

FUEL

Total SAVE £££ 0.3m ①
Open- M-Sat 0600-2200, Sun 1200-1600
Info- WC
Tel- 01792 222932

FOOD

The Old Inn £7.00 0.3m ②
Open- M-Sat 1200-2100, Sun 1200-1600
Info- Extensive hot & cold menu.
Tel- 01792 894097

ESSENTIALS

Morriston Hospital 3m
Dir'n- Signposted from the junction.
Tel- 01792 702222

Swansea Tourist Information Centre
Tel- 01792 468321

THINGS TO DO

Picnic Site Free 0.3m ③
Open- Daylight hours.
Info- Forestry Commission site.

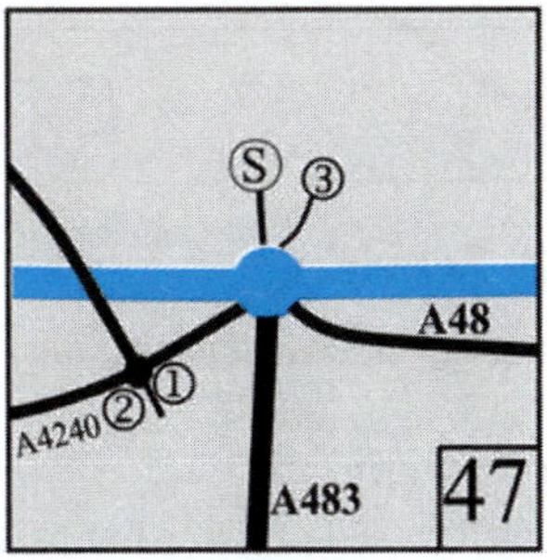

M4 Junction 48
Llanelli

FUEL

Shell SAVE £ 0.7m ①
Open- Daily 24 hours
Info- WC, cash machine.
Tel- 01792 885741

FOOD

Black Horse Inn £5.00 0.5m ②
Open- M-Sat 1200-2130, Sun 1200-1500
Info- Varied menu & real ales.
Tel- 01729 882239

ESSENTIALS

Fferyllfa Pharmacy 0.3m ③
Open- M-F 0845-1800, Sat 0900-1300
Tel- 01792 654405

Station Garage 0.6m ④
Open- M-F 0900-1700, Sat 0900-1300
Info- Small local garage for repairs.
Tel- 01792 885451

Jn 49 Services

This services is located just off the motorway.

FUEL **BP**

HGV fuelling and parking. Car parking £6 per 24 hours after first 2 hours.

FOOD ROADCHEF

onroute restaurant, Costa Coffee

Info- Cash machines

M4 Junction 49

Motorway Ends

ESSENTIALS

Morriston Hospital 11m

Dir'n- The nearest hospital is at Jn 46.

Tel- 01792 702222

M5-Birmingham to Exeter

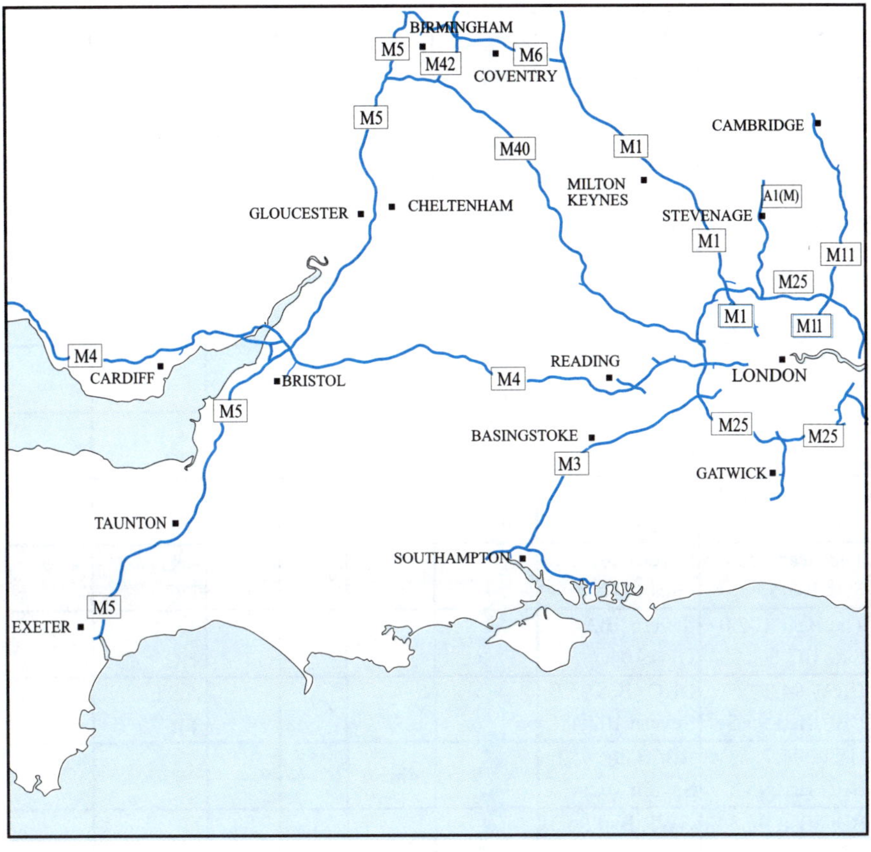

M5-Summary of Junctions

Radio stations & frequencies		Junction	Fuel	Food	Hotels	Essentials	Things to do
BBC Shrp 96.0 WOLF 107.7	B'con 103.1 Leic 104.9	1	24hr	✓	✓	A&E, TIC Pharm Svc	✓
Century 106.0 Galaxy 102.2	Saga 105.7 BRMB 96.4	2	24hr	✓	✓	Pharmacy Svc	
BH&W 104.0 BRMB 96.4	Saga 105.7 BBC WM 95.6	3	✓	✓		A&E	
BH&W 104.0 BRMB 96.4	Saga 105.7 BBC WM 95.6	S	24hr	✓	✓		
H&W 104.0 Severn 102.4	BRMB 95.6 Wyvern 102.8	4	24hr	✓	✓		
Saga 105.7 Wyvern 102.8	BBC WM 95.6 The Bear 102.0	4A				A&E	
Saga 105.7 Wyvern 102.8	BBC WM 95.6 The Bear 102.0	5	24hr	✓	✓	TIC	✓
Saga 105.7 BBC Glos 104.7	H&W 104.0 Wyvern 102.8	6		✓	✓	TIC	
H&W 104.0 Wyvern 102.8	Glos 104.7 WM 103.7	7	✓	✓		A&E	✓
H&W 104.0 Wyvern 102.8	Glos 104.7 WM 103.7	S	24hr	✓	✓	Svc	
Star 107.5 H&W 104.0	Severn 102.4 WM 103.7	8					
The Bear 102.0 Star 107.5	Severn 102.4 Glos 104.7	9	24hr	✓	✓	A&E TIC	✓
The Bear 102.0 Star 107.5	Severn 102.4 Glos 104.7	10					
The Bear 102.0 Star 107.5	Severn 102.4 Glos 104.7	11		✓	✓	A&E TIC	
The Bear 102.0 Star 107.5	Severn 102.4 Glos 104.7	11A				A&E TIC	✓
H&W 94.7 BBC Bstl 95.5	BBC Glos 95.0 Severn 102.4	12	✓	✓		A&E TIC	
H&W 94.7 BBC Bstl 95.5	BBC Glos 95.0 Severn 102.4	13	24hr	✓	✓		✓
BBC Bstl 95.5 BBC Glos 104.7	GWR Bstl 96.3 Severn 102.4	S	24hr	✓	✓		

Top Stops are highlighted

Radio stations & frequencies		Junction	Fuel	Food	Hotels	Essentials	Things to do
BBC Bstl 95.5 Glos 104.7	Bstl 96.3 Severn 102.4	14	✓	✓	✓	Svc	
BBC Bstl 95.5 BBC Glos 104.7	Bstl 96.3 REAL 105.4	15				TIC	
BBC Bstl 95.5 Star 107.3	Bstl 96.3 Vive 97.2	16	24hr	✓	✓	TIC	
Real 105.4 GWR Brstl 96.3	Star 107.3 Vive 101 97.2	17	✓	✓		A&E TIC	✓
Vibe 101 101.1 GTFM 106.9	Real 105.4 Red Dragon	18A					
Vibe 101 101.1 GTFM 106.9	Real 105.4 Dragon 97.4	18		✓	✓	A&E TIC Svc	
Vibe 101 101.1 GTFM 106.9	Real 105.4 Wales 103.9	19	24hr	✓	✓	TIC Svc	
Vibe 101 101.1 Dragon 97.4	GWR Bristol 96.3 BBC	20	✓	✓		Svc	✓
Vibe 101 101.1 Dragon 103.2	Star1077 107.7 Real 105.4	21	24hr	✓		A&E TIC Svc, Phar.	✓
Bristol 93.5 Dragon 103.2	Orchard 102.6 Wales 103.9	S	24hr	✓	✓	TIC	
Bristol 93.5 Dragon 103.2	Orchard 102.6 Wales 103.9	22	✓	✓	✓	A&E TIC	✓
Orchard 102.6 Dragon 103.2	Vibe 101 101.1 Bristol 93.5	23		✓	✓		✓
Bristol 93.5 Orchard 102.6	Vibe 101 101.1 Real 105.4	24 S	24hr	✓	✓		
Bristol 93.5 Orchard 102.6	BBC Cymru 96.8	25	24hr	✓	✓	A&E TIC	
Devon 103.4	Bristol 93.5	S	24hr	✓	✓		
Devon 103.4		26	✓			A&E	
Devon 103.4		27	✓	✓	✓	TIC	
Gemini E 97.0		28 S	24hr	✓	✓	Svc Pharmacy	
Gemini E 97.0		29				A&E Svc TIC	
Gemini E 97.0		30 S	24hr	✓		A&E TIC	
Gemini E 97.0		31					

M5 Junction Details

M5 Junction 1
West Bromwich

FUEL

Texaco SAVE £££ 0.3m ①
Open- *Daily 24 hours*
Info- *Cash machine.*
Tel- *0121 525 4100*

FOOD

McDonald's☞ £3.50 0.6m ②
Open- *M-Sat 0700-2300, Sun 0800-2300*
Tel- *0121 525 2885*

Pizza Hut☞ £6.00 0.6m ③
Open- *Daily 1130-2300*
Tel- *0121 500 5232*

Hwd Johnson Cafe-bar £7.00 0.8m ④
Open- *M-F 0630-1000, Sa/Sun 0730-1100*
Daily 1200-1400, 1800-2130
Info- *Drinks & light meals at the hotel.*
Tel- *0121 525 8333*

Others £4-6 <1m
Info- *There are many budget food outlets on the road to West Bromwich.*

ACCOMMODATION

Moat House Hotel☞ £137 0.6m ⑤
Info- *Bar & restaurant. Birmingham/West Bromwich location.*
Tel- *0121 609 9988*

Howard Johnson Hotel £67 0.8m ④
Info- *On-site cafe-bar*
Tel- *0121 525 8333*

ESSENTIALS

Sandwell Hospital 1.5m
Dir'n- *Signposted from the junction.*
Tel- *0121 553 1831*

Khaira Pharmacy 0.4m ⑥
Open- *M-F 0900-1900, Sat 0900-1700*
Tel- *0121 525 8333*

Birmingham Tourist Information Centre
Tel- *0121 693 6300*

Central Tyre 0.4m ⑦
Open- *M-F 0800-1800, Sat 0800-1700*
Info- *Tyres & exhausts.*
Tel- *0121 553 6684*

THINGS TO DO

West Bromwich Albion FC ⑧
Info- *Well known football ground.*

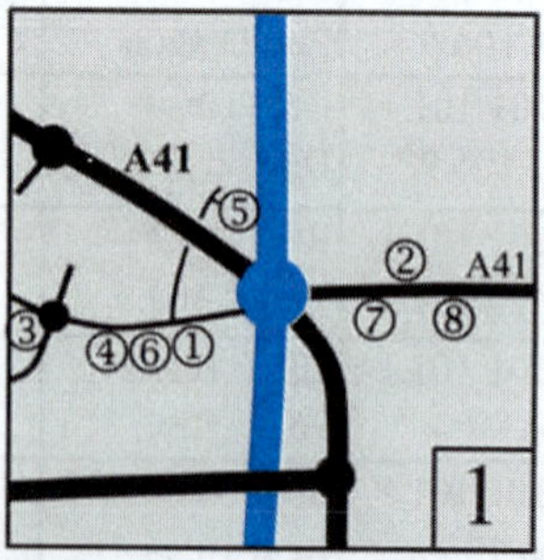

M5 Junction 2
Oldbury

FUEL

Total SAVE ££ 0.2m ①
Open- *Daily 0600-2200*
Info- *WC, carwash.*
Enter via A4034 to Oldbury.
Tel- *0121 552 6957*

BP SAVE ££ 0.8m ②
Open- *Daily 0600-2200*
Info- *WC, LPG, carwash.*
Tel- *0121 552 3709*

Texaco SAVE ££ 0.8m ③
Open- *Daily 0600-2300*
Info- *WC, cash machine.*
Tel- *0121 559 1217*

Sainsbury SAVE ££ 0.8m ④
Open- *M-Sat 0600-2230, Sun 0900-1700*
Info- *Carwash. WC, cafe, cash machines at store.*
Tel- *0121 665 2941*

FOOD

McDonald's☞ £3.50 0.2m ⑤
Open- *Daily 0630-2300*
Tel- *0121 541 2055*

Tom Cobleigh☞ £6.50 0.2m ①
Open- *M-Sat 1200-2200, Sun 1200-2130*
Info- *Enter next to Total garage on the Oldbury road.*
Tel- *0121 544 9621*

Bulls Head Pub £4.50 0.6m ⑥
Open- *Daily 1200-2030*
Info- *Varied pub menu.*
Tel- *0121 559 2637*

Whiteheath Gate Pub £3.00 0.6m ⑥
Open- *Daily 1100-2100*
Info- *Bar snacks.*
Tel- *0121 561 5733*

McDonald's no. 2☞ £3.50 0.6m ④
Open- *Daily 0630-2300*
Tel- *0121 552 9002*

Sainsbury Cafe☞ £3.50 0.6m ④
Open- *M-Sat 0800-1930, Sun 1000-1600*
Tel- *0121 665 2900*

Little Chef☞ £6.50 0.8m ②
Open- *Daily 0700-2200*
Tel- *0121 552 2494*

Wing Wah £10 0.9m ⑦
Open- *M-Sat 1200-1500, 1800-2300 Sun 1200-2200*
Info- *300 seat Chinese restaurant!*
Tel- *0121 552 0041*

KFC☞ £4.00 1m ⑧
Open- *Daily 1130-2400*
Tel- *0121 544 1819*

Brewsters☞ £6.50 1m ⑧
Open- *Daily 1130-2200*
Tel- *0121 552 3031*

ACCOMMODATION

Express by Hol. Inn☞ £45 1m ①
Info- *Birmingham Oldbury location. Well behaved dogs by arrangement.*
Tel- *0121 511 0000*

Travelodge☞ £45 0.8m ②
Info- *Oldbury location.*
Tel- *0870 191 1595*

Travel Inn☞ £45 1m ⑧
Info- *Oldbury location.*
Tel- *0870 197 7202*

ESSENTIALS

Halfords & AA service 0.3m ⑨
Open- *M-F 0800-2000, Sat 0900-1800, Sun 1000-1700 (AA open shorter hours).*
Info- *Car parts & service centre.*
Tel- *0121 552 6173*

Charlie Brown's Tyres 0.7m ⑩
Open- *M-Sat 0830-1800, Sun 1000-1600*
Info- *Tyres, exhausts & spare parts.*
Tel- *0121 544 2544*

HiQ Tyres & Exhausts 0.8m ❶
Open- *M-F 0830-1730, Sat 0830-1200*
Info- *Tyres & exhausts.*
Tel- *0121 552 1218*

Broomfield Garage 0.8m ③
Open- *M-F 0900-1700, Sat 0900-1300*
Info- *Servicing & repairs.*
Tel- *0121 559 1217*

Lloyds Pharmacy 0.9m ❷
Open- *M-F 0900-1900, Sat 0900-1700*
Tel- *0121 552 3215*

BMW Dealer 1m ⑦

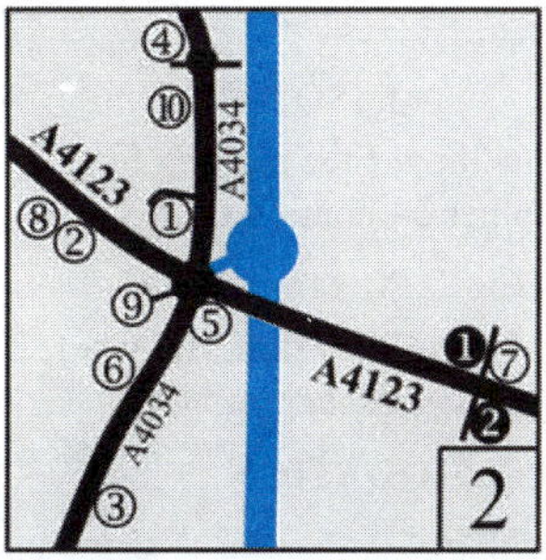

M5 Junction 3 Halesowen

FUEL

BP SAVE ££ 0.7m ①
Open- *M-F 0600-2200, Sat/Sun 0700-2200*
Info- *LPG , HGV fuelling, WC, carwash. Cash machine.*
Tel- *0121 585 5105*

FOOD

The Black Horse £6.50 1.3m ②

Open- *M-Sat 1130-2130, Sun 1130-2130. A Big Steak Pub.* ☞

Tel- *0121 550 1465*

ESSENTIALS

Selly Oak Hospital 6.5m

Dir'n- *Take the A456 towards Birmingham, and then the A4123 south to the A4040. The hospital is just past the A38 junction.*

Tel- *0121 627 1627*

Audi Dealer 1.7m ③

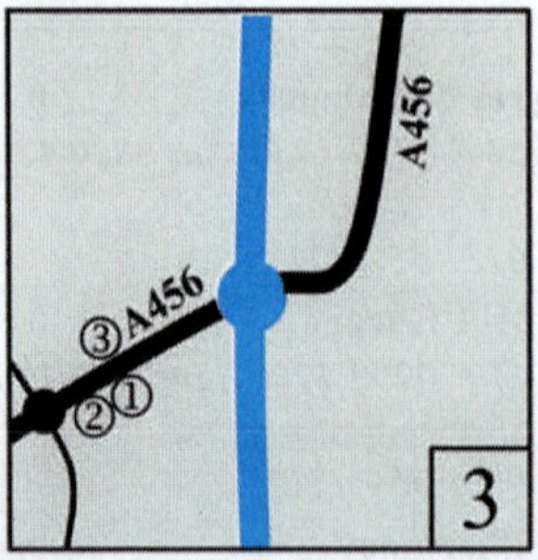

Frankley Services

This services has a roadbridge & footbridge.

FUEL ESSO

HGV fuelling. Free parking for 2 hours then £6 per 24 hours. Lorry park.

FOOD MOTO

Upper Crust, Ritazza, Little Chef, Harry Ramsden's, freshexpress.

ACCOMMODATION

Travelodge☞ £45

Info- *Birmingham South (Frankley) location.*

Info- *Cash machine (Link, Plus, Visa, Amex, Diners Club).*

Tel- *0870 905 6343*

M5 Junction 4
Bromsgrove North

FUEL

Total **SAVE** ££ 1.5m ①

Open- *Daily 24 hours*

Info- *WC, jetwash.*

Tel- *01527 839915*

FOOD

Miu Miu Takeaway £6.00 0.8m ①

Open- *M-Th 1700-2300, F/Sat 1700-2330, Sun 1700-2200*

Info- *Chinese takeaway meals.*

Tel- *0121 445 0938*

Toby Carvery☞ £7.00 0.9m ②

Open- *M-F 1200-1400, 1700-2200, Sat/Sun 1200-2200*

Tel- *01527 878060*

ACCOMMODATION

Home Farm B&B £40 0.3m ③

Info- *Price is for B&B.*

Tel- *01527 874964*

Hilton Hotel☞ £140 0.4m ④

Info- *On-site bar & brasserie. Bromsgrove location.*

Tel- *0121 447 7888*

Innkeeper's Lodge☞ £53 0.9m ②

Info- *Price includes cont. breakfast. Bromsgrove location.*

Tel- *01527 878060*

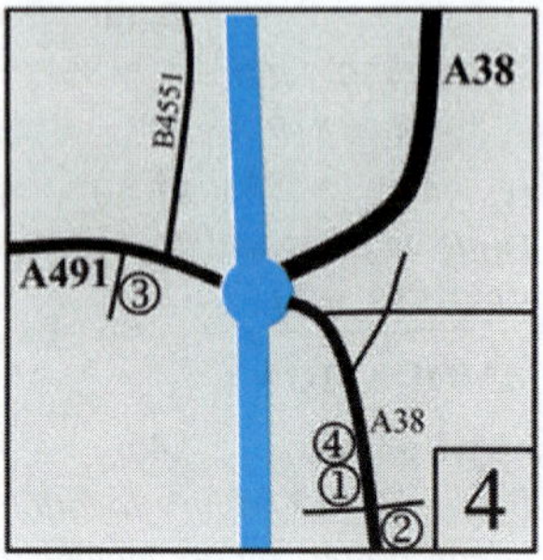

M5 Junction 4A
M5/M42 interchange

There is no access to local services at this junction.

ESSENTIALS

Alexandra Hospital 12m

Dir'n- *Take the M42 east, and then follow signs to Redditch where the hospital is signposted.*

Tel- *01527 503030*

M5 Junction 5
Droitwich Spa

FUEL

Murco SAVE ££ 0.6m ①

Open- *Daily 24 hours*

Info- *WC, jetwash*

Tel- *01527 839915*

FOOD

McDonald's☞ £3.50 0.2m ②

Open- *Daily 0700-2200*

Tel- *01527 869079*

The Robin Hood £8.00 0.3m ③

Open- *Daily 1200-2130.*

Info- *Extensive menu. A 'Vantage Inn'.*

Tel- *01527 861931*

Little Chef☞ £6.50 0.4m ④

Open- *Daily 0700-2000*

Tel- *01527 861594*

Burger King☞ £4.00 0.4m ④

Open- *Daily 1100-2100*

Tel- *01527 861594*

The Poacher's Pocket £7.00 0.5m ⑤

Open- *M-Sat 1200-2200, Sun 1200-2130*

Info- *Extensive hot & cold menu.*

Tel- *01527 861413*

Garden Room Rest. £6.00 0.5m ⑦

Open- *M-Sat 0900-1900, Sun 1030-1530*

Info- *Varied hot & cold menu at Webbs of Wychbold Garden Centre.*

Tel- *01527 860000*

ACCOMMODATION

Express by Hol. Inn☞ £66 0.2m ②

Info- *Droitwich location.*

Tel- *0870 4425658*

Travelodge☞ £55 0.4m ④

Info- *Droitwich location.*

Tel- *08701 911574*

Chateau Impney Hotel £90 1.3m ⑥

Info- *Price is B&B. On-site bar & restaurant. Impressive chateau setting & gardens.*

Tel- *01905 774411*

ESSENTIALS

Droitwich Tourist Information Centre

Tel- *01527 831809*

Saab/Seat Dealers 1.8m

Dir'n- *In Droitwich town centre.*

THINGS TO DO

Webbs of Wychbold 1.1m ⑦

Open- *M-Sat 0900-2000, Sun 1000-1630. Reduced opening hours Jan & Feb.*

Info- *Award winning garden centre, with a riverside walk & large restaurant.*

Tel- *01527 860000*

Droitwich 2m

Info- *This town is about 2m away, has a variety of facilities, and provides a good short break from the motorway.*

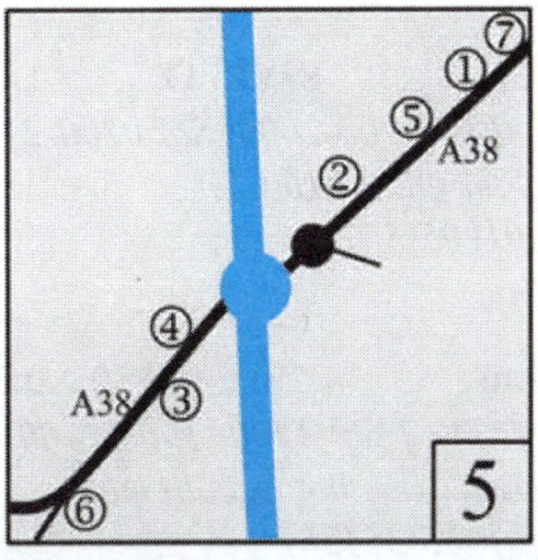

M5 Junction 6
Worcester North

FOOD

Beefeater☞ £7.00 0.3m ①

Open- *M-Sat 0700-0900, 1200-2200, Sun 0700-0900, 1200-2100*

Info- *Next to Travel Inn*

Tel- *01905 451240*

The Poacher's Pocket £7.00 1m ②

Open- *M-F 1200-2100, Sa/Sun 1200-2200*
Info- *Extensive menu & 'Poacher's Den' for children.*
Tel- *01905 458615*

ACCOMMODATION

Travel Inn☞ £45 0.2m ①

Info- *Worcester location.*
Tel- *08701 977278*

ESSENTIALS

Worcester Tourist Information Centre

Tel- *01905 726311*

M5 Junction 7
Worcester South

FUEL

BP SAVE ££ 1.1m ①

Open- *M-F 0700-2000, Sat 0700-2100, Sun 0800-2100*
Tel- *01905 351245*

FOOD

The Swan £7.50 0.5m ③

Open- *Daily 1200-1400, 1900-2100*
Info- *Extensive hot & cold menu.*
Tel- *01905 351361*

The Oak Apple Inn £5.00 1.1m ③

Open- *M-Sat 1100-2100, Sun 1200-2100*
Info- *Varied hot & cold meals.*
Tel- *01905 355121*

Other 1.5m

Info- *Worcester has a range of restaurants, pubs and cafes.*

ESSENTIALS

Worcester Royal Hospital 3m

Dir'n- *Signposted from junction.*
Tel- *01905 763333*

THINGS TO DO

Worcester Cathedral 1.5m

Info- *The cathedral is the highlight of nearby Worcester.*
Tel- *01905 726311*

Strensham Services

This services has a roadbridge, but no footbridge.

FUEL ESSO

HGV fuelling. Free parking for 2 hours then £6 per 24 hours. Lorry park.

FOOD ROADCHEF

Wimpy, onroute, Costa Coffee.
Other- Cash machine.

ACCOMMODATION

Travel Inn☞ £45

Info- *Tewkesbury Strensham location.*
Tel- *08701 977252*

ESSENTIALS

24 hour recovery £45

Info- *Erikson's Motor Services*
Tel- *01684 293006*

M5 Junction 8
M5/M50 interchange

There is no access to local services at this junction.

M5 Junction 9
Tewkesbury

FUEL

BP SAVE ££ 0.2m ①
Open- *Daily 24 hours*
Info- *LPG, WC, cash machine.*
Tel- *01684 293785*

Q8 SAVE £ 0.5m ②
Open- *M-Sat 0700-2000, Sun 0800-1900*
Info- *WC*
Tel- *01684 275555*

Safeway SAVE ££ 0.6m ③
Open- *M-F 0700-2200, Sat 0700-2100, Sun 0800-2000*
Info- *Carwash. WC, cafe at store.*
Tel- *01684 273268*

FOOD

Little Chef☞ £6.50 0.2m ①
Open- *Daily 0700-2300*
Tel- *01684 850270*

The Canterbury £4.00 0.6m ④
Open- *Daily 1200-2100*
Info- *Varied menu in local pub.*
Tel- *01684 297744*

Safeway Cafe☞ £3.50 1m ③
Open- *M-Sat 0800-2000, Sun 1000-1600*
Tel- *01684 273261*

ACCOMMODATION

Newton Farm B&B £40 0.5m ⑤
Info- *Price is for B&B.*
Tel- *01684 295903*

ESSENTIALS

Tewkesbury Hospital 2m
Info- *Minor injuries unit.*
Dir'n- *Signposted en-route to Tewkesbury.*
Tel- *01684 293303*

Tewkesbury Tourist Information Centre
Tel- *01684 295027*

THINGS TO DO

Tewkesbury 1.2m
Info- *Tewkesbury is a pleasant town with an interesting abbey, It offers a range of restaurants and cafes, as well as river walks and boat trips.*

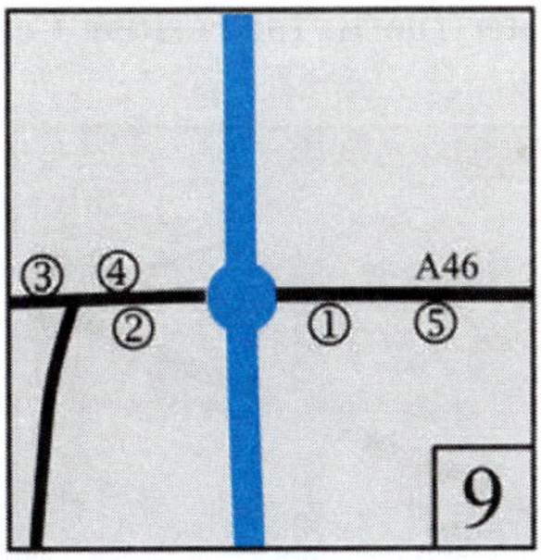

M5 Junction 10
Restricted

Vehicles can only exit the motorway heading southbound, and enter the motorway northbound.

M5 Junction 11
Restricted

Vehicles can only exit heading north on the motorway, and enter the motorway in the southbound direction.

FOOD

Burford Restaurant £15 1m ①
Open- *Daily 1200-1345, 1900-2145*
Info- *Refined dining at the Thistle Hotel.*
Tel- *01242 232691*

ACCOMMODATION

Briarfields Motel £36 1.2m ②
Info- *Motel & Caravan Pk. Dogs welcome.*
Tel- *01242 235324*

Thistle Hotel☞ £135 1m ①
Info- *On-site bar, restaurant & health club. Dogs at a £5 charge.*
Tel- *01242 232691*

ESSENTIALS

Cheltenham General Hospital 2.8m
Dir'n- *Take the A40 towards Cheltenham, where the hopsital is signposted to the right.*
Tel- *01242 222222*

Cheltenham Tourist Information Centre
Tel- *01242 522878*

Gloucester Tourist Information Centre
Tel- *01452 396572*

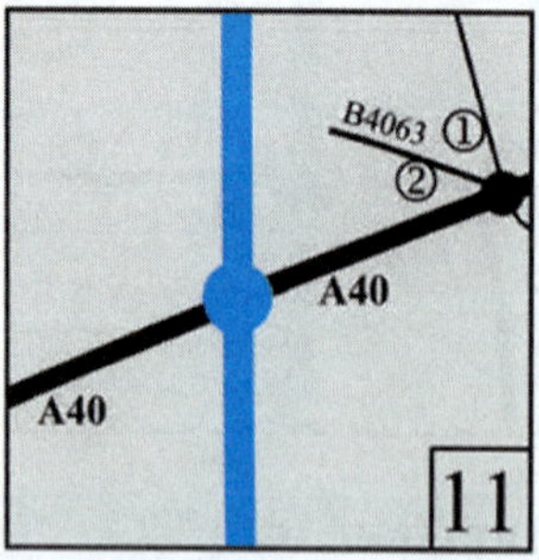

M5 Junction 11A
Restricted

No entrance to the northbound carriageway once you leave the motorway.

ESSENTIALS

Gloucester Royal Hospital 3m
Dir'n- *Follow signs to the Cathedral in Gloucester, and the hospital is signposted nearby.*
Tel- *01452 528555*

Gloucester Tourist Information Centre
Tel- *01452 396572*

THINGS TO DO

Gloucester 3m
Info- *Gloucester is an interesting city with an exceptional cathedral and a wide range of shops & restaurants. The National Waterways Museum is located near the centre.*

M5 Junction 12
Restricted

Vehicles can only exit the motoway heading northbound, and enter the motorway southbound.

FUEL

BP SAVE £ 0.5m ①
Open- *M-Sat 0600-2145, Sun 0700-2145*
Info- *WC, carwash, HGV fuelling.*
Tel- *01452 721470*

UK Fuels SAVE £ 0.6m ②
Open- *M-Fri 0800-1700, Sat 0800-1300, Sun 0800-1300*
Tel- *01452 720239*

FOOD

McDonald's☞ £3.50 0.5m ①
Open- *Daily 0700-1100*
Tel- *01452 723680*

ESSENTIALS

Gloucester Royal Hospital 5m
Dir'n- *Follow signs to the Cathedral in Gloucester, and the hospital is signposted nearby.*
Tel- *01452 528555*

Gloucester Tourist Information Centre
Tel- *01452 396572*

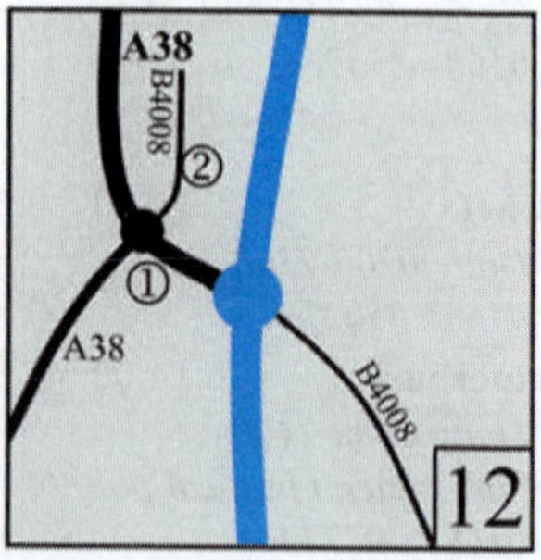

M5 Junction 13
Stroud

FUEL

Shell SAVE ££ 0.5m ①
Open- *Daily 24 hours.*
Info- *WC, carwash, HGV fuelling.*
Tel- *01452 794030*

Total SAVE £ 0.9m ②
Open- *Daily 24 hours.*
Info- *WC, carwash, HGV fuelling.*
Tel- *01452 740753*

FOOD

Little Chef☞ £6.50 0.5m ①
Open- *Daily 0700-2200*
Tel- *01453 828847*

Burger King☞ £4.00 0.5m ①
Open- *Daily 1000-2200*
Tel- *01453 828847*

Fromebridge Mill £9.00 0.5m ③
Open- *M-Sat 1200-2130, Sun 1200-2100*
Info- *Extensive menu in restored watermill.*
Tel- *01452 741796*

Old Forge Inn £8.00 1m ④
Open- *Tu-Sat 1200-1400, 1800-2100, Sun 1200-1400*
Info- *Real ales & extensive menu.*
Tel- *01452 741306*

ACCOMMODATION

Travelodge☞ £45 1.2m ①
Info- *Stonehouse location.*
Tel- *08701 911554*

THINGS TO DO

River Walk 2m ⑤
Info- *Pleasant walk along the river at Frampton-on-Severn.*

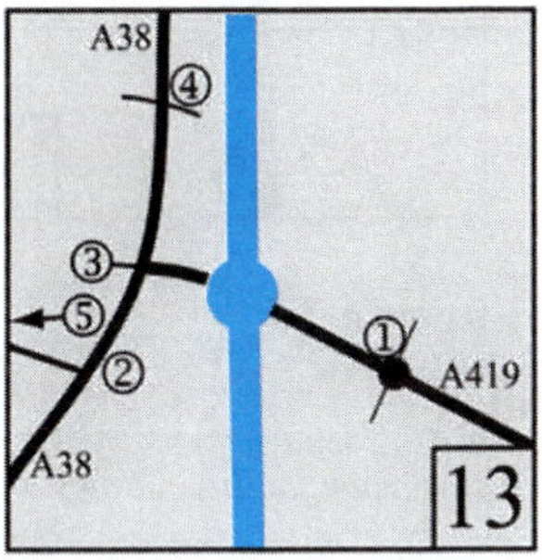

Michaelwood Services

This services has a footbridge.

FUEL BP
HGV fuelling. Free parking for 2 hours then £6 per 24 hours. Lorry park.

FOOD WELCOME BREAK
The Granary, Burger King, Coffee Express.
Other- Cash machine.

ACCOMMODATION

Days Inn☞ £45
Info- *Michaelwood location.*
Tel- *01454 261513*

M5 Junction 14
Charfield

FUEL

Total SAVE £ 0.7m ①
Open- *M-Sat 0630-2200*
Info- *WC, carwash.*
Tel- *01454 260284*

FOOD

Gables Hotel Restaurant £15 0.4m ②
Open- *M-Sat 1830-2130, Sun 1200-2030*
Info- *Refined dining & extensive menu.*
Tel- *01454 260502*

The Huntsman £5.50 0.4m ③
Open- *Daily 1200-1400, 1800-2130*
Info- *Varied range of hot & cold meals.*
Tel- *01454 260239*

ACCOMMODATION

The Gables Hotel £75 0.4m ②
Info- *On-site bar, restaurant & gym.*
Tel- *01454 260502*

ESSENTIALS

Fulford Garage 0.6m ④
Open- *M-F 0830-1700*
Info- *Local garage for repairs.*
Tel- *01454 260286*

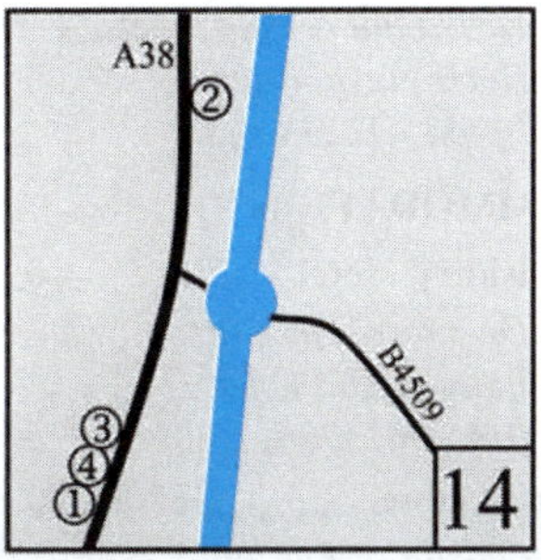

M5 Junction 15
M5/M4 interchange

There is no access to local services at this junction.

ESSENTIALS

Bristol Tourist Information Centre
Tel- *0117 926 0767*

M5 Junction 16
Bristol North

FUEL

Texaco SAVE £££ 1.5m ①
Open- *Daily 24 hours*
Info- *Carwash.*
Tel- *01454 453000*

FOOD

Oliver's Restaurant £12 0.5m ②
Open- *M-Sat 1200-1330, 1900-2130*
Info- *Almondsbury Hotel restaurant with extensive menu.*
Tel- *01454 613206*

Quarterjack's Restrnt £20 0.6m ③
Open- *Daily 1200-1400, 1930-2100*
Info- *Refined dining in the Aztec Hotel restaurant.*
Tel- *01454 201090*

The Black Sheep £6.00 0.6m ④
Open- *M-F 1200-1400, 1800-2045, Sat 1900-2045, Sun 1200-1400, 1900-2100*
Info- *Varied pub food.*
Tel- *01454 201592*

Travellers Restaurant £6.00 0.8m ⑤
Open- *Daily 1200-2200*
Info- *Varied hot & cold meals. A 'Hungry Horse' restaurant☞.*
Tel- *01454 612238*

ACCOMMODATION

Almondsbury Hotel £98 0.4m ②
Info- *On-site restaurant. Independent hotel.*
Tel- *01454 613206*

The Aztec Hotel £200 0.6m ③
Info- *On-site restaurant & bar. Spa facilities.*
Tel- *01454 201090*

Hilton Hotel☞ £129 0.5m ⑥
Info- *On-site restaurant & bar. Health club. Bristol location.*
Tel- *01454 201144*

Willow Hotel £60 1.6m ①
Info- *Bar & restaurant. Price is B&B. Independent hotel.*
Tel- *01454 612276*

The Jays Guest House £48 1.6m ①
Info- *Independent guest house. Price is B&B.*
Tel- *01454 612771*

Dove Court Mini Lodge £40 1.6m ①
Info- *Independent guest house. Includes continental breakfast.*
Tel- *01454 612271*

ESSENTIALS

Bristol Tourist Information Centre
Tel- *0117 926 0767*

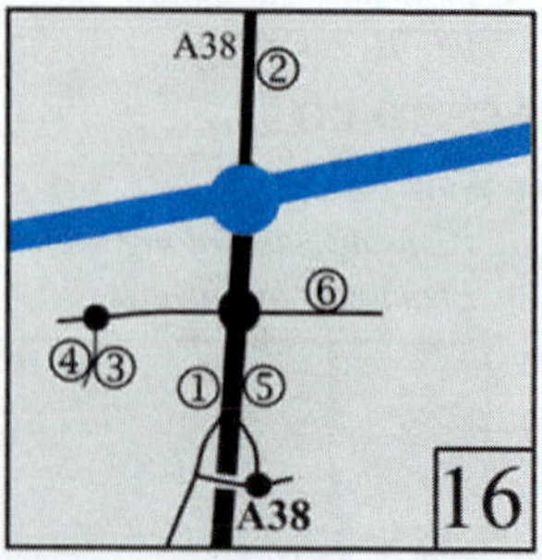

M5 Junction 17
Bristol

To help locate your facility follows signs to Retail Park ①, Cribbs Causeway ③, or The Mall ⑤.

FUEL

Asda SAVE £££ 0.8m ①
Open- *M-F 0700-2230, Sat 0700-2200, Sun 0900-1700. Daily 24 hours with credit card.*
Info- *WC, cash machines, cafe at store.*
Tel- *0117 969 3973*

FOOD

McDonald's☞ £3.50 0.4m ②
Open- *Daily 0730-2300*
Tel- *0117 950 1523*

KFC☞ £4.00 0.6m ①
Open- *Daily 1130-2300*
Tel- *0117 959 1492*

Burger King☞ £4.00 0.6m ③
Open- *Daily 1100-2200*
Tel- *0117 959 1492*

Chiquito☞ £8.50 0.8m ④
Open- *M-Sat 1200-2300, Sun 1200-2230*
Tel- *0117 959 1459*

Frankie & Benny's☞ £8.50 0.8m ④
Open- *M-Sat 1200-2300, Sun 1200-2230*
Tel- *0117 959 1180*

Bella Pasta☞ £7.00 0.8m ④
Open- *Sun-Th 1200-2200, F/Sat 1200-2300*
Tel- *0117 959 0982*

McDonald's☞ £3.50 0.8m ①
Open- *Daily 0700-2300*
Info- *Follow signs to retail superstore.*
Tel- *0117 950 3977*

ESSENTIALS

Southmead Hospital 3.5m
Dir'n- *Take the A4018 towards Bristol, and the hospital is signposted.*
Tel- *0117 950 5050*

Bristol Tourist Information Centre
Tel- *0117 926 0767*

THINGS TO DO

The Mall Shopping Centre 0.7m ⑤
Open- *M-F 1000-2000, Sat 0900-1900, Sun 1100-1700*
Info- *130 stores and 15 food outlets.*
Tel- *0117 903 0303*

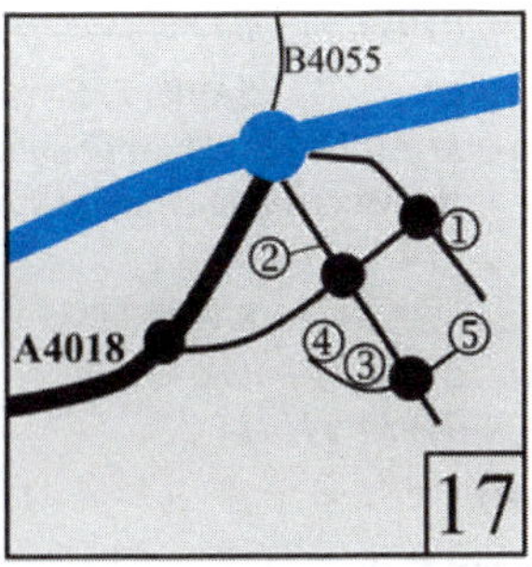

M5 Junction 18A
M5/M49 interchange

M5 Junction 18
Avonmouth

FOOD

The Miles Arms £5.50 0.7m ①
Open- *Daily 1230-1430, 1800-2030*
Info- *Varied hot & cold meals.*
Tel- *0117 982 2317*

ACCOMMODATION

The Miles Arms £55 0.7m ①
Info- *Rooms at this local pub.*
Tel- *0117 982 2317*

ESSENTIALS

Bristol Royal Infirmary 4m
Dir'n- *Take the A4 towards Bristol, and the hospital is signposted close to the centre.*
Tel- *0117 923 0000*

Bristol Tourist Information Centre
Tel- *0117 926 0767*

ATS 0.9m ②
Open- *M-F 0830-1730, Sat 0830-1230*
Info- *Tyre & exhaust centre.*
Tel- *0117 982 4707*

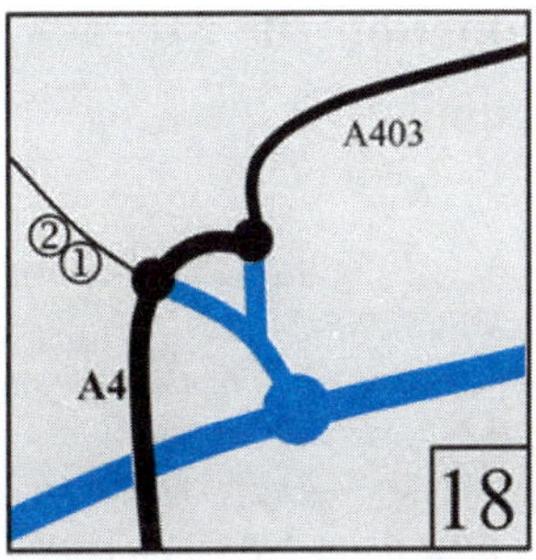

Jn 19-Gordano Services

The services are located off the motorway.

FUEL SHELL

HGV fuelling. Free parking for 2 hours then £6 per 24 hours. Lorry park.

FOOD WELCOME BREAK

'Granary' restaurant, 'bakery', Burger King & KFC. Cash machine (Link, Plus, Visa, Amex & Diners Club only).

ACCOMMODATION

Days Inn☞ £45
Info- Bristol West location.
Tel- 01275 373709

OTHER

Gordano Tourist Information Centre
Tel- 01275 373624

Auto Distress Car Repair Centre
Open- Daily 0800-2000
Info- Car repairs.
Tel- 01275 374807

M5 Junction 19
Portbury

There are no facilities close to this junction apart from Gordano Services.

M5 Junction 20
Clevedon

FUEL

Tesco☞ SAVE £££ 0.8m ①
Open- Daily 0700-2400
Info- WC, cash machines & cafe at store.
Tel- 01275 517400

Safeway☞ SAVE £££ 1.1m ②
Open- M-Sat 0600-2200, Sun 0800-2000
Info- Carwash.
Dir'n- From Safeway store follow signs to seafront.
Tel- 01275 875055

FOOD

Tandoori Nights £6.00 0.5m ③
Open- Daily 1200-1400,1730-2400
Info- Indian restaurant & takeaway.
Tel- 01275 342342

ESSENTIALS

Waterstone Tyre & Exhaust 0.5m ④
Open- M-F 0830-1800, Sat 0830-1700
Info- Tyre & exhaust centre.
Tel- 01275 342473

THINGS TO DO

Seafront Walk 2m
Info- The sea is easy to reach from this junction.

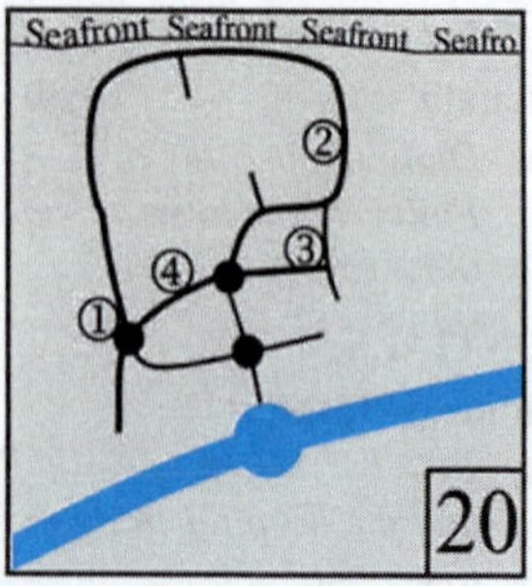

M5 Junction 21
Weston super Mare

FUEL

Safeway SAVE £££ 1.1m ①
Open- M-F 0600-2230, Sat/Sun 0800-2000
Info- Carwash. WC & cash machine at store.
Tel- 01934 515067

Sainsbury SAVE £££ 1.5m ②
Open- M-F 0600-2400, Sat/Sun 0800-1800
Info- WC & cash machine at store.
Tel- 01934 516088

BP SAVE ££ 1.7m ③
Open- Daily 24 hours
Tel - 01934 511414

FOOD

Safeway Cafe☞ £3.50 1.0m ①
Open- M-F 0700-1900, Sat 1000-1600, Sun 1000-1600
Info- Cash machine at store.
Tel- 01934 517883

The Bucket & Spade £6.50 1.0m ④

Open- *M-Sat 1100-2200, Sun 1200-2130*
Info- *Varied hot & cold meals. 'Wacky Warehouse' for children.*
Tel- *01934 521235*

McDonald's☞ £3.50 1.5m ②

Open- *Daily 0700-2300*
Tel- *01934 517846*

Sainsbury Cafe☞ £3.50 1.5m ②

Open- *M-Sat 0730-2000, Sun 0900-1530*
Tel- *01934 510495*

The Summerhouse £8.50 1.7m ⑤

Open- *M-Sat 1200-2200, Sun 1200-2100*
Info- *Pub-restaurant with extensive menu.*
Tel- *01934 520011*

ESSENTIALS

Weston General Hospital 4.5m

Dir'n- *Take the A370 towards Weston, then the A3033/Devonshire Rd. At the end turn right and the hospital is on the right.*
Tel- *01934 636363*

Safeway Pharmacy 1.1m ①

Open- *M-F 0800-2100, Sat 0800-2000, Sun 1000-1600*
Info- *In store pharmacy.*
Tel- *01934 521135*

Weston S.M. Tourist Information Centre

Tel- *01934 888 800*

Weston Recovery 1.2m ⑥

Info- *24 hour recovery service.*
Tel- *01934 517021*

Kwik Fit 1.6m ②

Open- *M-F 0800-1800, Sat 0800-1700, Sun 1000-1600.*
Info- *Tyre & exhaust centre.*
Tel- *01934 514777*

Worle Autos 1.6m ②

Open- *M-F 0830-1700, Sat 0900-1300*
Info- *Car servicing & repair.*
Dir'n- *Behind Kwik-Fit*
Tel- *01934 513808*

THINGS TO DO

Weston Super Mare 4.3m

Info- *The popular seaside resort is only a few miles away.*

Helicopter Museum 3m

Dir'n- *This is signposted from the junction.*
Tel- *01934 635227*

Sedgemoor Services

There is no roadbridge or footbridge at this services.

FUEL ESSO (SOUTHBOUND), SHELL (NORTHBOUND)

HGV fuelling. Free parking for 2 hours then £6 per 24 hours. Lorry park.

FOOD ROADCHEF / WELCOME BK

SOUTHBOUND- onroute restaurant & Costa Coffee.
NORTHBOUND- Granary restaurant & Burger King .
Info- *Cash machine.*

ACCOMMODATION

Welcome Lodge☞ (northbound) £45

Tel- *01934 750831*

OTHER

Tourist Information Centre (sthbound)

Info- *Somerset County Council TIC*
Tel- *01934 750833*

M5 Junction 22
Burnham on Sea

FUEL

Keyfuels SAVE £ 0.9m ①

Open- *M-Sat 0630-2000, Sun 0800-2000*
Info- *WC, jetwash.*
Tel- *01278 760542*

FOOD

The Fox & Goose £7.50 0.8m ②

Open- *M-Th 1130-1500, 1800-2130, Fr/Sat 1130-2200, Sun 1200-1930*

Info- *Extensive hot & cold menu*

Tel- *01278 760223*

The Goathouse rest. £6.50 1.1m ③

Open- *Tu-F 0900-1500, Th/Sat 1900-2300, Sun 0930-1500*

Info- *Varied hot & cold meals.*

Tel- *01278 760995*

ACCOMMODATION

Battleborough Grange £65 1.1m ④

Info- *On-site restaurant & bar. AA/RAC 2★. Independent hotel.*

Tel- *01278 760208*

ESSENTIALS

Weston General Hospital 7m

Dir'n- *Take the A38 north, then the A370 towards Weston. The hospital is signposted as you enter Weston.*

Tel- *01934 636363*

Burnham on Sea Tourist Info. Centre

Tel- *01278 427652*

THINGS TO DO

Burnham Seafront 2.5m

Info- *Burnham and its sandy beach and seaside amenities are close by.*

M5 Junction 23 Bridgwater North

FOOD

The Puriton Inn £7.00 0.2m ①

Open- *M-Sat 1200-1430, 1800-2100, Sun 1200-1500, 1700-2030*

Info- *Extensive hot & cold menu.*

Tel- *01278 683464*

The Admiral's Table £7.00 0.4m ②

Open- *Daily 1200-2300*

Info- *Extensive hot & cold menu.*

Tel- *01278 685671*

ACCOMMODATION

Room at the Inn☞ £50 0.4m ②

Info- *Bar & restaurant. Bridgwater location.*

Tel- *01278 685671*

THINGS TO DO

BCA Car Auctions 0.8m ③

Open- *Most Weds and Fridays at 1000.*

Info- *Watch a car auction!*

Tel- *01278 685511*

Jn 24 Bridgwater Services

This is located off the motorway.

FUEL BP

HGV fuelling. Free parking for 2 hours then £6 per 24 hours. Lorry park.

FOOD MOTO

Moto restaurant & Costa Coffee.

Info- *Cash machine.*

ACCOMMODATION

Travelodge☞ £45

Info- *Bridgwater location.*

Tel- *0870 191 1743*

Juntion 24
Bridgwater South

FUEL

Keyfuels SAVE ££ 0.6m ①
Open- *M-F 0700-2000, Sat/Sun 0700-1800*
Info- *HGV fuelling is available 24 hrs. HGV parking.*
Tel- *01278 663076*

BP SAVE ££ 0.8m ②
Open- *M-Sat 0600-2145, Sun 0700-2145*
Info- *WC*
Tel- *01278 427486*

FOOD

Compass Tavern £7.00 0.4m ③
Open- *M-Sat 1200-1500, 1800-2100, Sun 1200-2000*
Info- *Extensive hot & cold menu. Children welcome.*
Tel- *01278 662283*

Transport Cafe £3.50 0.6m ①
Open- *M-Th 0700-2030, Fr 0630-1700, Sat 0700-1100*
Tel- *01278 663052*

Boat & Anchor £7.00 1.0m ④
Open- *Daily 1200-1500, 1800-2100*
Info- *Extensive hot & cold menu at pub.*
Tel- *01278 662473*

ACCOMMODATION

Quantock View Gst Hs £40 0.4m ③
Info- *Private guest house. Price is B&B.*
Tel- *01278 663309*

Boat & Anchor £55 1.0m ④
Info- *En-suite rooms at the pub. Price is for B&B.*
Tel- *01278 662473*

ESSENTIALS

Car dealers
Info- *BMW and Skoda dealers en-route to the BP garage.*

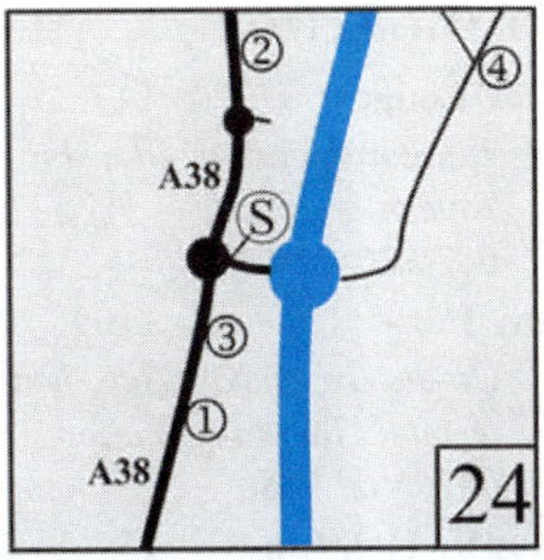

M5 Junction 25
Taunton

FUEL

Murco SAVE ££ 0.3m ①
Open- *Daily 24 hours*
Info- *WC, cash machine.*
Tel- *01823 332002*

Sainsbury SAVE ££ 0.5m ②
Open- *Daily 24 hours*
Info- *WC, cafe & cash machines at store.*
Tel- *01823 443163*

FOOD

Blackbrook Tavern £7.50 0.1m ③
Open- *M-Sat 1200-2200, Sun 1200-2130*
Info- *Extensive hot & cold menu. A 'Country Carvery' chain.*
Tel- *0870 990 6534*

Junction Restaurant £11 0.3m ④
Open- *M-F 0630-1100, 1230-1430, 1830-2300. Sat 0730-1100, 1830-2300, Sun 0730-1100, 1830-2130*
Info- *Holiday Inn restaurant.*
Tel- *0870 400 9080*

Harvester☞ £7.00 0.4m ⑤
Open- *M-Sat 1200-2200, Sun 1200-2100*
Tel- *01823 442221*

The Hankridge Arms £8.00 0.5m ⑥
Open- *Daily 1230-1400, 1800-2130*
Info- *Extensive hot & cold meals.*
Tel- *01823 444405*

McDonald's☞ £3.50 0.6m ⑦
Open- *Daily 0700-2300*
Dir'n- *Next to the cinema.*
Tel- *01823 443765*

ACCOMMODATION

Premier Lodge☞ £47 0.1m ③
Info- *Taunton location. Blackbrook Tavern attached.*
Tel- *0870 201 0203*

Holiday Inn☞ £109 0.3m ④
Info- *On-site restaurant, bar, health club, & pool. Taunton location.*
Tel- *0870 400 9080*

Express by Hol. Inn☞ £59 0.4m ⑤
Info- *Taunton location.*
Tel- *01823 624000*

Travelodge☞ £43 0.5m ⑧
Info- *Taunton location.*
Dir'n- *Turn right at the roundabout near to B&Q, then right again.*
Tel- *0870 191 1556*

ESSENTIALS

Taunton & Smrst Hospital 7m
Dir'n- *Follow signs to Taunton, and then towards Wellington on the A38. The hospital is on the left before leaving Taunton.*
Tel- *01823 333444*

Taunton Tourist Information Centre
Tel- *01823 336344*

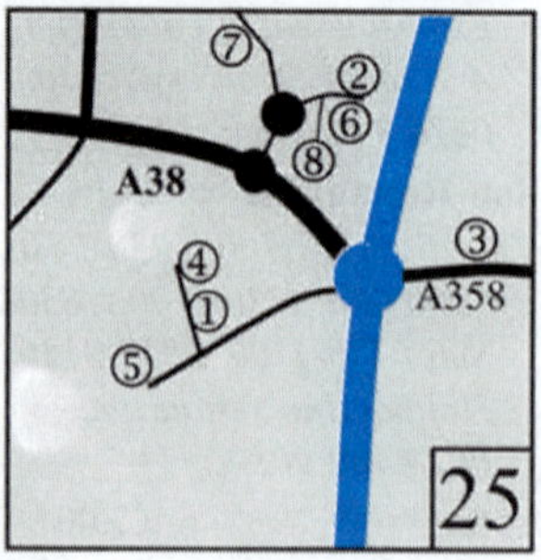

Taunton Deane Services

There is a footbridge between carriage-ways.

FUEL SHELL

HGV fuelling. Free parking for 2 hours then £6 per 24 hours. Lorry park.

FOOD ROADCHEF

onroute restaurant, Wimpy, Costa Coffee & Dr Beak's Kitchen. Cash machine (only Link cards).

ACCOMMODATION

Travel Inn☞ £45
Info- *Taunton Deane location.*
Tel- *0870 197 7250*

M5 Junction 26
Wellington

FUEL

Q8 **SAVE** £ 1.3m ①
Open- *M-Sat 0700-1900, Sun 0900-1600*
Info- *WC*
Tel- *01823 661469*

ESSENTIALS

Taunton & Smst Hospital 7m
Dir'n- *Take the A38 towards Taunton, where the hospital is on the right.*
Tel- *01823 333444*

Car Dealers
Nissan dealer as you head towards A38.

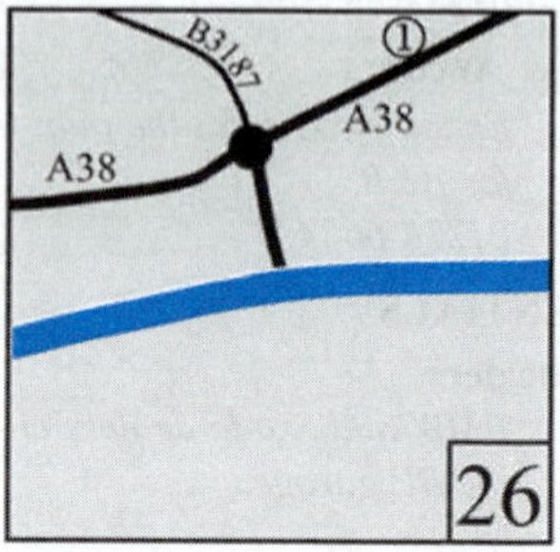

M5 Junction 27
Tiverton

FUEL

Shell SAVE £ 0.2m ①
Open- Daily 0600-2200
Info- WC, cash machine.
Tel- 01884 822010

FOOD

Burger King☞ £4.00 0.2m ①
Open- Daily 1000-2100
Tel- 01884 821205

Little Chef☞ £6.50 0.2m ①
Open- Daily 0900-2200
Tel- 01884 821205

Waterloo Cross Inn £8.00 0.5m ②
Open- Daily 1200-1400, 1800-2100
Info- Extensive hot & cold menu.
Tel- 01884 840328

The Globe Inn £7.50 1.0m ③
Open- M-Sat 1130-2300, Sun 1200-2230
Info- Extensive hot & cold menu.
Tel- 01884 821214

ACCOMMODATION

Travelodge☞ £43 0.2m ①
Info- Tiverton location.
Tel- 0870 191 1557

Waterloo Cross Hotel £55 0.5m ②
Info- Bar/restaurant on-site. 'Room at the Inn' group☞ .
Tel- 01884 840328

Parkway House £55 0.9m ④
Info- On-site restaurant & Bar. Independent country hotel.
Tel- 01884 820255

The Globe Inn £55 1.1m ③
Info- Price is for B&B.
Tel- 01884 821214

ESSENTIALS

Tiverton Tourist Information Centre
Tel- 01884 255827

Tiverton Parkway 0.9m ⑤
Info- About 1 train/hour to London. Journey time approx 2.5 hours.
Tel- 0845 748 4950

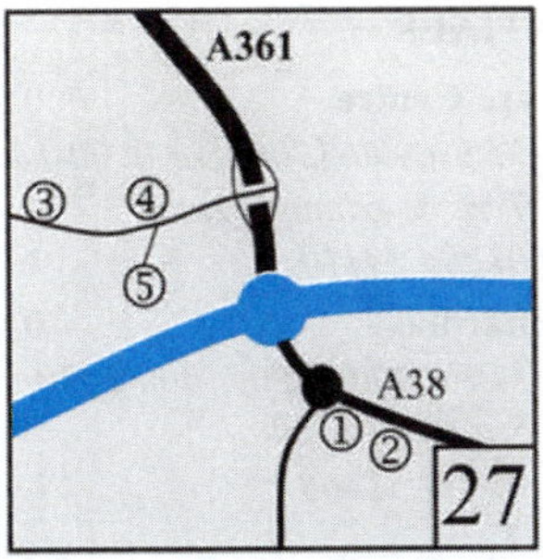

Cullompton Services

The services are located off the motorway, at ① & ③ at Junction 28.

FUEL BP
Info- WC, carwash, HGV fuelling, cash machine.

FOOD
Little Chef, McDonald's.
Open- Daily 0800-2100

M5 Junction 28
Cullompton

The small town of Cullompton is very close and has a number of pubs, though food options are limited.

FOOD

The Weary Traveller £7.00 0.2m ④
Open- M-F 1200-1400,1900-2100, Sat 1200-2100, Sun 1200-1500
Info- Varied hot & cold meals.
Tel- 01884 32317

The Manor Hotel £7.00 0.5m ②
Open- Daily 1200-1400, 1800-2100
Info- Restaurant & bar food.
Tel- 01884 32281

ACCOMMODATION

The Manor Hotel £60 0.5m ②
Info- On-site restaurant & bar. Independent hotel. AA/RAC 2 star.
Tel- 01884 32281

ESSENTIALS

NDT Tyre Centre 0.2m ⑤

Open- *M-F 0900-1700, Sat 0900-1300*
Info- *Tyre & exhaust centre.*
Tel- *01884 34110*

Moss Pharmacy 0.4m ⑥

Open- *M-F 0900-1300, 1400-1830, Sat 0900-1700*
Tel- *01884 32468*

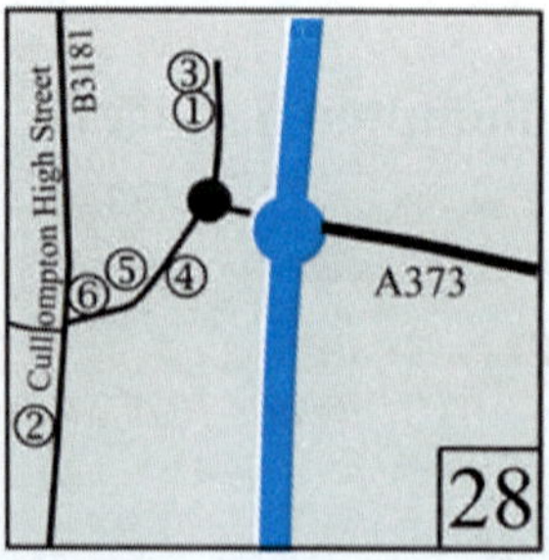

M5 Junction 29
Exeter North

FOOD

The Barnowl £7.00 0.4m ①

Open- *Daily 1200-2100*
Info- *Extensive hot & cold menu.*
Tel- *01392 449011*

The Black Horse Inn £7.50 0.7m ②

Open- *Daily 1200-1415, 1800-2115*
Info- *Extensive range of hot & cold food.*
Tel- *01392 366649*

ACCOMMODATION

Express by Hol. Inn £58 0.4m ①

Info- *Barnowl restaurant adjacent. Exeter location.*
Tel- *01392 261000*

ESSENTIALS

Royal D&E Hospital 2.5m

Dir'n- *Take the B3183 towards Exeter, and turn left on to Church Street where the hospital is signposted.*
Tel- *01392 411611*

Exeter Tourist Information Centre

Tel- *01392 265700*

Clyst Garage 0.7m ②

Open- *M-F 0830-1700, Sat 0900-1300*
Info- *Small car repairer.*
Tel- *01392 367235*

Car dealers 0.5m

Info- *Rover/MG dealer on the A3015 just beyond the Barn Owl.*

THINGS TO DO

Exeter 4m

Info- *Exeter has a cathedral and a wide range of shops and restaurants.*

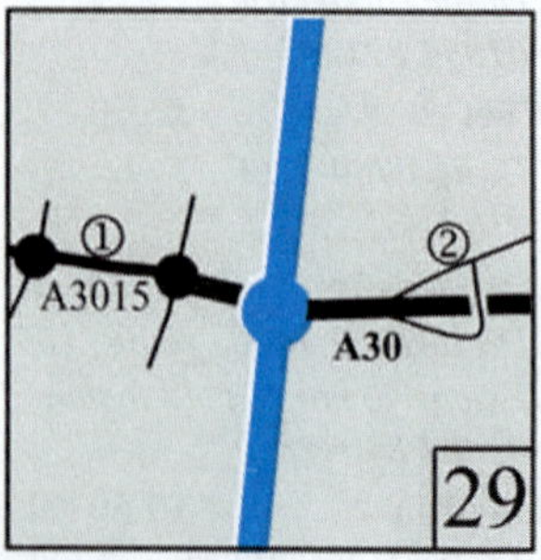

Exeter Services

The services are located off the motorway at Junction 30.

FUEL ESSO

HGV Fuelling & parking.

FOOD

Burger King, freshexpress, Harry Ramsden's

ACCOMMODATION

Travelodge £50

Info- *Exeter location.*
Tel- *0870 191 1727*

M5 Junction 30
Exeter East

FUEL

Tesco **SAVE** £ 1.2m ①

Open- *Daily 24 hours*
Info- *WC, cash machine, cafe at store.*
Tel- *0845 677 9263*

FOOD

The Blue Ball £7.00 1.2m ②

Open- *Daily 1200-1430, 1800-2130*
Info- *Extensive hot & cold menu.*
Tel- *01392 873401*

Tesco Cafe☞ £3.50 1.3m ①

Open- *M-F 0730-2000, Sat 0630-2000*
Sun 1000-1600
Tel- *0845 877 9263*

ESSENTIALS

Royal D&E Hospital 2.3m

Dir'n- *Follow the A379/Exeter road, and the hospital is well signposted.*
Tel- *01392 411611*

Exeter Tourist Information Centre

Tel- *01392 265700*

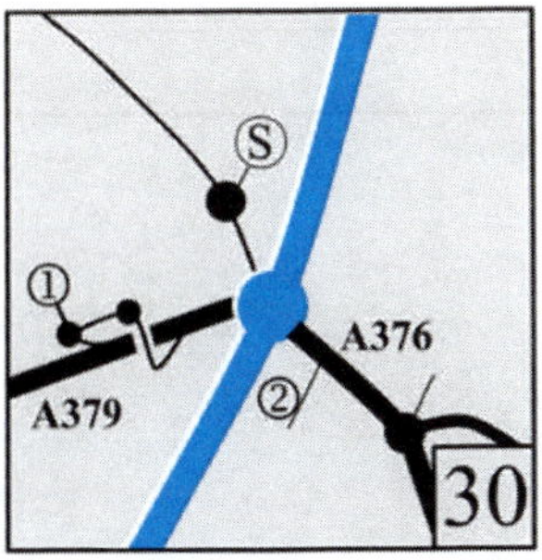

M5 Junction 31
Motorway ends

M6-Rugby to Carlisle

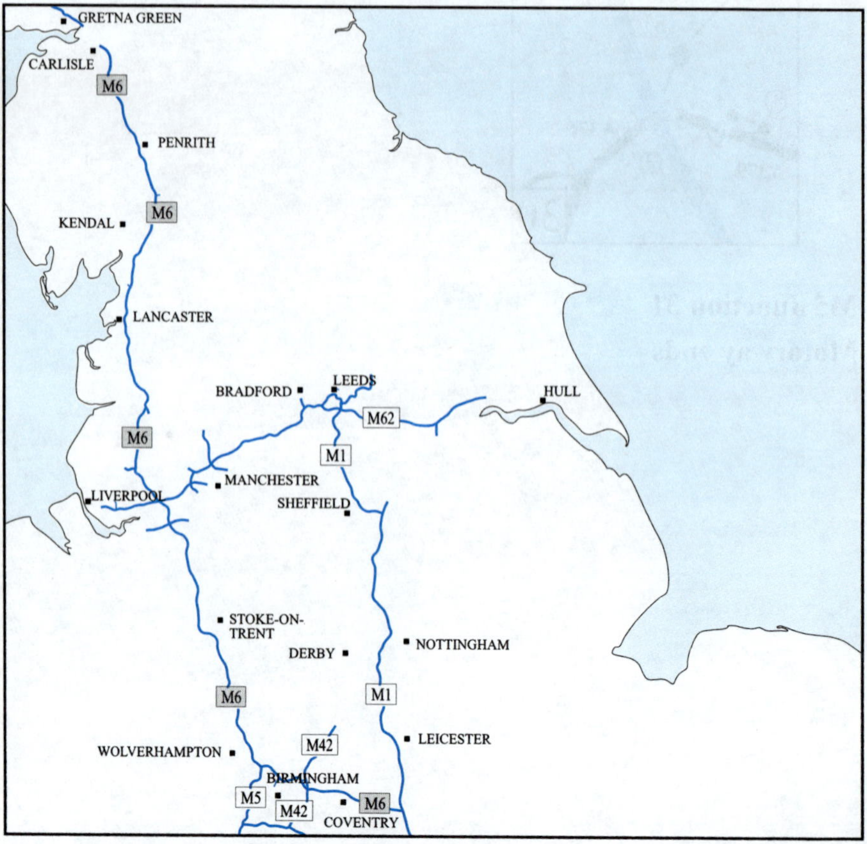

M6 Summary of Junctions

Radio stations & frequencies		Junction	Fuel	Food	Hotels	Essentials	Things to do
Heart Fm 100.7 BBC WM 94.8	Mercia 97.0 Rugby 107.1	0					
Heart Fm 100.7 BBC WM 94.8	Mercia 97.0 Rugby 107.1	1	✓	✓	✓	A&E TIC	
BBC WM 94.8 Mercia 97.0	KIX 96.2 Heart 100.7	2	24hr	✓	✓	Pharmacy A&E TIC	
BBC WM 94.8 Mercia 97.0	KIX 96.2 Heart 100.7	3	✓	✓	✓	A&E Svc	
BBC WM 94.8 Mercia 97.0	KIX 96.2 Heart 100.7	S	24hr	✓			
BBC WM 94.8 Galaxy 102.2	BRMB 96.4 Beacon 103.1	4					✓
BBC WM 94.8 Galaxy 102.2	BRMB 96.4 Beacon 103.1	4A					
BBC WM 94.8 Galaxy 102.2	BRMB 96.4 Beacon 103.1	5					
BBC WM 94.8 Mercia 97.0	KIX 96.2 BBC Leics 104.9	6				A&E TIC	
BBC WM 95.6 BRMB 96.4	Shrop 96.0 Beacon 97.2	7	24hr	✓	✓	Pharmacy	
BBC WM 95.6 BRMB 96.4	Shrop 96.0 Beacon 97.2	8					
BBC WM 95.6 BRMB 96.4	Shrop 96.0 Beacon 97.2	9	24hr	✓	✓	Pharmacy TIC	
BBC WM 95.6 BRMB 96.4	BBC Shrp 96.0 Beacon 97.0	10	✓	✓	✓	A&E Svc, TIC	
BBC WM 95.6 BRMB 96.4	BBC Shrp 96.0 Beacon 97.0	10A	24hr	✓	✓		
BBC WM 95.6 BRMB 96.4	SAGA 105.7 FLR 106.3	S	24hr	✓	✓		
Heart Fm 100.7 WOLF 107.7	SAGA 105.7 FLR 106.3	11	Diesel only				
Signal 1 96.9 Beacon 97.2	BBC WM 95.6 BBC Stke 94.6	12	✓	✓	✓	Svc	
Signal 1 96.9 B'Con 103.1	BBC WM 95.6 Stafford 103.6	13	✓	✓	✓	A&E TIC	✓
BBC Stke 104.1 B'Con 103.1	Cymru 104.3 Stafford 103.6	14	✓	✓	✓	A&E TIC	✓
BBC Stke 104.1 B'Con 103.1	Cymru 104.3 Stafford 103.6	S	24hr	✓	✓		

Top Stops are highlighted

Radio stations & frequencies		Junction	Fuel	Food	Hotels	Essentials	Things to do
BBC Stke 94.6 GMR 102.6	BBC Stke 94.6 GMR 102.6	15	✓	✓	✓	A&E, TIC	
BBC Stke 94.6 GMR 102.6	BBC Stke 94.6 GMR 102.6	S	24hr	✓			
BBC Stke 94.6 GMR 102.6	BBC Stke 94.6 GMR 102.6	16	✓	✓	✓	A&E, TIC	
BBC Stke 94.6 GMR 102.6	BBC Stke 94.6 GMR 102.6	S	24hr	✓			
BBC Stke 94.6 BBC Shrp 96.0	MFM 193.4 Signal 1 96.4	17	24hr	✓	✓	A&E	✓
BBC Stke 94.6 Shrp 96.0	MFM 193.4 Signal 1 96.4	18	✓	✓			
BBC Stke 94.6	Key 103 103.0	S	24hr	✓	✓		
BBC Stke 94.6	Key 103 103.0	19	24hr	✓	✓	TIC	
Lanc 103.9 WIRE 107.2	Tower 107.4 Century 105.4	20 S	24hr	✓	✓	A&E, TIC	
Lanc 103.9 WIRE 107.2	Tower 107.4 Century 105.4	21		✓	✓	A&E, TIC	
WIRE 107.2 Mrsy 95.8	GMR 95.1 Rock FM 97.4	21A				A&E, TIC	
WIRE 107.2 Mrsy 95.8	GMR 95.1 Rock FM 97.4	22		✓	✓		
Lanc 103.9 Silk FM 106.9	WIRE 107.2 Galaxy 102.0	23	24hr	✓	✓		✓
Lanc 103.9 Silk FM 106.9	WIRE 107.2 Galaxy 102.0	24					
KEY 103.0 Lanc 103.9	Tower 107.4 Imagine 104.9	25					
GMR 95.1 WISH 102.4	Tower 107.4 Imagine 104.9	26		✓	✓	A&E, Pharmacy	
Lanc 103.9 Century 105.4	Rock FM 97.4 WISH 102.4	27	24hr	✓	✓	A&E	
BBC Lanc 103.9 Century 105.4	Rock FM 97.4 WISH FM	S	24hr	✓	✓		
The Bay 96.9 ROCK 97.4	Lanc 103.9 Dune 107.9	28	24hr	✓	✓	A&E	✓
The Bay 96.9 ROCK 97.4	Lanc 103.9 Dune 107.9	29	✓	✓	✓	Pharmacy	✓
Century 105.4 ROCK 97.4	Lanc 103.9	30					

Radio stations & frequencies		Junction	Fuel	Food	Hotels	Essentials	Things to do
Lanc 104.5 Century 105.4	Cmbr 96.1 WAVE 96.5	31	24hr	✓	✓		TIC
Lanc 104.5 Century 105.4	Cmbr 96.1 WAVE 96.5	31A			✓	A&E	
Lanc 104.5 Century 105.4	Lanc 104.5 WAVE 96.5	32				A&E	TIC
Lanc 104.5		S	24hr	✓	✓		
Lanc 104.5		33		✓		A&E Svc	
Lanc 104.5		34	24hr	✓	✓	A&E, Svc	
Lanc 104.5 Bay 96.9	Cmbr 96.1	35	24hr	✓	✓		
Cmbr 96.1 Bay 96.9	Lanc 104.5	S	24hr	✓			
Cmbr 96.1 Bay 96.9	Lanc 104.5	36	24hr	✓	✓	A&E, TIC Svc	
Cmbr 96.1 Bay 96.9		S	24hr	✓	✓	TIC	✓
Cmbr 96.1		37				A&E, TIC	✓
Cmbr 96.1	BBC Scot 93.5	38	24hr	✓	✓	Svc	
Cmbr 96.1	BBC Scot 93.5	S	24hr	✓	✓		
BBC Scot 93.5		39		✓	✓		
BBC Scot 94.7 BBC Cmbr 95.6		40	24hr	✓	✓	TIC Svc	✓
BBC Scot 94.7 BBC Cmbr 95.6	CFM 96.4 West Snd 97.0	41	✓	✓			
BBC Scot 94.7 BBC Cmbr 95.6	CFM 96.4 West Snd 97.0	S	24hr	✓	✓	TIC Svc	
BBC Scot 94.7 BBC Cmbr 95.6	CFM 96.4	42	24hr	✓	✓	A&E, TIC Svc	
BBC Scot 94.7 BBC Cmbr 95.6	CFM 96.4	43	24hr	✓	✓	A&E, TIC	✓
BBC Scot 94.7 BBC Cmbr 95.6	CFM 96.4	44	24hr	✓	✓	A&E, TIC	

M6 Junction Details

M6 Junction 0
M6/M1/A14 interchange

This is a restricted interchange. Traffic is not allowed from the M6 to the M1 north, or the M1 south to the M6.

M6 Junction 1
Rugby

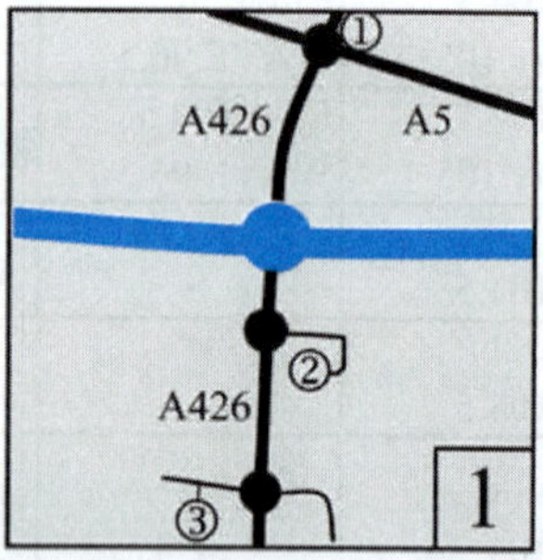

FUEL

Texaco SAVE ££ 1.3m ①
Open- *M-F 0830-2200, Sat-Sun 0700-2200*
Info- *WC, jetwash, postbox, cash machine.*
Tel- *01788 861500*

FOOD

Brewsters☞ £6.50 0.3m ②
Open- *M-Sat 1130-2200, Sun 1200-2200*
Tel- *01788 565930*

Harvester☞ £7.00 1.5m ③
Open- *M-Sat 1200-2200, Sun 1200-2100*
Tel- *01788 569466*

ACCOMMODATION

Travel Inn☞ £43 0.3m ②
Info- *Breakfast available at extra charge. Brewsters restaurant attached. Rugby location.*
Tel- *0870 238 3344*

Express by Hol. Inn☞ £57 1.5m ③
Info- *Free continental breakfast. Harvester restaurant adjacent. Rugby location.*
Tel- *01788 550333*

ESSENTIALS

Hospital of St Cross 3.7m
Dir'n- *From M6 head towards Rugby, and the hospital is signposted.*
Tel- *01788 572831*

Rugby Tourist Information Centre
Tel- *01788 534970*

M6 Junction 2
M6/M69 interchange

FUEL

Asda☞ SAVE £££ 1.3m ①
Open- *M-Sat 0600-2230 Sun 0800-1700*
Info- *Carwash. WC, coffee shop at store.*
Tel- *024 7661 7241*

Texaco☞ SAVE ££ 1.3m ②
Open- *Daily 24 hours*
Info- *WC, cash machine.*
Dir'n- *Turn right at McDonald's then left.*
Tel- *024 7684 1990*

FOOD

Big W Cafe☞ £4.00 0.9m ③
Open- *M-Sat 0900-1700, Sun 1030-1530*
Info- *Cafe in Woolworths store. Sandwiches & snacks.*

Burger King☞ £4.00 1.0m ③
Open- *Daily 1000-2200*
Tel- *024 766 03661*

Pizza Hut☞ £6.00 1.0m ③
Open- *M-Th 1200-2300, F-Sat 1200-2330, Sun 1200-2200*
Tel- *024 7660 3040*

Asda Coffee Shop☞ £2.00 1.3m ①
Open- *M-Sat 0730-2100, Sun 1000-1500*
Info- *Sandwiches, cakes & drinks.*
Tel- *024 7662 5800*

Frankie & Benny's ☞ £8.50 1.1m ③
Open- *M-Sat 1200-2300, Sun 1200-2230*
Tel- *024 7660 4900*

Traders Restaurant £10 1.1m ④
Open- *M-Fr 0630-1000, Sat-Sun 0730-1030, M-Sat 1830-2200, Sun 1900-2130*
Info- *Pleasant dining at the Holiday Inn.*
Tel- *0870 400 9021*

Mount Pleasant Inn £7.00 1.3m ⑤
Open- *Su-Th 1200-2100, Fr/Sa 1200-2200*
Info- *Varied menu. A 'New English Inn'.*
Tel- *024 7661 2406*

McDonald's ☞ £3.50 1.3m ⑥
Open- *Sun-Th 0700-2300, F/Sa 0700-2400*
Tel- *024 7661 2492*

ACCOMMODATION

Hilton Hotel ☞ £118 0.5m ⑦
Info- *On-site bar, restaurant, health club & pool. Coventry location.*
Tel- *024 7660 3000*

Holiday Inn ☞ £100 1.1m ④
Info- *On-site bar, restaurant & health club. Coventry location.*
Tel- *0870 400 9021*

Campanile ☞ £42 1.5m ⑧
Info- *On-site bar & restaurant. Coventry location.*
Tel- *024 7662 2311*

ESSENTIALS

Coventry & Warks Hospital 7m
Dir'n- *Follow the A4600 to Coventry, and turn north on the A4053, where the hospital is signposted.*
Tel- *024 7622 4055*

Asda Pharmacy ①
Open- *M-F 0800-2200, Sat 0800-2000, Sun 1000-1600*
Tel- *024 7662 5817*

Coventry Tourist Information Centre
Tel- *024 762 27264*

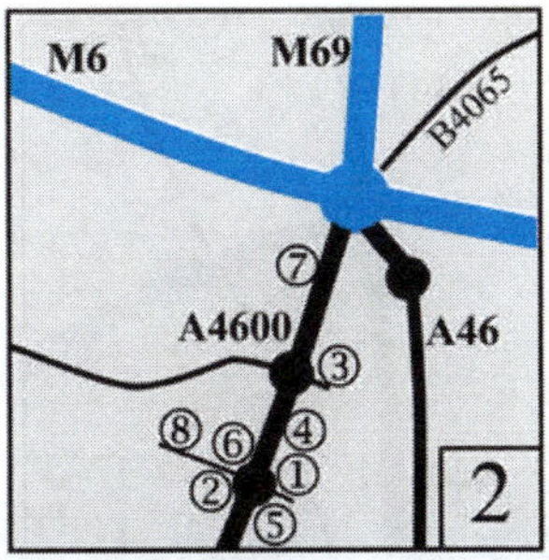

M6 Junction 3
Coventry North

FUEL

Texaco SAVE £ 1.0m ①
Open- *M-F 0645-2230, Sat 0645-2230, Sun 0745-2230*
Info- *WC*
Tel- *024 7649 4300*

FOOD

Novotel Brasserie £7.50 0.2m ②
Open- *M-F 0600-2330, Sat/Sun 0700-2230*
Info- *Extensive menu and dining all day.*
Tel- *024 7636 5000*

Morgan's Eatery £2.00 0.9m ③
Open- *M-F 0830-1400*
Info- *Cold & fried sandwiches.*
Tel- *024 7636 6933*

ACCOMMODATION

Novotel ☞ £70 0.2m ②
Info- *On-site bar & brasserie. Outdoor pool. Coventry location.*
Tel- *024 7636 5000*

ESSENTIALS

Coventry & Warks Hospital 7m
Dir'n- *Follow the A444 to Coventry, and turn right onto the B4113, where the hospital is signposted on the left.*
Tel- *02476 224055*

BDK Motor Services ④
Info- *Repairs & 24 hour recovery.*
Tel- *024 7668 7646*

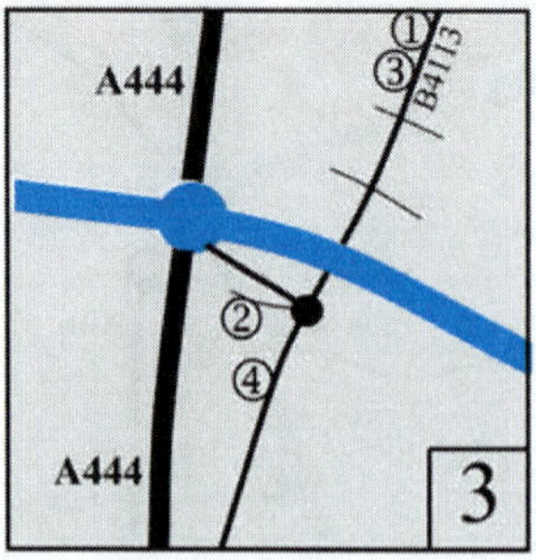

Corley Services

There is a footbridge between carriage-ways at this services.

FUEL SHELL

HGV fuelling. Free parking for 2 hours then £6 per 24 hours. Lorry park.

FOOD WELCOME BREAK

Coffee Primo, 'bakery', Coffee Express, Burger King & KFC.

Info- Cash machine (Link, Plus, Visa, Amex & Diners Club only).

M6 Junction 4
NEC

There are no services within a mile of this junction.

THINGS TO DO

NEC 1.5m
Info- The National Exhibition Centre.
Dir'n- This is well signposted.

M6 Junction 4A
M6/M42 interchange

There is no access to any local services at this junction.

M6 Junction 5
Restricted

This junction only allows exit from the west, and entrance eastbound.

M6 Junction 6
Spaghetti Junction

The complexity of this junction makes access to the limited local services impractical.

ESSENTIALS

Birmingham Heartlands Hosp. 5m
Dir'n- Take the A38(M) towards Birmingham, then the A4540 to the B4128. The hospital in on the right on the A4158.
Tel- 0121 424 2000

Birmingham Tourist Information Centre
Tel- 0121 693 6300

M6 Junction 7
Great Barr

FUEL

Total SAVE ££ 0.5m ①
Open- Daily 24 hours
Info- WC, carwash.
Tel- 0121 358 8800

Shell SAVE ££ 0.6m ②
Open- Daily 0700-2300
Info- WC
Tel- 0121 358 4622

FOOD

Harvester☞ £7.00 0.4m ③
Open- Daily 1200-2200
Tel- 0121 357 2567

The Basmati Restrnt. £9.50 0.4m ③
Open- M-Sa 1200-1430, 1800-2400, Sun 1200-1430, 1800-2330
Info- Indian restaurant & takeaway.
Tel- 0121 358 8898

Scotts Arms Balti £7.50 0.7m ④
Open- Su-Th 1700-2400, F/Sat 1700-0030
Info- Indian takeaway.
Tel- 0121 358 3792

New Sandwell £7.50 0.7m ④
Open- M/W/Th/Fr Sa 1700-2400, Tu 1700-2100, Sun 1800-2400
Info- Takeaway Indian meals.
Tel- 0121 358 3792

Scott Arms £3.50 0.8m ⑤

Open- *M-Sat 1200-1400*
Info- *Pub lunches.*
Tel- *0121 357 8780*

ACCOMMODATION

Holiday Inn☞ £130 0.4m ⑥

Info- *On-site restaurant, bar, health club & pool. Birmingham J7 location.*
Tel- *0870 400 9009*

Express by Hol. Inn☞ £55 0.4m ③

Info- *Harvester nearby. Birmingham North location.*
Tel- *0121 358 4044*

ESSENTIALS

Lloyds Pharmacy 0.7m ④

Open- *M-F 0900-1800*
Tel- *0121 357 1384*

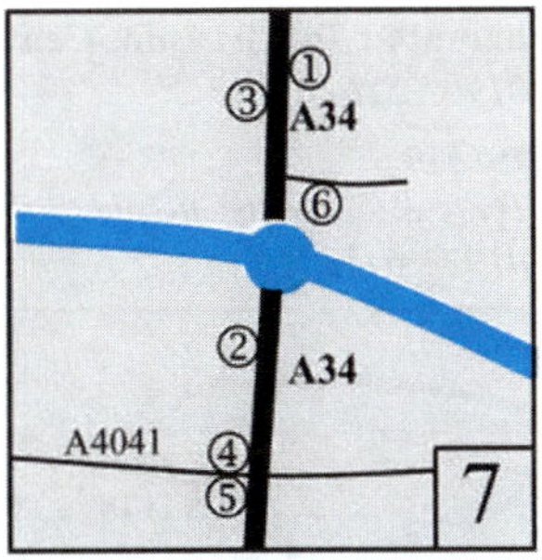

M6 Junction 8
M6/M5 interchange

There is no access to any local services at this junction.

M6 Junction 9
Walsall South

FUEL

Morrisons SAVE £££ 0.4m ①

Open- *M-F 0600-2230, Sa/Sun 0700-2200*
Info- *Carwash. WC, cash machines at store.*
Tel- *01922 638571*

Safeway SAVE ££ 1.0m ②

Open- *Daily 24 hours*
Info- *WC, carwash. No store attached.*
Tel- *0121 505 2205*

FOOD

Morrisons Cafe £3.50 0.4m ①

Open- *M-W 0830-1800, Th/F 0800-1800, Sat 0800-1800, Sun 0930-1530*
Info- *Fried meals in supermarket cafe.*
Tel- *01922 616177*

The Imperial £12 0.4m ③

Open- *M-Sa 1200-1430, 1700-2330, Sun 1200-2300*
Info- *Cantonese & Thai restaurant.*
Tel- *0121 502 2218*

Burger King☞ £4.00 0.5m ④

Open- *M-Sat 0900-2100, Sun 0900-1900*
Dir'n- *Follow signs to superstores.*
Tel- *0121 556 2100*

Pizza Hut☞ £6.00 0.5m ④

Open- *Sun-Th 1100-2300, F-Sat 1100-2400*
Dir'n- *Follow signs to superstores.*
Tel- *0121 556 6533*

KFC☞ £4.00 0.5m ④

Open- *Sun-Th 1100-2300, F/Sa 1100-2400*
Dir'n- *Follow signs to superstores.*
Tel- *0121 556 6634*

McDonald's☞ £3.50 0.7m ④

Open- *Su-Th 0730-2200, F/Sat 0730-2330*
Tel- *01922 635747*

ACCOMMODATION

Bescot Hotel £54 0.1m ⑤

Info- *Small private hotel with restaurant & bar. Price is B&B.*
Tel- *01922 622447*

Abberley Hotel £60 0.4m ⑥

Info- *Small private hotel. Price is B&B.*
Tel- *01922 627413*

ESSENTIALS

Moss Pharmacy £3.50 0.4m ①

Open- *M-Sat 0900-2000, Sun 1000-1600*
Info- *At Morrisons supermarket.*
Tel- *01922 611008*

Walsall Tourist Information Centre

Tel- *01922 625540*

Halfords £7.00 0.7m ⑦

Open- *M-F 0900-2000, Sat 0900-1800, Sun 1000-1700*
Tel- *01922 646046*

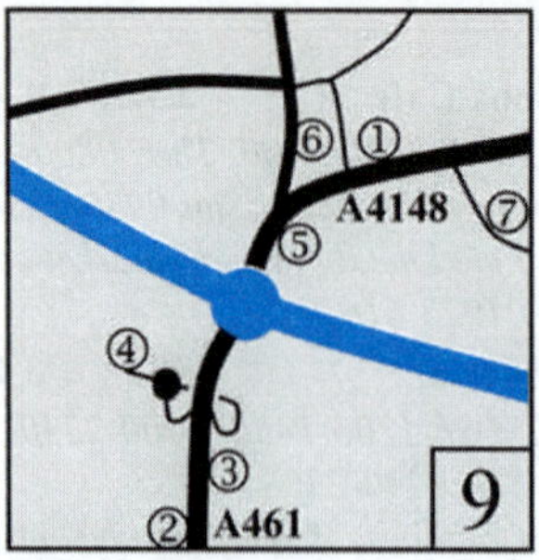

M6 Junction 10
Walsall West

FUEL

Esso SAVE £££ 0.8m ①
Open- *M-F 0600-2300, Sat/Sun 0630-2200*
Info- *WC*
Tel- *01922 634532*

FOOD

Transport Cafe £3.00 0.2m ②
Open- *M-F 0730-1500, Sat 0730-1030*
Info- *Fried meals.*
Tel- *01922 722593*

The Parkbrook £3.00 0.4m ③
Open- *M-Sat 1200-1400, 1800-2000*
Info- *Pub food.*
Tel- *01922 622970*

Choices Restaurant £12 0.4m ④
Open- *M-Sat 0700-0930, 1900-2200, M-F 1200-1400, Sun 0730-1000, 1200-1400, 1900-2130*
Info- *Dining at the Quality Inn Rest.*
Tel- *01922 724444*

Cinnamon Court £7.00 0.6m ⑤
Open- *Daily 1800-2330*
Info- *Extensive Indian menu.*
Tel- *0121 568 6664*

Brewsters☞ £6.50 0.7m ⑥
Open- *M-Sat 1130-2200, Sat 1200-2200, Suns 1200-2130*
Info- *Travel Inn adjacent.*
Tel- *01922 724485*

Railway Tavern £6.00 0.8m ⑦
Open- *M-Sat 1200-1400, 1830-2100, Sun 1200-1500*
Info- *Varied hot & cold menu.*
Tel- *0121 526 2604*

ACCOMMODATION

Quality Inn☞ £115 0.4m ④
Info- *On-site bar, restaurant, health club & pool. Walsall location.*
Tel- *01922 724444*

Travel Inn☞ £45 0.7m ⑥
Info- *Brewsters restaurant adjacent. Walsall location.*
Tel- *08701 977258*

ESSENTIALS

Manor Hospital 1m
Dir'n- *Signposted en-route to Walsall.*
Tel- *01922 721172*

Wolverhampton Tourist Info. Centre
Tel- *01902 556110*

HiQ Tyres etc 1.0m ⑧
Info- *Tyres & exhausts. Return difficult.*
Tel- *01922 645374*

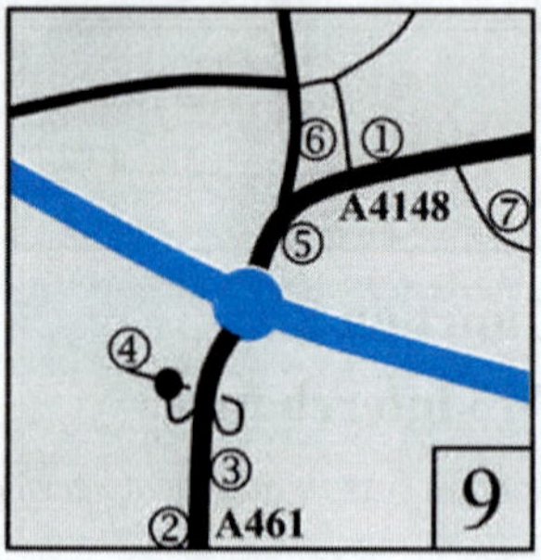

M6 Junction 10A
M6/M54 interchange

This is a restricted junction, and only allows access from the M6 northbound to the M54, and to the M6 southbound. There is no access to any local services at this junction.

Hilton Park Services

There are a footbridge and a roadbridge at this services.

FUEL BP

HGV fuelling & parking. Free parking for 2 hours then £6 per day.

FOOD MOTO

Burger King, freshexpress, Harry Ramsden's

Info- Cash machines.

ACCOMMODATION

Travelodge☞ £53

Info- B'ham North (Hilton Pk) location.

Tel- 08701 911566

M6 Junction 11 Cannock South

There are major roadworks at this junction in 2004, so expect congestion around here.

FUEL

UK Fuel SAVE £ 0.5m ①

Open- Sun 2200-Fr 2200 open for 24 hours per day, Sat 0700-1200

Info- HGV fuelling centre. LNG & shop.

Tel- 01922 412995

FOOD

The Elms Pub £7.00 0.8m ②

Open- M-Sat 1200-1400, 1800-2100, Sun 1200-1700

Info- Varied hot & cold meals.

Tel- 01922 412063

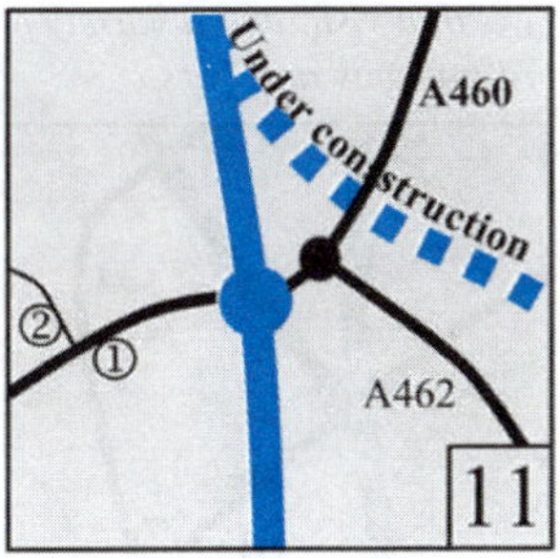

M6 Junction 12 Cannock

FUEL

Texaco SAVE £ 0.8m ①

Open- M-Sat 0800-2300, Sun 0800-2300

Info- WC, jetwash.

Tel- 01902 791172

FOOD

Hollies Transport Cafe £3.00 1m ②

Open- Daily 24 hours

Info- Good value meals. HGV parking..

Tel- 01543 503435

The Spread Eagle £8.00 1m ③

Open- M-Sat 1130-2200, Sun 1200-2200

Info- Extensive menu at a 'Table Tavern'.

Tel- 01902 790212

ACCOMMODATION

Bed & Breakfast £50 0.3m ④

Info- Price includes breakfast. Camping & caravan site attached.

Tel- 01543 500770

Oak Farm Hotel £53 1.1m ⑤

Info- Independent hotel & restaurant. Restaurant open 1830-2100.

Tel- 01543 462045

ESSENTIALS

Galley Recovery 0.3m

Info- 24 hour vehicle recovery.

Tel- 01902 790589

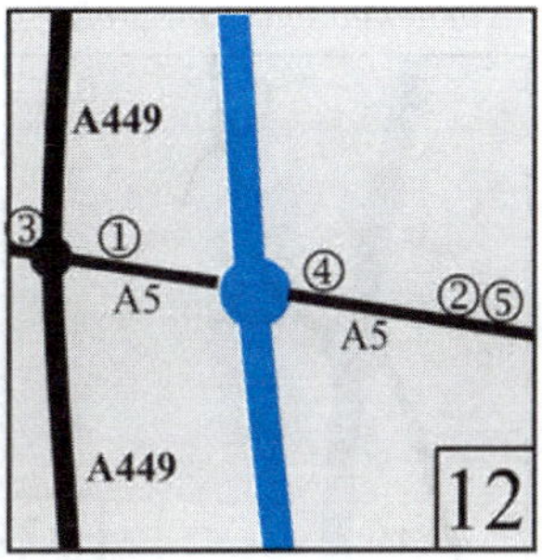

M6 Junction 13
Stafford South

FUEL

Total **SAVE** ££ 0.7m ①
Open- *M-F 0600-2300, Sat/Sun 0800-2200*
Info- *WC*
Tel- *01785 782900*

FOOD

Tom Cobleigh☞ £6.50 0.1m ②
Open- *M-Sat 1200-2200, Sun 1200-2130*
Info- *Children's 'Play Barn'.*
Tel- *01785 245867*

ACCOMMODATION

Express by Hol. Inn☞ £62 0.1m ②
Info- *Stafford South location.*
Tel- *01785 212244*

ESSENTIALS

Staffordshire General Hospital 5m
Info- *Take the A449 towards Stafford, then the A518 east in Stafford, from where the hospital is signposted.*
Tel- *01785 257731*
Stafford Tourist Information Centre
Tel- *01785 619619*

THINGS TO DO

Stafford 2.5m
Info- *Stafford has an old centre that is worth a visit, and a variety of restaurants and bars. The one way system can make parking difficult.*

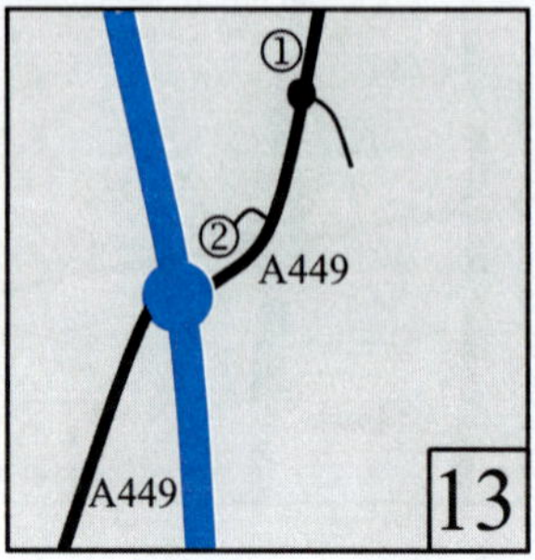

M6 Junction 14
Stafford North

FUEL

Total **SAVE** £££ 1m ①
Open- *M-Sat 0700-2300, Sun 0800-2200*
Info- *No other facilities*
Tel- *01785 240010*

FOOD

Tillington Hall Htl rest. £13 0.2m ②
Open- *Daily 1200-1400, 1900-2130*
Info- *Refined dining in the hotel.*
Tel- *01785 253531*

McDonald's☞ £3.50 1m ③
Open- *Daily 0700-2300*
Tel- *01785 254482*

ACCOMMODATION

Tillington Hall Hotel £80 0.6m ②
Info- *On-site bar, restaurant, health club & pool. A Best Western Hotel☞*
Tel- *01785 253531*

ESSENTIALS

Staffordshire General Hospital 5m
Info- *Drive towards central Stafford, then the A518/Uttoxeter Road, where the hospital is signposted.*
Tel- *01785 257731*
Stafford Tourist Information Centre
Tel- *01785 619619*
Ford Dealer ③

THINGS TO DO

Stafford 2.3m
Info- *Stafford has an old centre that is worth a visit, and a variety of restaurants and bars.*

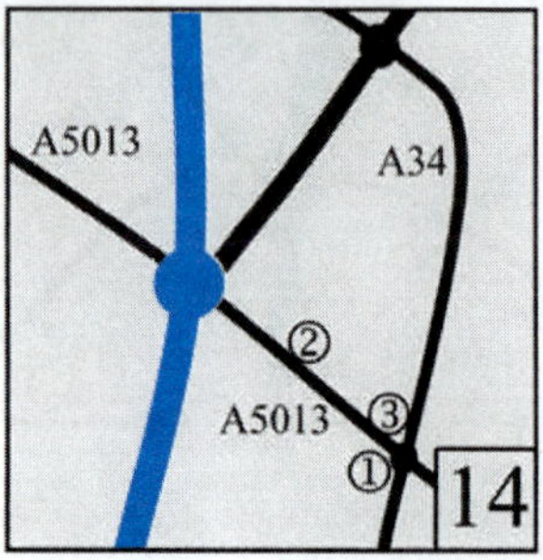

Stafford Services

There is no footbridge or roadbridge at this services.

FUEL ESSO/BP

HGV fuelling & parking. Free parking for 2 hours then £6 per day.

FOOD MOTO/ROADCHEF

Wimpy, Costa Coffee, Dr Beak's Chicken, onroute. (southbound)
Burger King, Little Chef (northbound)
Info- *Cash machines.*

ACCOMMODATION

Travel Inn☞ £45
Info- *Stafford (southbound) location.*
Tel- *08701 977239*

Travelodge☞ £50
Info- *Stafford (northbound) location.*
Tel- *08701 911605*

M6 Junction 15
Stoke South

FUEL

BP SAVE ££ 0.5m ①
Open- *Daily 0700-2100*
Info- *WC*
Tel- *01782 713308*

Esso SAVE £££ 1m ②
Open- *M-F 0600-2300, Sat/Sun 0700-2200*
Info- *WC*
Tel- *01782 613189*

FOOD

Traders restaurant £10 0.3m ③
Open- *M-F 0630-1000, 1230-1400, 1830-2200, Sat/Sun 0730-1100, Sun 1830-2100*
Info- *Refined dining at the Holiday Inn.*
Tel- *0870 400 9077*

Westbury Tavern £4 0.8m ④
Open- *Daily 1200-1430, 1730-2000*
Info- *Bar meals at local pub.*
Tel- *01782 638766*

Arts restaurant £10 1m ②
Open- *M-F 0730-0930, Sa/Sun 0800-1000, M-Sat 1900-2130, Sun 1900-2030*
Info- *Refined dining at the Jarvis Hotel.*
Tel- *01782 613093*

ACCOMMODATION

Holiday Inn☞ £95 0.3m ③
Info- *Bar/rest, health club, pool. Stoke location.*
Tel- *0870 400 9077*

Jarvis Hotel☞ £95 1m ②
Info- *Bar & restaurant.*
Tel- *01782 613093*

ESSENTIALS

North Staffordshire Hospital 3m
Dir'n- *Take the A500 towards Stoke, then the A52 towards Newcastle Under Lyme. The hospital is signposted off the A52, about 1 mile from the centre of Stoke.*
Tel- *01782 715444*

Stoke Tourist Information Centre
Tel- *01782 236000*

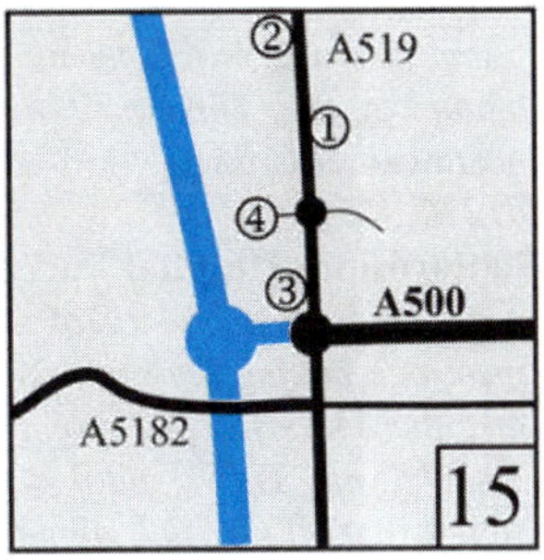

Keele Services

This services has a footbridge.

FUEL SHELL

LPG (southbound) HGV fuelling & parking. Free parking for 2 hours then £6 per day.

FOOD WELCOME BREAK

foodconnection, Burger King, The Granary, KFC.
Info- *Cash machine.*

M6 Junction 16
Stoke North

FUEL

Total SAVE ££ 0.2m ①
Open- *M-F 0630-2230, Sat 0700-2300, Sun 0800-2200*
Info- *WC*
Tel- *01270 872952*

FOOD

Little Chef☞ £6.50 0.2m ①
Open- *Daily 0700-2200*
Tel- *01270 883115*

Burger King☞ £4.00 0.2m ①
Open- *Daily 1100-2100*
Tel- *01270 883115*

ACCOMMODATION

Travelodge☞ £50 0.2m ①
Info- *Crewe location.*
Tel- *08701 911571*

ESSENTIALS

Leighton Hospital 7.5m
Dir'n- *Signposted westwards from motorway exit. The hospital is northwest of Crewe.*
Tel- *01270 255141*

North Staffordshire Hospital 7.5m
Dir'n- *Take the A500 towards Stoke, then then on reaching the centre of Stoke take the A52 towards Newcastle Under Lyme. The hospital is signposted off the A52, about 1 mile from the centre of Stoke.*
Tel- *01782 715444*

Crewe/Nantwich Tourist Info. Centre
Tel- *01270 610983*

Newcastle U LymeTourist Info. Centre
Tel- *01782 297313*

Stoke Tourist Information Centre
Tel- *01782 236000*

Sandbach Services

There is a footbridge at this services.

FUEL ESSO
HGV fuelling & parking. Free parking for 2 hours then £6 per day.

FOOD ROADCHEF
onroute, Costa Coffee, Wimpy
Info- *Cash machine.*

M6 Junction 17
Sandbach

FUEL

Texaco SAVE £ 0.2m ①
Open- *Daily 24 hours*
Info- *Carwash, jetwash, cash machine.*
Tel- *01270 758980*

FOOD

Cafe Symphony £10 0.9m ②
Open- *M-F 1200-1400, 1730-2200, Sat 1730-2200, Sun 1200-2100*
Info- *Restaurant & wine bar.*
Tel- *01270 763664*

Casa Vecchia £7.00 1m ③
Open- *M-Th 1200-1400, 1800-2230, F/Sa 1200-1400, 1800-2300, Sun 1630 - 2230*
Info- *Independent Italian restaurant.*
Tel- *01270 761077*

Old Hall Restaurant £12 0.9m ③
Open- *Tu-Sun 1200-1430, 1830-2130*
Info- *Refined dining at the hotel rest.*
Dir'n- *Follow signs to Sandbach crosses.*
Tel- *01270 761221*

China Kitchen £5.50 1m ③

Open- *Daily 1700-2400, Th-Sa 1200-1400*
Info- *Chinese takeaway.*
Dir'n- *Near the crosses in Sandbach.*
Tel- *01270 762777*

ACCOMMODATION

Saxon Cross Hotel £60 0.4m ④

Info- *On-site bar, restaurant. Independent hotel.*
Tel- *01270 763281*

Old Hall Hotel £70 0.9m ③

Info- *On-site bar, restaurant. The hotel is in a lovely timber-framed building.*
Dir'n- *Follow signs to Sandbach crosses.*
Tel- *01270 761221*

ESSENTIALS

Leighton Hospital 9m

Dir'n- *Take the A534 towards Crewe, and then right on the A532 west. Next take the B5076, where the hospital is on the left.*
Tel- *01270 255141*

THINGS TO DO

Sandbach

Info- *This has two ancient stone crosses in the centre, & is worth a quick visit. There is a range of pubs and small restaurants, mostly at the cheaper end.*

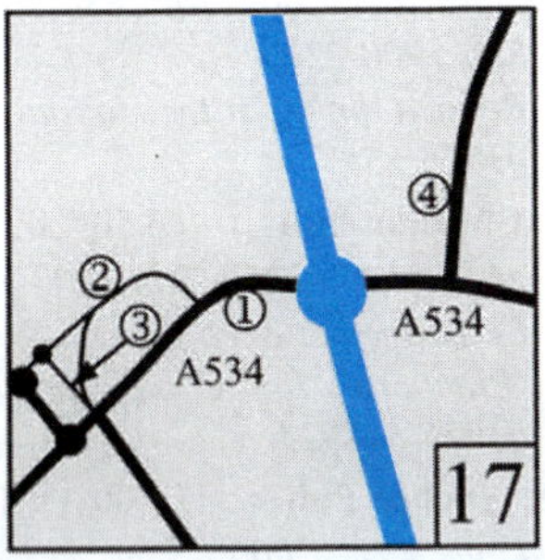

M6 Junction 18 Holmes Chapel

FUEL

Texaco SAVE £ 0.6m ①

Open- *M-F 0600-2200, Sat/Sun 0700-2100*
Info- *WC, carwash, jetwash, cash machine, postbox.*
Tel- *01477 536910*

FOOD

Fox & Hounds £7.00 0.6m ②

Open- *Daily 1200-1430, Tu-Sat 1800-2100, Sun 1800-2000*
Info- *Extensive hot & cold menu.*
Tel- *01606 832303*

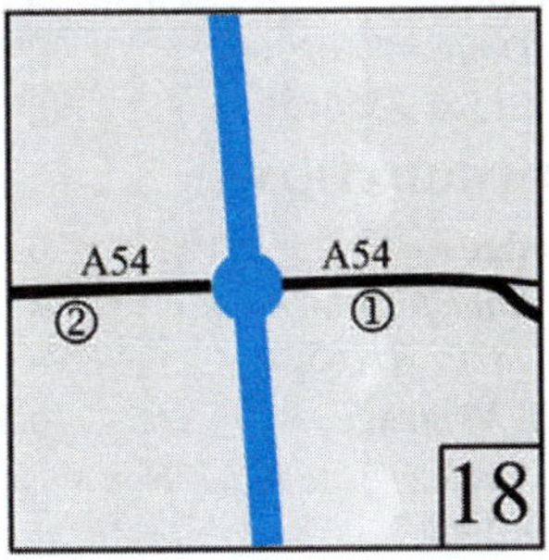

Knutsford Services

There are a footbridge and a roadbridge at this services.

FUEL BP

LPG, HGV fuelling & parking. Free parking for 2 hours then £6 per day.

FOOD MOTO

Burger King, Little Chef, freshexpress, Upper Crust, Harry Ramsden's

Info- *Cash machine.*

ACCOMMODATION

Travelodge☞ £50

Info- *Knutsford M6 location.*
Tel- *08701 911653*

M6 Junction 19 Knutsford

FUEL

Shell SAVE £££ 0.1m ①

Open- *Daily 24 hours*
Info- *WC, cash machine (Link, Plus, Diners Club, Amex).*
Tel- *01565 621735*

BP **SAVE** £ 0.2m ②
Open- *Daily 0600-2200*
Info- *Carwash.*
Tel- *01565 755127*

FOOD

The Windmill Pub £6.50 0.1m ③
Open- *Daily 1200-2100*
Info- *Varied menu in local pub.*

Little Chef☞ £6.50 0.2m ②
Open- *Daily 0700-2300*
Tel- *01565 755049*

ACCOMMODATION

Travelodge☞ £50 0.2m ②
Info- *Knutsford location.*
Tel- *08701 911652*

The Old Vicarage £65 0.3m ④
Info- *Small private hotel. Non smoking. AA 4◆*
Tel- *01922 652221*

ESSENTIALS

Knutsford Tourist Information Centre
Tel- *01565 632611*

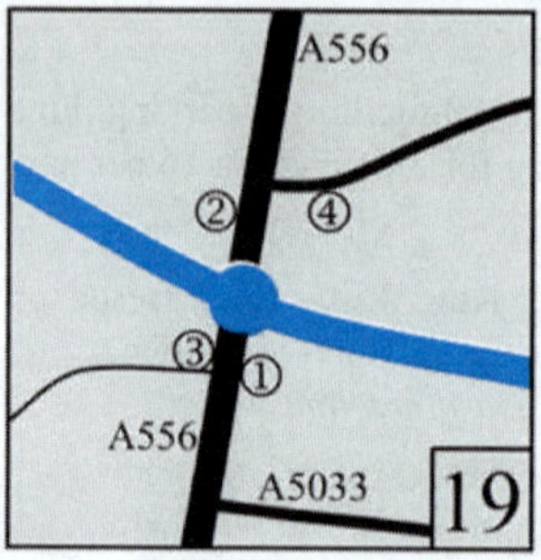

Junction 20 Services

These are located just off the motorway, and there are no other facilities close to this junction.

FUEL TOTAL

HGV fuelling & parking. Free parking for 2 hours then £6 per day.

FOOD

'Poplar' food bar, 'Pop Inn' licensed bar. McDonald's (0700-2330 only)
Info- *Cash machine & Barbershop.*

Services continued

ACCOMMODATION

Travelodge☞ £43
Info- *Lymm location.*
Tel- *01925 754478*

M6 Junction 20
M6/M56 interchange

Apart from the services above there are no facilities close to this junction.

ESSENTIALS

Warrington Hospital 6.5m
Dir'n- *Follow signs to Warrington and then the A57 west, where the hospital is signposted.*
Tel- *01925 635911*

Manchester Tourist Information Centre
Tel- *0161 234 3157*

Warrington Tourist Information Centre
Tel- *01925 442180*

M6 Junction 21
Warrington East

FOOD

Junction Restaurant £12 0.2m ①
Open- *M-F 0630-1000, Sat/Sun 0730-1130, M-F 1230-1430, Sun 1200-1500, M-F 1830-2030, Sun 1900-2200*
Info- *Refined dining at the Holiday Inn.*
Tel- *01925 838779*

Muscrat Manor Pub £6.50 0.2m ②
Open- *M-Sat 1200-2200, Sun 1000-2130*
Info- *Extensive hot & cold menu & a 'Playbarn'. Tom Cobleigh chain☞.*
Tel- *01925 812923*

Rope & Anchor Pub £6.00 1m ②
Open- *Daily 1200-2000*
Info- *Varied menu at local pub. Real ale.*
Tel- *01925 814996*

ACCOMMODATION

Premier Lodge☞ £48 0.2m ④
Info- *Warrington Central location.*
Tel- *0870 990 6524*

Holiday Inn☞ £96 0.2m ①

Info- *On-site bar & restaurant. Warrington location.*

Tel- *01925 838779*

ESSENTIALS

Warrington Hospital 6m

Dir'n- *Follow the A57 past Warrington town centre where the hospital is signposted.*

Tel- *01925 635911*

Manchester Tourist Information Centre

Tel- *0161 234 3157*

Warrington Tourist Information Centre

Tel- *01925 442180*

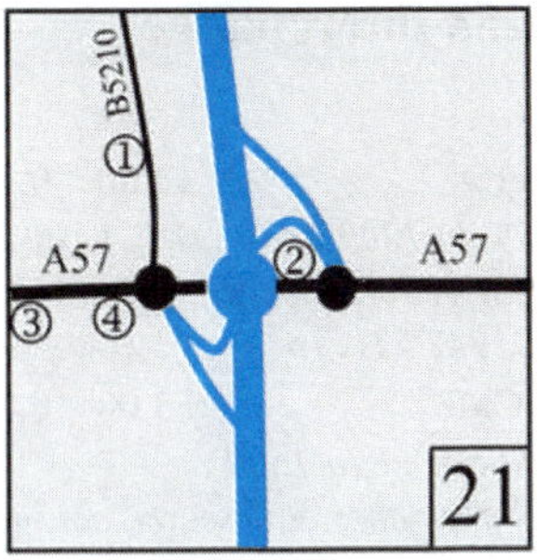

M6 Junction 21A
M6/M62 interchange

There is no access to local services at this junction.

ESSENTIALS

Warrington Hospital 6m

Info- *Drive to Junction 9 of the M62, and then towards Warrington, and the hospital is signposted en-route.*

Tel- *01925 635911*

Manchester Tourist Information Centre

Tel- *01612 343157*

Warrington Tourist Information Centre

Tel- *01925 442180*

M6 Junction 22
Newton Le Willows

FOOD

Burger King☞ £7.00 1.2m ①

Open- *M-F 0800-2200, Sa/Sun 1000-2200*

Tel- *01925 573387*

Chef & Brewer☞ £8.00 0.6m ②

Open- *Daily 1100-2230, M-F 0700-0930, Sat-Sun 0800-1000*

Info- *Next to Premier Lodge.*

Tel- *0870 990660*

ACCOMMODATION

Premier Lodge☞ £48 1.2m ②

Info- *Warrington North location.*

Tel- *0870 990660*

M6 Junction 23
Haydock

FUEL

Shell SAVE ££££ 0.2m ①

Open- *Daily 24 hours*

Info- *WC, LPG, HGV, jetwash, carwash, cash machine.*

Tel- *01925 293690*

Total SAVE ££££ 1.3m ②

Open- *Daily 24 hours*

Info- *WC, jetwash, carwash.*

Tel- *01942 408912*

FOOD

Holiday Inn Rest. £10 0.4m ③

Open- *M-F 0630-1000, 1200-1430, 1830-2200, Sat 0730-1000, 1830-2200, Sun 0730-1100, 1230-1500, 1830-2130*

Info- *Refined dining at the Holiday Inn.*

Tel- *0870 400 9039*

Thistle Hotel Rest. £14 0.6m ④

Open- *M-F 0700-1000, 1230-1400, 1900-2200, Sat 0700-1100, 1900-2200, Sun 0800-1100, 1300-1500, 1900-2130*

Info- *Refined dining at the Thistle Hotel.*
Tel- *01942 272000*

Millers Kitchen☞ £6.50 1m ⑤
Open- *Sat-Th 1200-2130, Fr 1200-2200*
Tel- *0870 010203*

Little Chef☞ £6.50 1.3m ②
Open- *Daily 0700-2100*
Info- *Harry Ramsden's & Upper Crust.*
Tel- *01942 272048*

Burger King☞ £4.00 1.3m ②
Open- *Daily 1100-2200*
Tel- *01942 272048*

ACCOMMODATION

Holiday Inn☞ £100 0.4m ③
Info- *Restaurant, bar & health club. Haydock location.*
Tel- *0870 400 9039*

Thistle Hotel☞ £137 0.6m ④
Info- *Restaurant, bar & health club. Haydock location.*
Tel- *01942 272000*

Premier Lodge☞ £48 1m ⑤
Info- *Wigan South location.*
Tel- *0870 990 6582*

Travelodge☞ £43 1.3m ②
Info- *Haydock location.*
Tel- *0870 191 1645*

THINGS TO DO

Haydock Races £5.00 0.7m ⑥
Info- *Regular horseracing.*
Tel- *01942 270879*

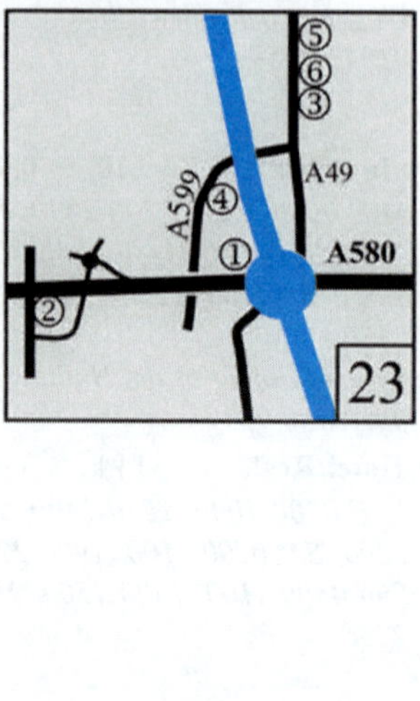

M6 Junction 24 Restricted

This junction only allows entrance to the motorway northbound, and exit southbound.

M6 Junction 25 Restricted

This junction only allows entrance to the motorway southbound, and exit northbound.

M6 Junction 26 M6/M58 interchange

FOOD

Beefeater☞ £7.00 0.7m ①
Open- *Daily 1200-1430, M-F 1730-2200, Sat 1730-2300, Sun 1730-2100*
Tel- *01942 211516*

Piccolo Cafe £3.00 0.9m ②
Open- *M-Sat 0830-1600*
Info- *Sandwiches & desserts, eat in or take away.*
Tel- *01942 216444*

Sorrento Trattoria £6.00 1m ③
Open- *M-Sat 1730-2200, Sun 1400-2200*
Info- *Extensive Italian menu.*
Tel- *01942 218555*

The Stag Inn £5.00 1m ③
Open- *M-Sat 1730-2200, Sun 1400-2200*
Info- *Varied pub menu. Satellite TV.*

KFC☞ £4.00 1m ④
Open- *Daily 1100-2400*
Tel- *01942 216849*

ACCOMMODATION

Travel Inn☞ £45 0.7m ①
Info- *Wigan West location.*
Tel- *01942 211516*

ESSENTIALS

Wigan Infirmary 5m
Dir'n- *Follow signs towards Wigan and then north towards Standish on the A49, where the hospital is on the left.*

Info- *Full hospital name is Royal Albert Edward Infirmary.*
Tel- *01942 244000*

Co-op Pharmacy 1m ⑤
Open- *M-F 0900-1800, Sat 0900-1300*
Tel- *01942 223175*

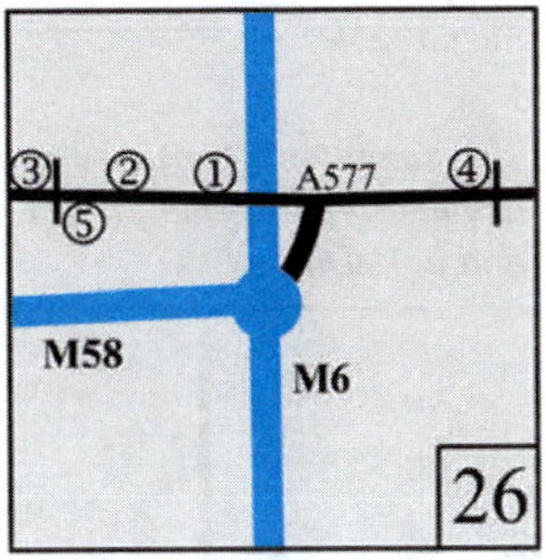

M6 Junction 27
Standish

FUEL

BP SAVE £££ 0.2m ①
Open- *Daily 24 hours*
Info- *WC, LPG, HGV, cash machine.*
Tel- *01257 421390*

Total SAVE ££££ 0.6m ②
Open- *Daily 24 hours*
Info- *Jetwash.*
Tel- *01257 473660*

FOOD

Charnley Arms £6.50 0.6m ③
Info- *Extensive menu at this local pub.*
Tel- *01257 424619*

Forresters Arms £6.50 0.6m ④
Open- *Su-Th 1200-2100, F/Sa 1130-2200*
Info- *Extensive menu including stir fries & pizzas.*
Tel- *01257 421337*

Hesketh Arms £6.50 0.6m ④
Open- *Tu-Th 1200-1400, 1700-2100, F/Sa 1200-2100, Sun 1200-2000*
Info- *Extensive menu in local pub, children's play area & 'pets'.*
Tel- *01257 402211*

Moat House restaurant £7.50 0.6m ⑤
Open- *Daily 0700-1000, M-Sat 1900-2130, Sun 1900-2100*
Info- *Extensive menu at the hotel.*
Tel- *01257 499988*

Bennets restaurant £14 0.6m ⑥
Open- *W-Sat 1830-2115, Sun 1230-1515*
Info- *Refined dining at the Wrightington Country Club.*
Tel- *01257 478244*

ACCOMMODATION

Wrightington Ctry Club £78 0.6m ⑥
Info- *Restaurant, health club & pool. A Best Western hotel.* ☞
Tel- *01257 425803*

Moat House Hotel £70 0.6m ⑤
Info- *Restaurant & bar. Wigan/Standish location. Price is B&B. Dogs at manager's discretion.*
Tel- *01257 499988*

Premier Lodge £48 0.6m ③
Info- *Wigan North location.*
Tel- *0870 990 6474*

ESSENTIALS

Wigan Infirmary 5m
Dir'n- *Take the A5209 to Standish, and then the A49 to Wigan. The hospital is signposted on the right off the A49.*
Info- *Full name is Royal Albert Edward Infirmary.*
Tel- *01942 244000*

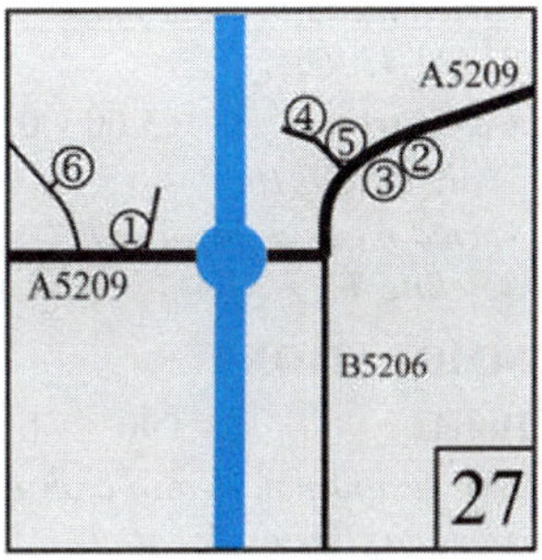

Charnock Richard Services

There are a footbridge and a roadbridge at this services.

FUEL SHELL

LPG (southbound) HGV fuelling & parking. Free parking for 2 hours then £6 per day.

FOOD WELCOME BREAK

foodconnection, Burger King, KFC

ACCOMMODATION

Welcome Lodge☞ £49
Info- *Charnock Richard location.*
Tel- *01257 791746*
Info- *Cash machine.*

M6 Junction 28
Leyland

FUEL

Total SAVE ££££ 0.2m ①
Open- *M-F 0600-2200, Sa/Sun 0700-2100*
Info- *Carwash.*
Tel- *01772 425902*

Shell SAVE ££££ 0.5m ②
Open- *Daily 24 hours*
Info- *WC, cash machine, carwash.*
Tel- *01772 450940*

FOOD

The Hayrick £5.50 0.3m ③
Open- *Daily 1200-2100*
Info- *Varied menu in local pub.*
Tel- *01772 434668*

Waggon & Horses £5.00 0.3m ④
Open- *Daily 1200-2100*
Info- *Varied menu in local pub. Satellite TV.*

ACCOMMODATION

Jarvis Hotel £90 0.2m ⑤
Info- *Bar, restaurant, health club & pool. Leyland/Preston location.*
Tel- *01772 422922*

ESSENTIALS

Chorley General Hospital 4.5m
Dir'n- *Take the B5256 east, and then the A6 south, where the hospital is on the right.*
Tel- *01257 261222*

THINGS TO DO

Country Park £nil 1m ⑥
Info- *Large country park with river & picnic tables.*

Leyland 1m ⑦
Info- *This small town is nearby and has a number of pubs, small takeaways and a McDonald's.*

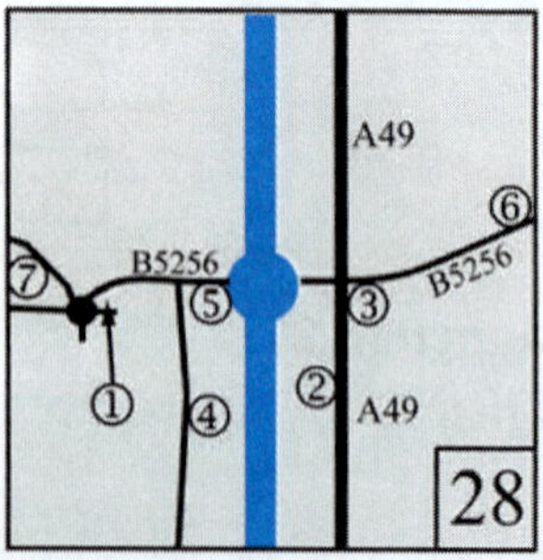

M6 Junction 29
M6/M65 interchange

FUEL

Sainsbury SAVE ££££ 0.5m ①
Open- *M-F 0600-2400, Sa/Sun 0700-2200*
Info- *Jetwash, carwash, cash machine, cafe at store.*
Tel- *01772 697352*

FOOD

The Brasserie £10 0.2m ②
Open- *Daily 0630-2200*
Info- *Dining at the Novotel.*
Tel- *01772 313331*

Millers Kitchen☞ £6.50 0.5m ③
Open- *M-Sat 1200-2200, Sun 1200-2100*
Tel- *01772 324100*

Burger King☞ £4.00 0.5m ④
Open- *Daily 0800-2200*
Tel- *01772 337192*

Sainsbury Cafe☞ £3.50 0.5m ①
Open- *M/Tu/W/Sat 0800-1900, Th-F 0800-2000, Sun 0930-1600*
Tel- *01772 627726*

The Olde Hob Inn £6.50 0.6m ⑤

Info- *Extensive menu & real ales.*
Open- *Tu-Sat 1200-1400, 1800-2100, Sun 1200-2100*
Tel- *01772 336863*

ACCOMMODATION

Novotel☞ £60 0.2m ②

Info- *Bar & restaurant. Preston location.*
Tel- *01772 313331*

ESSENTIALS

Boots Pharmacy 1m ⑥

Open- *M-Sat 0900-1730*
Tel- *01772 335458*

THINGS TO DO

Church Road Park 0.6m ⑤

Info- *Small park opposite The Olde Hob Inn.*

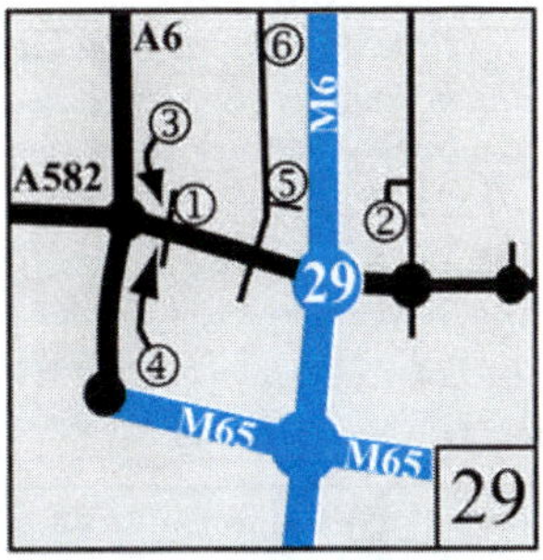

M6 Junction 30
M6/M61 interchange

This is a motorway interchange and there is no access to any local services.

M6 Junction 31
Preston

FUEL

BP SAVE £££ 0.2m ①

Open- *Daily 24 hours*
Info- *Jetwash, HGV fuelling.*
Tel- *01772 877656*

BP#2 SAVE ££££ 0.8m ②

Open- *Daily 24 hours*
Info- *Carwash, cash machine, HGV fuelling.*
Tel- *01772 794212*

FOOD

Campions £10 1.2m ③

Open- *Tu-Th 1200-1400, 1800-2100, F/Sa 1200-1400, 1800-2130, Sun 1200-2100*
Info- *Restaurant & bar, extensive menu.*
Dir'n- *Follow signs to Roach Bridge.*
Tel- *01772 877641*

New Hall Tavern £6.00 1.2m ④

Open- *Daily 1200-1400, 1800-2100*
Info- *Extensive menu at local pub.*
Dir'n- *Follow signs to Roach Bridge.*
Tel- *01772 877217*

ACCOMMODATION

Tickled Trout Hotel £65 0.2m ①

Info- *Restaurant & bar. A 'MacDonald' hotel☞.*
Tel- *01772 877671*

ESSENTIALS

Preston Tourist Information Centre

Tel- *01772 253731*

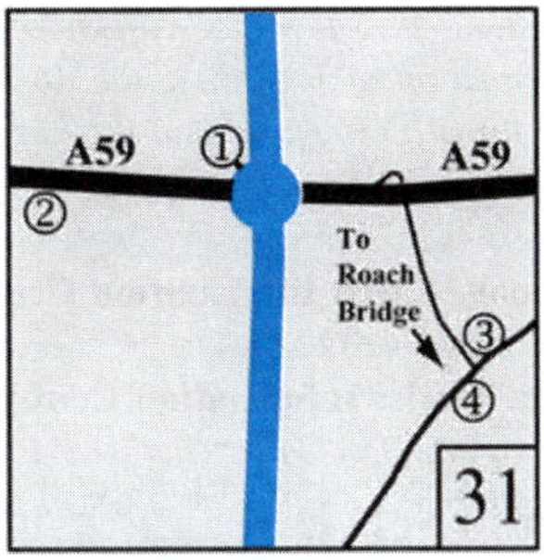

M6 Junction 31A
Restricted

This junction only allows exit northbound, and entry southbound.

ACCOMMODATION

Travel Inn☞ £45 0.6m ①

Info- *Restaurant & bar, extensive menu. Preston East location.*
Dir'n- *Follow the route to the M6 southbound from the northbound turn off, and the hotel is on the left.*
Tel- *0870 197 7215*

ESSENTIALS

Royal Preston Hospital 3m

Dir'n- *Take B6242 west, and turn right on Sharoe Green Lane, where the hospital is on the left.*

Tel- *01772 716565*

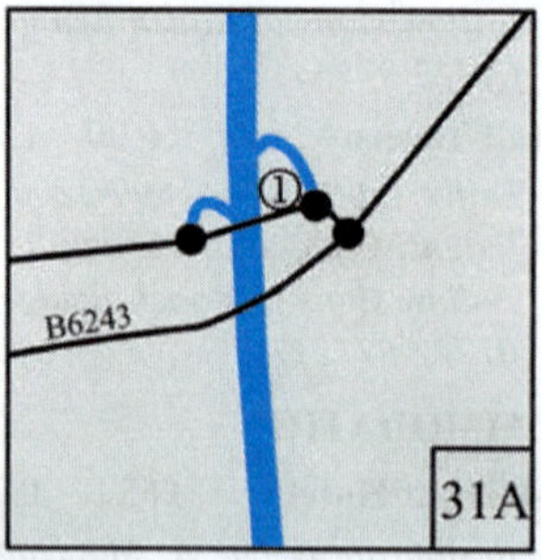

M6 Junction 32
M6/M55 interchange

ESSENTIALS

Royal Preston Hospital 2.5m

Dir'n- *Take M55 towards Blackpool and turn off at Jn 1. Take the A6 towards Preston, and the hospital is signposted on the left.*

Tel- *01772 716565*

Blackpool Tourist Information Centre

Tel- *01253 478222*

Preston Tourist Information Centre

Tel- *01772 253731*

Forton Services

There are a footbridge and a roadbridge at this services.

FUEL SHELL

LPG, HGV fuelling & parking. Free parking for 2 hours then £6 per day.

FOOD MOTO

freshexpress, Burger King, Little Chef, Harry Ramsden's

Info- *Cash machines.*

ACCOMMODATION

Travelodge☞ £50

Info- *Lancaster Forton location.*

Tel- *0870 191 1654*

M6 Junction 33
Galgate

FOOD

The Plough £5.50 0.8m ①

Open- *Daily 1200-2030*

Info- *Varied hot & cold menu, real ales.*

Tel- *01524 751337*

Bay Horse Inn £5.50 0.8m ②

Open- *M-Sat 1200-1400, 1900-2100, Sun 1200-1500*

Info- *Extensive hot & cold menu. Real ales.*

Dir'n- *Turn left at 'Trough of Bowland' sign on A6.*

Tel- *01524 791204*

ESSENTIALS

Royal Lancaster Infirmary 4.5m

Dir'n- *Take the A6 towards Lancaster, and the hospital is signposted near the centre.*

Tel- *01524 583100*

France Motor Services 0.9m ③

Info- *Tyres.*

Tel- *01524 751251*

Seat Dealer 1.1m ④

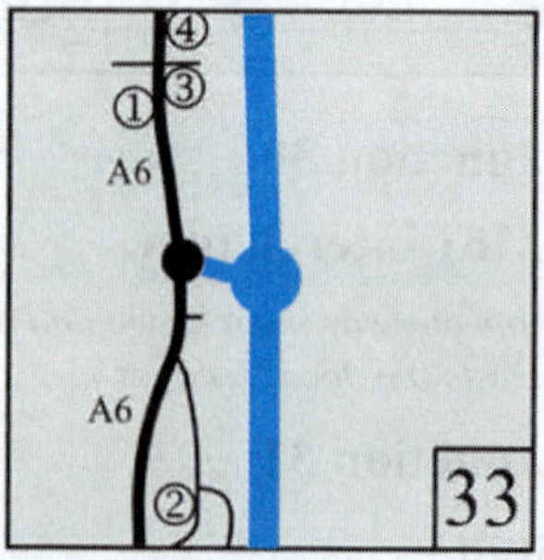

M6 Junction 34
Lancaster

FUEL

Shell **SAVE** £££ 0.6m ①

Open- *Daily 24 hours*

Info- *WC*

Tel- *01524 590900*

FOOD

Holiday Inn restaurant £10 0.2m ②

Open- *M-F 0630-1000, 1200-1430, 1800-2145, Sat 0730-1100, 1800-2145, Sun 0730-1100, 1230-1430, 1800-2130*

Info- *Extensive menu at the Holiday Inn.*

Tel- *0870 400 9047*

Brewsters☞ £6.50 0.3m ③

Info- *Next to Travel Inn.*

Tel- *0870 197 7290*

ACCOMMODATION

Holiday Inn☞ £93 0.2m ②

Info- *Bar, restaurant & health club.*

Tel- *0870 400 9047*

Travel Inn☞ £45 0.3m ③

Info- *Lancaster location.*

Tel- *0870 197 7290*

Lancaster Town House £45 0.7m ④

Info- *Private guest house. AA/ETC 3◆*

Tel- *01524 65527*

ESSENTIALS

Royal Lancaster Infirmary 3m

Dir'n- *Take the A683 towards Lancaster, and then the A6 south, where the hospital is signposted.*

Tel- *01524 583100*

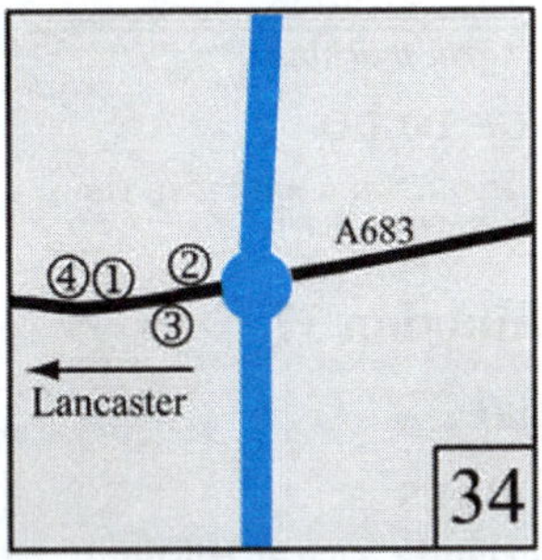

M6 Junction 35
Carnforth

FUEL

Esso/Truckhaven SAVE £ 1.5m ①

Open- *Daily 24 hours*

Info- *WC, cafe, HGV parking.*

Tel- *01524 736699*

FOOD

Pine Lake Rest. £10 1.2m ②

Open- *Daily 0930-1430, 1800-2100*

Info- *Extensive menu at this resort restaurant. Visitors welcome.*

Tel- *01524 736191*

Truckhaven restaurant £10 1.5m ①

Open- *M-Sat open 24 hours, Sun 0700-2300*

Info- *Varied menu at above average truckstop.*

Tel- *01524 736699*

ACCOMMODATION

Pine Lake Resort £80 1.2m ②

Info- *Overnight bookings of 6 berth holiday cabins sometimes available. Price is per cabin.*

Tel- *01524 736191*

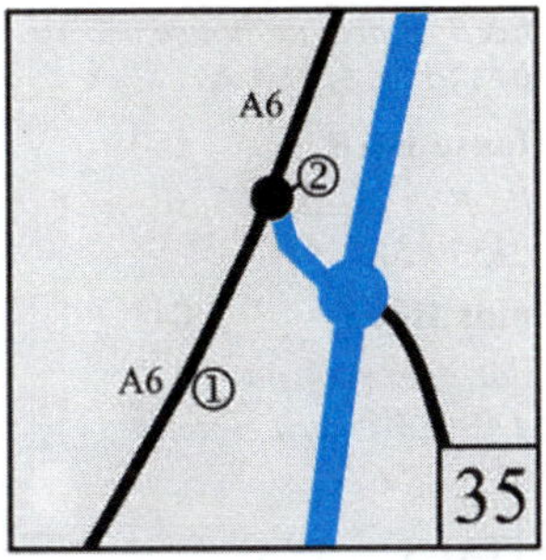

Burton In Kendal Services (Northbound only)

FUEL ESSO

HGV fuelling. Free parking for 2 hours then £6 per 24 hours. Lorry park.

FOOD MOTO

freshexpress, Harry Ramsden's, Uppercrust.

Info- Cash machine.

M6 Junction 36
Milnthorpe

FUEL

Shell SAVE ££ 0.5m ①
Open- *Daily 24 hours*
Info- *LPG, WC, cafe, HGV fuelling & fuel bunkering.*
Tel- *01539 567280*

FOOD

Crooklands Rest. £10 1m ②
Open- *Daily 1200-1400, 1900-2100*
Info- *Extensive bar & restaurant menu at the Crooklands Hotel.*
Tel- *01539 567432*

ACCOMMODATION

Beckside B&B £40 1m ③
Info- *B&B in private house.*
Tel- *01539 567387*

Spout House B&B £50 1m ④
Info- *B&B in private house.*
Tel- *01539 567135*

Crooklands Hotel £48 1m ②
Info- *Bar & restaurant. A Best Western Hotel.* ☞
Tel- *01539 567432*

ESSENTIALS

Westmorland Gen. Hospital 7.5m
Dir'n- *Take A591, and then the A6 to Kendal where the hospital is signposted.*
Info- *Minor injuries unit only.*
Tel- *01539 732288*

Kendal Tourist Information Centre
Tel- *01539 725758*

JAS 24 Hour Recovery 0.5m ①
Info- *Local recovery service.*
Tel- *01539 567401*

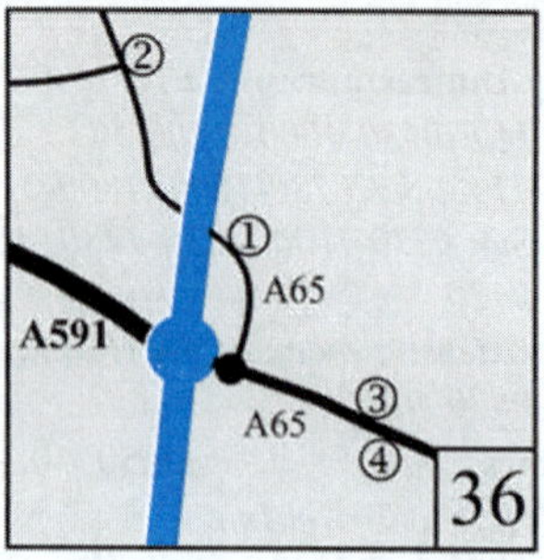

Killington Services (Southbound only)

FUEL BP
HGV fuelling & parking. Free parking for 2 hours then £6 per day.

FOOD ROADCHEF
onroute, Costa Coffee, Wimpy
Open- *Daily 0730-2200*

ACCOMMODATION

Travel Inn☞ £45
Info- *Kendal/Killington Lake location.*
Tel- *0870 197 7145*

ESSENTIALS

Killington Lake Tourist Information
Tel- *01539 620138*
Info- *Cash machine.*

THINGS TO DO
Info- *Picnic area with lake view.*

M6 Junction 37
Kendal

ESSENTIALS

Westmorland General Hospital 8m
Dir'n- *Take A684 to Kendal where the hospital is signposted.*
Info- *Minor injuries unit only.*
Tel- *01539 732288*

Kendal Tourist Information Centre
Tel- *01539 725758*

THINGS TO DO

Lanbrigg Wind Farm 0.4m ①

Info- *View the windfarm from the road.*

Kendal & the Lakes 6m

Info- *Kendal is at the south of the Lake District and has a good range of shops, restaurants & pubs.*

M6 Junction 38
Tebay

FUEL

M6 Diesel **SAVE** ££ 0.2m ①

Open- *Daily 24 hours*

Info- *LPG, petrol & diesel. WC, cafe, HGV fuelling & bunkering.*

Tel- *01539 624336*

FOOD

Transport Cafe £4.50 0.2m ①

Open- *Daily 24 hours except Sat 2230-Sun 0700*

Info- *Varied menu at transport cafe.*

Tel- *01539 624505*

Cross Keys Inn £7.00 0.5m ②

Open- *Daily 1200-1430, 1800-2100*

Info- *Extensive menu & real ales.*

Tel- *01539 624240*

ACCOMMODATION

High Bank House £42 0.3m ③

Info- *Small guest house. Price is B&B.*

Tel- *01539 624651*

Cross Keys B&B £45 0.5m ②

Info- *B&B at local pub.*

Tel- *01539 624240*

ESSSENTIALS

JAS Garage/Recovery 0.2m ④

Info- *Garage & 24 hour recovery.*

Tel- *01539 567401*

Tebay Services

There is a roadbridge between carriageways. This is an unusually pleasant services, with great views, accommodation, and lack of mass catering.

FUEL TEXACO

LPG, HGV fuelling. Free parking for 2 hours then £6 per 24 hours. Lorry park.

FOOD

Self service restaurant with great views & a coffee shop.

Info- *Cash machine. Yards away is the :-*

Westmorland Hotel restaurant £14

Open- *Daily 1900-2100*

Info- *Refined dining in this* **AA Rosette** *restaurant. Bar meals 24 hours.*

ACCOMMODATION

Westmorland Hotel £63

Info- *Restaurant & bar. Pets welcome at extra charge.*

M6 Junction 39
Shap

FOOD

Greyhound Hotel £8.00 1.5m ①

Open- *Daily 1200-1400, 1800-2100*

Info- *Extensive menu at this village pub restaurant. Real ales.*

Tel- *01931 716474*

ACCOMMODATION

Greyhound Hotel £56 1.5m ①
Open- *Daily 1200-1400, 1800-2100*
Info- *On site bar & restaurant. Party accommodation in bunkhouse.*
Tel- *01931 716474*

Brookfields B&B £48 1.3m ②
Info- *B&B in village home.*
Tel- *01931 716397*

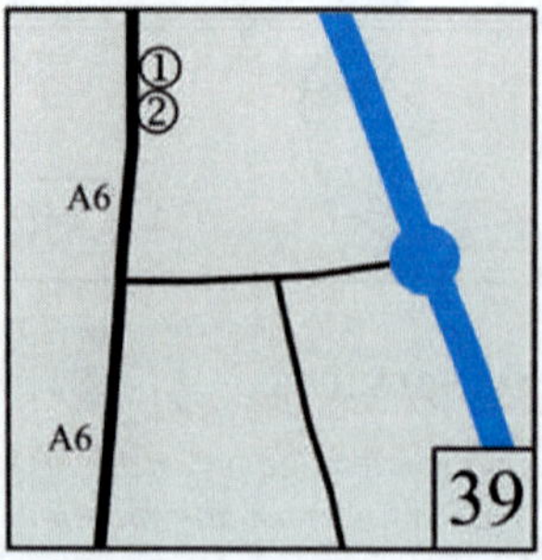

M6 Junction 40
Penrith

FUEL

Red Rooster SAVE £ 0.3m ①
Open- *M-F 0700-2100, Sa/Sun 0800-2000*
Info- *HGV fuelling. Transport cafe adjacent.*
Tel- *01768 892906*

Ullswater Garage SAVE nil 0.3m ①
Open- *M-F 0830-1730, Sat 0830-1200*
Info- *LPG only (& car repairs).*
Dir'n- *Just behind the 'Red Rooster'.*
Tel- *01768 864546*

J40 Services SAVE ££ 0.6m ②
Open- *Daily 24 hours*
Info- *Diesel only. HGV parking, repairs. Truckwash & 24 hour recovery.*
Tel- *01768 867101*

Safeway SAVE ££ 0.8m ③
Open- *Daily 24 hours*
Info- *Cafe at nearby store.*
Tel- *01768 891162*

Texaco SAVE ££ 0.8m ④
Open- *Daily 24 hours*
Info- *WC, carwash, jetwash.*
Tel- *01768 899303*

Shell SAVE ££ 1m ⑤
Open- *Daily 24 hours*
Info- *WC, jetwash, cash machine.*
Tel- *01768 212900*

Texaco no. 2 SAVE ££ 1m ⑥
Open- *Daily 24 hours*
Info- *WC*
Tel- *01768 860023*

FOOD

Red Rooster £4 0.3m ①
Open- *M-Sa 0700-1800, Sat 0800-1800*
Info- *Hot & cold meals at transport cafe.*
Tel- *01768 895818*

Little Chef☞ £6.50 0.5m ⑦
Open- *Daily 0700-2200*
Info- *Harry Ramsden's & Upper Crust.*
Tel- *01768 868303*

Burger King☞ £4.00 0.5m ⑦
Open- *Daily 1100-2100*
Tel- *01768 864196*

McDonald's☞ £3.50 0.7m ③
Open- *Daily 0700-2300*
Tel- *01768 868347*

ACCOMMODATION

Travelodge £50 0.5m ⑦
Info- *Penrith location.*
Tel- *0870 191 1667*

North Lakes Hotel £55 0.7m ⑧
Info- *Bar, restaurant & health club. AA 4◆*
Tel- *01768 868111*

The Limes £50 0.7m ⑨
Info- *Country house hotel. Pets welcome.*
Tel- *01768 863343*

Others 1m
Info- *Penrith has a number of small hotels and B&Bs.*

ESSENTIALS

Penrith Tourist Information Centre
Tel- *01768 867466*

Kwik Fit 0.3m ①
Info- *Tyre & exhaust centre.*
Dir'n- *Behind the 'Red Rooster'.*
Tel- *01768 864545*

Halfords 0.7m ②
Open- *M-F 0900-2000, Sa/Sun 0900-1800*
Info- *Car spares.*
Tel- *01768 892960*

THINGS TO DO

Castle Park & Penrith Castle 0.7m ⑩
Info- *Pleasant town centre park with 14th century ruins open for free viewing.*

'Rheged' £5.50 1m ⑥
Open- *Daily 1000-1730*
Info- *Discovery Centre dedicated to local history & culture, & exploration. Cafe & shops.*
Tel- *01768 868000*

Penrith & the Lake District 1m
Info- *Penrith is at the northern edge of the Lake District and has a range of shops and accommodation.*

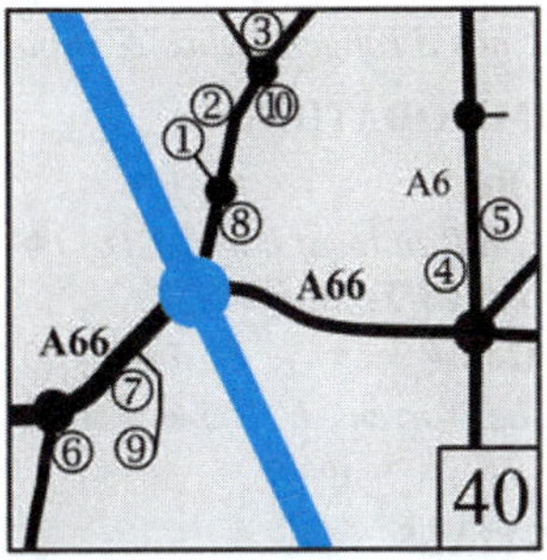

M6 Junction 41
Penrith North

FUEL

Texaco SAVE Nil 0.3m ①
Open- *M-F 0830-1800, Sat 0830-1300*
Info- *WC*
Tel- *01768 864019*

FOOD

Stonybeck Inn £7.00 1.1m ②
Open- *M-F 1100-1500, 1800-2130, Sa/Sun 1100-2130*
Info- *Extensive hot & cold menu.*
Tel- *01768 862369*

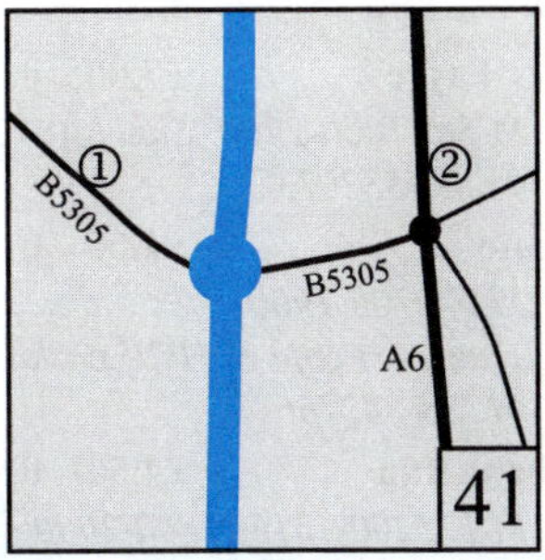

Southwaite Services

There is a roadbridge between carriage-ways.

FUEL ESSO

HGV fuelling. Free parking for 2 hours then £6 per 24 hours. Lorry park.

FOOD

Harry Ramsden's, Upper Crust, Ritazza
Info- *Cash machines.*

ACCOMMODATION

Travelodge☞ £50
Info- *Carlisle Southwaite location.*
Tel- *0870 191 1628*

ESSENTIALS

Egerton's Recovery
Info- *24 hr recovery & repairs. Northbound direction.*
Tel- *01565 873196*

Carlisle Tourist Information Centre
Tel- *01228 625600*

M6 Junction 42
Carlisle South

FUEL

BP SAVE ££ 0.3m ①
Open- *Daily 24 hours.*
Info- *HGV fuelling & parking.*
Tel- *01228 542766*

BP#2 SAVE ££ 0.4m ②
Open- *M-Sat 0700-2200, Sun 1200-2000*
Tel- *01228 592479*

FOOD

Brewers Fayre☞ £7.00 0.3m ③
Open- *M-Sat 1000-2200, Sun 1200-2200*
Tel- *01228 532073*

JK's Cafe £4.00 0.3m ①
Open- *M-F 0700-1900*
Info- *Transport cafe & HGV parking.*
Tel- *01228 542766*

Greenbank Inn £4.50 0.9m ④
Open- *M-F 1200-1315, 1800-2000, Sat/Sun 1200-1400, 1700-2000*
Info- *Pub meals.*
Tel- *01228 528846*

Dhaka Tandoori £8.00 0.9m ④
Open- *M-Sat 1200-1400, 1800-2400, Sun 1200-2400*
Info- *Indian restaurant & takeaway.*
Tel- *01228 523855*

ACCOMMODATION

Travel Inn☞ £45 0.3m ③
Info- *Carlisle South location.*
Tel- *0870 197 7054*

ESSENTIALS

Cumberland Royal Infirmary 4m
Dir'n- *Follow the A6 to Carlisle town centre, and the hospital is signposted.*
Tel- *01228 523444*

Carlisle Tourist Information Centre
Tel- *01228 625600*

Carleton Service Station 0.6m ⑤
Open- *M-F 0830-1700*
Info- *24 hour recovery service.*
Tel- *01228 527287*

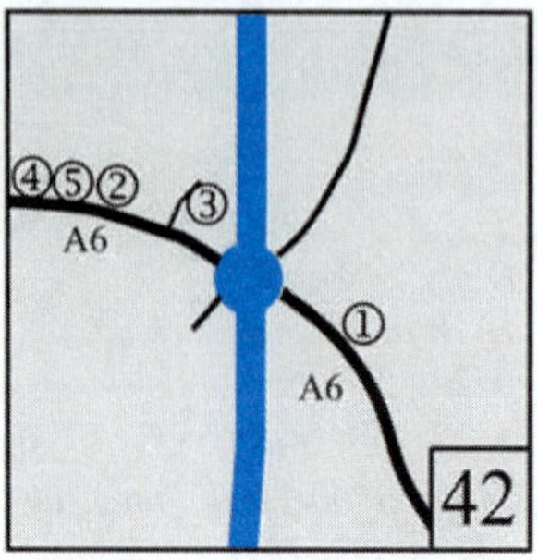

M6 Junction 43
Carlisle

FUEL

Tesco **SAVE** ££££ 0.3m ①
Open- *Daily 24 hours*
Info- *Cafe & cash machine at store.*
Tel- *0845 677 9125*

Esso **SAVE** ££££ 0.7m ②
Open- *Daily 24 hours*
Info- *WC, carwash.*
Tel- *01228 528715*

FOOD

Tesco Cafe☞ £3.50 0.9m ①
Open- *M 0800-1900, Tu-Sat 0700-1900, Sun 1000-1600*
Tel- *0845 677 9125*

Others 2.5m
Carlisle has a range of pubs & restaurants.

ACCOMMODATION

Dalroc B&B £36 0.7m ④
Info- *B&B in local home. ETC 3◆*
Tel- *01228 542805*

Guest House £40 0.7m ⑤
Info- *'The Warren', ETC 3◆. Price is B&B.*
Tel- *01228 533663*

ESSENTIALS

Cumberland Infirmary 3.2m
Dir'n- *Follow the A69 to Carlisle, and the hospital is signposted*
Tel- *01228 523444*

Carlisle Tourist Information Centre
Tel- *01228 625600*

Car Dealers 0.3m ⑥
Info- *Landrover, Rover, MG, Mercedes.*

THINGS TO DO

Carlisle 2.5m
Info- *Carlisle has an interesting centre with a Castle and Cathedral to see.*

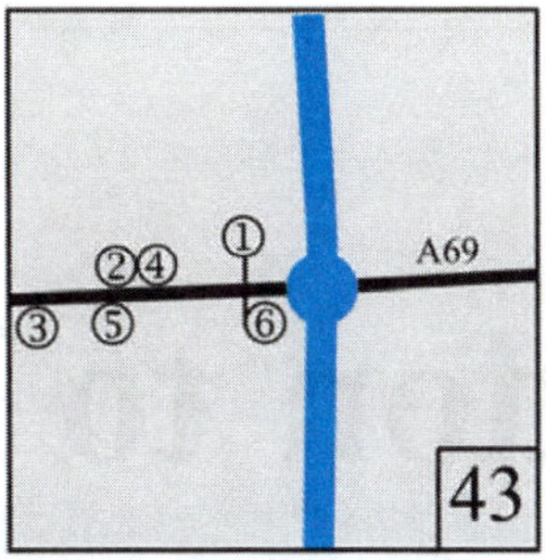

M6 Junction 44
M6/A74 Merge

FUEL

BP SAVE ££££ 0.4m ①
Open- *Daily 0600-2200*
Info- *WC*
Tel- *01228 523031*

BP Truckstop SAVE ££ 0.5m ②
Open- *Daily 24 hours*
Info- *HGV fuel only. Cafe, HGV parking & accommodation.*
Tel- *01228 534192*

Asda SAVE ££££ 0.6m ③
Open- *Daily 24 hours with credit cards.*
Info- *Cafe & cash machine at store.*
Tel- *01228 514926*

FOOD

McDonald's☞ £3.50 0.3m ④
Open- *Daily 0700-2300*
Tel- *01228 513309*

Holiday Inn rest. £10 0.3m ⑤
Open- *M-F 0630-1000, 1230-1400, Sat/Sun 0730-1100, M-Sat 1800-2200, Sun 1900-2200*
Info- *Refined dining at hotel restaurant.*
Tel- *0870 400 9018*

BP Truckstop £4.00 0.5m ②
Open- *Daily 24 hours except Sat 1400-Sun 0600*
Info- *Hot & cold meals at transport cafe.*
Tel- *01228 534192*

Asda Cafe☞ £3.00 0.6m ③
Open- *M-Sat 0800-1930, Sun 1000-1400*
Info- *Cash machines.*
Tel- *01228 526550*

Millers Kitchen☞ £6.50 0.8m ⑥
Open- *M-Th 1200-2130, F/Sa 1200-2200, Sun 1200-2130*
Tel- *0870 990 6502*

ACCOMMODATION

Holiday Inn☞ £90 0.3m ⑤
Info- *Bar, restaurant & health club. Carlisle location.*
Tel- *0870 400 9018*

BP Truckstop £18 0.5m ②
Info- *Value accommodation, no en-suite.*
Tel- *01228 534192*

Newfield Grange Motel £40 0.5m ⑦
Info- *Private motel with restaurant. ETC 3◆*
Tel- *01228 819926*

Premier Lodge☞ £48 0.8m ⑥
Info- *Carlisle location.*
Tel- *0870 990 6502*

Travelodge☞ £50 2.0m ⑧
Info- *Carlisle North location.*
Dir'n- *Take the A74 north. The hotel is on the Southbound carriageway.*
Tel- *0870 191 1627*

ESSENTIALS

Cumberland Infirmary 3.2m
Dir'n- *Follow the A7 to Carlisle, and the hospital is signposted.*
Tel- *01228 523444*

Carlisle Tourist Information Centre
Tel- *01228 625600*

Car Dealers 0.3m
Info- *BMW, Chrysler, Citroen, ERF, FIAT, Ford, Honda, Hyundai, Jaguar, Lexus, Mazda, Skoda, Suzuki, Toyota, Volkswagen, Volvo.*
Dir'n- *All between Asda & Premier Lodge.*

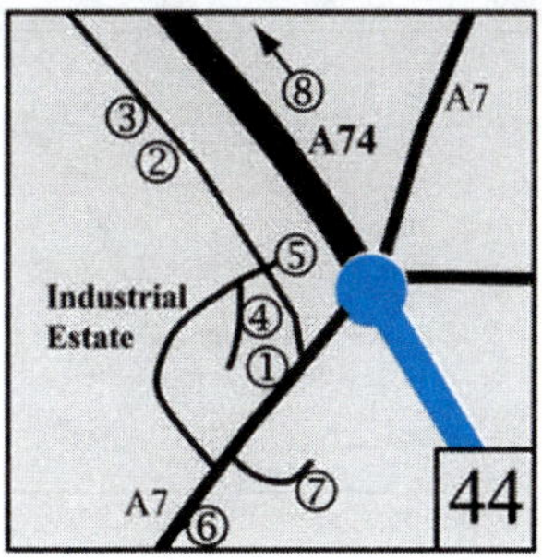

M11-London to Cambridge

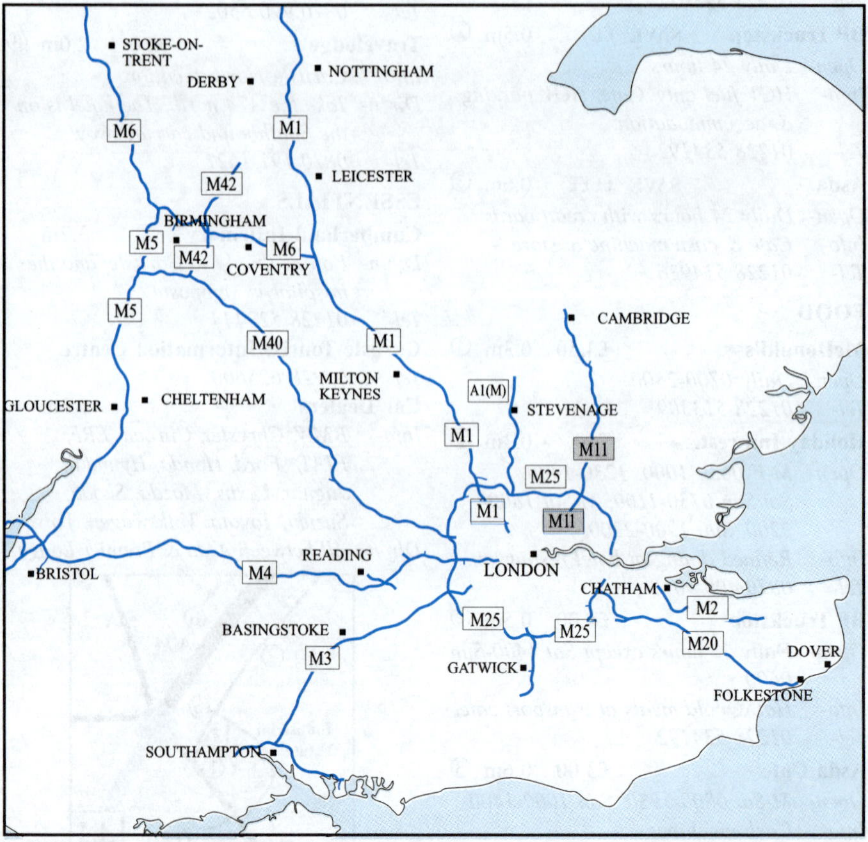

M11 Summary of Junctions

Radio stations & frequencies		Junction	Fuel	Food	Hotels	Essentials	Things to do
Capital 95.8 Magic 105.4	LBC 97.3 Heart 106.2	4	Motorway starts			A&E, TIC	
Capital 95.8 Magic 105.4	LBC 97.3 Heart 106.2	5					
Capital 95.8 Magic 105.4	LBC 97.3 Heart 106.2	6					
Heart 106.2 Essex FM 102.6	Capital 95.8 Ten-17 101.7	7	24hr	✓	✓	A&E	✓
Heart 106.2 Essex FM 102.6	Capital 95.8 Ten-17 101.7	8 S	24hr	✓	✓	TIC	✓
Vibe FM 105.6 Q103 103.0	Star 107.9 BBC 3CR 95.5	9				TIC	
Vibe FM 105.6 Q103 103.0	Star 107.9 BBC 3CR 95.5	10	24hr	✓	✓		✓
Vibe FM 105.6 Q103 103.0	Star 107.9 BBC 3CR 95.5	11	✓	✓		A&E, TIC Pharmacy	✓
Vibe FM 105.6 Q103 103.0	Star 107.9 BBC 3CR 95.5	12	✓	✓		A&E TIC	✓
Vibe FM 105.6 Q103 103.0	Star 107.9 BBC 3CR 95.5	13					
Vibe FM 105.6 Q103 103.0	Star 107.9 BBC 3CR 95.5	14	Motorway ends				✓

Top Stops are highlighted

M11 Junction Details

M11 Junctions 1,2,3
Non-existent

Junction 4
Motorway starts

This is a restricted access junction allowing access only to & from the A406/North Circular.

ESSENTIALS

Whipps Cross Hospital 2.5m
Dir'n- *Take the A406 west & then the A104 south, where the hospital is signposted.*
Tel- *0208 539 5522*

Southwark Tourist Information Centre
Tel- *0207 375 2549*

M11 Junction 5
Restricted

This is a restricted access junction allowing access only to the southbound direction, and from the northbound direction.

M11 Junction 6
M11/M25 interchange

M11 Junction 7
Harlow

FUEL

Shell SAVE £ 0.4m ①
Open- *Daily 24 hours*
Info- *WC, LPG, HGV fuelling.*
Tel- *01279 635980*

BP SAVE ££ 0.6m ②
Open- *Daily 24 hours*
Info- *WC, cash machine, HGV fuelling.*
Tel- *01279 432391*

Keyfuels SAVE £ 1.3m ③
Open- *M-Sat 0700-1930*
Info- *WC, HGV fuelling, hand carwash during weekdays.*
Tel- *01992 578284*

FOOD

McDonald's☞ £3.50 0.2m ④
Open- *Daily 0700-2300*
Tel- *01279 454367*

Little Chef☞ £3.50 0.6m ①
Open- *Daily 0700-2200*
Tel- *01279 417057*

Beefeater☞ £7.00 0.6m ⑤
Open- *M-Sat 1200-2230, Sun 1200-2100*
Tel- *01279 424495*

Rainbow & Dove Pub £6.00 0.7m ⑥
Open- *Daily 1230-1400, 1700-2100*
Info- *Extensive hot & cold menu. In the Good Pub Guide.*
Tel- *01279 415419*

CrossKeys Cafe £3.50 1.1m ⑦
Open- *M-F 0700-1400, Sat/Sun 0700-1500*
Info- *Transport cafe. Mainly fried food.*

ACCOMMODATION

Moat House Hotel☞ £140 0.8m ⑧
Info- *Bar & restaurant. Harlow location.*
Tel- *01279 829988*

ESSENTIALS

Princess Alexandra Hospital
Dir'n- *Follow signs to Harlow town centre (A414/A1025), and the hospital is well signposted.*
Tel- *01279 444455*

THINGS TO DO

North Weald Market 2.5m
Open- *Every Sat. and Bank Holiday Mon.*
Info- *Large market on the North Weald airfield.*
Dir'n- *Follow the A414 towards Chelmsford & the market is signposted.*

Nth Weald Air Museum £3.50 2.8m
Open- *Mar 29-Oct 6, Sat-Sun 1200-1700*

Info- *Museum of this WW2 airfield.*
Tel- *01992 523010*
Dir'n- *Follow the A414 to North Weald Bassett, then the B181 to Epping. Ad Astra House is on Hurricane Way (the former entrance to the airfield), accessed via North Weald Village, and not the present airfield entrance.*

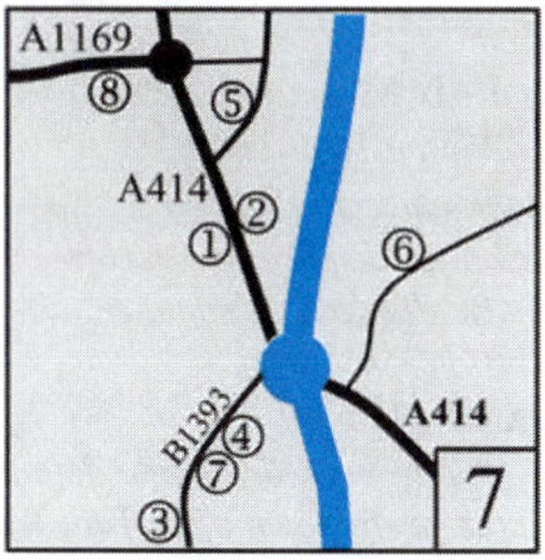

Jn 8 -Birchanger Svcs

This services is located just off the motorway.

FUEL SHELL

LPG. Car parking £6 for 24 hours after first 2 hours. HGV parking and fuelling.

FOOD WELCOME BREAK

KFC, Red Hen, Burger King, The Granary
Info- *Cash machines.*

ACCOMMODATION

Welcome Lodge☞ £69 0.6m
Info- *Birchanger Green location.*
Tel- *0800 028 0400*

M11 Junction 8
Stansted Airport

The pleasant town of Bishop's Stortford is less than 2 miles away and has a wide range of facilities.

FUEL

Esso **SAVE** £ 0.3m ①
Open- *Daily 24 hours*
Info- *WC, cash machine.*
Tel- *01279 503959*

FOOD

Three Willows Pub £7 1.0m ②
Open- *M-Sat 1200-1400, 1800-2130*
Info- *Extensive hot & cold menu. Featured in Good Pub Guide.*
Tel- *01279 815913*

ACCOMMODATION

Stansted Manor Hotel £115 1m ③
Info- *On-site restaurant. Independent hotel. AA/RAC 3★*
Tel- *01279 859800*

Pearse House £ 75 0.9m ④
Info- *On-site restaurant. Off airport parking in grounds. Price is for B&B. Independent hotel.*
Tel- *01279 757400*

The Cottage Guest Hs £68 1.8m ⑤
Info- *Price is B&B. ETC Gold award. In the 'Which B&B' guide.*
Tel- *01279 812349*

Hilton Hotel☞ £155 0.9m ⑥
Info- *On site restaurant & bar. Health club. Special deals with airport parking. Stansted Airport location.*
Dir'n- *Follow signs to long term car park which is next to the hotel.*
Tel- *01279 680800*

ESSENTIALS

Bishops Stortford Tourist Info. Centre
Tel- *01279 655831*

24 hour Recovery 1.6m
Info- *Rowland Ridgewell Recovery.*
Dir'n- *Follow signs to Hertford/A120, then turn left at the B1383 junction.*
Tel- *01279 654408*

Car Dealers & Service
Info- *Ford, BMW, Vauxhall, Toyota, VW, Audi, LandRover, Mercedes dealers.*
Dir'n- *Most are close by in Bishop's Stortford. The Mercedes dealer is about 1 mile away on the A120 east to Takeley/Great Dunmow.*

THINGS TO DO

Hatfield Forest £3 3m
Open- *Most daylight hours*
Info- *National Trust Forest, lakes & nature reserve. Cafe at peak hours.*

Price is per car.
Dir'n- *Signposted from A120 heading east.*
Tel- *01279 870678*

Saffron Walden 12m
Info- *A long but worthwhile detour to see the pretty town of Saffron Walden which has a good supply of restaurants and small shops. Nearby is Audley End House and an HDRA organic kitchen garden. Rejoin the motorway at Junction 10.*

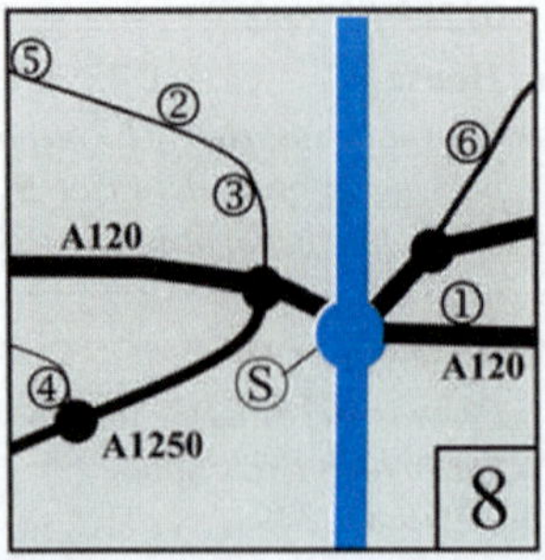

M11 Junction 9
Restricted

This junction does not allow entry to & from the northbound direction of the M11.

ESSENTIALS

Saffron Walden Tourist Info. Centre
Tel- *01799 510444*

M11 Junction 10
Duxford

FUEL

Texaco **SAVE** nil 0.3m ①
Open- *Daily 0600-2000*
Info- *WC, cash machine.*
Tel- *01223 499100*

BP **SAVE** £ 1.8m ②
Open- *Daily 24 hours*
Info- *WC, LPG, cash machine, HGV fuelling.*
Tel- *01223 832996*

FOOD

McDonald's☞ £3.50 1.8m ②
Open- *Daily 0700-2300*
Tel- *01223 836947*

ACCOMMODATION

Red Lion Hotel £60 1.5m ③
Info- *Varied pub meals available. Family run hotel. Folk evenings on Fridays.*
Tel- *01223 832047*

THINGS TO DO

Duxford Air Museum £8.50 0.2m ④
Open- *Winter 1000-1600, Summer 1000-1800*
Info- *Large display of aircraft. Air displays in summer.*
Tel- *01223 835000*

Saffron Walden 9m
Info- *A long but worthwhile detour to see the pretty town of Saffron Walden which has a good supply of restaurants and small shops. Nearby is Audley End House and an HDRA organic kitchen garden. Rejoin the motorway at Jn 8.*

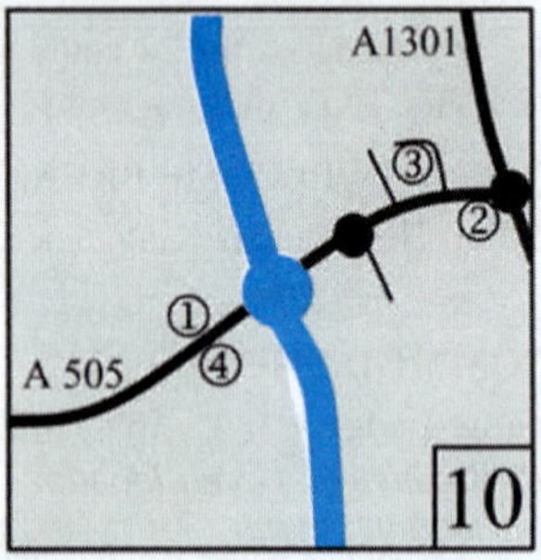

M11 Junction 11
Cambridge South

FUEL

Shell **SAVE** ££ 1.2m ①
Open- *Daily 0600-2400*
Info- *WC, cash machine.*
Tel- *01223 846990*

Esso **SAVE** ££ 1.5m ②
Open- *Daily 0630-2200*
Info- *WC*
Tel- *01223 872287*

FOOD

Waitrose Cafe £4.00 0.9m ③
Open- *M-Sa 0830-2030, Sun 1000-1530.*
Info- *Light meals & snacks.*
Tel- *01223 845777*

Good Luck Takeaway £5.00 1.2m ④
Open- *M-Sat 1200-1400, 1700-2200*
Info- *Chinese meals to take away.*
Tel- *01223 841353*

Old English Gentleman £5.00 1.2m ⑤
Open- *Daily 1730-2300*
Info- *Pub with Tandoori takeaway meals.*
Tel- *01223 870287*

The Green Man £6.00 2m ⑥
Open- *Daily 1200-1430, 1800-2100*
Info- *Varied pub menu. Cash machine inside pub.*
Tel- *01223 841178*

Other
Info- *There are three other pubs in Grantchester which serve food, and several other pubs which serve food, as you drive into Cambridge.*

ESSENTIALS

Addenbrookes Hospital 3m
Dir'n- *Follow signs into Cambridge and then signs to the hospital via the ring road.*
Tel- *01223 245151*

Gregory Pharmacy 0.9m ①
Open- *M/Th/F 0900-1730, Tu/W 0900-1330, Sat 0900-1300*
Tel- *01223 841109*

Cambridge Tourist Information Centre
Tel- *01223 322640*

Car Dealers
Info- *Volvo dealer en-route to the Esso filling station, and Saab dealer just beyond.*

THINGS TO DO

Grantchester River Walk 2m
Info- *Relaxing stroll by the River Cam.*
Dir'n- *Park near The Green Man.*

Cambridge City Centre 3m
Info- *This famous city has an attractive centre, and is well equipped with visitor facilities.*

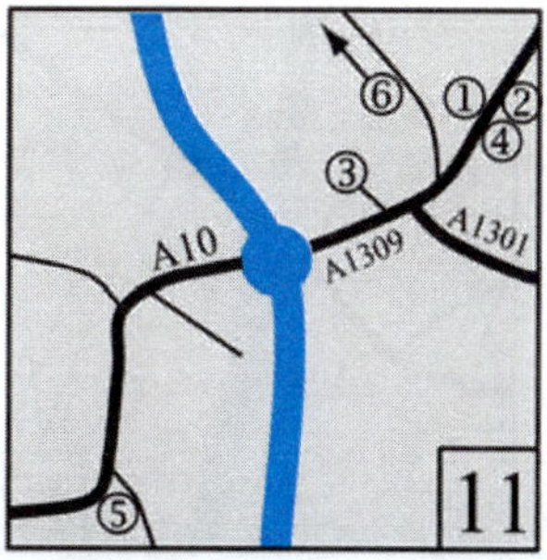

M11 Junction 12
Cambridge Southwest

FUEL

Q8 SAVE £ 1m ①
Open- *Daily 0700-2130*
Info- *Cash machine (Link only).*
Tel- *01223 263911*

FOOD

The White Horse £6.50 1m ②
Open- *Daily 1200-2200*
Info- *Varied hot & cold meals. Limited accommodation.*
Tel- *01223 262327*

The Green Man £6.00 1.4m ③
Open- *Daily 1200-1430, 1800-2100*
Info- *Varied pub menu. Cash machine inside pub.*
Dir'n- *Go right on entering Grantchester.*
Tel- *01223 841178*

ESSENTIALS

Addenbrookes Hospital 4.5m
Dir'n- *Follow signs into Cambridge and then signs to the hospital via the ring road.*
Tel- *01223 245151*

Cambridge Tourist Information Centre
Tel- *01223 322640*

THINGS TO DO

Grantchester River Walk 2m
Info- *Relaxing stroll by the River Cam.*
Dir'n- *Park near The Green Man.*

Cambridge City Centre 2.5m
Info- *This famous city has an attractive centre, and is well equipped with visitor facilities.*

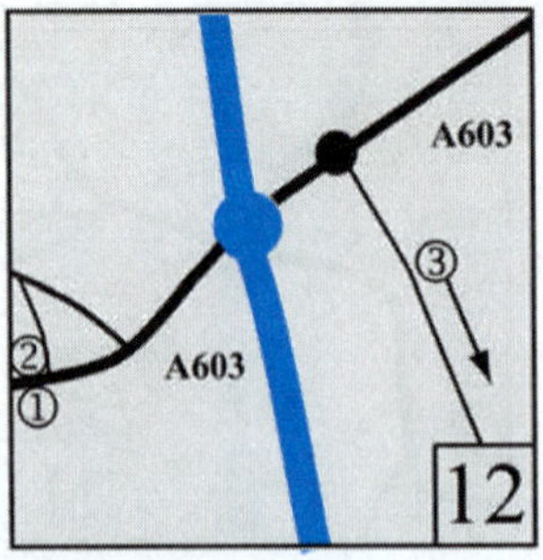

M11 Junction 13
Restricted

This is a restricted access junction, allowing access only to the M11 south.

M11 Junction 14
M11/A14 interchange

There are no facilities easily available at this junction.

ESSENTIALS

Cambridge Tourist Information Centre

Tel- *01223 322640*

THINGS TO DO

Cambridge City Centre 3m

Info- *This famous city has an attractive centre, and is well equipped with visitor facilities.*

M20-London to Folkestone

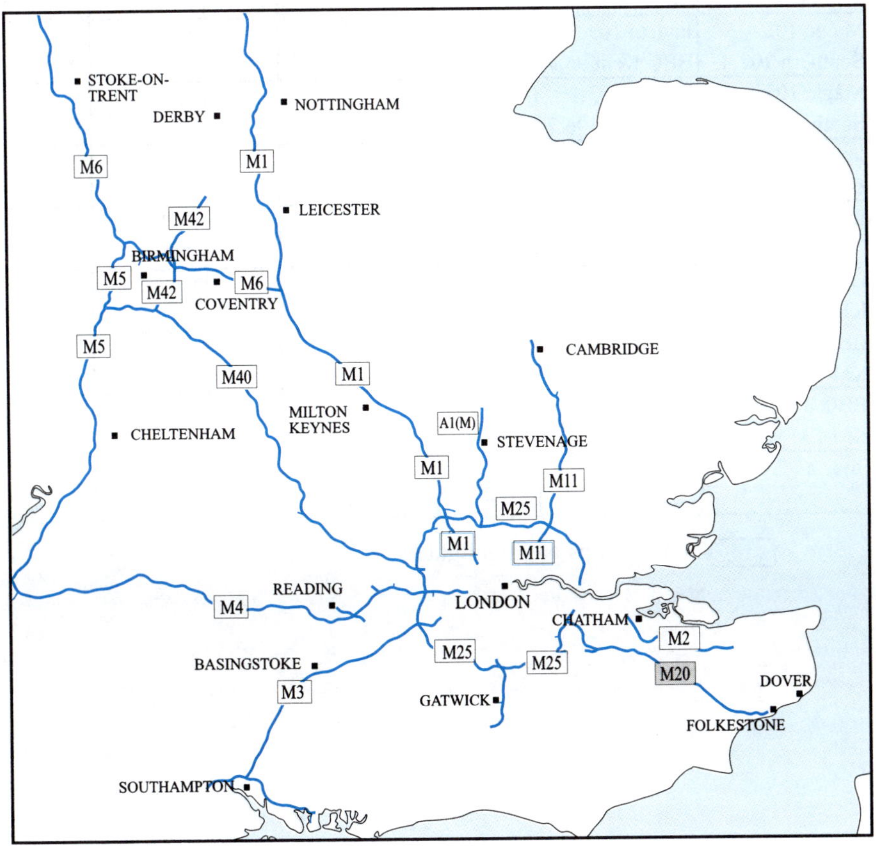

M20 Summary of Junctions

Radio stations & frequencies		Junction	Fuel	Food	Hotels	Essentials	Things to do
BBC Kent 96.7 Heart 106.2	Magic 105.4 Virgin 105.8	1	24hr	✓		A&E	
Invicta 103.1 BBC SCR 104.5	KM-FM 101.6 BBC Kent 96.7	2					
Invicta 103.1 BBC SCR 104.5	KM-FM 101.6 BBC Kent 96.7	3					
BBC Kent 96.7 Invicta 103.1	KM-FM 101.6	4	24hr	✓	✓	TIC Svc	✓
BBC Kent 96.7 Invicta 103.1	KM-FM 101.6 BBC LDN 94.9	5	24hr	✓	✓	A&E Svc	
BBC Kent 96.7 Invicta 103.1	BBC LDN 94.9 Magic 105.4	6	24hr	✓	✓	A&E TIC	✓
Magic 105.4 Southern 102.4	Invicta 103.1 BBC Kent 96.7	7		✓	✓	A&E	✓
Magic 105.4 Southern 102.4	Invicta 103.1 BBC Kent 96.7	8 S	24hr	✓	✓	TIC	✓
Invicta 96.1 BBC Kent 104.2	Southern 102.4 BBC SCR 104.	9	24hr	✓	✓	TIC	
Invicta 96.1	BBC Kent 96.7	10	24hr	✓	✓	A&E TIC	
BBC Kent 97.6 KM-FM 96.4	Kent 104.2 Invicta 97.0	11				TIC	
BBC Kent 97.6 KM-FM 96.4	Kent 104.2 Invicta 97.0	11A					
BBC Kent 97.6 KM-FM 96.4	Kent 104.2 Invicta 97.0	12	24hr	✓	✓	TIC	
Invicta 97.0	Kent 104.2	13	✓	✓	✓	TIC	

Top Stops are highlighted

M20 Junction Details

M20 Junction 1
M20/M25 interchange

FUEL

Jet SAVE ££ 0.7m ①
Open- *Daily 24 hours*
Info- *Carwash, jetwash.*
Tel- *01322 662955*

FOOD

The Olympic £4 0.7m ②
Open- *Daily 1200-1430, F/Sat 1800-2100*
Info- *Council managed bar with food.*
Tel- *01322 615126*

Others 1m
Info- *The town of Swanley is nearby and has a few restaurants and an Asda store in the centre (with cafe), but the relatively low number of facilities combined with parking difficulties do not make this a particularly good stop.*

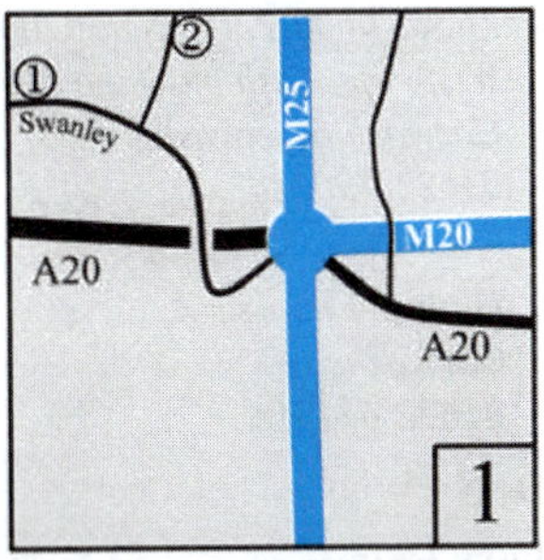

ESSENTIALS

Queen Mary's Hospital 5m
Dir'n- *From the junction take the A20 west towards London. After about 4 miles take the A222 towards Sidcup, and the hospital is signposted shortly afterwards.*
Tel - *0208 3022678*

M20 Junction 2
Restricted

This junction only allows access to the motorway heading westbound, and exit heading eastbound.

M20 Junction 3
M20/M26 interchange

This is a restricted junction. Exit is allowed eastbound, and entry westbound.

M20 Junction 4
Leybourne

FUEL

Shell SAVE £ 0.7m ①
Open- *Daily 24 hours*
Info- *WC, HGV fuelling.*
Tel- *01634 247920*

Total SAVE £ 1.7m ②
Open- *Daily 24 hours*
Info- *WC, LPG.*
Tel- *01732 840000*

FOOD

Brewsters☞ £6.50 0.3m ③
Open- *M-Sat 1100-2130, Sun 1200-2130*
Tel- *01732 521630 or 0870 197 7170*

Henry's Table ☞ £8.50 0.6m ④
Open- *M-Sat 1200-1430, 1800-2130, Sun 1200-2130*
Info- *Extensive hot & cold menu.*
Dir'n- *Next left after Brewsters.*
Tel- *01732 844888*

Pad Thai £9.00 1.6m ⑤
Open- *Tu-Sun 1200-1400, 1730-2300*
Info- *Restaurant with takeaway.*
Tel- *01732 870000*

Imperial Dynasty £9.5 1.6m ⑥
Open- *Daily 1200-1400, 1730-2300*
Info- *Chinese restaurant & takeaway.*
Tel- *01732 840402*

Gandhi Tandoori £8.50 1.6m ⑥
Open- *Daily 1800-2330*
Info- *Indian restaurant & takeaway.*
Tel- *01732 845600*

The Bakery Restaurant £6.00 1.6m ⑤
Open- *M-F 1030-1430, 1830-2230, Sat 1830-2200, Sun 1200-1500*
Info- *Restaurant with varied menu.*
Tel- *01732 845567*

The Assembly Rooms £9.50 1.6m ⑥
Open- *M-Sat 1800-2200, Sun 1900-2130*
Info- *Mexican & Cajun restaurant.*
Tel- *01732 845567*

Bombay Cuisine £9.50 1.8m ⑦
Open- *Daily 1800-2100*
Info- *Indian restaurant with takeaway.*
Tel- *01732 871256*

'Lovely' Takeaway £6.00 1.8m ⑧
Open- *Wed-Mon 1700-2300*
Info- *Chinese takeaway meals.*
Tel- *01732 873800*

Mackenzie's Cafe Bar £8.00 1.8m ⑦
Open- *M-Sat 1000-2230, Sun 1300-2100*
Info- *Extensive Italian menu.*
Tel- *01732 847100*

The Lobster Pot £10.00 1.8m ⑨
Open- *Tu-Sat 1200-1400, Sun 1200-1500, Tu-Th 1900-2100, F/Sat 1900-2130*
Info- *Pub-rest. Varied menu & real ales.*
Tel- *01732 843265*

Ragamuffins Cafe £4.00 1.8m ⑧
Open- *M 1000-1600, Tu-F 0800-1600, Sat 0900-1700*
Info- *Light meals, sandwiches & cakes.*
Tel- *01732 891870*

ACCOMMODATION

Travel Inn☞ £45 0.3m ③
Info- *Maidstone (Leybourne) location. Next to Brewsters.*
Tel- *0870 197 7170*

ESSENTIALS

Rochester Tourist Information Centre
Tel- *01634 843666*

Mid-Kent Citroen 1.7m ②
Open- *M-F 0900-1700, Sat 0900-1300*
Info- *Small garage. Citroen specialists.*
Dir'n- *Just behind Total garage.*
Tel- *01732 845264*

West Malling Garage 1.6m ⑥
Open- *M-F 0900-1700, Sat 0900-1300*
Info- *Small garage for repairs.*
Tel- *01732 874350*

THINGS TO DO

West Malling 1.6m
Info- *West Malling is a pretty village for a break from the motorway.*
Dir'n- *Signposted off the A228 south.*

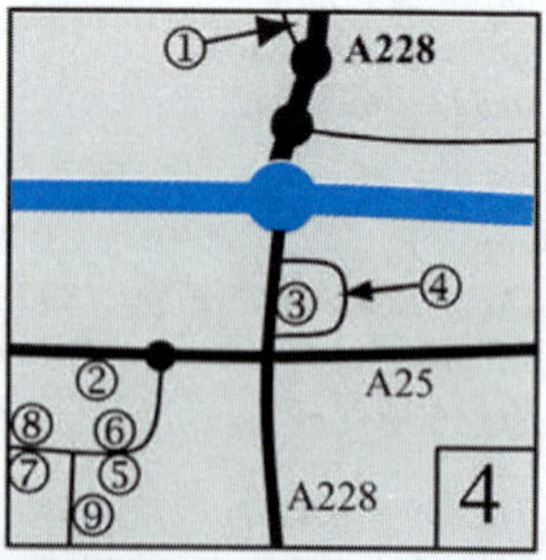

M20 Junction 5 Maidstone West

FUEL

Sainsbury SAVE £ 0.7m ①
Open- *M-Sat 0600-2200, Sun 0700-2130*
Info- *WC, cafe, cash machine at store. Carwash & jetwash.*
Tel- *01622 790224*

BP SAVE £ 1.0m ②
Open- *Daily 24 hours.*
Info- *Carwash.*
Tel- *01622 682416*

FOOD

Sainsbury Cafe☞ £3.50 0.7m ①
Open- *M/T/W/Sat 0800-1900, Th/Fr 0800-2000, Sun 0930-1530*
Tel- *01622 790223*

Beefeater☞ £7.00 0.8m ③
Open- *M-F 1200-1430, 1700-2200, Sat 1200-2230, Sun 1200-2100*
Tel- *0870 197 7168*

ACCOMMODATION

Travel Inn☞ £45 0.8m ③
Info- *Maidstone (Allington) location. Next to the Beefeater.*
Tel- *0870 197 7168*

Conway House £50 1.2m ④
Info- *Small B&B. AA/ETC 4◆. Price is for B&B.*
Dir'n- *Turn right after the BP garage.*
Tel- *01622 688287*

ESSENTIALS

Maidstone Hospital 2.5m
Dir'n- *Signposted on the A20 west.*
Tel- *01622 729000*

Car Dealers 0.7m ⑤
Info- *BMW, Nissan, VW & Audi dealers near to Sainsbury store.*

Halfords/AA Workshop 0.7m ⑥
Open- *M-F 0800-1800, Sat 0900-1800, Sun 1000-1500*
Info- *Car parts & service/repair.*
Tel- *01622 715333 (Halfords)*
01622 715321 (AA workshop)

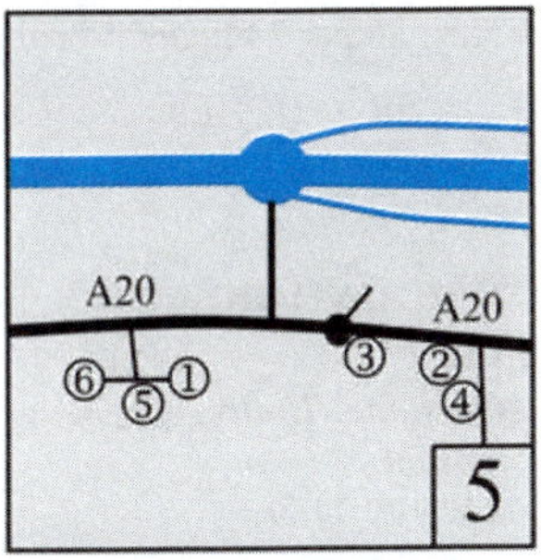

M20 Junction 6
Maidstone

FUEL

Shell SAVE £ 1.2m ①
Open- *Daily 24 hours*
Info- *WC*
Tel- *01634 661900*

FOOD

Harvester☞ £7.00 0.4m ②
Open- *Daily 1200-2200*
Tel- *01622 752975*

Beefeater☞ £7.00 0.5m ③
Open- *Daily 1200-2130*
Tel- *01622 717251*

Lower Bell £6.00 0.6m ④
Open- *Daily 1200-1430,1800-2130*
Info- *Varied menu, Good Beer Guide, real ales.*
Tel- *01634 861127*

Kit's Brasserie £13.5 0.8m ⑤
Open- *M-Fri 1200-1400, 1900-2130, Sat 1900-220, Sun 1200-1430*
Info- *Refined dining. No children.*
Dir'n- *Take the first slip road off the A229, then bear right at the junction.*
Tel- *01634 684445*

ACCOMMODATION

Travel Inn☞ £45 0.5m ③
Info- *Maidstone (Sandling) location. Next to the Beefeater.*
Tel- *0870 197 7308*

ESSENTIALS

Maidstone Hospital 4.5m
Dir'n- *Take the A429 to Maidstone, then the A26 west, where the hospital is signposted.*
Tel- *01622 729000*

Maidstone Tourist Information Centre
Tel- *01622 602169*

THINGS TO DO

Museum of Kent Life £5.50 0.5m ③
Open- *March-Oct Daily 1000-1730. Winter Sat/Sun 1000-1500*
Dir'n- *Well signposted. Near to Travel Inn.*
Tel- *01622 763936*

River Walk & Boat Trips. 0.5m ③
Info- *Pleasant river walk near the museum. Boat trips Easter-Oct.*
Tel- *01622 753740*

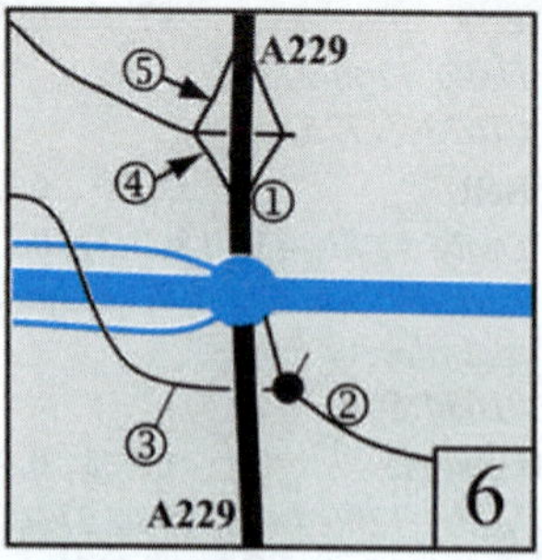

M20 Junction 7
Maidstone East

FOOD

Noble House Rest. £8.00 0.4m ①
Open- *Daily 1200-1400, 1700-2230*
Info- *Chinese restaurant & takeaway.*
Tel- *01622 631268*

Newnham Court Inn £8.00 0.4m ①
Open- *M-Th 1200-1430, 1800-2100, Fr 1200-2130, Sat-Sun 1200-2130*
Info- *Extensive menu. A 'Henry's Table' pub/restaurant☞.*
Tel- *01622 734211*

Seasons Restaurant £12 1.0m ②
Open- *M-Sat 0700-1000, 1230-1400, 1900-2130, Sun 0730-1030, 1230-1430, 1900-2130*
Info- *Refined dining at the Hilton Hotel.*
Tel- *01622 734600*

Chiltern Hundreds £7.50 0.8m ③
Open- *M-Sat 1100-2130, Sun 1200-2100*
Info- *Extensive hot & cold menu. A Chef & Brewer family pub/rest☞.*
Tel- *01622 752335*

ACCOMMODATION

Hilton Hotel☞ £110 1.0m ②
Info- *Restaurant, bar, health club & pool. Maidstone location. Dogs welcome.*
Tel- *01622 734322*

ESSENTIALS

Maidstone Hospital 4.5m
Dir'n- *Take the A429 to Maidstone, then the A26 west. The hospital is signposted from here.*
Tel- *01622 729000*

THINGS TO DO

Maidstone
Info- *The town centre is about 2 miles away and offers many facilities.*

Shopping Mall ①
Info- *Newnham Court shopping mall. About 10 shops & a vet.*

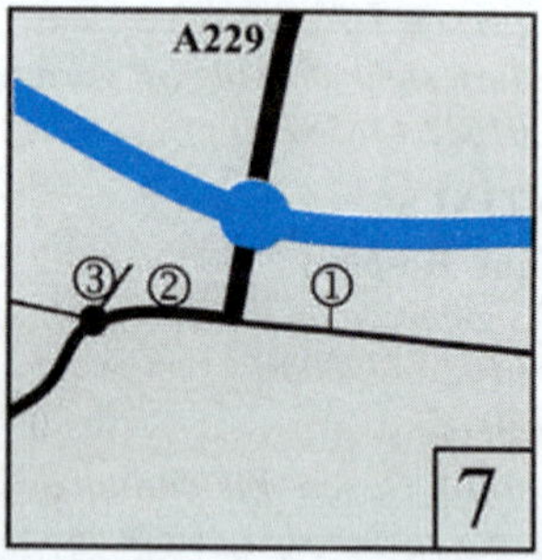

Junction 8 Services

This services is located just off the motorway junction.

FUEL ESSO

HGV fuelling, car wash. Free parking for 2 hours then £6 per 24 hours. Lorry park.

FOOD ROADCHEF

onroute, Wimpy, Costa Coffee
Info- *Cash machine.*

ACCOMMODATION

Travel Inn☞ £45
Info- *Maidstone (Hollingbourne) location.*
Tel- *0870 197 7169*

ESSENTIALS

Tourist Information Centre
Tel- *01622 602048*

M20 Junction 8
Leeds Castle

FOOD

Rick's Bar & Grill £10 0.4m ①
Open- *Daily 0700-0930, 1230-1400, Sun-Th 1900-2200, Fr/Sa 1830-2200*
Info- *Refined dining at the Ramada Hotel*
Tel- *01622 631163*

Park Gate Inn £8.00 0.8m ②

Open- *Daily 1200-2100*
Info- *Extensive menu. Real ales. Six Continents Group.*
Tel- *01622 880985*

The Windmill £8.00 0.9m ③

Open- *M-F 1200-1500, 1800-2200, Sat 1200-2200*
Info- *Extensive menu in village pub. Real ales.*
Tel- *01622 880280*

The Sugar Loaves £6.00 1.0m ④

Open- *M-Sat 1200-2200, Sun 1200-2130*
Info- *Varied menu in village pub. Real ales.*
Tel- *01622 880220*

ACCOMMODATION

Ramada Hotel☞ £120 0.5m ①

Info- *Maidstone location. Restaurant, bar, health club & pool.*
Tel- *01622 631163*

THINGS TO DO

Leeds Castle £11 2.2m

Info- *Historic castle & grounds.*
Dir'n. *Well signposted on A20 east.*
Tel- *01622 765400*

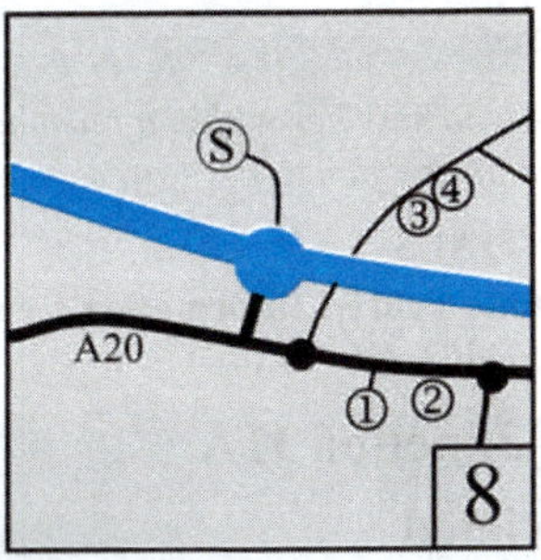

M20 Junction 9 Ashford

FUEL

Sainsbury SAVE £ 0.4m ①

Open- *Daily 24 hours*
Info- *WC, cafe at store.*
Tel- *01233 610841*

FOOD

Sainsbury Cafe☞ £3.50 0.4m ①

Open- *Sat-W 0700-1900, Th/F 0700-2100, Sun 0900-1530*
Tel- *01233 610841*

Pizza Hut☞ £6.00 0.4m ②

Open- *Sun-Fr 1200-2300, Sat 1200-2330*
Tel- *01233 650650*

KFC☞ £4.00 0.4m ②

Open- *Sun-Th 1130-2400, F-Sat 1130-0300*
Tel- *01233 663138*

Little Chef☞ £4.00 0.4m ②

Open- *Daily 0700-2200*
Tel- *01233 661936*

Burger King☞ £4.00 0.4m ②

Open- *Daily 0700-2200*
Tel- *01233 663942*

Frankie & Benny's☞ £8.50 0.4m ②

Open- *Daily 0700-2200*
Tel- *01233 662814*

ACCOMMODATION

Ashford Int. Hotel £110 0.3m ③

Info- *On-site bar, restaurant, pool & health club. AA/ETC 4★.*
Tel- *01233 219988*

Travelodge☞ £60 0.4m ②

Info- *Maidstone location. Close to cinema & food outlets.*
Tel- *01870 1911504*

ESSENTIALS

Ashford Tourist Information Centre

Tel- *01233 629165*

Halfords ①

Info- *Parts for your vehicle.*
Tel- *01233 664513*

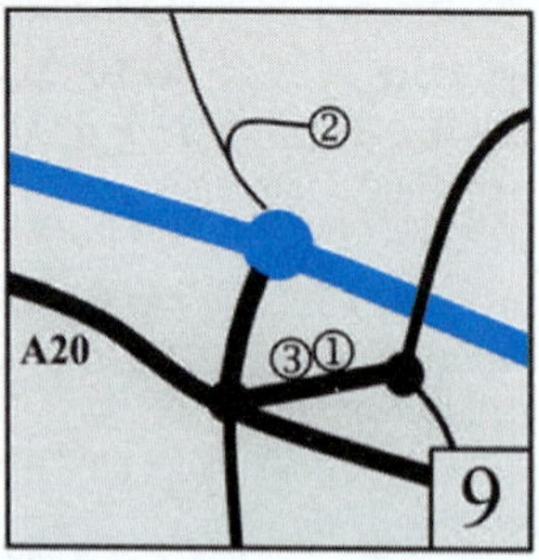

M20 Junction 10
Ashford East

FUEL

Tesco SAVE £ 0.2m ①
Open- *Daily 24 hours*
Info- *WC & cafe at store.*
Tel- *01233 207 445*

Esso SAVE £ 0.5m ②
Open- *Daily 24 hours*
Info- *Close to several cheap takeaways.*
Tel- *01233 623946*

FOOD

Tesco Cafe☞ £3.50 0.2m ①
Open- *Mon 0800-1800, Tu-Sat 0700-1800, Sun 1000-1600*
Info- *Filling station adjacent.*
Tel- *0845 677 9008*

Blacksmith's Arms £7.00 0.3m ③
Open- *M-Sat 1200-1400, 1800-2130, Sun 1200-1800*
Info- *Extensive menu & real ales.*
Tel- *01233 623975*

The White Horse £7.00 0.3m ④
Open- *Daily 1100-2100*
Info- *Varied menu & real ales.*
Tel- *01233 624257*

Lee's Takeaway £5.00 0.5m ⑤
Open- *Sun-Th 1630-2200, Fr-Sat 1200-1430, 1630-2200*
Info- *Chinese food to take away.*
Tel- *01622 646198*

Willesboro' Tandoori £5.00 0.5m ⑤
Open- *Daily 1700-2200*
Info- *Indian meals to take away.*
Tel- *01622 638333*

Tim's Fish Bar £4.00 0.5m ⑤
Open- *M-Sat 1700-2200, F/Sat 1200-1330*
Info- *Fish meals to take away.*

ACCOMMODATION

Warren Cottage Hotel £80 0.4m ⑥
Info- *Bar, restaurant. Small private hotel.*
Tel- *01233 621905*

ESSENTIALS

William Harvey Hospital 0.3m ⑦
Dir'n- *Signposted from the exit.*
Tel- *01233 633331*

Folkestone Tourist Information Centre
Tel- *01303 258594*

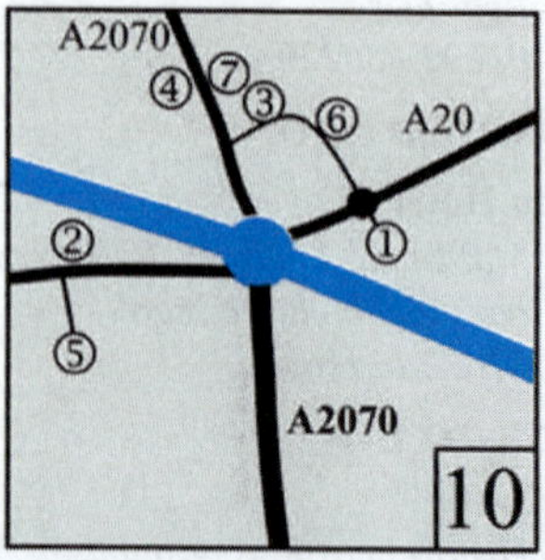

M20 Junction 11
Hythe

There are no services within a reasonable distance of this junction.

ESSENTIALS

Folkestone Tourist Information Centre
Tel- *01303 258594*

M20 Junction 11A
Restricted

Channel Tunnel passengers only.

M20 Junction 12
Folkestone

FUEL

Tesco SAVE £ 0.3m ①
Open- *Daily 24 hours*
Info- *WC, cash machine, cafe at store.*
Tel- *01303 719445*

BP SAVE £ 0.3m ②

Open- *Daily 24 hours*
Info- *WC, carwash, cash machine.*
Tel- *01303 276006*

FOOD

White Lion Hotel £6.50 0.7m ③

Open- *M-Sat 0700-0900, 1200-2300, Sun 1200-2200. B&B available.*
Info- *Pub-restaurant. Varied menu & real ales.*
Tel- *01303 270007*

ACCOMMODATION

White Lion Hotel £90 0.7m ③

Info- *Pub-restaurant offering B&B.*
Tel- *01303 270007*

ESSENTIALS

Folkestone Tourist Information Centre

Tel- *01303 258594*

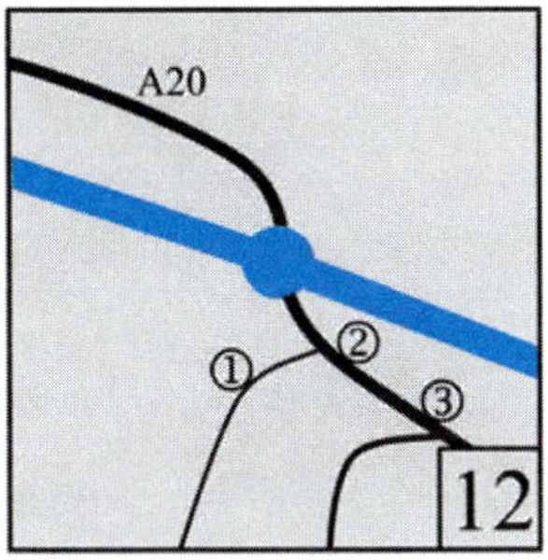

M20 Junction 13
End of Motorway

FUEL

Sainsbury SAVE £ 0.8m ①

Open- *Daily 0600-2400*
Info- *WC, cash machine & cafe at store.*
Tel- *01303 850810*

FOOD

Brewsters☞ £6.50 0.2m ②

Open- *M-Sat 1130-2200, Su 1200-2200*
Tel- *01303 273619*

Burger King☞ £4.00 0.2m ②

Open- *Daily 1100-2200*
Tel- *01303 274275*

ACCOMMODATION

Travel Inn☞ £45 0.2m ②

Info- *Folkestone location.*
Tel- *0870 197 7103*

ESSENTIALS

Folkestone Tourist Information Centre

Tel- *01303 258594*

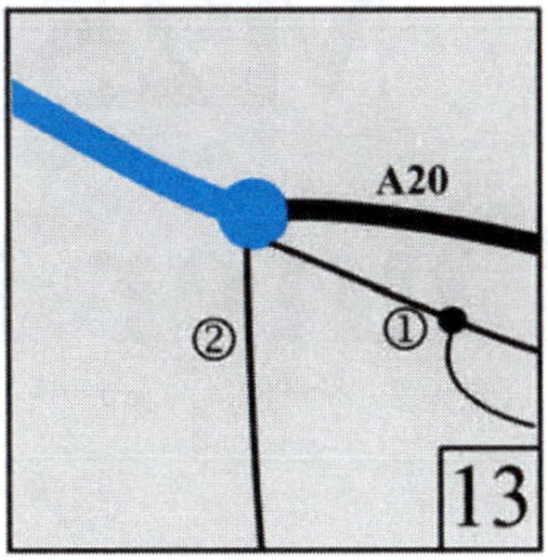

M25-London Outer Ring Road

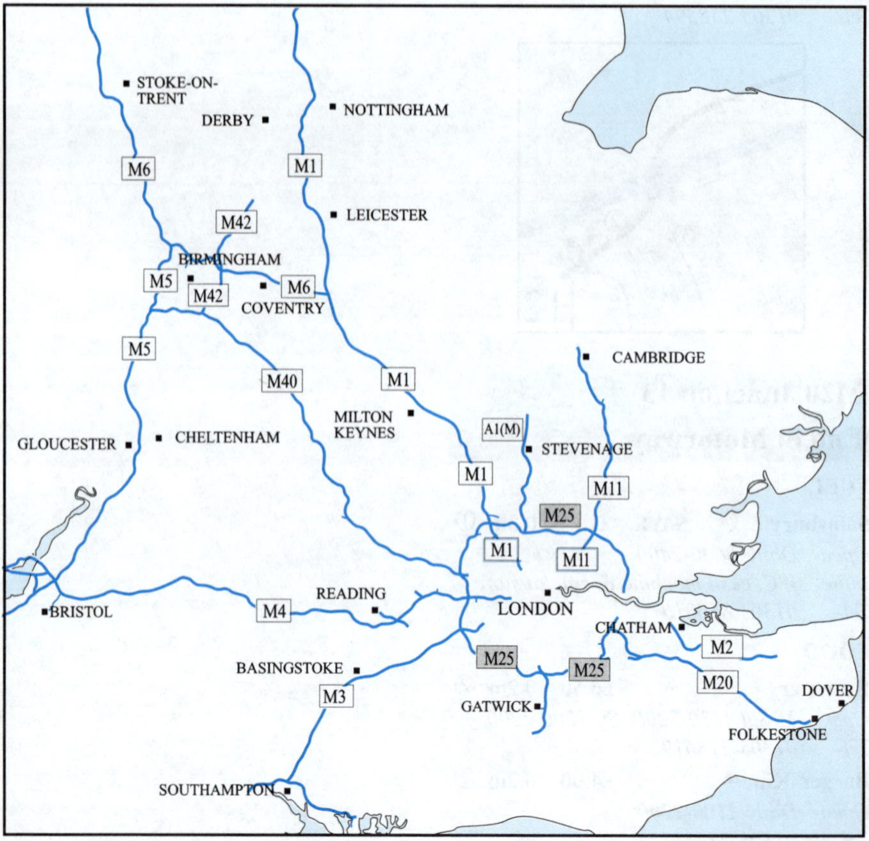

M25 Summary of Junctions

Radio stations & frequencies		Junction	Fuel	Food	Hotels	Essentials	Things to Do
Heart 106.2 Capital 95.8	Essex 102.6 BBC LDN 94.9	1			✓		✓
Heart 106.2 Capital 95.8	Essex 102.6 BBC LDN 94.9	1B	24hr	✓		A&E TIC	
Heart 106.2 Capital 95.8	Essex 102.6 BBC LDN 94.9	2	24hr	✓		A&E TIC	
BBC Kent 96.7 Heart 106.2	Magic 105.4 LBC 97.3	3	24hr	✓		A&E TIC	
BBC Kent 96.7 Heart 106.2	Magic 105.4 Virgin 105.8	4				A&E	
Capital 95.8 KISS 100	LDN 94.9 BBC Kent 96.7	5				TIC	
Capital 95.8 KISS 100	LDN 94.9 BBC Kent 96.7	S	24hr	✓	✓	TIC	
Capital 95.8 BBC SCR 104.5	Mercury 102.7 BBC Kent 96.7	6	24hr	✓	✓		✓
Mercury 102.7 Heart 106.2	BBC SCR 104	7				A&E	
Mercury 102.7 Heart 106.2	BBC SCR 104	8	24hr	✓	✓	A&E	
Heart 106.2 BBC LDN 94.9	Jazz FM 102.2 KISS 100	9	24hr	✓	✓	A&E Svc	✓
Capital 95.8 LBC 97.3	Jazz FM 102.2 BBC LDN 94.9	10					✓
Capital 95.8 LBC 97.3	Jazz FM 102.2 KISS 100	11	✓	✓		A&E	
Heart 106.2 964 Eagle 96.4	Star 106.6 Capital 95.8	12					
Virgin 105.8 LBC 97.3	Magic 105.4 BBC LDN 94.9	13	24hr	✓	✓	A&E Svc	✓
Virgin 105.8 LBC 97.3	Magic 105.4 BBC LDN 94.9	14		✓		A&E	
Virgin 105.8 Freeze 92.7	Heart 106.2 Capital 95.8	15				A&E	
Virgin 105.8 Freeze 92.7	Heart 106.2 Capital 95.8	16				A&E TIC	

Top Stops are highlighted

Radio stations & frequencies		Junction	Fuel	Food	Hotels	Essentials	Things to do
Virgin 105.8 Freeze 92.7	Heart 106.2 LDN 94.9	17		✓			
Mercury 96.6 Capital 95.8	Chiltern 97.6 LDN 94.9	18	24hr	✓		A&E	✓
Mercury 96.6 Capital 95.8	Chiltern 97.6 LDN 94.9	19	24hr	✓	✓	A&E	
Mercury 96.6 Capital 95.8	Chiltern 97.6 BBC LDN 94.9	20	24hr	✓	✓	A&E TIC Pharmacy	
Mercury 96.6 Capital 95.8	KISS 100.0 LDN 94.9	21				A&E TIC	
BBC 3CR 94.9 London 94.9	KISS 100.0 Mercury 96.6	21a	24hr	✓	✓	A&E TIC Pharmacy	✓
BBC 3CR 94.9 London 94.9	Chiltern 97.6 Mercury 96.6	22	24hr	✓	✓	TIC	✓
Virgin 105.8 Jazz FM 012.2	BBC 3CR 94.9 LGR 103.3	23 S	24hr	✓	✓	Svc A&E	
Heart 106.2 Kiss 100	Capital 85.8 Jazz FM 102.2	24	24hr	✓		A&E Svc Pharmacy	✓
Heart 106.2 Virgin 105.8	KISS 100 Choice-N 107.1	25	24hr	✓		A&E TIC Svc	✓
Heart 106.2 Capital 95.8	KISS 100 Jazz FM 102.2	26	24hr	✓	✓	TIC	✓
Heart 106.2 Soulcity 107.5	Virgin 105.8 KM FM 107.9	27					
Virgin 105.8 Essex 102.6	Magic 105.4 Heart 106.2	28	24hr	✓	✓	A&E TIC Svc	
KISS 100 Essex FM 96.3	Heart 106.2 LBC 97.3	29			✓	A&E Svc	
KISS 100 Essex FM 96.3	Heart 106.2 LBC 97.3	30 S	24hr	✓	✓	TIC	✓
KISS 100 Essex FM 96.3	Heart 106.2 Capital 95.8	31	24hr	✓	✓		✓

M25 Junction Details

M25 Junction 1
Bluewater

ACCOMMODATION

Hilton☞ £99 0.5m ①
Info- *On-site restaurant & bar.*
Dartford Crossing location.
Tel- *01322 288225*

Campanile☞ £ 47 0.7m ②
Info- *On-site restaurant & bar.*
Dartford Bridge location.
Dir'n- *Follow signs to Ferry Terminal.*
Tel- *01322 278925*

Holiday Inn☞ £68 0.7m ③
Info- *Bar & supper menu available.*
Cont. breakfast inclusive.
Dartford Bridge location.
Dir'n- *Follow signs to Crayford/A206, and watch for hotel sign on left.*
Tel- *01322 290333*

Travelodge☞ £ 59 1.8m ④
Info- *Burger King adjacent.*
Dartford location.
Tel- *0870 191 1525*

THINGS TO DO

Greenhithe 2m ⑤
Info- *For a good view of the river and bridge drive to Greenhithe.*
Dir'n- *After the tolls follow the signs to Swanscombe/A206, and then signs to Bluewater. Just after the Asda store turn left and the village of Greenhithe is soon after. Parking is available at the far end of the village, or the Asda car park.*

Bluewater Retail Park 2.4m ⑤
Open- *M-F 1000-2100, Sat 0900-2000, Sun 1100-1700*
Info- *Large shopping complex with a wide range of food outlets.*
Dir'n- *Take the A206 east towards Greenhithe and then follow the signs to Bluewater.*
Tel- *01322 623300*

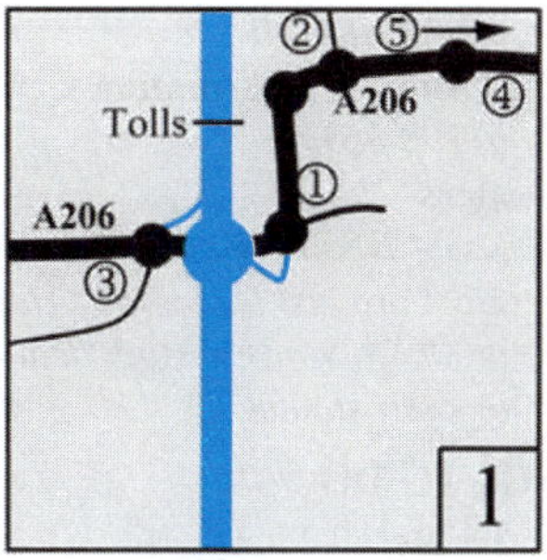

M25 Junction 1B
Dartford

This is linked to Junction 2 by a road that runs parallel to the M25. See the map for Junction 2.

ESSENTIALS

Darent Valley Hospital 3.3m
Dir'n- *Take the A296 east and turn right at the first roundabout where the hospital is signposted.*
Tel- *01322 428100*

Dartford Tourist Information Centre
Tel- *01708 863733*

M25 Junction 2
Dartford

FUEL

Esso SAVE ££ 0.2m ①
Open- *Daily 24 hours*
Info- *HGV fuelling.*
Tel- *01322 220250*

BP SAVE £££ 0.3m ②
Open- *Daily 24 hours*
Info- *Carwash, cash machine.*
Tel- *01322 290379*

FOOD

Harvester☞ £ 7.00 0.2m ③
Open- *Daily 1200-2130*
Tel- *01322 287766*

ESSENTIALS

Darent Valley Hospital 3.8m

Dir'n- *This is well signposted from the motorway exit.*

Tel- *01322 428100*

Dartford Tourist Information Centre

Tel- *01708 863733*

Car Dealers

Info- *Saab, Nissan, Vauxhall, Audi.*

Dir'n- *Most are just beyond the Harvester on the A296 west. Audi dealer next to Esso station.*

THINGS TO DO

Bluewater Retail Park 2.4m

Open- *M-F 1000-2100, Sat 0900-2000, Sun 1100-1700*

Info- *Large shopping complex with a wide range of food outlets.*

Dir'n- *Take the A2 east towards Rochester and Bluewater is signposted.*

Tel- *01322 623300*

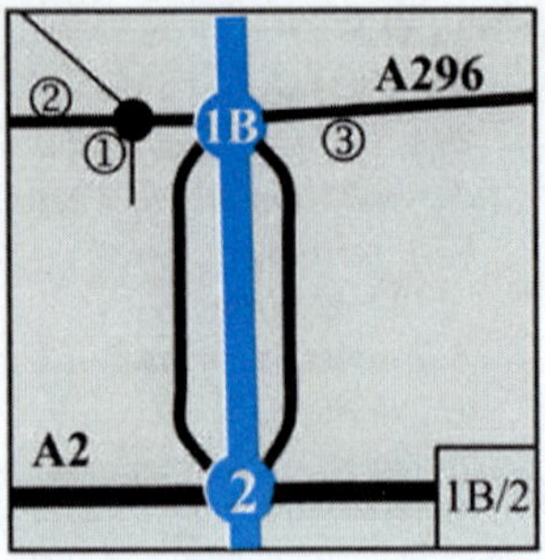

M25 Junction 3
M25/M20 interchange

When travelling southbound be careful not to take the M20 sliproad which is just before the main Junction 3 turnoff.

FUEL

Jet SAVE ££ 0.7m ①

Open- *Daily 24 hours*

Info- *Carwash, jetwash.*

Tel- *01322 662955*

FOOD

The Olympic £4 0.7m ②

Open- *Daily 1200-1430, F/Sat 1800-2100*

Info- *Council managed bar with food.*

Tel- *01322 615126*

Other 1m

Info- *The town of Swanley is nearby and has a few restaurants and an Asda store in the centre (with cafe), but the relatively low number of facilities, combined with parking difficulties, do not make this a particularly good stop.*

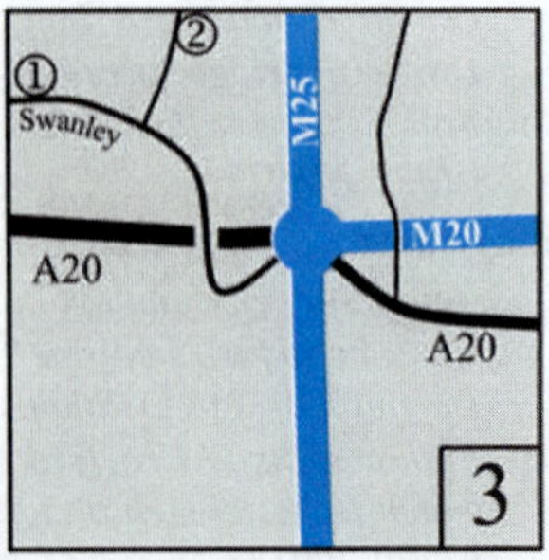

ESSENTIALS

Queen Mary Hospital 5m

Dir'n- *From the junction take the A20 west towards London. After about 4.5 miles take the A222 towards Sidcup, and the hospital is signposted shortly afterwards.*

Tel - *0208 302 2678*

Swanley Tourist Information Centre

Tel- *01322 614660*

M25 Junction 4
Orpington

There are no facilities within a reasonable distance of this junction.

ESSENTIALS

Farnborough Hospital 5m

Dir'n- *Take the A21 west and the hospital is on the right.*

Tel - *01689 863000*

M25 Junction 5
M25/M26 interchange

This junction only allows exit to the A21, and it is difficult to reach the return carriageway.

ESSENTIALS

Sevenoaks Tourist Information Centre
Tel- 01732 450305

Clackett Lane Services

There is a roadbridge to the hotel.

FUEL **Total**

HGV fuelling. Free parking for 2 hours then £6 per day. Lorry park.

FOOD WELCOME BREAK

onroute, Wimpy, Costa Coffee, Coffee Primo
Info- Cash machine.

ACCOMMODATION

Travel Inn☞ £50
Info- Westerham location.
Tel - 0870 197 7265

ESSENTIALS

Clackett Lane Tourist Information
Tel - 01959 565063

M25 Junction 6
Godstone

FUEL

Shell SAVE ££ 0.4m ①
Open- Daily 24 hours
Info- WC, cash machine.
Tel- 01883 741700

FOOD

The Old Forge Cafe £4.00 0.8m ②
Open- M-Sat 0730-1500
Info- Hot & cold snacks, dine in & take away.
Tel- 01883 743230

Beefeater☞ £7.00 0.8m ③
Open- M-Sat 1200-1430, 1700-2230, Sun 1200-2100
Info- 'The White Hart'
Tel- 01883 742521

The Hare & Hounds £7.00 0.9m ②
Open- M-Th 1200-1500, 1900-2130, F-Sun 1200-2030
Info- Village pub with extensive menu.
Dir'n- In the centre of Godstone follow the one way system to the right, past the village green, to return to the motorway. The Hare and Hounds is just past the village green.
Tel- 01883 742296

ACCOMMODATION

The Godstone Hotel £65 0.9m ④
Info- Restaurant. Independent hotel.
Dir'n- Opposite The Bell pub.
Tel- 01883 742461

THINGS TO DO

Godstone
Info- This is a quiet village with a green and pond, and is worth considering for a short break from the motorway.

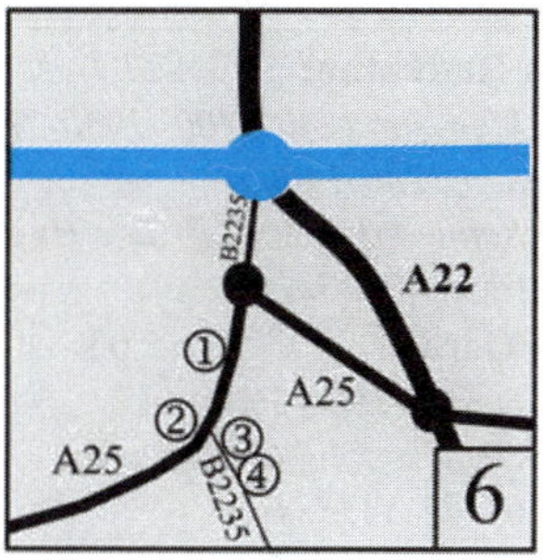

M25 Junction 7
M25/M23 interchange

ESSENTIALS

East Surrey Hospital, Redhill 6m
Dir'n- From the junction head north on the M23, then take a southward direction to the A23/Redhill. Continue past Redhill and the hospital is signposted on the left.
Tel- 01737 768511

M25 Junction 8
Reigate

FUEL

Esso SAVE ££ 0.9m ①
Open- Daily 24 hours
Info- WC, cash machine.
Tel- 01737 221150

Total SAVE ££ 0.9m ②
Open- M-F 0700-2200, Sat/Sun 0700-2100
Info- WC, carwash.
Tel- 01737 831952

BP SAVE £ 1.0m ③
Open- Daily 24 hours
Info- LPG, WC, carwash.
Dir'n- Return journey is 2 miles.
Tel- 01737 832048

Texaco SAVE ££ 2.0m ④
Open- Daily 24 hours
Info- LPG, WC, carwash, cash machine.
Dir'n- Return journey is 1 mile.
Tel- 01737 831800

FOOD

Lanni's Restaurant £27 0.4m ⑤
Open- Mon-Sat 1230-1400, 1930-2100, Sun 1230-1400
Info- Refined dining at Bridge Hs Hotel.
Tel- 01737 244821

Chau's Garden £5.00 1.1m ③
Open- Daily 1700-2300
Info- Chinese food to take away.
Tel- 01737 833374

ACCOMMODATION

Bridge House Hotel £115 0.4m ⑤
Info- Restaurant. Price is B&B.
Tel- 01737 244821

Reigate Manor Hotel £125 0.9m ⑥
Info- Restaurant. AA 3◆. Best Western☛
Tel- 01737 240125

ESSENTIALS

East Surrey Hospital, Redhill 5m
Dir'n- From the junction take the A217 south, and then take the A25 east towards Redhill. On reaching the A23, turn right along this road and the hospital will be signposted to the left.
Tel- 01737 768511

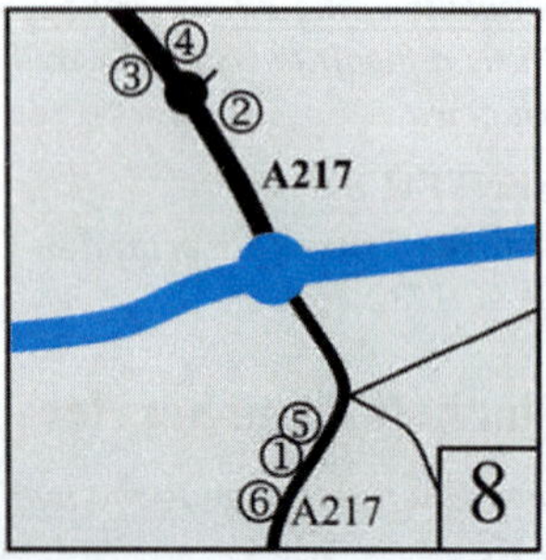

M25 Junction 9
Leatherhead

Junction 9 is really two restricted exits situated very close to each other. The easiest way to find most of the facilities marked is by following signs to the Industrial Area in Leatherhead.

FUEL

Tesco SAVE ££ 0.3m ①
Open- Daily 0600-2400
Info- WC at store.
Dir'n- At westbound exit take Cobham A215 Industrial Parks turn off the first round about, and then turn right at the next roundabout.
Tel- 01372 859400

Esso SAVE £ 0.6m ②
Open- Daily 24 hours
Info- WC
Tel- 01372 361562

Shell SAVE £ 0.8m ③
Open- Daily 0700-2300
Info- WC, carwash.
Tel- 01372 225110

FOOD

The Plough £5.50 0.4m ④
Open- M-Sat 1100-2300, Sun 1200-2230
Info- Pub offering Thai meals.
Tel- 01372 377608

Papa John's Pizza £5.0 0.5m ⑤
Open- Daily 1130-2300

Info- *Takeaway pizza chain.*
Dir'n- *At westbound exit take Cobham A215 Industrial Parks turn off the first roundabout, and then go straight across the next roundabout.*
Tel- *01372 370370*

BB's Sandwich Shop £5.00 0.5m ⑤
Open- *M-F 0800-1400*
Info- *Hot & cold meals, eat in & take away.*
Tel- *01372 360511*

Caesar's Restaurant £7 1.4m
Open- *Daily 1130-2230*
Info- *American restaurant.*
Dir'n- *Follow the signs to the town centre. Caesar's is located in Church St.*
Tel- *01372 379915*

Others 1.4m
Info- *The centre of Leatherhead has a fair range of shops and 3-4 other restaurants all within an easy walk of the car parks.*

ACCOMMODATION

Swan Guest House £48 0.7m ②
Info- *Private guest house. Price is B&B.*
Tel- *01372 376332*

ESSENTIALS

Epsom Hospital 5m
Dir'n- *From the junction follow signs to the A24/Epsom, where you will find the hospital off the A24 to the right.*
Tel- *01372 735735*

ATS 0.4m ④
Open- *M-F 0830-1730, Sat 0830-1600*
Info- *Tyre & exhaust centre.*
Tel- *01372 372003*

Car dealers ⑥
Info- *Honda and Volvo dealers.*

THINGS TO DO

World of Adventure £23 3m
Open- *Most days 1100-1700 or 1000-1930 depending on time of year.*
Info- *Well known theme park.*
Dir'n- *Follow the A243 towards London, and park is signposted on the left.*
Tel- *0870 444 7777*

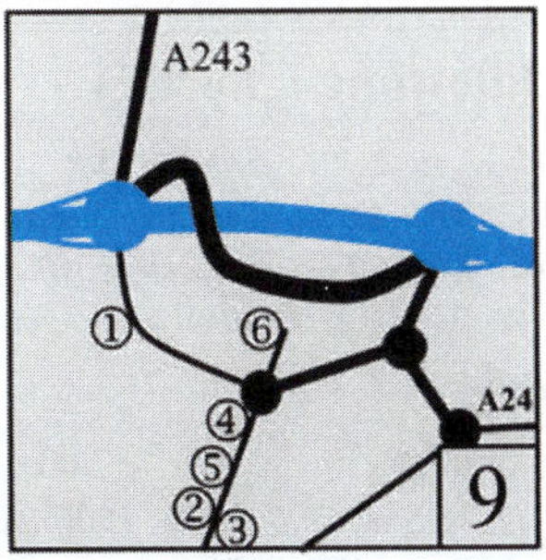

M25 Junction 10
Cobham/A3

This junction links to the A3, but there are no services nearby, and the dual carriageway prevents an easy return to the motorway.

THINGS TO DO

Ockham Common
Info- *Extensive woods & lakes.*
Dir'n- *Follow signs to the Semaphore Tower to find a car park.*

Semaphore Tower £2.00 0.7m
Open- *Weekends 23rd March-6th October between 1200-1700.*
Info- *Great views and an exhibition at this old signalling station. The tower is a walk of about 1000m from the car park.*
Dir'n- *Just follow the signs from the A3 as you head towards Wisley gdns.*
Tel - *01732 458822*

RHS Wisley Garden £6.00 2m
Open- *M-F 1000-1630, Sat-Sun 0900-1800. Reduced opening Nov- Feb. RHS members only on Sundays.*
Info- *Royal Horticultral Society specimen garden. Flowers, fruits, vegetables and cultivar trial beds.*
Dir'n- *Follow the A3 south/Guildford direction, and then return to the motorway at the first roundabout. Wisley is on the left as you return, and is well signposted.*
Tel- *01483 224234*

M25 Junction 11
Addlestone-Chertsey

Total SAVE ££ 1.1m ①
Open- *M-F 0630-2300, Sa-Sun 0700-2300*
Info- *LPG, WC, carwash, cash machine.*
Tel- *01932 839960*

FOOD

The George £7.00 1.1m ②
Open- *M-Sat 1200-1400, 1900-2130, Sun 1200-1430*
Info- *Extensive hot & cold menu.*
Tel- *01932 820784*

ESSENTIALS

St Peter's Hospital 1.5m ③
Dir'n- *Follow signs towards Woking on the A320 West, and the hospital is signposted right at the first roundabout after leaving the motorway junction.*
Tel- *01932 872000*

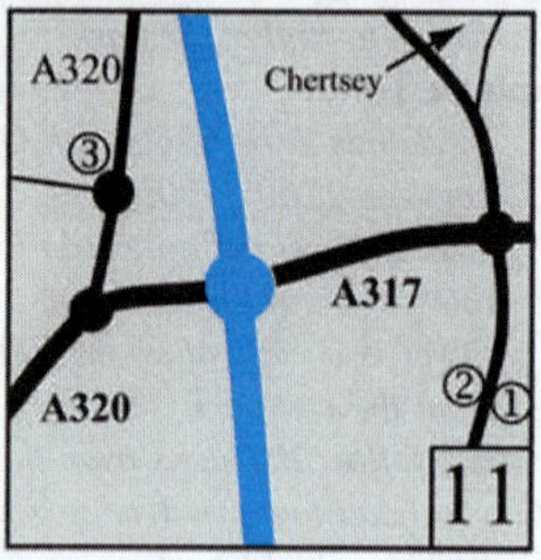

M25 Junction 12
M25/M3 interchange

There is no access to local services at this junction.

M25 Junction 13
Staines

This junction is made up from two exits which combine to give full motorway access.

FUEL

Total SAVE £ 1.0m ①
Open- *Daily 0700-2300*
Info- *WC, jetwash.*
Tel- *01784 430763*

Shell SAVE £ 1.4m ②
Open- *Daily 24 hours*
Info- *WC, cash machine (not Maestro).*
Tel- *01784 441020*
Dir'n- *Take the A30 towards Staines and then take the first turn off, and then turn right on the A308.*

FOOD

Panahar Restaurant £7.50 0.7 ③
Open- *Tu-Sun 1200-1430, 1800-2300*
Info- *Tandoori & balti rest & takeaway.*
Tel- *01784 483951*

Bem-Vindo a Nando's £7.00 1.3m ④
Open- *Su-Th 1200-2330, F/Sat 1200-2400*
Info- *Popular Mexican chain.*
Dir'n- *Between Waitrose & the cinema.*
Tel- *01784 441678*

Yellow River £8.00 1.3m ④
Open- *M-Sat 1030-2300, Sun 1100-2300*
Info- *Varied Asian menu. This is Ken Hom's Yellow River.*
Dir'n- *Between Waitrose & the cinema.*
Tel- *01784 224660*

Spur Steak & Grill £7.00 1.3m ④
Open- *M-Th 1200-2130, Fr/Sat 1200-2230, Sun 1200-2100.*
Info- *Steak & grill chain.*
Dir'n- *Opposite the Yellow River.*
Tel- *01784 492111*

Oasis Restaurant £6.00 1.0m ⑤
Open- *M-Th 1200-2300, F/Sat 1200-0100, Sun 1200-2230.*
Info- *Offers a few rooms at £60 per night.*
Tel- *01784 432183*

Left Bank Restaurant £14 1.3m ⑥
Open- *Daily 1200-1430, M-Sat 1900-220*
Info- *Refined dining at hotel restaurant. Dinner/dance on Saturdays.*
Tel- *01784 436171*

Other
Info- *Staines has a variety of eating opportunities.*

Dir'n- *Drive to Staines via the B376 and then follow the signs to the Two Rivers car park. Park in the car park of Waitrose which is just opposite. Small parking charge applies.*

ACCOMMODATION

Travelodge☞ £70 1.3m ⑦
Info- *Staines location.*
Tel- *0870 191 1746*

Runnymede Hotel £210 1.3m ⑥
Info- *'Left Bank' restaurant on-site. Hotel has health club and spa. AA/RAC 4★.*
Tel- *01784 436171*

ESSENTIALS

Ashford Hospital 4m
Dir'n- *From Junction 13 take the A30 east towards Staines. The hospital is on the left after about 4 miles.*
Tel- *01784 884488*

Bell Weir Garage 0.6m ⑧
Open- *M-F 0830-1800, Sat 0830-1300*
Info- *Repairs, recovery and tyres.*
Tel- *01784 483555*

THINGS TO DO

Runnymede 1.5m
Info- *Historic site where the Magna Carta was signed in 1215.*
Dir'n- *Follow the A308 towards Maidenhead and the site is on the left.*
Tel- *01784 884488*

JFK Memorial 2.4m
Info- *Memorial to John F Kennedy.*
Dir'n- *Follow the A308 towards Maidenhead and after about 1.5 miles turn left on the A328. The monument is signposted on the left.*

RAF Memorial 1.9m
Info- *Memorial to over 20,000 RAF personnel killed in action.*
Dir'n- *Follow the A30 towards Camberley, and turn right after about 1 mile. Go along this road and the memorial is signposted.*

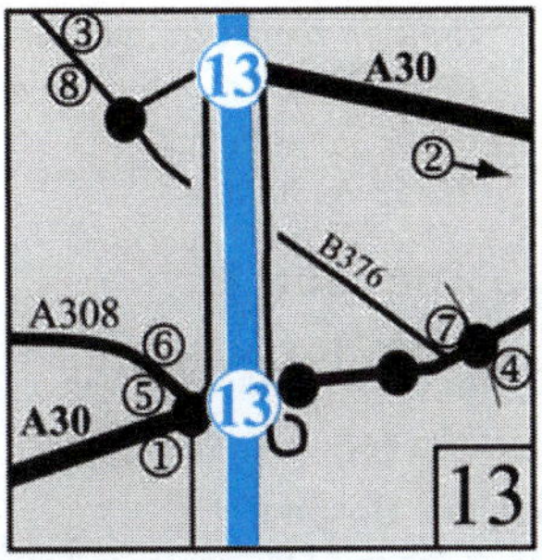

M25 Junction 14
Heathrow Terminal 4

FOOD

Golden Cross Pub £4.50 0.6m ①
Open- *M-F 1200-2100, Sat-Sun 1200-1800*
Info- *Varied hot & cold menu.*
Tel- *01753 682231*

ESSENTIALS

Ashford Hospital 3.2m
Dir'n- *Follow signs to Heathrow T4 from the junction, and then turn right onto the A3044 at the first roundabout. The hospital is signposted to the left (Stanwell B378) along this road.*
Tel- *01784 884488*

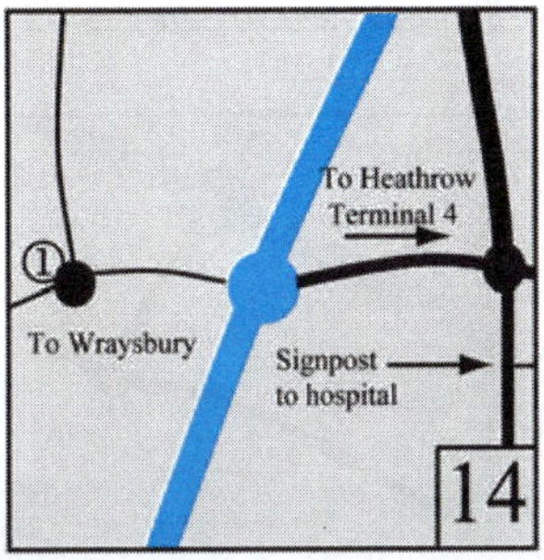

M25 Junction 15
M25/M4 interchange

ESSENTIALS

Wexham Park Hospital 6.5m
Dir'n- *Take the M4 west to Junction 5 and*

then the A4 towards Slough. Turn right on the B416, and the hospital is signposted to the right before you reach Stoke Poges.
Tel- *01753 633000*

M25 Junction 16
M25/M40 interchange

ESSENTIALS

Hillingdon Hospital 7.5m
Dir'n- *Take the M40 towards London, and at the roundabout take the A4020 to Hillingdon. Turn off at Royal Lane and the hospital is soon after.*
Tel- *01895 238282*

Hillingdon Tourist Information Centre
Tel- *01895 250706*

M25 Junction 17
Rickmansworth

FOOD

The Cross pub £4 1.0 ①
Open- *Daily 1200-2000*
Info- *Features low price steak meals.*
Tel- *01923 773266*

Transport Cafe £3.50 1.0m ①
Open- *M-F 0700-1500, Sat 0800-1200*
Info- *Good value fried food.*
Dir'n- *Situated next to 'The Cross'.*
Tel- *01923 778637*

M25 Junction 18
Chorleywood

FUEL

Shell SAVE £ 0.2m ①
Open- *Daily 24 hours*
Info- *WC, jetwash, cash machine (not Maestro).*
Tel- *01923 285010*

FOOD

White Horse Pub £7.00 0.2m ②
Open- *M-Sat 1200-1415, 1800-2100, Sun 1200-1500*
Info- *Varied hot & cold meals.*
Tel- *01923 282227*

Jenny Wren pub £7 0.5m ③
Open- *M-Sat 1200-2200, Sun 1200-2130*
Info- *Extensive range of hot & cold food.*
Tel- *01923 282053*

ESSENTIALS

Watford General Hospital 6m
Dir'n- *Take the A404 towards Rickmansworth, and then the A412 towards Watford. The hospital is signposted near to the town centre.*
Tel- *01923 244366*

THINGS TO DO

Chorleywood Pk Estate Free 0.7m ④
Info- *Wooded park which has a footpath to the River Chess.*

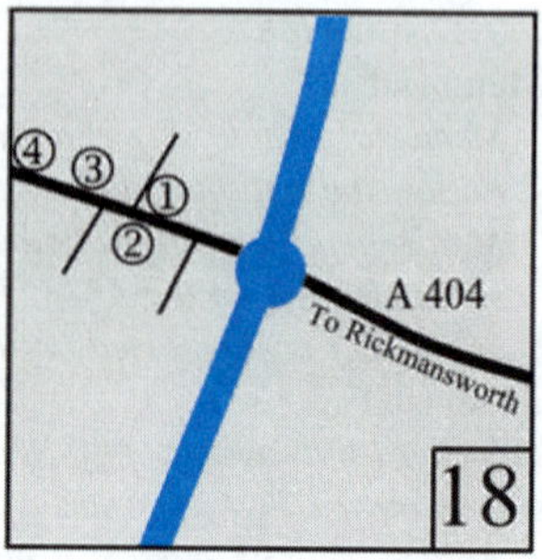

M25 Junction 19
Restricted

This junction is a long motorway slip road to Watford, but provides good access in both directions to Junction 20 via the A41 if the traffic is not congested.

FUEL

Total SAVE £££ 0.7m ①
Open- *Daily 24 hours*
Info- *WC, carwash.*
Tel- *01923 680024*

FOOD

King's Lodge Hotel rest. £10 0.9m ②
Open- *Daily 1200-1430, 1900-2130, Sun 1200-2000*
Info- *Varied hot & cold meals.*
Tel- *01923 441141*

The King's Head £5 0.9m ②
Open- *Daily 1200-2000*
Info- *Varied hot & cold bar meals.*
Tel- *01923 262307*

ACCOMMODATION

King's Lodge Hotel £60 0.9m ②
Info- *On-site restaurant. Price is B&B. Small independent hotel.*
Tel- *01923 441141*

ESSENTIALS

Watford General Hospital 3m
Dir'n- *Follow signs to Watford via the A411. The hospital is well signposted en-route.*
Tel- *01923 244366*

M25 Junction 20
Kings Langley

FUEL

Total SAVE £££ 0.8m ①
Open- *Daily 24 hours*
Info- *WC, carwash.*
Tel- *01923 680024*

FOOD

King's Lodge Hotel rest. £10 0.7m ②
Open- *M-Sat 1200-1430, 1900-2130, Sun 1200-2000*
Info- *Varied hot & cold meals.*
Tel- *01923 441141*

The King's Head £5 0.7m ②
Open- *Daily 1200-2000*
Info- *Varied hot & cold bar meals.*
Tel- *01923 262307*

Rose & Crown £7.50 0.7m ③
Open- *Daily 1200-2000*
Info- *Extensive hot & cold menu. This is an 'Ember Inn'.*
Tel- *01923 290229*

La Cassetta £11 0.8m ④
Open- *Tu-Fr 1200-1400, Tu-Sat 1700-2200*
Info- *Independent Italian restaurant.*
Tel- *01923 263823*

Taste of India £6.50 0.8m ⑤
Open- *Daily 1200-1430, 1800-2330*
Info- *Indian restaurant & takeaway.*
Tel- *01923 270668*

Oscar's Pizza Bar £7.50 0.8m ⑤
Open- *Daily 1200-2230*
Info- *Pizza restaurant & takeaway.*
Tel- *01923 263800*

Langley Fish Bar £4.00 1.1m ⑥
Open- *M-F 1130-1400, 1630-2200, Sat 1130-2200*
Info- *Takeaway fish meals.*
Tel- *01923 262445*

Millers Pub & Rest. £7.50 1.3m ⑥
Open- *M-Sat 0700-0930, Sun 0800-1000, M-F 1200-2200, Sun 1200-2100*
Info- *Extensive hot & cold menu.*
Tel- *01923 263150*

ACCOMMODATION

King's Lodge Hotel £60 0.7m ②

Info- *On-site restaurant. Price is B&B. Independent small hotel.*

Tel- *01923 441141*

Premier Lodge☞ £50 1.3m ⑥

Dir'n- *Next to the Millers Pub-Restaurant. Kings Langley location.*

Tel- *0870 990 6372*

ESSENTIALS

Watford General Hospital 3m

Dir'n- *Take the A41 south and the hospital is well signposted.*

Tel- *01923 244366*

Hemel General Hospital 3.5m

Dir'n-Follow signs to Hemel Hempstead via the A41, and the A&E is signposted.

Tel- *01442 213141*

Moss Pharmacy 0.8m ④

Open- *M-F 0900-1730, Sat 0900-1300*

Tel- *01923 262430*

Hemel Hempstead Tourist Info. Centre

Tel- *01442 234222*

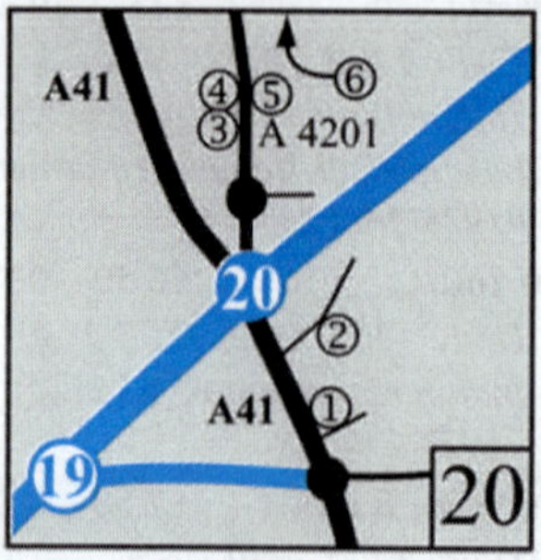

M25 Junction 21
M25/M1 interchange

This is a restricted junction that does not allow access to the M1 southbound. This southbound access is available at junction 21A nearby.

ESSENTIALS

Hemel General Hospital 3m

Dir'n- *Follow signs to Hemel Hempstead, and then A&E is well signposted.*

Tel- *01442 213141*

St Albans Tourist Information Centre

Tel- *01727 864511*

M25 Junction 21A
Bricket Wood

FUEL

Shell **SAVE** ££££ 0.5m ①

Open- *Daily 24 hours*

Info- *WC, carwash.*

Tel- *01727 819900*

Total **SAVE** ££££ 0.3m ②

Open- *Daily 24 hours*

Info- *WC, carwash.*

Tel- *01923 680024*

FOOD

Three Hammers Pub £7.00 1.1m ③

Open- *Daily 1200-2000*

Info- *Varied food menu. An 'Ember Inn'. Children 14+ welcome for meals.*

Tel- *01727 846218*

Rami Indian Takeaway £7.00 1.1m ③

Open- *Daily 1700-2300*

Info- *Tandoori & balti takeaway.*

Tel- *01727 884170*

Flamelight £6.00 1.1m ③

Open- *M-Sat 1200-1400, 1700-2245, Sundays 1700-2245*

Info- *Indian takeaway meals.*

Tel- *01727 852288*

Little Chef☞ £6.50 0.8m ④

Open- *Daily 0700-2200*

Tel- *01923 661842*

Harvester☞ £6.50 1.7m ⑤

Open- *Sun-F 1200-2130, Sat 1200-2200*

Tel- *01923 672061*

TGIF☞ £11 1.8m ⑥

Open- *Daily 1200-2300*

Dir'n- *Enter via A412, just before the parade of shops on the left hand side.*

Tel- *01923 672310*

Other food

Info- *Arcade just beyond TGIF has fish & chip shop, sandwich bar, and a Chinese takeaway.*

ACCOMMODATION

Thistle Hotel☞ £113 0.5m ⑦

Info- *On-site restaurant & bar. St Albans location.*

Tel- *0870 333 9144*

Travel Inn☞ £55 1.8m ⑥

Info- *Watford location.*

Tel- *0870 1977261*

Dir'n- *Enter via A412, before the parade of shops on the left hand side.*

ESSENTIALS

Watford General Hospital 5m

Dir'n- *Head to Watford on A405, and the hospital is well signposted.*

Tel- *01923 244366*

Nash Chemists 1.1m ③

Open- *M-F 0900-1300, 1400-1800, Saturdays 0900-1300*

St Albans Tourist Information Centre

Tel- *01727 864511*

THINGS TO DO

St Albans City Centre 3.5m

Info- *Historic city with a cathedral, remains of a Roman settlement, and a pleasant shopping area.*

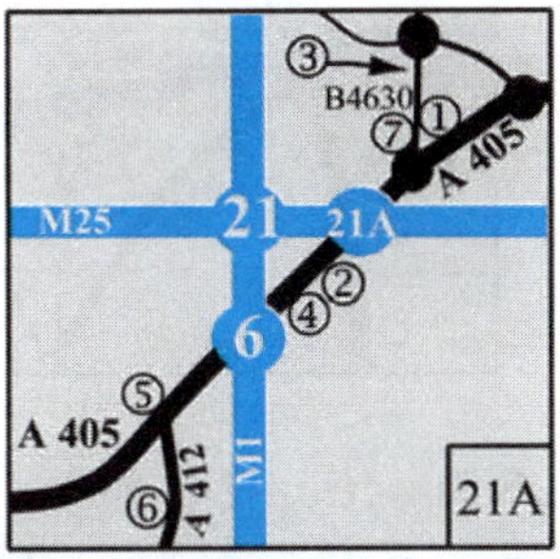

M25 Junction 22
London Colney

FUEL

Sainsbury SAVE ££ 0.2m ①

Open- *Daily 24 hours*

Info- *LPG, carwash. WC, cash machine at store.*

Tel- *01727 828151*

FOOD

McDonald's☞ £3.50 0.2m ②

Open- *Daily 0700-2300*

Tel- *01727 827948*

Sainsbury Cafe☞ £3.50 0.2m ①

Open- *M-F 0800-2000, Sat 0800-1900*

Info- *Inside the store.*

Tel- *01727 744400*

Starbucks☞ £3.50 0.2m ①

Open- *M-F 0800-2000, Sat 0900-2000, Sun 1100-1700,*

Info- *Inside Sainsbury store.*

Tel- *01727 828112*

The Colney Fox £6.50 0.5m ③

Open- *M-Sat 1200-2200, Sun 1200-2130*

Info- *'Vintage Inn' pub chain.*

Tel- *01727 823698*

Other food 0.7m

Info- *The village of Colney has several pubs which serve food, in addition to those mentioned here.*

ACCOMMODATION

Innkeeper's Lodge £57.50 0.5m ③

Info- *St Albans location.*

Dir'n- *Next to the Colney Fox.*

Tel- *01727 823698*

ESSENTIALS

St Albans Tourist Information Centre

Tel- *01727 864511*

THINGS TO DO

Aircraft Museum £5 1.7m ④

Open- *Tu,Th,Sa 1400-1730, Su 1030-1730. First Sunday in March to last Sunday in October.*

Info- *Museum dedicated to the Mosquito & other DeHavilland aircraft.*

Tel- *01727 822051*

Willows Farm Village 0.3m ⑤

Open- *Daily 1000 - 1730 (shop). Farm open from 5th April to 2nd Nov. inclusive.*

Info- *Meet farm animals. Tractor rides, bouncy haystacks etc. Rest. & shop.*

Tel- *01727 822444*

St Albans City Centre 4m ⑥

Info- *Historic city with a cathedral, remains of a Roman settlement, and a pleasant shopping area.*

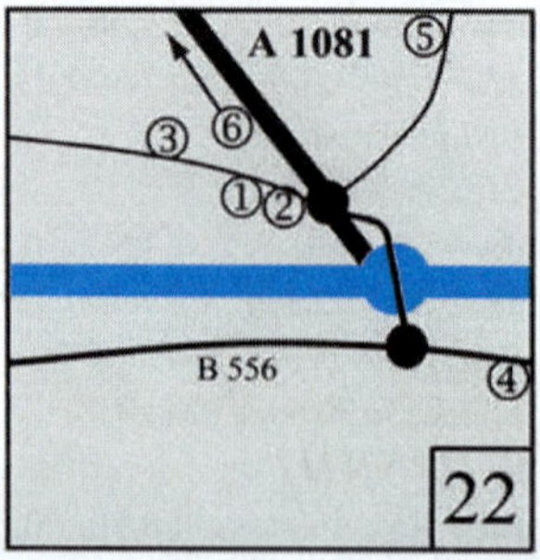

J23 South Mimms Services

This services is located just off the motorway at Junction 23.

FUEL BP

Cash machine, HGV fuelling & parking. Free parking for 2 hours then £6 per day.

FOOD WELCOME BREAK

Red Hen, KFC, Burger King, Coffee Primo, The Granary Restaurant

Info- *Cash machines.*

ACCOMMODATION

Days Inn☞ £45

Info- *South Mimms location.*

Tel- *01707 665440*

M25 Junction 23
South Mimms

FUEL

Murco SAVE £ 0.7m ①

Open- *M-Sat 0600-2300, Sun 0800-2200*

Info- *WC, jetwash.*

Tel- *01707 654610*

FOOD

The Green Dragon £5.00 1.2m ②

Open- *M-Sat 1200-2200, Sun 1200-2130*

Info- *Bar & restaurant.*

Tel- *01208 4492972*

The White Hart £6.00 0.7m ③

Open- *M-Sat 1200-1430, 1830-2100, Sun 1200-1800*

Info- *Extensive hot & cold menu.*

Tel- *01707 642122*

ACCOMMODATION

Holiday Inn☞ £96 0.2m ④

Info- *On-site restaurant. South Mimms location.*

Tel- *0870 400 9072*

ESSENTIALS

Barnet Hospital 8m

Dir'n- *From exit follow A1 south, then A411 east. The hospital is signposted on the right in Wellhouse Lane.*

Tel- *0208 216 4000*

Lantern Recovery 0.3m ⑤

Open- *Daily 24 hours*

Dir'n- *Just beyond the Holiday Inn.*

Tel- *01707 644691*

Lantern Car Hire 0.3m ⑤

Dir'n- *Just beyond the Holiday Inn.*

Tel- *01707 654465*

M25 Junction 24
Potters Bar

FUEL

Tesco SAVE £ 0.5m ①

Open- *Daily 24 hours*

Info- *Cash machines & cafe at store.*

Tel- *01707 347500*

BP SAVE nil 0.7m ②

Open- *Daily 24 hours*

Info- *Carwash, jetwash, cash machine.*

Tel- *01707 661375*

FOOD

Tesco Cafe☞ £3.50 0.7m ①
Open- *M-Sat 0800-1800, Sun 0900-1600*
Info- *Cash machines in the store (open 24 hours).*
Tel- *0845 677 9556*

Mediterranean £7.00 0.7m ④
Open- *M-Fr 1200-1500, 1700-2300, Sat/Sun 1600-2300*
Info- *Italian restaurant & takeaway.*
Tel- *01707 660654*

Pubali Tandoori £3.50 0.7m ⑤
Open- *Daily 1200-1430, 1830-2330*
Info- *Indian food to eat in or take away.*
Tel- *01707 655272*

Out & Out Pub/rest☞ £7.00 1.0m ⑥
Open- *Daily 1200-1900*
Info- *Extensive bar & restaurant menu.*
Tel- *01707 664035*

Other food
Info- *Potters Bar has an abundance of restaurants, cafes and sandwich shops, in addition to those mentioned here, and is a recommended stop for those wishing to find food off the motorway.*

ESSENTIALS

Chase Farm Hospital 4.5m
Dir'n- *Take the A1005 towards Enfield and the hospital is on the left.*
Tel- *0208 366 6600*

Questmoor Pharmacy 0.9m ⑦
Open- *M-F 0830-1815, Sat 0830-1730*
Tel- *01707 659120*

KwikFit 0.7m ⑤
Open- *M-F 0800-1800, Sat/Sun 0900-1700*
Tel- *01707 649500*

THINGS TO DO

Oakmere Park 1.0m ④
Info- *Small park with a lake and children's playground.*

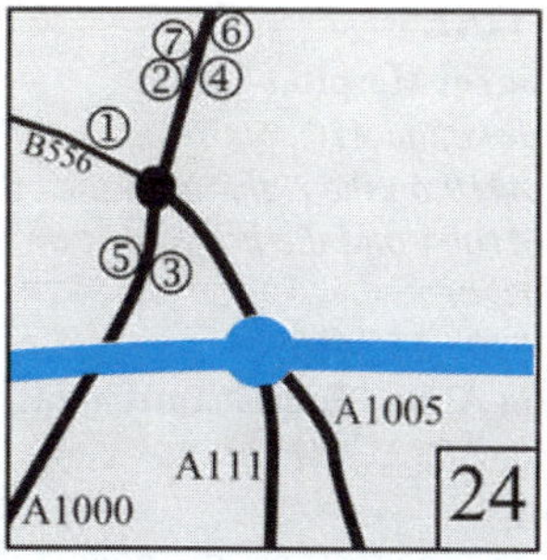

M25 Junction 25
Cheshunt

FUEL

Total SAVE ££ 0.4m ①
Open- *Daily 24 hours*
Info- *WC, carwash.*
Tel- *01992 659780*

BP SAVE £ 0.4m ②
Open- *Daily 24 hours*
Info- *Carwash, cash machine.*
Tel- *01992 700778*

Total #2 SAVE ££ 1.3m ③
Open- *M-Sat 0600-2200, Sun 0800-2200*
Info- *Carwash.*

Esso SAVE ££ 1.5m ④
Open- *Daily 24 hours*
Info- *WC, carwash.*
Tel- *0208 363 6494*

FOOD

McDonald's☞ £3.50 0.4m ②
Open- *Daily 0700-2300*
Tel- *01992 788261*

Burger Kg Drive Thru £4.00 0.4m ②
Open- *Daily 0800-2300*
Info- *Fish & chip shop opposite.*
Tel- *01992 652666*

Little Chef☞ £6.50 1.0m ⑤
Open- *Daily 0700-2200*
Tel- *01992 630788*

Other 1.3m
Info- *Several low price takeaways and cafes near to ③.*

ESSENTIALS

Chase Farm Hospital 5m

Dir'n- *Take the A10 south and then the A110 on the right. Next take the A1005 and the hospital is on the right.*

Tel- *0208 366 6600*

Waltham Abbey Tourist Info. Centre

Tel- *0870 225 4845*

KwikFit 1.2m ④

Open- *M-F 0800-1800, Sat 0800-1700, Sundays 1000-1600*

Info- *Tyre & exhaust centre.*

Tel- *01992 629075*

THINGS TO DO

Capel Manor Gardens £5.00 0.6m ⑥

Open- *Daily March-April 1000-1800. Weekdays November to February.*

Info- *30 acres of gardens.*

Tel- *0208 366 4442*

M25 Junction 26
Waltham Abbey

FUEL

Shell **SAVE** £ 1.4m ①

Open- *Daily 24 hours*

Info- *WC, cash machine.*

FOOD

The Volunteer £7.00 0.3m ②

Open- *Daily 1200-2100*

Info- *Pub with Chinese and British meals.*

Tel- *01992 713705*

The Woodbine £6.00 0.4m ①

Open- *M-Sat 1200-1500, 1830-2130, Sun 1200-1600*

Info- *Pub with varied hot & cold meals.*

Tel- *01992 713050*

Old Orleans £9.00 1.4m ④

Open- *M-Sat 1200-2300, Sun 1200-2230*

Info- *American 'Southern style' chain.*

Tel- *01992 812618*

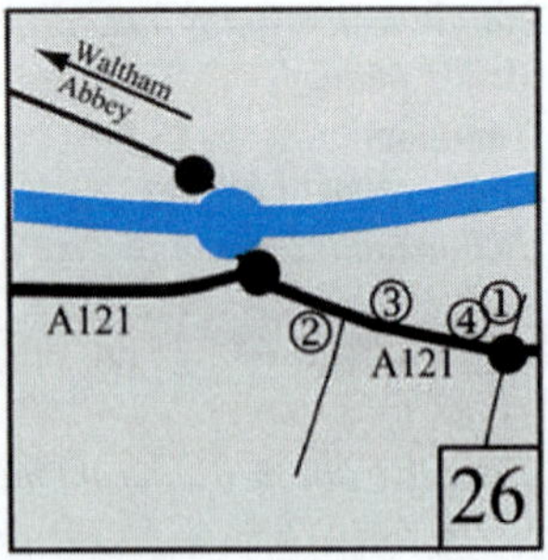

ACCOMMODATION

Marriott Hotel☛ £90 0.3m ⑤

Info- *On-site restaurant & health club. Waltham Abbey location.*

Tel- *0870 400 7259*

ESSENTIALS

Waltham Abbey Tourist Info. Centre

Tel- *01992 652295*

THINGS TO DO

Epping Forest 1.4m

Info- *Take a walk in the woods!*

Dir'n- *Turn right just after The Volunteer or just before the Old Orleans. Parking is 0.8 miles on.*

Waltham Abbey 2m

Info- *The remains of this ancient abbey can be seen in the town centre.*

M25 Junction 27
M25/M11 interchange

There is no access to local services at this junction.

M25 Junction 28
Brentwood

FUEL

Total **SAVE** £ 0.2m ①
Open- *Daily 24 hours*
Info- *Carwash, post box.*
Tel - *01277 233819*

FOOD

Little Chef☞ £6.50 0.2m ①
Open- *Daily 0700-2300*
Tel- *01277 201519*

Burger King☞ £4.0 0.2m ①
Open- *Daily 1000-2100*
Tel- *01277 201519*

Nag's Head £7.50 0.6m ②
Open- *M-Sat 1200-2200, Sun 1200-2130*
Info- *Varied hot & cold menu.*
Tel- *01277 260005*

Harvester☞ £7.00 0.9m ③
Open- *M-Sat 1200-2200, Sun 1200-2130*
Tel- *01277 224511*

Marygreen Manor £19 1.0m ⑤
Open- *Daily 1230-1415, 1930-2130*
Info- *Dining in the hotel restaurant.*
Tel- *01277 225252*

ACCOMMODATION

Holiday Inn☞ £149 0.4m ④
Info- *On-site restaurant, bar, health club. Brentwood location.*
Tel- *0870 400 9012*

Marygreen Manor Htl £145 1.0m ⑤
Info- *On-site restaurant & bar. Afternoon teas. AA/RAC 4◆. Pantheon Hotels*
Tel- *01277 225252*

ESSENTIALS

Oldchurch Hospital 6m
Dir'n- *Take the A12 west, and then the A125 to Romford. The hospital is signposted off the A125.*
Tel- *01708 746090*

Brentwood Tourist Information Centre
Tel- *01277 200300*

KwikFit 0.9m ⑥
Open- *M-F 0800-1800, Sat 0800-1700, Sun 1000-1600*
Info- *Tyres & exhausts.*
Tel- *01227 227602*

Car Dealers
Info- *Vauxhall & Saab dealers.*
Dir'n- *En-route to KwikFit.*

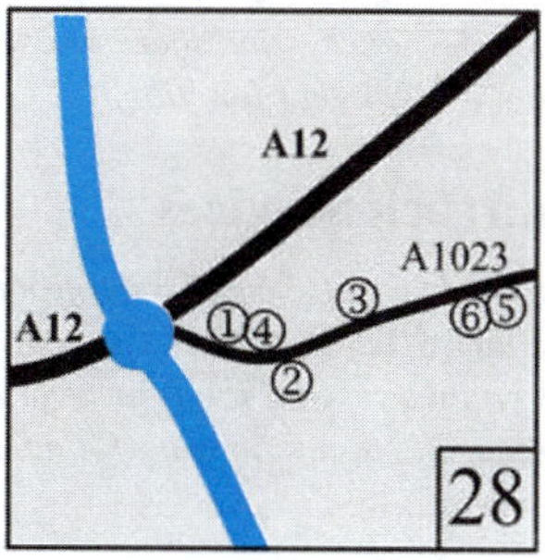

M25 Junction 29
Upminster

This junction does not allow easy return.

ACCOMMODATION

Brick House Hotel £55 0.8m ①
Info- *Price is for B&B. Independent hotel. Return to motorway is over 4 miles.*
Tel- *01277 217107*

ESSENTIALS

Oldchurch Hospital 6.5m
Dir'n- *Take the A127, then A12 west, and then the A125 to Romford. The hospital is signposted off the A125.*
Tel- *01708 746090*

D&G recovery 1.3m ②
Open- *Daily 24 hours*
Info- *Return to motorway is over 4 miles.*
Tel- *01708 225800*

M25 Junction 30

Restricted

This junction allows exit southbound and entry northbound. The missing exits are at Junction 31 nearby, and there are services en-route & near that junction.

Thurrock Services

This services can be accessed from Junctions 30 and 31 of the motorway. Alternative fuel and food are available at Junction 31, less than a half a mile from the services.

FUEL ESSO

HGV fuelling. Free parking for 2 hours then £6 per day. HGV parking.

FOOD MOTO

freshexpress, Burger King, Harry Ramsden's

Info- *Cash machine.*

ACCOMMODATION

Travelodge☞ £60

Info- *Thurrock location.*
Tel - *0870 191 1715*

ESSENTIALS

Thurrock Tourist Information Centre

Info- *At the service area.*
Tel- *01708 863733*

M25 Junction 31

Restricted

This Junction allows entry southbound and exit northbound. The missing exits are at Junction 30 nearby.

FUEL

Tesco SAVE ££ ①

Open- *Daily 24 hours*
Info- *WC and cafe at store.*
Dir'n- *Follow signs to services but at the roundabout leading to the services take the second turn off.*
Tel- *01708 791445*

FOOD

McDonald's☞ £3.50 0.3m ①

Open- *Daily 0700-2300*
Dir'n- *See Tesco fuel entry.*
Tel- *01708 860241*

Pizza Hut☞ £6.00 0.3m ①

Open- *M-Sat 1200-2300, Sun 1200-2200*
Dir'n- *See Tesco fuel entry.*
Tel- *01708 869155*

Tesco Cafe☞ £3.50 0.3m ①

Open- *M-Sat 0800-1900, Sun 1000-1600*
Dir'n- *See Tesco fuel entry.*
Tel- *0845 677 9209*

Others 0.3m ①

Info- *Harry Ramsden's and Starbucks cafes.*
Dir'n- *In 'Borders' near to McDonald's.*

ACCOMMODATION

Premier Lodge☞ £55 0.2m ②

Info- *On site bar & restaurant. Thurrock location.*
Tel- *0870 700 1380*
Dir'n- *Follow signs to A1090 (Purfleet) and hotel is on the right.*

Thurrock Hotel £70 0.4m ③

Info- *On site restaurant & bar. Independent hotel.*
Tel- *01708 868901*

THINGS TO DO

Lakeside Retail Park 0.8m ④

Open- *M-F 1000-2200, Sat 0900-1930, Sun 1100-1700*
Info- *Large shopping centre with over 300 stores & 30 cafes/restaurants.*
Tel- *01708 869933*

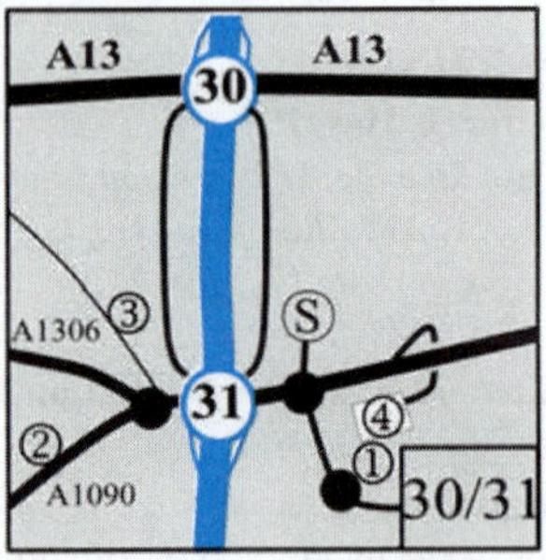

M40-London to Birmingham

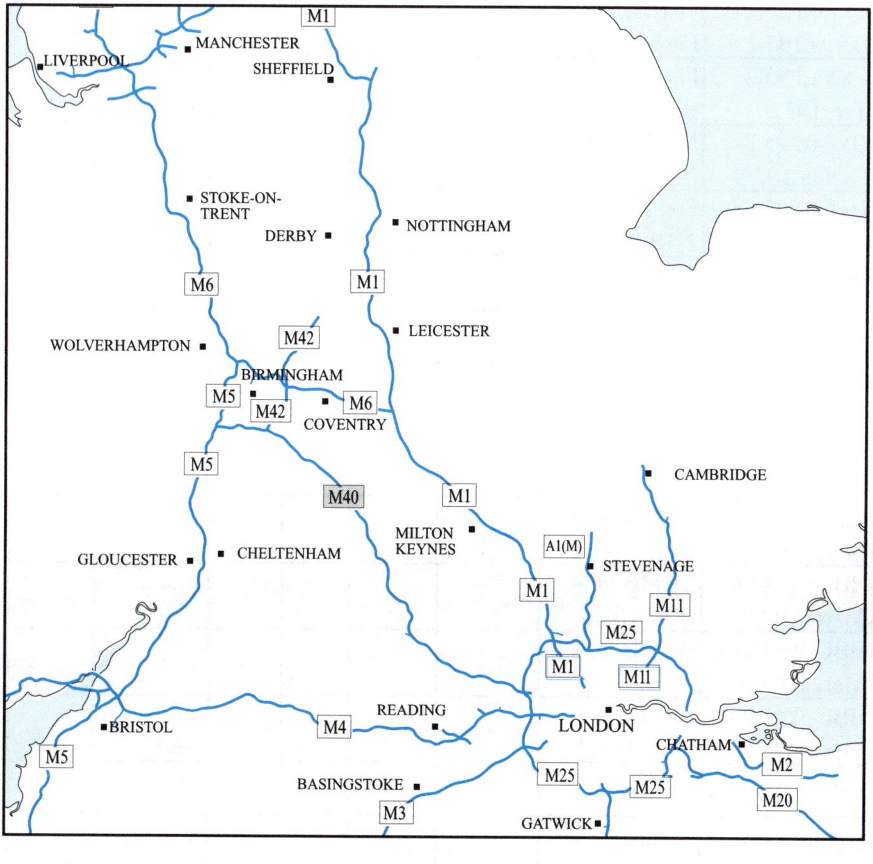

M40 Summary of Junctions

Radio stations & frequencies		Junction	Fuel	Food	Hotels	Essentials	Things to do
Heart 106.2 Jazz FM 102.2	KISS 100 XFM 104.9	1	24hr	✓		A&E TIC	✓
Heart 106.2 Freeze 92.7	Star 106.6 Swan 107.4	1A					
Heart 106.2 Freeze 92.7	Star 106.6 Berks 94.6	2		✓	✓	A&E TIC Svc	
Berks 94.6 Capital 95.8	LDN 94.9 KISS 100	3					
Berks 94.6 Capital 95.8	LDN 94.9 LBC 97.3	4	✓	✓	✓	A&E TIC	
KISS 100.0 2-Ten FM	Swan 107.4 Fox FM 102.6	5	✓	✓	✓		
Oxford 95.2 Berks 104.1	Fox FM 102.6 Fusion 107.9	6		✓	✓		
Oxford 95.2 2- Ten 102.9	Fox FM 102.6 Berks 104.1	7	Diesel only			Svc A&E	
Oxford 95.2 Fusion 107.9	Fox FM 102.6 2-10 FM	8				TIC A&E	✓
Oxford 95.2 Fusion 107.9	Fox FM 102.6 2-10 FM	8A S	24hr	✓	✓	A&E TIC	✓
Fox FM 102.6	Oxford 95.2	9	24hr				
Fox FM 102.6	Oxford 95.2	10 S	24hr	✓	✓	TIC	
Oxford 95.2	Fox FM 102.6	11	24hr	✓		TIC A&E	✓
BBC WM 94.8 Mercia 97.0	BRMB 96.4 Heart 100.7	12	✓	✓			✓
BBC WM 94.8 Mercia 97.0	BRMB 96.4 Heart 100.7	S	24hr	✓	✓		
BBC WM 94.8 Mercia 97.0	BRMB 96.4 Bear 102.0	13				TIC	
BBC WM 94.8 Mercia 97.0	BRMB 96.4 Heart 100.7	14				TIC	
BBC WM 94.8 Mercia 97.0	BRMB 96.4 Saga 105.7	15		✓	✓	TIC A&E	
BBC WM 94.8	BRMB 96.4	16				TIC	
BBC WM 94.8	BRMB 96.4	17				A&E, TIC	

Top Stops are highlighted

M40 Junction Details

M40 Junction 1
Uxbridge

FUEL

Esso SAVE £ 0.3m ①
Open- *Daily 24 hours*
Info- *WC, carwash, cash machine.*
Tel- *01895 831616*

BP SAVE £ 0.3m ②
Open- *Daily 24 hours*
Info- *Carwash, cash machine.*
Tel- *01895 832221*

Esso no. 2 SAVE £ 0.8m ③
Open- *Daily 0700-2200*
Info- *WC*
Tel- *01895 256378*

Texaco SAVE £ 0.7m ④
Open- *Daily 0600-2200*
Info- *WC, carwash, cash machine.*
Tel- *01895 451940*

FOOD

The Swan £10 1.0m ⑤
Open- *Daily 1200-1400, 1900-2200*
Info- *Refined pub dining, extensive menu.*
Tel- *01895 832085*

Indian Summer Brsrie £9 0.4m ⑥
Open- *Daily 1200-1430, 1730-2400*
Info- *Indian brasserie with takeaway.*
Tel- *01895 255025*

The Beijing £8 1.0m ③
Open- *M-Sat 1200-1430, 1730-2400, Sun 1200-2400*
Info- *Cantonese/Peking restaurant & takeaway.*
Tel- *01895 814188*

Other 1.5m
Info- *Uxbridge is nearby & has a wide range of restaurants & pubs.*

ESSENTIALS

Hillingdon Hospital 4.5m
Dir'n- *Take the A4020 towards Hillingdon. Turn off at Royal Lane and the hospital is soon after.*
Tel- *01895 238282*

Hillingdon Tourist Info. Centre
Tel- *01895 250706*

ATS 0.8m ③
Open- *M-F 0830-1730, Sat 0830-1230*
Info- *Tyre & exhaust centre.*
Tel- *01895 233705*

THINGS TO DO

Denham Village 1m
Info- *Pretty village with 3 pleasant pubs, each of which serve food.*

Uxbridge 1.5m
Info- *This town is well equipped with shops, and there is a canalside walk before you reach the town.*

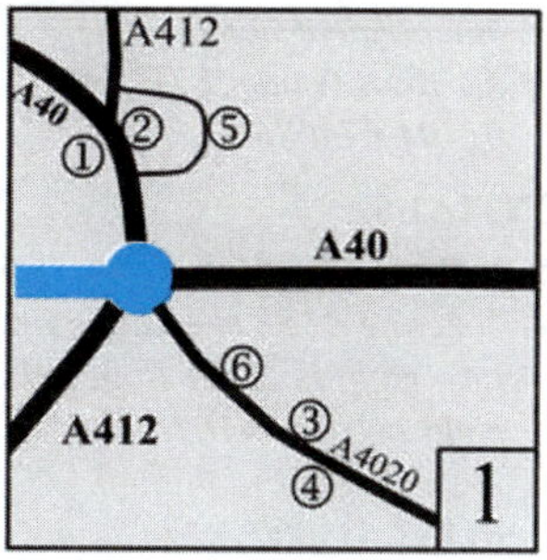

M40 Junction 1A
M40/M25 interchange

M40 Junction 2
Beaconsfield

FOOD

Loch Fyne Fish rest. £9 0.9m ①
Open- *Daily 1200-2200*
Info- *Fish and shellfish restaurant.*
Tel- *01494 679960*

Old White Swan £5.50 0.9m ①
Open- *M-F 1200-1430, 1800-2100, Sat 1200-1430, Sun 1200-1500*
Info- *Varied hot & cold meals.*
Tel- *01494 673800*

Pizza Organic £7.50 0.9m ①
Open- *M-Sat 1100-2300, Sun 1200-2200*
Info- *Organic pizzas and Italian meals.*
Tel- *01494 677758*

Tout a Manger £3.50 1.0m ②
Open- *M-F 0700-1430, Sat 0800-1400*
Info- *Sandwiches & hot snacks takeaway.*
Tel- *01494 673425*

Other food outlets 1.1m
Info- *There are an Indian restaurant, a Beefeater restaurant, a Pizza Express and numerous other pubs & restaurants near the George Hotel.*

ACCOMMODATION

The Broadway Hotel £72 1.2m ③
Info- *On-site restaurant. Independent hotel.*
Tel- *01494 678571*

The George Hotel £148 1.2m ④
Info- *On-site restaurant. No smoking independent hotel.*
AA B&B Guide. ETC 4◆.
Tel- *01494 673086*

ESSENTIALS

Wexham Park Hospital 6.5m
Dir'n- *Take the A355 to Slough, and then turn right to Stoke Poges. Turn right on the B416, and the hospital is signposted to the left.*
Tel- *01753 633000*

Beaconsfield Tourist Info. Centre
Tel- *01628 771542*

AJ Dunlop Garage 0.9m ①
Open- *M-F 0800-1700, Sat 0800-1300*
Info- *Car repairs and servicing.*
Tel- *01494 675616*

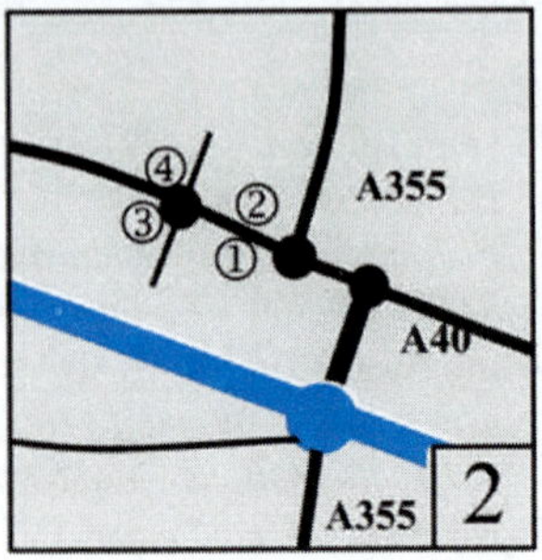

M40 Junction 3
Restricted

This is a restricted access junction, only allowing motorway entry towards London and exit from the London direction.

M40 Junction 4
High Wycombe

FUEL

Asda **SAVE** £££ 0.7m ①
Open- *M-F 0600-2300, Sat 0630-2200 Sun 0800-1800*
Info- *WC, McDonald's & cash machines at nearby store.*
Tel- *01494 441611*

FOOD

Beefeater Restaurant☞ £7.00 0.3m ②
Open- *Su-Th 1200-2100, F-Sat 1200-2200*
Tel- *01494 525323*

Frankie & Benny's☞ £8.50 0.4m ③
Open- *M-Sat 1200-2300, Sun 1200-2230*
Tel- *01494 511958*

TGIF☞ £10.00 0.7m ④
Open- *Sun-Th 1200-2230, F/Sat 1200-2330*
Tel- *01494 450067*

ACCOMMODATION

Holiday Inn £160 0.3m ③
Info- *On-site restaurant & bar. High Wycombe location.*
Tel *0870 400 9042*

ESSENTIALS

Wycombe Hospital 1.5m
Dir'n- *Take the A404 towards High Wycombe and the hospital is signposted to the right.*
Tel- *01494 526161*

High Wycombe Tourist Info. Centre
Tel- *01494 421892*

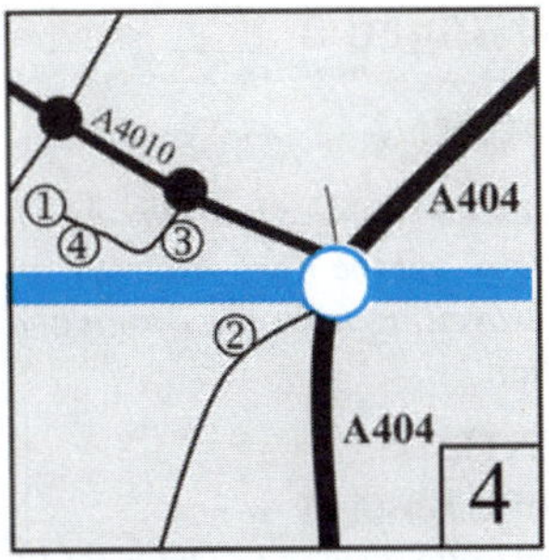

M40 Junction 5
Stokenchurch

FUEL

Total SAVE ££ 0.3m ①
Open- *Sun-Fr 0600-2200, Sat 0700-2200*
Info- *WC, carwash.*
Tel- *01494 480950*

FOOD

Fleur De Lis £5 0.4m ②
Open- *M-F 1200-1400, 1730-2030, Sat 1200-1430, 1730-2030, Sun 1200-1630*
Info- *Varied hot & cold pub meals.*
Tel- *01494 482269*

Four Horseshoes £5 0.4m ②
Open- *Daily 0930-2000*
Info- *Breakfasts and pub meals.*
Tel- *01494 482265*

Black Olive Restaurant £7 0.4m ③
Open- *M-F 0700-0900, 1100-2200, Sat/Sun 0800-1000 and 1100-2200*
Info- *Breakfasts & extensive meal menu at the Kings Arms Hotel.*
Tel- *01494 609090*

ACCOMODATION

The Kings Arms Hotel £130 0.4m ③
Info- *On-site restaurant (see Black Olive). Best Western☞.*
Tel- *01494 609090*

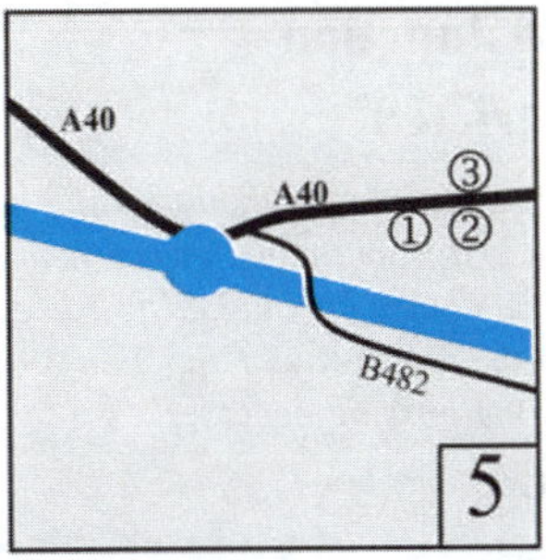

M40 Junction 6
Lewknor

FOOD

Ye Olde Leather Bottel £7.00 0.5m ①
Open- *F-Sa 1800-2200, Sun-Th 1900-2130, M-Sun 1200-1400,*
Info- *Extensive hot & cold menu. AA Pub Guide & Good Pub Guide.*
Tel- *01844 351482*

The Lambert Arms £8.00 0.5m ②
Open- *M-Sat 1200-1400, 1900-2100, Sun 1200-1400*
Info- *Varied pub meals & restaurant.*
Tel- *01844 351496*

ACCOMMODATION

Tower Cottage B&B £50 0.8m ③
Info- *Price is for B&B.*
Tel- *01844 354676*

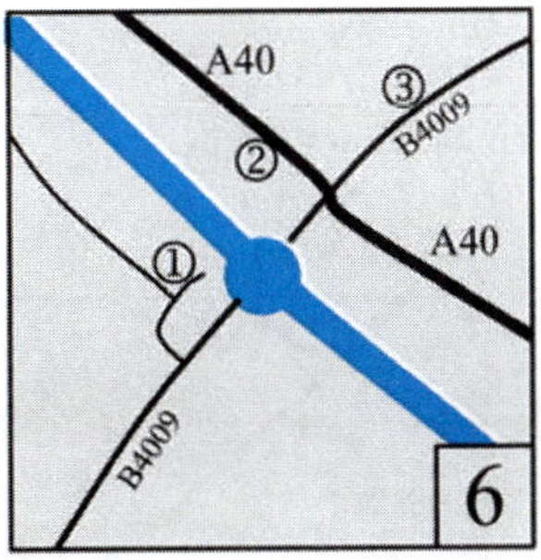

M40 Junction 7
Restricted

This is a restricted junction which only allows exit from the motorway heading west, and entry heading east. It is easy to rejoin the motorway at Junction 8A which offers the missing accesses.

FUEL

Keyfuels SAVE £ 0.4m ①
Open- *Daily 0900-1800*
Info- *Diesel only. HGV fuelling.*
Tel- *01844 279336*

ACCOMMODATION

The Oxford Belfry £130 0.3m ②
Info- *On site restaurant & bar meals. Leisure club. Oxford location.*
Tel- *01844 279381*

Langsmeade House £50 1.5m ③
Info- *Price is for B&B.*
Tel- *01844 278727*

ESSENTIALS

Radcliffe Hospital 6.5m
Dir'n- *Follow signs to Oxford/A40, then take the A420 where the hospital is signposted.*
Tel- *01865 741166*

SVS Services 0.2m ④
Open- *M-F 0800-1800, Sat 0900-1700, Sun 1000-1500.*
Info- *Van servicing.*
Tel- *01844 279648*

Lantern 24 Hours Recovery 0.4m ①
Info- *Vehicle recovery.*
Tel- *01844 279336*

M40 Junction 8
Restricted

This junction merges with the A40 heading to Oxford and the west. No entry or exit for those travelling from the Birmingham direction.

ESSENTIALS

Radcliffe Hospital 6m
Dir'n- *Follow signs to Oxford/A40, then take the A420 where the hospital is signposted.*
Tel- *01865 741166*

Oxford Tourist Information Centre
Tel- *01865 726871*

THINGS TO DO

Oxford 7m
Info- *Renowned university town with a wide range of restaurants and hotels.*
Dir'n -Follow signs from the motorway.

Oxford Services

This services is located just off the motorway at junction 8A.

FUEL BP
HGV fuelling. Free parking for 2 hours then £6 per 24 hours. Lorry park.

FOOD WELCOME BREAK
foodconnection, Burger King, KFC, Coffee Primo, Red Hen.
Info- *Cash machine.*

ACCOMMODATION

Days Inn☞ £60
Info- *Oxford location.*
Tel- *01865 877000*

M40 Junction 8A
Restricted

Exit only for those heading from the west, and entry heading towards the west. It is easy to drive to Junction 7 and rejoin the motorway if heading towards London.

FUEL

Keyfuels SAVE £ 0.8m ①
Open- *Daily 0900-1800*
Info- *Diesel only. HGV fuelling.*
Tel- *01844 279336*

ACCOMMODATION

The Oxford Belfry £130 1.6m ②
Info- *On site restaurant & bar meals. Leisure club. Oxford location.*
Tel- *01844 279381*

Langsmeade House £50 0.6m ③
Info- *Price is for B&B.*
Tel- *01844 278727*

ESSENTIALS

Radcliffe Hospital 6.5m
Dir'n- *Follow signs to Oxford/A40, then take the A420 where the hospital is signposted.*
Tel- *01865 741166*

Oxford Tourist Information Centre
Tel- *01865 726871*

SVS Services 1.8m ④
Open- *M-F 0800-1800, Sat 0900-1700, Sun 1000-1500.*
Info- *Van servicing.*
Tel- *01844 279648*

Lantern 24 Hours Recovery 2.0m ①
Info- *Vehicle recovery*
Tel- *01844 279336*

THINGS TO DO

Oxford 6m
Info- *Renowned university town with a wide range of restaurants and hotels.*
Dir'n -Follow signs from the motorway.

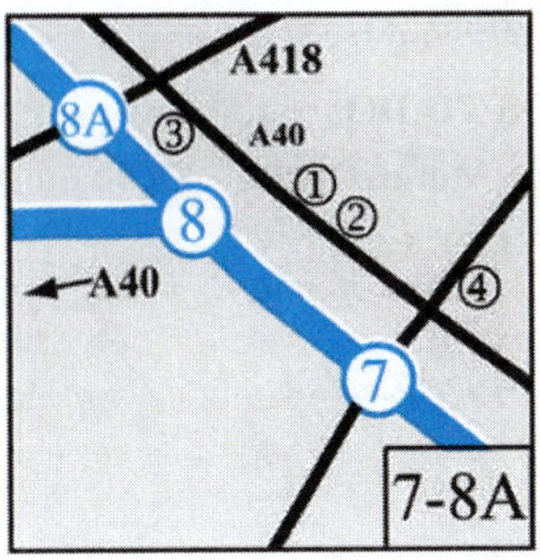

M40 Junction 9
Bicester

The Esso filling station is the nearest facility to this junction.

FUEL

Esso SAVE ££ 2.6m
Open- *Daily 24 hours*
Info- *WC*
Tel- *01869 324451*
Dir'n- *Head towards Bicester on the A41, and the filling station is on the left.*

ESSENTIALS

Oxford Tourist Information Centre
Tel- *01865 726871*

Junction 10 Services

The services at this junction are just off the motorway.

FUEL Esso
HGV fuelling. Free parking for 2 hours then £6 per 24 hours. Lorry park.

FOOD MOTO
freshexpress, Burger King, Little Chef, Upper Crust and Harry Ramsden's.
Info- Cash machines.

ACCOMMODATION

Travelodge☞ £50
Info- *Towcester/Silverstone location.*
Tel- *0870 191 1612*

OTHER

Cherwell Valley Tourist Info. Centre
Tel- *01869 345888*

M40 Junction 10
Ardley

FUEL

Esso SAVE ££ 0.7m ①
Open- *Daily 24 hours*
Info- *WC.*
Tel- *01869 345312*

FOOD

Fox & Hounds £5 0.3m ②

Open- *M-Sat 1200-1415, 1800-2100, Sun 1200-1430.*
Info- *Varied pub meals.*
Tel- *01869 346883*

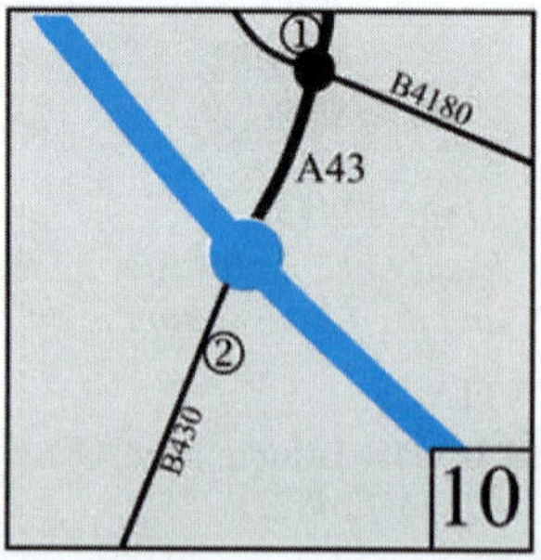

M40 Junction 11
Banbury

FUEL

Esso SAVE £ 0.6m ①

Open- *Daily 24 hours*
Info- *WC, car wash, HGV fuelling.*
Tel- *01295 279989*

Tesco SAVE £ 1.3m ②

Open- *Daily 24 hours*
Info- *WC at store.*
Tel- *01295 457400*

FOOD

Tesco Cafe☞ £3.50 1.4m ②

Open- *M-Sat 0800-1800, Sun 1000-1600*
Info- *Cash machine at store.*
Tel- *0845 677 9030*

Burger King☞ £4.00 1.3m ②

Open- *M-F 0900-2200, Sat/Sun 1000-2100*
Tel- *01295 275744*

ESSENTIALS

Horton Hospital 3.5m

Dir'n- *Head towards Banbury, and then the A4260 south. The hospital is well signposted.*
Tel- *01295 275500*

Banbury Tourist Information Centre

Tel- *01295 259855*

THINGS TO DO

Castle Quays Shopping Centre 1.5m ③

Info- *Covered shopping centre & strolls by adjacent canal. Car parking 60p*
Dir'n- *Drive towards Tesco or A422/ Banbury, and turn left as you pass the second roundabout.*

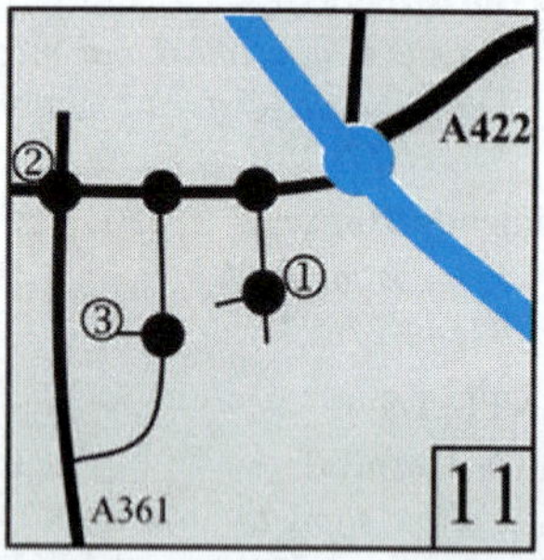

M40 Junction 12
Gaydon

FUEL

Esso SAVE ££ 0.4m ①

Open- *Daily 0600-2300*
Info- *WC, jetwash.*
Tel- *01926 642278*

FOOD

Gaydon Inn £5.00 0.4m ②

Open- *M-Th 1200-1430, 1800-2030, F-Sat 1730-2100, Sun 1200-1500*
Info- *Varied hot & cold meals.*
Tel- *01926 640388*

The Malt Shovel £7.50 0.5m ③

Open- *Daily 1200-1400, 1830-2100*
Info- *Varied hot & cold meals.*
Tel- *01926 641221*

THINGS TO DO

Heritage Motor Centre £8.00 1.0m ④

Open- *Daily 1000-1700*
Info- *Museum of motoring with 'off road experience'.*
Tel- *01926 641188*

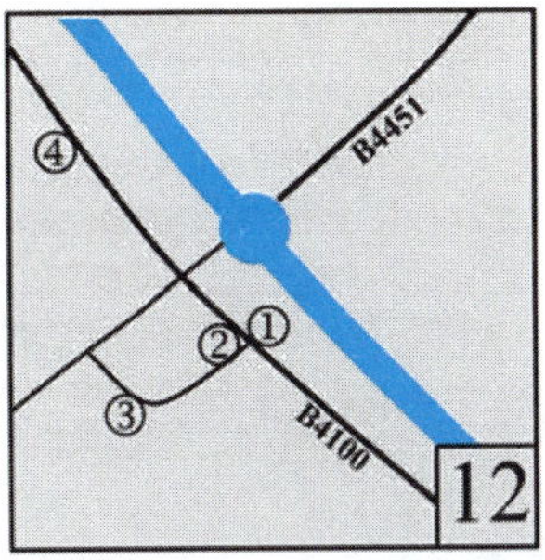

Warwick Services

No foot or road connection between carriageways.

FUEL BP

LPG, HGV fuelling. Free parking for 2 hours then £6 per 24 hours. Lorry park.
Info- Cash machine.

FOOD WELCOME BREAK

foodconnection, Burger King, Coffee Express, Coffee Primo, bakery.
Info- Cash machines.

ACCOMMODATION

Days Inn☞ (northbound) £50
Info- Warwick Northbound location.
Tel- 01926 651681
Welcome Lodge☞ (southbound) £50
Info- Warwick Southbound location.
Tel 01926 650168

M40 Junction 13
Restricted Access

This allows connection with the motorway only to and from the south.

ESSENTIALS

Leamington Spa Tourist Info. Centre
Tel- 01926 742762

M40 Junction 14
Restricted Access

This allows connection with the motorway only to and from the north.

ESSENTIALS

Leamington Spa Tourist Info. Centre
Tel- 01926 742762

M40 Junction 15
Warwick

FOOD

Porridge Pot £6.50 0.5m ①
Open- M-Sat 1200-2200, Sun 1200-2130
Info- Tom Cobleigh chain.☞
Tel- 01926 401697

ACCOMMODATION

Hilton Hotel☞ £98 0.5m ②
Info- On-site restaurant, bar, pool, gym. Warwick location.
Tel- 01926 499555
Express by Hol. Inn☞ £69 0.6m ①
Info- Warwick location. Includes b/fast.
Tel- 01926 483000

ESSENTIALS

Warwick Hospital 3m
Dir'n- Take the A429 towards Warwick, and then Coventry. The hospital is on the left off Coventry Road.
Tel- 01926 495321
Warwick Tourist Information Centre
Tel- 01926 492212
Stratford Tourist Information Centre
Tel- 01789 293127

THINGS TO DO

Warwick 3m
Info- The town of Warwick with its historic Castle is nearby.

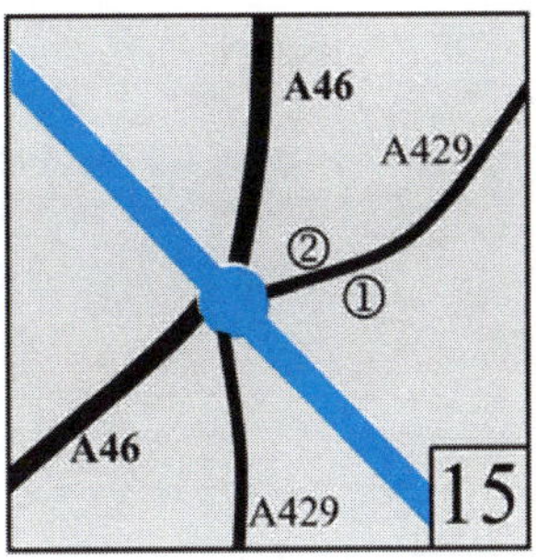

M40 Junction 16
Restricted Access

This junction allows connection only to and from the west of the motorway.

ESSENTIALS

Birmingham Tourist Info. Centre
Tel- *0121 693 6300*

M40 Junction 17
M40/M42 interchange

ESSENTIALS

Solihull General Hospital **6m**
Dir'n- *Take the M42 north to Junction 5, and then follow signs on entering Solihull.*
Tel- *0121 424 2000*
Birmingham Tourist Information Centre
Tel- *0121 693 6300*

M42-Birmingham SE Ring Road

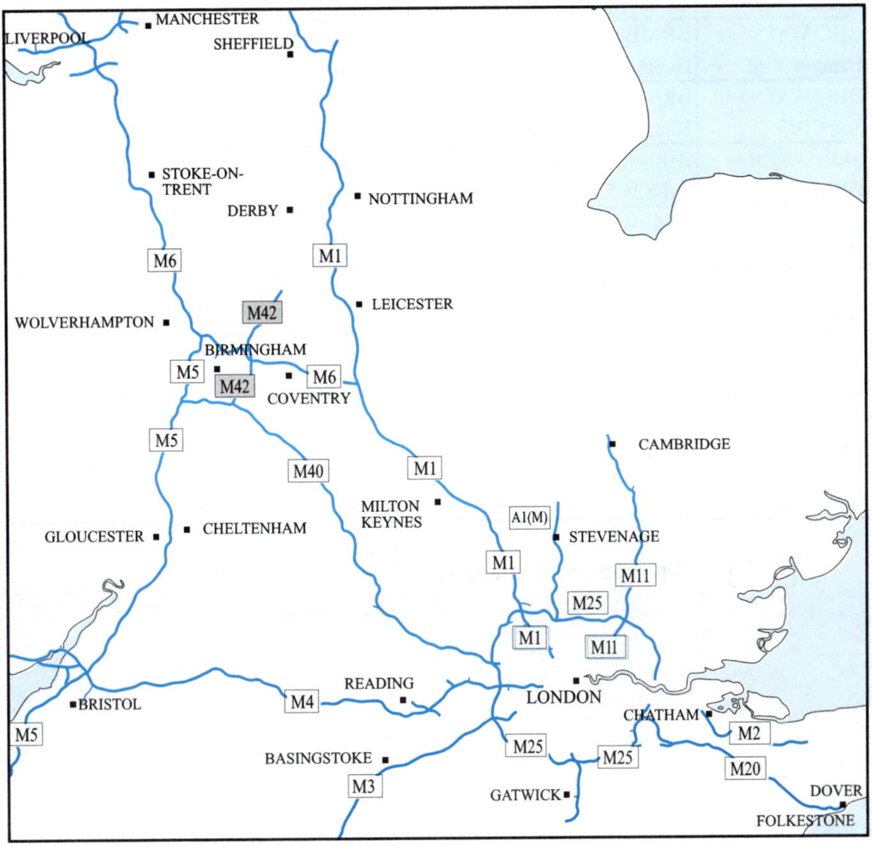

M42 Summary of Junctions

Radio stations & frequencies		Junction	Fuel	Food	Hotels	Essentials	Things to do
Heart FM 100.7 Wyvern 102.8	The Bear 102.0 WM 103.7						
Heart FM 100.7 Wyvern 102.8	The Bear 102.0 WM 103.7	1				TIC A&E	
Heart FM 100.7 Wyvern 102.8	The Bear 102.0 WM 103.7	2 S	24hr	✓	✓	TIC Svc A&E	
BBC WM 95.6 Beacon 97.2	BRMB 96.4 Heart 100.7	3	24hr	✓	✓	Svc A&E	
BRMB 96.4 Heart 100.7	BBC WM 95.6 Beacon 97.2	3A					
BBC WM 95.6 Beacon 97.2	BRMB 96.4 Heart 100.7	4	24hr	✓	✓		
BBC WM 95.6 Saga 105.7	BRMB 96.4 Heart 100.7	5	✓	✓		A&E	
Mercia 97.0 BRMB 96.4	BBC WM 95.6 Saga 105.7	6	24hr		✓		✓
Mercia 97.0 BRMB 96.4	BBC WM 95.6 Saga 105.7	7					
BBC WM 95.6 Beacon 97.2	BRMB 96.4 Heart 100.7	8					
BBC WM 95.6 Beacon 97.2	BRMB 96.4 Heart 100.7	9		✓	✓		
Centre FM 101.6 BBC Leics 104.9	Galaxy 102.2 Saga 105.7	10 S	24hr	✓	✓	A&E TIC Svc	
Fosseway 107.9 BRMB 96.4	BBC WM 95.6	11	24hr	✓	✓		

Top Stops are highlighted

M42 Junction Details

M42 Junction 0
M42/M5 interchange

There are no services accessible at this junction.

M42 Junction 1
Restricted

Entry to the motorway only for eastbound traffic, and exit only for westbound traffic.

ESSENTIALS

Bromsgrove Tourist Info. Centre
Tel- *01527 831809*

Alexandra Hospital 8m
Dir'n- *Take the A38 south and then the A448 towards Redditch. In Redditch take the A441 south, and the hospital is signposted.*
Tel- *01527 503030*

Birmingham Tourist Info. Centre
Tel- *0121 693 6300*

Junction 2 Services

The services are just off the motorway at Junction 2.

FUEL BP

HGV fuelling. Free parking for 2 hours then £6 per 24 hours. Lorry park.

FOOD WELCOME BREAK

Burger King, Red Hen, foodconnection, Coffee Primo.
Info- *Cash machine.*

M42 Junction 2
Alvechurch

FUEL

Texaco **SAVE** ££ 0.9m ①
Open- *M-F 0600-2200, Sat-Sun 0700-2200*
Info-
Tel- *0121 445 6173*

FOOD

Hopwood House Inn £7.50 1.0m ②
Open- *Su-Th 1200-2100, F-Sa 1200-2200*
Info- *Banks's family pub, on canalside.*
Tel- *0121 445 1716*

Westmead Restaurant £11 1.2m ③
Open- *Daily 1900-2130, M-F & Sun 1230-1400, M-F 0700-0930, Sat-Sun 0800-1030*
Info- *Dining at the Westmead Hotel.*
Tel- *0870 609 6119*

ACCOMMODATION

Westmead Hotel £108 1.2m ③
Info- *On-site restaurant & bar. Birmingham South location. A Corus Hotel☞*
Tel- *0870 609 6119*

ESSENTIALS

Alexandra Hospital 5.5m
Dir'n- *Take the A441 south to Redditch, and the hospital is signposted.*
Tel- *01527 503030*

Redditch Tourist Information Office
Tel- *01527 60806*

Bridge Garage 0.9m ①
Open- *M-F 0815-1700*
Info- *Small garage for repairs.*
Tel- *0121 445 1451*

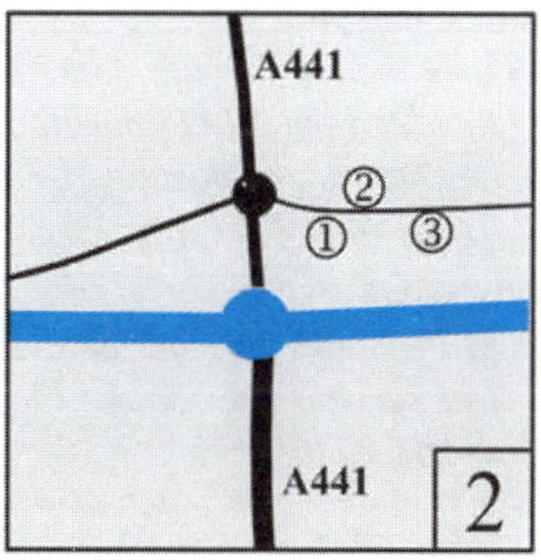

M42 Junction 3
Tanners Green

FUEL

Total SAVE ££ 0.2m ①
Open- *M-Sat 0600-2200, Sun 0700-2200*
Tel- *01564 824685*

Texaco SAVE ££ 2.0m ②
Open- *Daily 24 hours*
Info- *WC, LPG, HGV fuelling, carwash, HGV wash, cash machine.*
Tel- *01564 825110*

FOOD

Big Steak Pub☞ £6.50 0.4m ③
Open- *M-Sat 1100-2200, Sun 1200-2130*
Info- *Varied hot & cold menu. 'Wacky Warehouse' next door for children.*
Dir'n- *Turn left just after Total filling station, then right.*
Tel- *01564 822308*

Beckets Restaurant £7.00 1.3m ④
Open- *M-Th 0800-1730, F/Sat 0800-2200, Sun 0900-1700*
Info- *Extensive hot & cold menu.*
Tel- *01564 823402*

ACCOMMODATION

Inkford Hotel £75 0.7m ⑤
Info- *Small independent hotel. Price includes breakfast.*
Tel- *01564 824330*

ESSENTIALS

Alexandra Hospital 6.5m
Dir'n- *Take the A435 south, and then in Redditch the B4093 north, and the hospital is signposted.*
Tel- *01527 503030*

Edgingtons Garage 2.2m ②
Open- *M-F 0830-1700, Sat 0900-1300*
Info- *Car servicing & repair.*
Tel- *01564 824058*

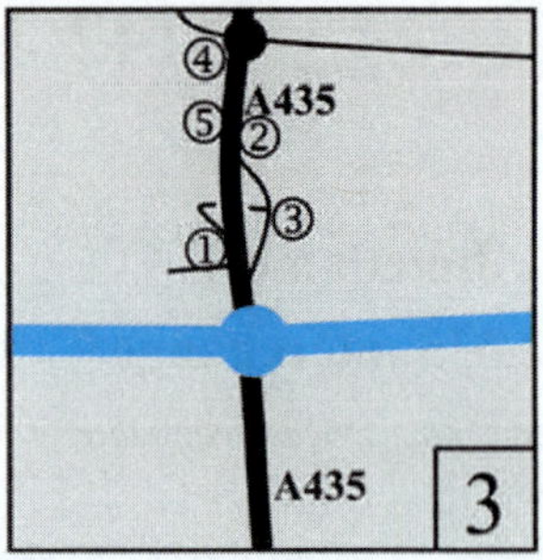

M42 Junction 3A
M42/M40 interchange

M42 Junction 4
Chiswick Green

FUEL

Tesco SAVE ££ 0.2m ①
Open- *Daily 24 hours*
Info- *WC, cash machines at 24 hr store.*
Tel- *0121 253 7500*

FOOD

Tesco Cafe☞ £3.50 0.4m ①
Open- *M-F 0800-1900, Sat 0800-1800*
Info- *Cash machines at 24 hour store.*
Tel- *0845 677 9624*

Beefeater☞ £7.00 0.7m ②
Open- *Su-Th 1200-2200, F-Sat 1200-2300, M-F 0700-0900, Sa-Su 0800-1000*
Tel- *0121 744 2942*

Jeffersons £8.50 0.9m ③
Open- *M-Th 1200-2300, F-Sat 1200-0030, Sun 1200-2230*
Info- *American/Mexican bar-restaurant.*
Tel- *0121 733 1666*

McDonald's☞ £3.50 1.7m ④
Open- *Daily 0700-2300*
Tel- *0121 733 6327*

ACCOMMODATION

Travel Inn☞ £45 0.7m ②
Info- *Solihull (Hockley Heath) location.*
Dir'n- *Next to Beefeater restaurant.*
Tel- *0870 197 7230*

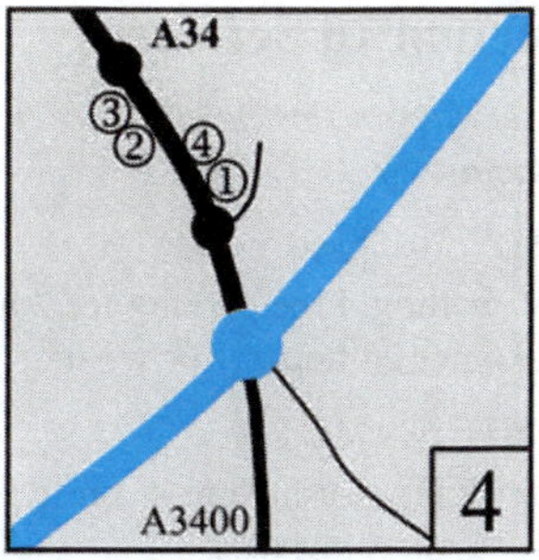

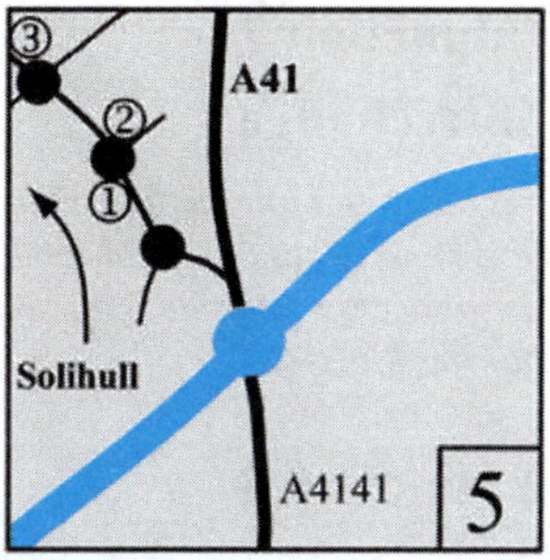

M42 Junction 5
Solihull

FUEL

BP SAVE ££ 1.3m ①
Open- *Daily 0600-2200*
Info- *WC*
Tel- *0121 704 0878*

FOOD

Bar Co pub £4.50 1.0m ②
Open- *M-F 1100-1800, Sat 1000-1700*
Info- *Varied menu & satellite TV.*
Tel- *0121 704 1567*

Rennaissance Htl rest. £13 1.9m ③
Open- *Daily 1230-1415, 1800-2145. Closed Saturday lunchtimes.*
Info- *Refined dining in hotel restaurant.*
Tel- *0121 711 3000*

ACCOMMODATION

Rennaissance Hotel £120 1.9m ③
Info- *On-site restaurant, bar & health club. Solihull location.*
Tel- *0121 711 3000*

ESSENTIALS

Solihull Hospital 2m
Dir'n- *Follow signs on entering Solihull.*
Tel- *0121 424 2000*

M42 Junction 6
NEC

FUEL

Esso SAVE ££ 0.8m ①
Open- *Daily 24 hours*
Info- *WC, cash machine.*
Tel- *01675 443498*

ACCOMMODATION

Arden Hotel £115 1.0m ①
Info- *On-site restaurant & bar. Leisure club. Independent hotel.*
Tel- *01675 443221*

THINGS TO DO

NEC 0.7m ②
Open- *Times vary with the event.*
Info- *National Exhibition Centre.*

Nat'l Motorcycle Msm £5 0.2m ③
Open- *Daily 1000-1800*
Info- *Motorcycle museum & cafe. A serious fire in late 2003 may affect entry to this museum.*
Tel- *01675 443311*

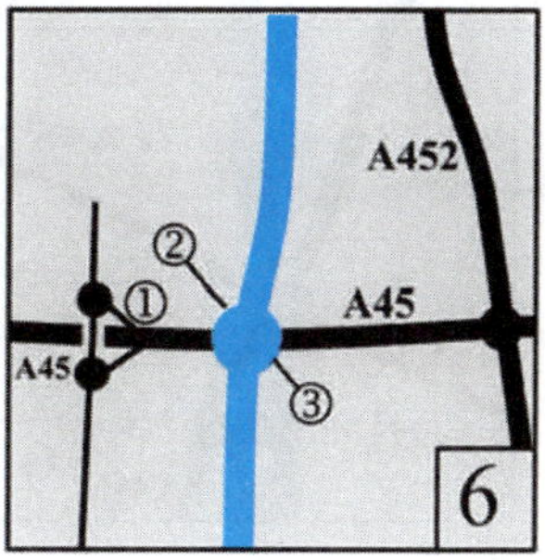

M42 Junction 7
M6 interchange

This is a restricted interchange with the M6 and there is no access to local facilities. There is no access from the M42 southbound to the M6.

M42 Junction 8
M6 interchange

This is an interchange with the M6 and there is no access to local facilities. You can only join the M42 from the M6 southbound and exit from the M42 southbound to the M6 northbound.

M42 Junction 9
Curdworth

FOOD

The White Horse £7.00 0.7m ①
Open- *M-Sat 1200-2200, Sun 1200-2130*
Info- *Varied hot & cold menu.*
Tel- *01675 470227*

ACCOMMODATION

Water Park Lodge £57.50 0.4m ②
Info- *Private hotel. Prices are for B&B.*
Tel- *01675 470533*

Reindeer Park Lodge £57.50 0.5m ②
Info- *Private hotel, RAC /ETC 4◆. Prices are for B&B. Free airport parking for guests.*
Tel- *01675 470811*

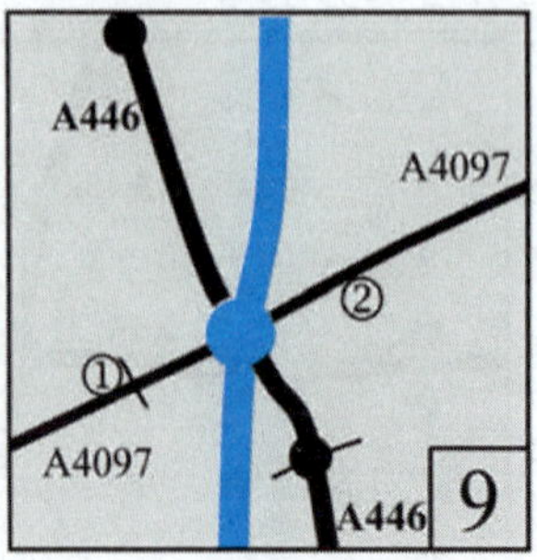

Junction 10 Services

The services at this junction are just off the motorway.

FUEL Esso
HGV fuelling. Free parking for 2 hours then £6 per 24 hours. Lorry park.

FOOD MOTO
Burger King, freshexpress, Little Chef.
Info- *Cash machines.*

ACCOMMODATION

Travelodge☞ £50 0.3m
Info- *Tamworth location.*
Tel- *0870 085 0950*

M42 Junction 10
Tamworth

FUEL

Murco **SAVE** £ 0.3m ①
Open- *M-F 0830-1730, Sat 0900-1700*
Tel- *01827 280089*

FOOD

Brewers Fayre☞ £7.00 0.4m ②
Open- *M-Sat 1130-2200, Sun 1200-2200*
Dir'n- *Make sure to take the first slip road.*
Tel- *01827 260587*

ESSENTIALS

George Eliot Hospital 10m
Dir'n- *Take the A5, and then A444 to south of Nuneaton where the hospital is signposted.*
Tel- *02476 351351*

Tamworth Tourist Info. Centre
Tel- *01827 709581*

Kinsall Green Garage 0.4m ①
Open- *M-F 0830-1730, Sat 0900-1700*
Info- *Small garage for repairs.*
Tel- *01827 280089*

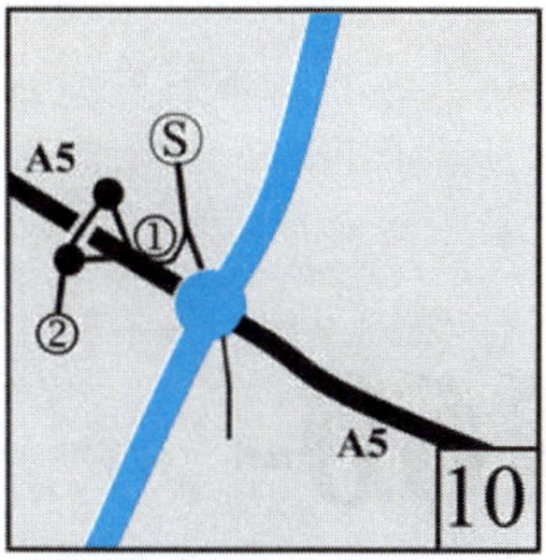

M42 Junction 11
Motorway ends

FUEL

Total SAVE £ 0.2m ①

Open- *Daily 24 hours*
Info- *LPG, HGV fuelling, cash machines. Postbox.*
Tel- *01530 271660*

FOOD

Arts Restaurant & Bar £8.00 0.2m ②

Open- *M-Sat 1800-2145, Sun 1900-2130, Daily 1000-1400.*
Info- *Restaurant at the Hotel Metro.*
Tel- *01530 279500*

McDonald's☞ £3.50 0.2m ①

Open- *Sun-Th 0600-2330, F-Sat 0600-2400*
Tel- *01530 273197*

ACCOMMODATION

Hotel Metro £40 0.2m ②

Info- *On-site restaurant & bar. Independent hotel.*
Tel- *01530 279500*

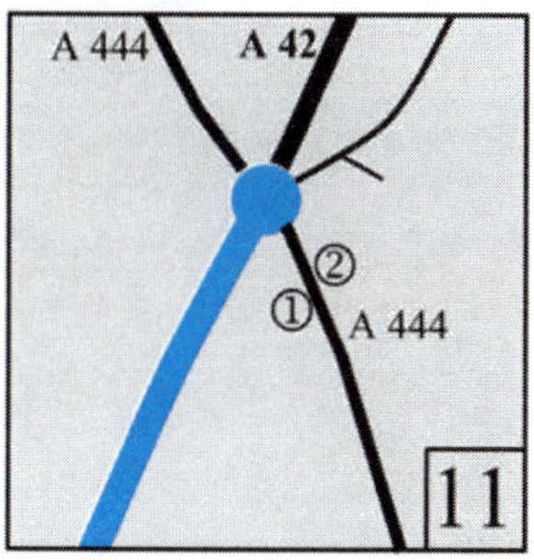

M62/M60-
Liverpool to Hull

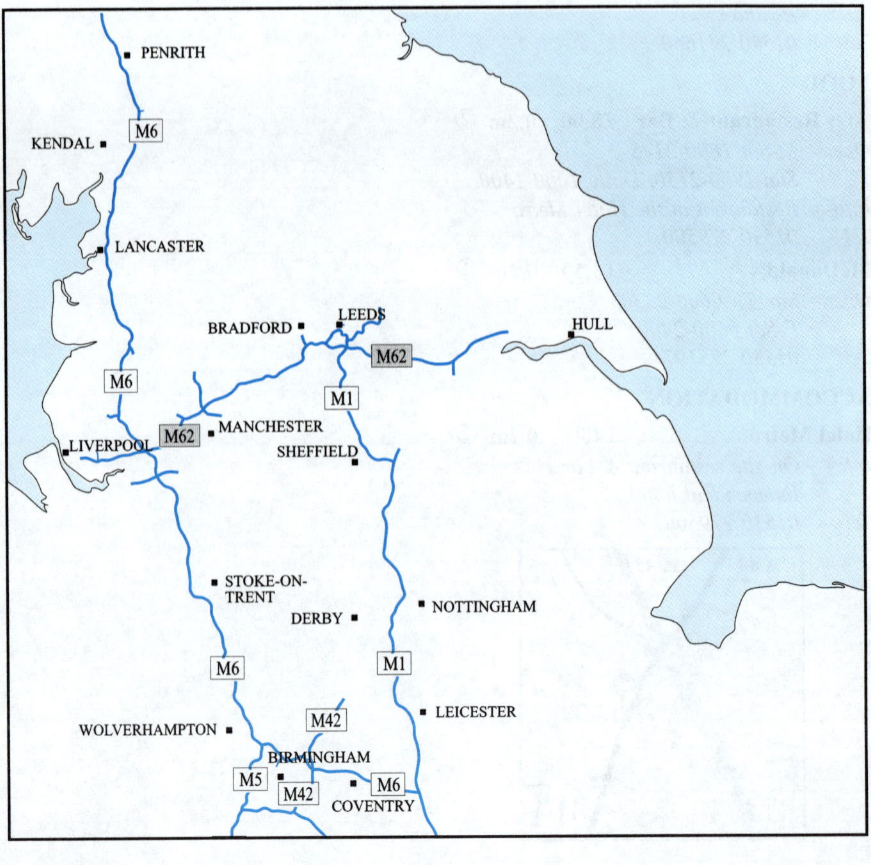

M62/M60 Summary of Junctions

Radio stations & frequencies		Junction	Fuel	Food	Hotels	Essentials
Mrsy 95.8 Lanc 103.9	City 96.7 Signal 1 102.6	4				TIC
Mrsy 95.8 Lanc 103.9	City 96.7 Signal 1 102.6	5	✓	✓	✓	Pharmacy
Mrsy 95.8 Lanc 103.9	Juice 107.6 City 96.7	6	24hr	✓	✓	A&E
Signal 1 102.6 Lanc 103.9	Key 103 103.0 City 96.7	7	24hr	✓	✓	A&E
Signal 1 102.6 Lanc 103.9	Key 103 103.0 City 96.7	8				
Rock FM 97.4 Lanc 103.9	Key 103 103.0 City 96.7	S	24hr	✓	✓	
BBC Leed 92.4 Mrsy 95.8	GMR 95.1 City 96.7	9	24hr	✓	✓	A&E TIC, Svc
BBC Leed 92.4 Mrsy 95.8	GMR 95.1 City 96.7	10				
BBC Stk 94.6 Mrsy 95.8	Rock FM 97.4 City 96.7	11				
BBC Stk 94.6 Mrsy 95.8	Rock FM 97.4 City 96.7	12				A&E TIC
BBC Leed 92.4 Mrsy 95.8	GMR 95.1 City 96.7	13	24hr	✓	✓	
BBC GMR 95.1 ALL FM 96.9	The Rev 96.2 Key103 103.0	14				
BBC GMR 95.1 ALL FM 96.9	The Rev 96.2 Key103 103.0	15				A&E
BBC Stk 94.6 BBC Lanc	GMR 95.1 Signal 1 102.6	16				
BBC GMR 95.1 ALL FM 96.9	The Rev 96.2 Key103 103.0	17	24hr	✓		Pharmacy Svc
BBC Leed 92.4 Galaxy 102.0	GMR 95.1 Key103 103.1	18				
BBC GMR 95.1 ALL FM 96.9	The Rev 96.2 Key103 103.0	S	24hr	✓	✓	TIC

Top Stops are highlighted

Radio stations & frequencies		Junction	Fuel	Food	Hotels	Essentials	Things to do
BBC Leed 92.4 Galaxy 102.0	GMR 95.1 Key103 103.1	19	24hr				
BBC GMR 95.1 Century 105.4	Rock FM 97.4 Cymru 104.3	20				A&E TIC	
BBC GMR 95.1 Century 105.4	Rock FM 97.4 Cymru 104.3	21	24hr	✓	✓		
BBC Leed 92.4 Viking 95.9	GMR 95.1 Humb 95.9	22					✓
BBC Leed 92.4 Viking 95.9	GMR 95.1 Humb 95.9	23				A&E	
BBC Leed 92.4 Viking 95.9	GMR 95.1 Humb 95.9	24	24hr	✓	✓	A&E TIC	
BBC Leed 92.4 Pulse 102.5	Home 107.9 GMR 95.1	25	✓	✓	✓		
BBC Leed 92.4 Pulse 102.5	Home 107.9 GMR 95.1	S	24hr	✓	✓		
Galaxy 105.8	Real 106.2	26		✓	✓	A&E TIC Svc	
BBC Leed 92.4 BBC GMR 95.1	Pulse 102.5 Galaxy 105.8	27	24hr	✓	✓	A&E TIC Svc	✓
BBC Leed 92.4 BBC York	Pulse 102.5 Galaxy 105.8	28			✓		
BBC Leed 92.4 BBC York	Pulse 102.5 Galaxy 105.8	29				A&E	
Humb 95.9 Viking 96.9	Rad Aire 96.3 Pulse! 102.5	30				A&E TIC	
Ridings 106.8 Galaxy 105.11	Pulse! 102.5 Real 106.2	31		✓	✓		
BBC Leed 92.4 Viking 96.9	Humb 95.9 Pulse! 102.5	32	24hr	✓	✓	Svc	✓
Humb 95.9 Pulse! 102.5	Rad Aire 96.3 Real 106.2	33 S	24hr	✓	✓	Svc	
York 103.7 Minster 104.7	Viking 96.9 Galaxy 105.1	34	✓	✓		Svc	
Humb 95.9 Hallam 103.4	Viking 96.9 York 103.7	35					
Humb 95.9 Hallam 103.4	Viking 96.9 York 103.7	36	24hr	✓	✓	A&E	

Radio stations & frequencies		Junction	Fuel	Food	Hotels	Essentials	Things to do
Humb 95.9 Minster 104.7	Viking 96.9 York 103.7	37	24hr	✓	✓		✓
Humb 95.9 Minster 104.7	Viking 96.9 York 103.7	38	End of Motorway		✓	TIC	

M62/M60 Junction Details

M62 Junction 4
Motorway starts

ESSENTIALS

Liverpool Tourist Information Centre
Tel- *0151 707 0986*

M62 Junction 5
Huyton

FUEL

Murco SAVE ££ 0.9m ①
Open- *Daily 0700-2300*
Info- *Carwash, WC.*
Tel- *0151 489 6211*

Q8 SAVE £ 1m ②
Open- *Daily 0600-2300*
Info- *Jetwash, WC.*
Tel- *0151 481 0188*

FOOD

The Crofters £3.25 0.9m ①
Open- *Daily 1200-1500*
Info- *Bar food at local pub.*
Tel- *0151 482 4951*

ACCOMMODATION

Premier Lodge☞ £48 0.7m ③
Info- *Liverpool South-East location.*
Tel- *0870 990 6596*

ESSENTIALS

Pharmacy 0.9m ④
Open- *M-F 0900-1300, 1400-1900, Sat 0900-1300, 1400-1730*
Tel- *0151 489 5817*

THINGS TO DO

Nat'l Wildflower Centre £3.00 0.6m ⑤
Open- *April 1-Sept 30, daily 1000-1700.*
Tel- *0151 737 1819*

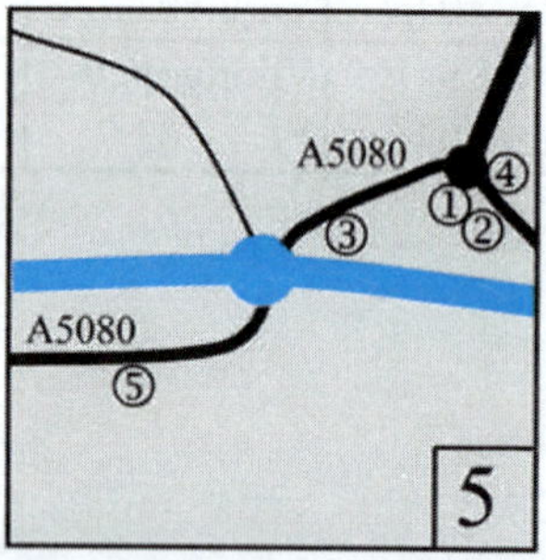

M62 Junction 6
M62/M57 interchange

FUEL

Esso SAVE £££ 0.5m ①
Open- *Daily 24 hours.*
Info- *Carwash, cash machine.*
Tel- *0151 489 2053*

FOOD

Sallingers Restaurant £8.50 0.3m ②
Open- *Daily 1200-1400, 1700-2200*
Info- *Dining at the Village Hotel restaurant.*
Tel- *0151 449 2341*

Brewsters☞ £6.50 0.4m ③
Open- *M-F 1130-2200, Sun 1200-2200*
Tel- *0151 480 9614*

Hare & Hounds £6.00 0.7m ④
Open- *Daily 1200-1400, 1900-2130*
Info- *Varied pub menu & 'Fun Factory'.*
Tel- *0151 489 3046*

ACCOMMODATION

Village Hotel☞ £45 0.3m ②
Info- *On-site bar, restaurant, pool, leisure club. Part of 'Village Hotel' chain.*
Tel- *0151 449 2341*

Travel Inn☞ £45 0.4m ③
Info- *Tarbock location.*
Tel- *0870 197 7159*

ESSENTIALS

Whiston Hospital 2m

Dir'n- This is well signposted from the motorway.

Tel- 0151 426 1600

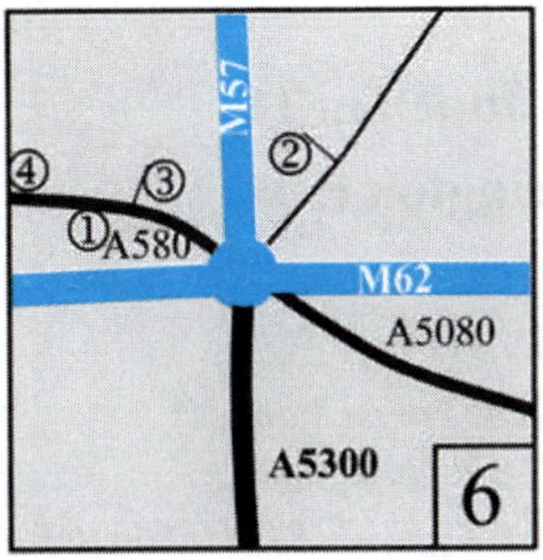

M62 Junction 7
Widnes

FUEL

Shell SAVE £ 0.6m ①

Open- Daily 24 hours.

Info- WC, jetwash.

Tel- 0151 426 4199

FOOD

Henry's Table☛ £7.50 0.7m ②

Open- Daily 1200-2200

Tel- 0151 426 4165

Brewsters☛ £6.50 1m ③

Open- Daily 1100-2200

Info- The Micklehead Green.

Tel- 01744 818971

ACCOMMODATION

Premier Lodge☛ £48 0.7m ②

Info- Liverpool East location.

Tel- 0870 201 0203

Travel Inn☛ £45 1m ③

Info- St Helens location.

Tel- 0870 197 7237

ESSENTIALS

Whiston Hospital 2.5m

Dir'n- Take the A57 north-west towards Whiston, and the hospital is on the left.

Tel- 0151 426 1600

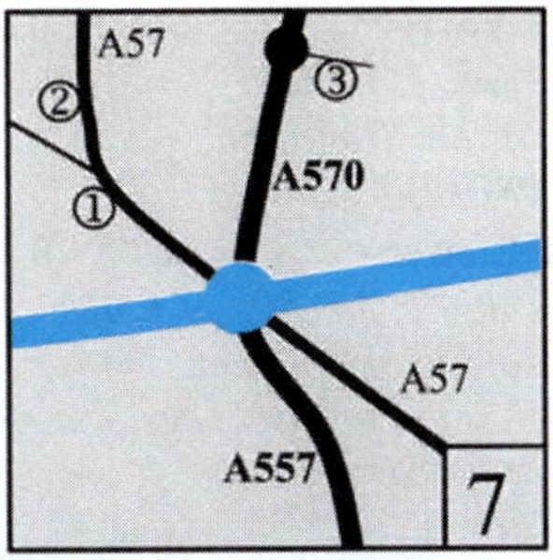

M62 Junction 8
Warrington West

There are no facilities close to this junction.

Burtonwood Services

There is no footbridge or roadbridge at this services.

FUEL SHELL

HGV fuelling & parking. Free parking for 2 hours then £6 per day.

FOOD WELCOME BREAK

Granary, Red Hen

Info- Cash machine.

ACCOMMODATION

Travelodge☛ £40

Info- Manchester North location. Dogs welcome.

Tel- 0870 191 1661

M62 Junction 9
Warrington North

FUEL

Safeway SAVE ££ 1m ①

Open- Daily 24 hours.

Info- LPG, WC, carwash.

Tel- 01925 634255

FOOD

Burger King☛ £7.00 0.2m ②

Open- M-F 0800-2200, Sat-Sun 1000-2200

Tel- 01925 573387

Brewers Fayre☞ £7.00 0.6m ③
Open- Daily 1130-2200
Info- Next to Travel Inn.
Tel- 0870 197 7260

Chef & Brewer☞ £8.00 0.6m ④
Open- Daily 1100-2230, M-F 0700-0930, Sat-Sun 0800-1000
Info- Next to Premier Lodge.
Tel- 0870 990 6600

Pizza Hut☞ £6.00 1m ⑤
Open- Daily 1200-2300
Tel- 01925 574220

KFC☞ £4.00 1m ⑤
Open- Daily 1100-2100
Tel- 01925 419786

ACCOMMODATION

Travel Inn☞ £45 0.6m ③
Info- Warrington North location.
Tel- 08701 977260

Premier Lodge☞ £48 0.6m ④
Info- Warrington North location.
Tel- 0870 990 6600

ESSENTIALS

Warrington Hospital 3.5m
Info- This is well signposted from the motorway turnoff.
Tel- 01925 635911

Warrington Tourist Information Centre
Tel- 01925 442180

Charlie Brown's 1m ①
Info- Tyres, exhausts & car repairs.
Tel- 01925 240520

Hyundai Dealer 1m ①
Info- Next to Charlie Brown's.

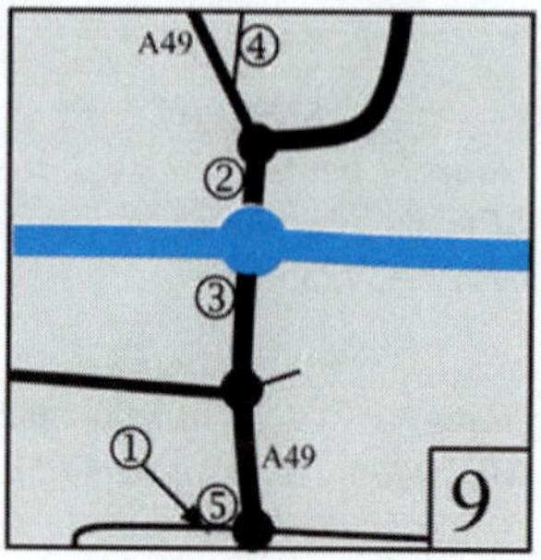

M62 Junction 10
M62/M6 interchange

There is no access to local services at this junction.

M62 Junction 11
Warrington East

There are no facilities close to this junction.

THINGS TO DO

Birchwood Forest Park 1m ①
Open- Daylight hours.
Info- Large country park with play areas.

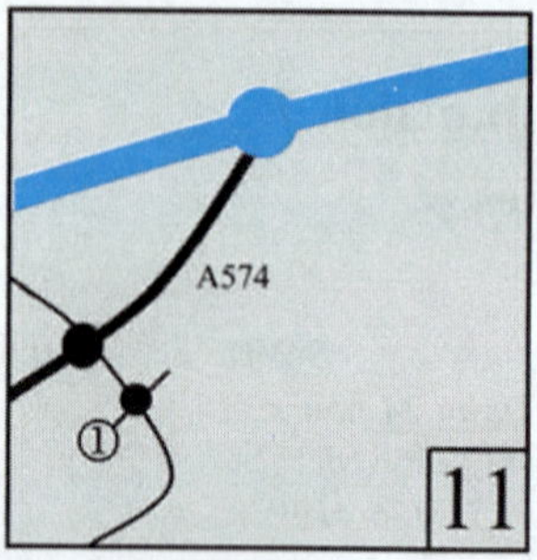

M62 Junction 12
M60/M62/M602 interchange

There is no access to local services at this junction.

ESSENTIALS

Hope Hospital 3m
Dir'n- Take the M602 towards Manchester and take the A576 at Junction 2, where the hospital is signposted.
Tel- 0161 789 7373

Manchester Tourist Information Centre
Tel- 0161 234 3157

M60 Junction 13
Worsley

FUEL

Texaco SAVE ££ 0.6m ①
Open- *Daily 24 hours.*
Info- *WC, jetwash, cash machine.*
Tel- *0161 7894665*

Esso SAVE ££ 0.7m ②
Open- *Daily 24 hours.*
Info- *Cash machine.*
Tel- *0161 702 0370*

FOOD

Tapas Bar £7.50 0.2m ③
Open- *M-Sat 1700-2300*
Info- *Extensive Spanish menu.*
Tel- *0161 793 6003*

The John Gilbert £8.00 0.2m ④
Open- *Daily 1130-2230*
Info- *Extensive menu & carvery.*
Tel- *0161 703 7733*

Bridgewater Hotel £6.50 0.3m ⑤
Open- *M-Sat 1100-2130, Sun 1200-2000*
Info- *Varied pub menu. Satellite TV.*
Tel- *0161 794 0589*

Milan restaurant £14 0.3m ⑤
Open- *M-F 1200-1430, 1730-2230, Sat 1730-2330, Sun 1200-2230*
Info- *Refined dining. Italian menu.*
Tel- *0161 794 5444*

Barton Arms £7.00 0.4m ⑥
Open- *Daily 1200-2000*
Info- *Extensive menu. An 'Ember Inn'.*
Tel- *0161 727 9318*

Marriott restaurant £15 0.4m ⑦
Open- *Su-Fr 1200-1400, 1900-2145, Sat 1900-2145*
Info- *Hotel restaurant with* ***AA Rosette****.*
Tel- *0870 400 7270*

Brewers Fayre☞ £7.00 0.4m ⑦
Open- *Daily 1200-2200*
Tel- *0161 799 2960*

Henry's Table☞ £7.50 0.7m ②
Open- *Daily 1200-2130*
Tel- *0161 790 2381*

ACCOMMODATION

Novotel☞ £72 0.2m ④
Info- *Bar & restaurant. Manchester West location.*
Tel- *0161 799 3535*

Marriott Hotel ☞ £115 0.4m ⑦
Info- *Bar, restaurant, pool, health club & golf in this 'country club'. Worsley Park location.*
Tel- *0870 400 7270*

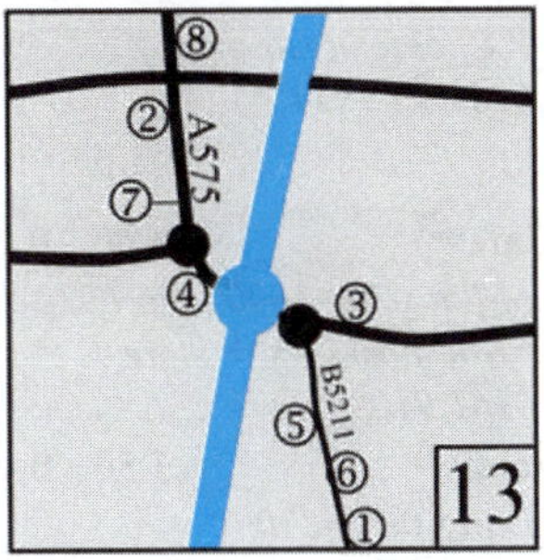

M60 Junction 14
Restricted

This gives limited access to the A580, and exiting for local facilities is not advised.

M60 Junction 15
M60/M61 interchange

This is a restricted junction and there is no access to local services.

ESSENTIALS

Royal Bolton Hospital 4.5m
Dir'n- *Take the M61 west and turn off at Junction 4. Take the northwards turn off to the B6199 east, where the hospital is signposted.*
Tel- *01204 390390*

M60 Junction 16
Restricted

This junction allows entry to the motorway only from the A666 towards Manchester, and exit only to the A666 towards Manchester.

M62 Junction 17
Manchester North

FUEL

BP SAVE £££ 0.6m ①
Open- *Daily 24 hours.*
Info- *LPG, cash machine.*
Tel- *0161 772 9969*

Tesco SAVE £££ 0.5m ②
Open- *Daily 24 hours.*
Info- *WC, cafe at store.*
Tel- *0161 910 9445*

FOOD

Tesco Cafe☞ £3.50 0.5m ②
Open- *M-Sat 0700-2000, Sun 0930-1600*
Info- *Cash machines at store.*
Tel- *0161 910 9400*

McDonald's☞ £3.50 0.4m ③
Open- *Daily 0800-2300*
Tel- *0161 767 9731*

Hong Kong Takeaway £6.00 0.4m ③
Open- *Tu-Sat 1700-2230*
Info- *Chinese meals to take away.*
Tel- *0161 766 8088*

The Mogul £5.00 0.4m ④
Open- *Daily 1800-2300*
Info- *Halal Indian restaurant & takeaway.*
Tel- *0161 796 0403*

Dawat Tandoori £5.00 0.6m ⑤
Open- *Su-Th 1700-2400, F/Sat 1700-0100*
Info- *Indian takeaway.*
Tel- *0161 796 5976*

Peppers £5.50 0.6m ⑤
Open- *Tu-F 1700-2300, Sa/Sun 1700-2400*
Info- *Pizzeria and pasta restaurant.*

Roma Restaurant £5.50 0.7m ⑥
Open- *M-F 0915-1800, Sat 0915-1700*
Info- *Italian restaurant & coffee shop.*
Tel- *0161 766 2941*

Pizza Base £6.50 0.8m ⑥
Open- *Daily 1700-2330*
Info- *Takeaway pizzas.*
Tel- *0161 796 6266*

ESSENTIALS

Tesco Pharmacy 0.5m ②
Open- *M-Sat 0800-2200, Sun 1000-1600*
Tel- *0161 910 9447*

Tyre & Exhaust Centre 0.4m ⑦
Open- *M-F 0900-1800, Sat 0900-1300*
Info- *Minor repairs.*
Tel- *0161 767 9921*

Vauxhall Dealer ⑧

Mercedes Dealer ⑨

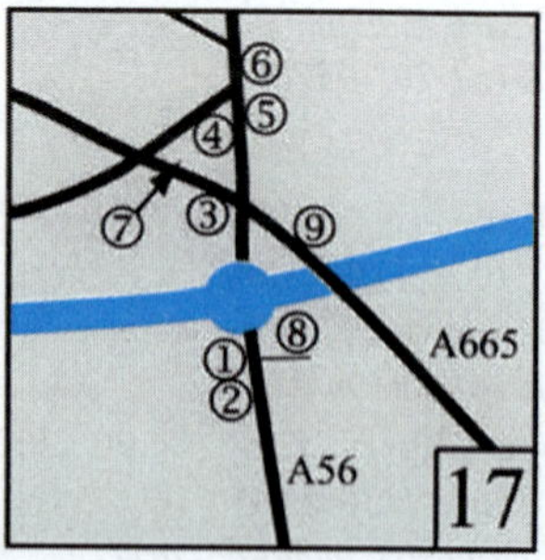

M62 Junction 18
M62/M60 interchange

There is no access to local services at this junction.

ESSENTIALS

Bury Tourist Information Centre
Tel- *01204 364333*

Manchester Tourist Information Centre
Tel- *0161 234 3157*

Birch Services

This services has a footbridge.

FUEL ESSO
HGV fuelling & parking. Free parking for 2 hours then £6 per day.

FOOD MOTO
Harry Ramsden's, Ritazza, freshexpress, Burger King, Little Chef, Upper Crust.
Info- *Cash machine.*

ACCOMMODATION

Travelodge☞ £45
Info- *On both carriageways. Manchester North location.*
Tel- *0870 191 1661*

M62 Junction 19
Heywood

FUEL

Texaco SAVE ££ 0.3m ①

Open- *Daily 24 hours.*
Info- *WC, jetwash, cash machine.*
Tel- *01706 692100*

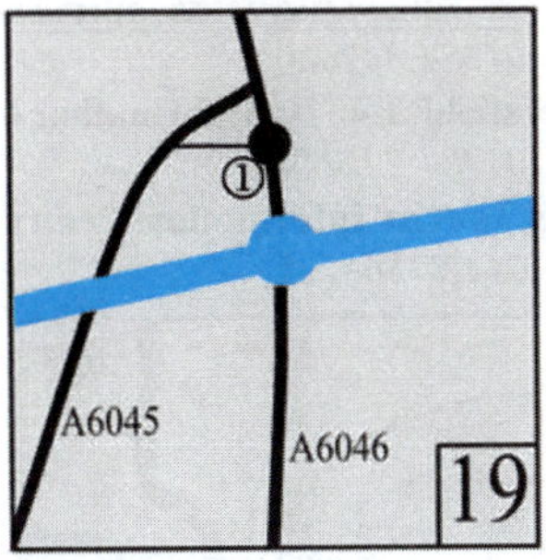

M62 Junction 20
Restricted

This is no access to local services at this junction.

ESSENTIALS

Royal Oldham Hospital 3m

Dir'n- *Take the A627(M) towards Manchester, and then the turn off to the A627/A663. The hospital is signposted close to the turn off, on the A627.*
Tel- *0161 624 0420*

Oldham Tourist Information Centre

Tel- *0161 627 1024*

Rochdale Tourist Information Centre

Tel- *01706 356592*

M62 Junction 21
Milnrow

FUEL

BP SAVE ££ 0.9m ①

Open- *Daily 24 hours.*
Info- *WC, carwash, cash machine.*
Tel- *01706 641132*

FOOD

Hungry Horse Pub☞ £3.00 0.4m ②

Open- *M-Sat 1200-2100, Sun 1200-2030*
Info- *Satellite TV.*
Tel- *01706 355405*

Brewers Fayre☞ £7.00 0.6m ③

Open- *M-Sat 1100-2200, Sun 1200-2200*
Info- *Next to Travel Inn.*
Tel- *01706 299999*

ACCOMMODATION

Travel Inn☞ £45 0.6m ③

Info- *Next to Brewers Fayre.*
Tel- *01706 299999*

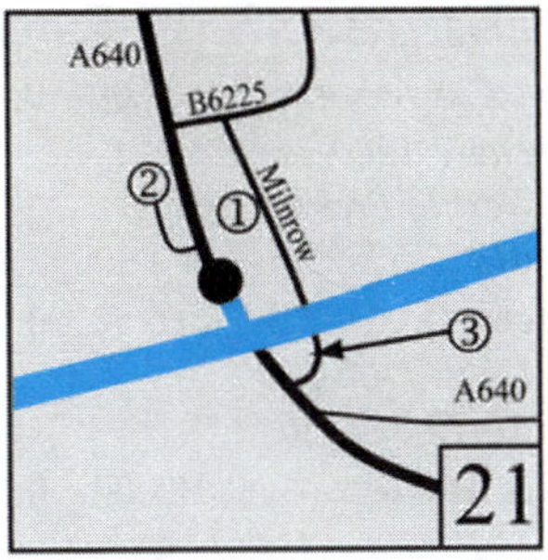

M62 Junction 22
Saddleworth Moor

There are no services close to this junction.

THINGS TO DO

Saddleworth Moor

Info- *Just off the motorway junction. Good views 0.5 miles south.*

M62 Junction 23
Restricted

This junction allows entry to the motorway westbound only, and exit only from the motorway eastbound.

ESSENTIALS

Huddersfield Royal Infirmary 3m

Dir'n- *Eastbound travellers take the A640 towards Huddersfield. The hospital is signposted near the town centre.*
Tel- *01484 342000*

M62 Junction 24
Huddersfield

FUEL

BP SAVE £££ 0.7m ①
Open- *Daily 24 hours.*
Info- *WC, carwash, cash machine.*
Tel- *01484 451362*

FOOD

Olympic Restaurant £13 0.3m ②
Open- *Daily 1230-1345, 1900-2145*
Info- *Refined dining at the Cedar Court Hotel.*
Tel- *01422 375431*

Country Carvery☞ £7.00 0.4m ③
Open- *Daily 1200-2100*
Info- *Next to Premier Lodge.*
Tel- *01422 373758*

Brewsters☞ £6.50 0.4m ④
Open- *Daily 1100-2200*
Tel- *01422 374360*

The Grey Horse £5.00 0.5m ⑤
Open- *M-F 1200-1430, 1730-2030, Sat 1200-2030, Sun 1200-2000*
Info- *Varied menu in local pub.*
Tel- *01422 314941*

Tamanna's Brasserie £7.00 0.5m ⑥
Open- *M-Sa 1730-2400, Sun 1600-2300*
Info- *Extensive menu at local brasserie.*
Tel- *01422 374616*

Da Sandro's Rest £8.00 0.7m ⑦
Open- *M-Sat 1200-1400. 1800-2230, Sun 1230-2145*
Info- *Pizza & Pasta restaurant.*
Tel- *01484 512845*

ACCOMMODATION

Cedar Court Hotel £95 0.3m ②
Info- *On-site bar, restaurant, pool, health club.*
Tel- *01422 375431*

Premier Lodge☞ £48 0.4m ③
Info- *Next to Country Carvery bar/ restaurant. Huddersfield location.*
Tel- *0870 990 6488*

Briar Court Hotel £72 0.7m ⑦
Info- *ETC 3◆. The Da Sandro restaurant is adjacent.*
Tel- *01484 519902*

ESSENTIALS

Huddersfield Royal Infirmary 3m
Dir'n- *Take the A629 towards Huddersfield, and the hospital is signposted as you approach the town centre.*
Tel- *01484 342000*

Huddersfield Tourist Information Centre
Tel- *01484 222444*

Halifax Tourist Information Centre
Tel- *01422 368725*

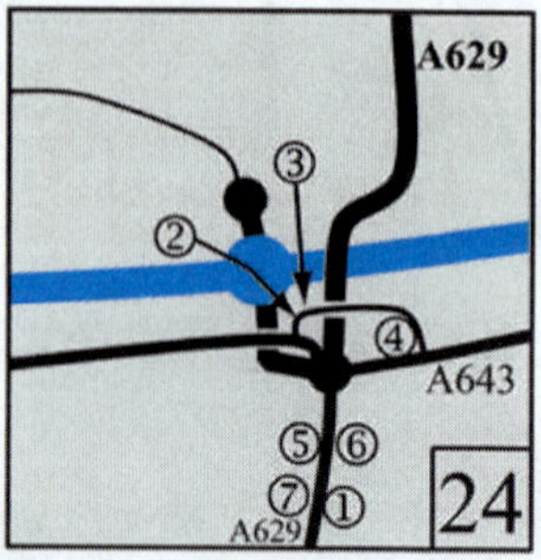

M62 Junction 25
Brighouse

FUEL

Shell SAVE ££ 0.9m ①
Open- *Daily 0600-2130*
Info- *WC, carwash.*
Tel- *01484 720371*

FOOD

The Junction Restaurant £10 0.3m ②
Open- *M-F 0630-1000, Sa/Sun 0730-1100, Sun-F 1200-1400, 1830-2200, Sat 1830-2200*
Info- *Refined dining at the Holiday Inn.*
Tel- *0870 400 9013*

ACCOMMODATION

Holiday Inn☞ £105 0.3m ②
Info- *On-site bar, restaurant, health club. Leeds Brighouse location.*
Tel- *0870 400 9013*

Chef & Brewer☞ £8.00 0.6m ③
Open- *Daily 1200-2100*
Tel- *01484 402161*

Hartshead Moor Services

This services has a footbridge.

FUEL SHELL

HGV fuelling & parking. Free parking for 2 hours then £6 per day.

FOOD WELCOME BREAK

Burger King, KFC, Coffee Primo, Granary.

Info- *Cash machine (Plus, Amex, Diners Club, Link, Visa Debit).*

ACCOMMODATION

Days Inn☞ £45
Info- *On eastbound carriageway.*
Tel- *01274 851706*

M62 Junction 26
M62/M606 interchange

FOOD

Brewsters☞ £6.50 0.3m ①
Open- *M-Sat 1100-2300, Sun 1200-2230*
Tel- *0870 197 7037*

ACCOMMODATION

Travel Inn☞ £45 0.3m ①
Info- *Next to the Brewsters restaurant. Bradford South location.*
Tel- *0870 197 7037*

ESSENTIALS

St Luke's Hospital 4.5m
Dir'n- *Take the M606, and then follow signs to the the city centre/A641. The hospital is signposted near the centre.*
Tel- *01274 734744*

Bradford Tourist Information Centre
Tel- *01274 753678*

MID Accident/Repair 0.4m ②
Open- *M-F 0900-1700, Sat 0900-1200*
Info- *Vehicle recovery & repair.*
Tel- *01274 869739*

Rover Dealer 0.5m ③

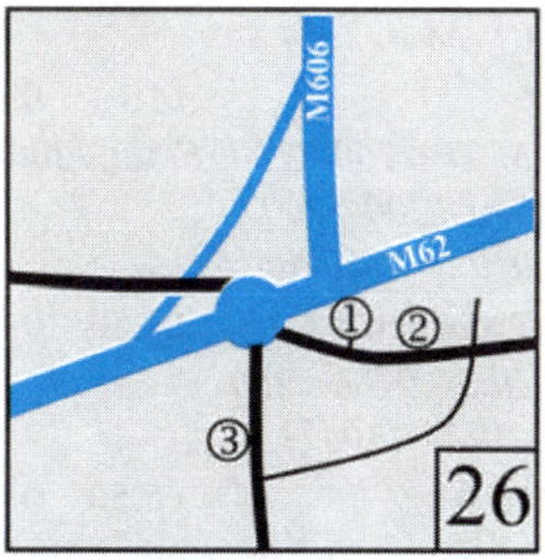

M62 Junction 27
M62/M621 interchange

FUEL

Murco SAVE £ 0.3m ①
Open- *M-F 0600-2200, Sat/Sun 0800-2200*
Info- *WC, carwash.*
Tel- *01924 441687*

Total SAVE £££ 0.8m ②
Open- *Daily 24 hours*
Info- *Carwash & postbox.*
Tel- *01132 383343*

FOOD

McDonald's☞ £3.50 0.3m ③
Open- *Daily 0700-2400*
Tel- *01924 422024*

The Exchange £10 0.3m ③
Open- *M-F 1200-2230, Sat/Sun 1200-2300*
Info *American Bar & Grill*
Tel- *01924 373758*

Pizza Hut☞ £6.00 0.3m ③
Open- *Daily 1130-2300*
Tel- *01924 420460*

Frankie & Benny's☞ £8.50 0.3m ④
Open- *M-Sat 1200-2200, Sun 1200-2230*
Tel- *01924 423747*

Chiquito☞ £8.50 0.3m ④
Open- *M-Sat 1200-2300, Sun 1200-2230*
Tel- *01924 359292*

Bella Pasta☞ £7.00 0.3m ④
Open- *M-Sat 1200-2300, Sun 1200-2230*
Tel- *01924 422374*

KFC☞ £4.00 0.3m ④
Open- *Daily 1100-2400*
Tel- *01924 422634*

TGIF☞ £10 0.3m ⑤
Open- *M-Th 1200-2230, F/Sat 1200-2300, Sun 1200-2200*
Tel- *01924 475000*

Harry Ramsden's☞ £3.50 0.5m ⑥
Open- *Daily 0700-2200*
Tel- *01924 440621*

Brewster's☞ £6.50 0.5m ⑦
Open- *M-Sat 1130-2200, Sun 1200-2200*
Info- *With childrens 'Fun Factory'.*
Tel- *0870 197 7152*

Hadley's Bistro £7.00 0.8m ②
Open- *M-Fr 1200-1430, 1700-2300, Sat 1830-2300, Sun 1230-1530*
Info- *Bar & bistro. Varied menu.*
Tel- *01132 521828*

The Millhouse £6.50 0.9m ⑧
Open- *M-Sat 1200-2030, Sun 1200-1930*
Info- *Extensive menu & real ales.*
Tel- *01132 383810*

Toby Carvery☞ £7.00 0.7m ⑨
Open- *M-F 1200-1400, 1700-2200, Sat/Sun 1200-2200*
Tel- *01132 533115*

ACCOMMODATION

Travel Inn☞ £45 0.5m ⑦
Info- *Next to the Brewsters restaurant. Leeds Bradford South location.*
Tel- *0870 197 7152*

Innkeeper's Lodge☞ £40 0.7m ⑨
Info- *Next to the Toby Inn.*
Tel- *01132 533115*

ESSENTIALS

Leeds General Infirmary 6m
Dir'n- *Take the M621 and at Junction 2 turn off and follow signs to the city centre. The hospital is signposted, close to the university.*
Tel- *01132 432799*

Bradford Tourist Information Centre
Tel- *01274 753678*

Leeds Tourist Information Centre
Tel- *01132 425242*

Highway Recovery 0.5m ⑥
Info- *24 hour recovery service.*
Dir'n- *Just opposite Harry Ramsden's.*
Tel- *01924 422177*

THINGS TO DO

West Yorkshire Retail Park 0.3m ⑤
Info- *Numerous stores near to TGIF.*

M62 Junction 28
Leeds

FOOD

Beefeater☞ £7.00 0.1m ①
Open- *M-F 1200-1500, 1700-2200 Sat/Sun 1200-2200*
Tel- *01132 532768*

Chaw's Chinese rest. £5.00 0.4m ②
Open- *Tu-Sun 1700-2330*
Info- *Chinese takeaway.*
Tel- *01132 526066*

Tingley Fish Restrnt. £7.00 0.8m ③
Open- *Daily 1130-2030*
Info- *Fish restaurant with a traditional atmosphere.*
Tel- *01132 533774*

Brewsters☞ £6.50 0.9m ④
Open- *M-Sa 1130-2200, Sun 1200-2200*
Tel- *01132 523720*

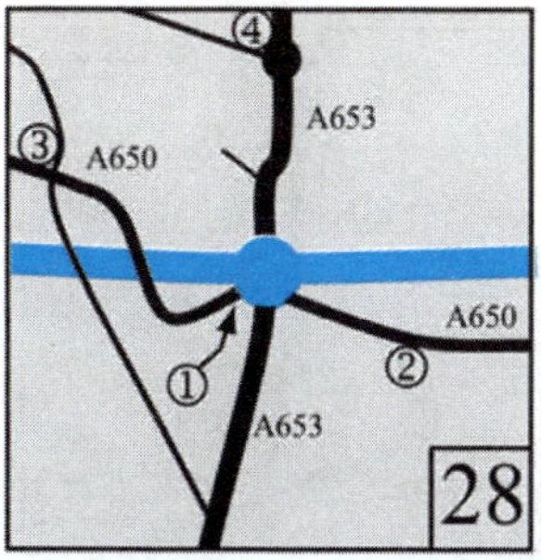

M62 Junction 29
M62/M1 interchange

ESSENTIALS

Leeds General Infirmary 7m
Dir'n- *Take the M1 north, and at the next junction take the M621. At Junction 4 turn off and follow signs to the city centre. The hospital is signposted, close to the university.*
Tel- *01132 432799*

M62 Junction 30
Rothwell

There are no facilities close to this junction.

ESSENTIALS

Pinderfields Hospital 3m
Dir'n- *Take the A642 south towards Wakefield, and the hospital is on the right.*
Tel- *01924 201688*

Wakefield Tourist Information Centre
Tel- *01924 787787*

M62 Junction 31
Normanton/Castleford

FOOD

The Village £6.50 0.2m ①
Open- *Daily 1200-2200*
Info- *Part of the Millhouse chain.* ☞ *Extensive pub-restaurant menu.*
Tel- *01924 897171*

The Trading Post £7.50 0.6m ②
Open- *M-Sat 1200-2130, Sun 1200-2100*
Info- *Extensive pub & restaurant menu.*
Tel- *01977 519587*

The Rising Sun £6.50 0.8m ③
Open- *M-F 1200-2200, Sun 1200-2100*
Info- *Extensive pub & restaurant menu.*
Tel- *01977 554766*

ACCOMMODATION

Village Motel☞ £40 0.2m ①
Info- *Normanton location of the Millhouse chain.* ☞
Tel- *01924 897171*

Premier Lodge☞ £48 0.6m ②
Info- *Next to Trading Post pub-restaurant. Castleford location.*
Tel- *0870 990 6592*

M62 Junction 32
Castleford/Pontefract

FUEL

BP SAVE ££ 0.5m ①
Open- *Daily 24 hours*
Info- *Carwash, HGV fuelling.*
Tel- *01977 553489*

Texaco SAVE ££ 0.7m ②
Open- *Daily 24 hours*
Info- *WC*
Tel- *01977 552718*

FOOD

McDonald's no. 1☞ £3.50 0.3m ③
Open- *Daily 0730-2200*
Tel- *01977 555692*

Pizza Hut☞ £6.00 0.3m ③
Open- *Su-Th 1130-2200, F/Sa 1130-2300*
Tel- *01977 520333*

Furlong Inn £50 0.4m ④
Open- *M-Sat 1200-1400, 1800-2100, Sun 1200-2100*
Info- *Inn next to hotel. Extensive menu.*
Tel- *01977 709911*

Tom Cobleigh Inn☞ £6.50 0.6m ②
Open- *M-Sat 1200-2200, Sun 1200-2130*
Tel- *01977 668383*

McDonald's no. 2☞ £3.50 0.9m ⑤
Open- *Sun-Th 0730-2300, F/Sa 0730-2400*
Tel- *01977 602919*

ACCOMMODATION

Parkside Hotel £50 0.4m ④
Info- *On-site bar-restaurant. Independent hotel.*
Tel- *01977 709911*

ESSENTIALS

Car Dealers 0.3m
Info- *Ford, Fiat & Vauxhall dealers.*
Dir'n- *Ford/Fiat next to and opposite Pizza Hut. Vauxhall next to BP garage.*

Simpsons Car Repair Centre 0.7m
Open- *M-F 0900-1700, Sat 0900-1300*
Dir'n- *Just before the Texaco station.*
Tel- *01977 511601*

Halfords 0.9m ⑤
Open- *M-F 0900-2000, Sat 0900-1800, Sun 1000-1700*
Info- *Car parts.*
Tel- *01977 703224*

THINGS TO DO

Pontefract Racecouse 0.8m ⑥
Info- *Horse races year round.*
Tel- *01977 703224*

'Freeport' Outlet Mall 0.4m ③
Open- *M-F 1000-2000, Sat 1000-1800, Sun 1200-1700*
Info- *Outlet centre with a cafe.*
Tel- *01977 520153*

M62 Junction 33 Pontefract

FUEL

Texaco SAVE ££ 1.3m ①
Open- *Daily 24 hours*
Info- *WC, carwash, cash machine.*
Tel- *01977 636600*

FOOD

Brewsters☞ £6.50 1.3m ②
Open- *M-Sat 1130-2200, Sun 1200-2200*
Info- *Next to Travel Inn & has 'Fun Factory' for children.*
Tel- *0870 197 7209*

ACCOMMODATION

Travel Inn☞ £45 1.4m ②
Info- *Pontefract location. Next to Brewsters.*
Tel- *0870 197 7209*

ESSENTIALS

Motorcity 1.3m ①
Open- *M-F 0830-1800, Sat 0930-1400*
Info- *Tyres, exhausts & repairs.*
Tel- *01977 670411*

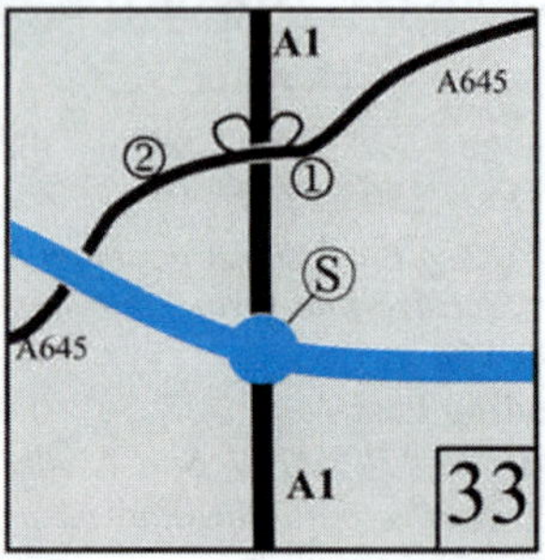

Junction 33 Services

This is located just off the motorway.

FUEL ESSO

HGV fuelling & parking. Free parking for 2 hours then £6 per day.

FOOD MOTO

Burger King, Harry Ramsden's, Ritazza, Little Chef, freshexpress.

Info- Cash machine.

ACCOMMODATION

Travelodge☞ £50

Info- Pontefract Ferrybridge location. Meeting room for hire.

Tel- 0870 191 1669

M62 Junction 34 Whitley

FUEL

Independent SAVE £ 0.5m ①

Open- M-F 0715-1830, Sat 0800-1400

Info- Small local garage. No cheques.

Tel- 01977 661256

FOOD

George & Dragon £5.00 0.6m ②

Open- Daily 1200-1400, 1900-2100

Info- Varied hot & cold food.

Tel- 01977 661319

Jolly Miller £4.50 0.5m ③

Open- M-F 1800-2030, Sun 1130-1430, Sat 1200-1400, 1800-2030

Info- Pub food.

Tel- 01977 661348

ESSENTIALS

Station Garage/Recovery 0.5m ①

Open- M-F 0715-1830, Sat 0800-1400

Info- Small local garage & 24 hour recovery. No cheques.

Tel- 01977 661256

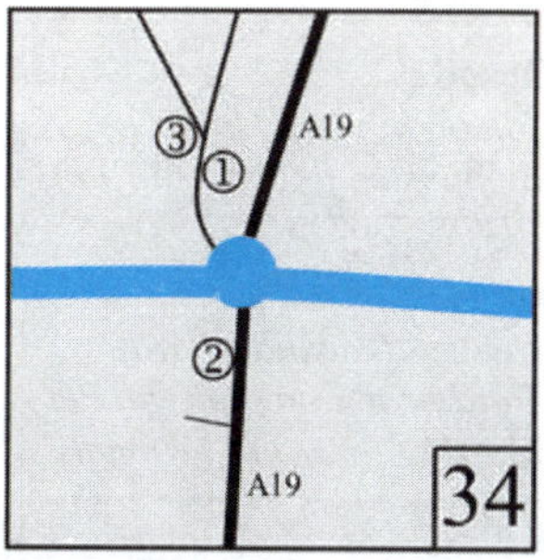

M62 Junction 35 M62/M18 interchange

There is no access to any services at this junction.

M62 Junction 36 Goole West

FUEL

Shell SAVE £ 0.2m ①

Open- Daily 24 hours

Info- WC, carwash, HGV fuelling.

Tel- 01405 764525

Total SAVE £ 0.9m ②

Open- M-Sat 0600-2200, Sun 0700-2200

Info- Carwash.

Tel- 01405 721702

FOOD

Brewer's Fayre☞ £7.00 0.2m ①

Open- M-Sat 1130-2200, Sun 1200-2200

Dir'n- Next to Travel Inn.

Tel- 01405 722660

McDonald's☞ £3.50 0.3m ①

Open- Su-Th 0700-2330, F/Sat 0700-2400

Info- Cash machine nearby.

Tel- 01405 766747

Woodside Cafe £3.00 0.9m ②

Open- M-F 0600-1700

Info- Transport cafe & HGV parking.

Tel- 01405 839321

ACCOMMODATION

Travel Inn☞ £45 0.2m ①

Info- Next to Brewer's Fayre. Goole location.

Tel- 0870 197 7177

ESSENTIALS

Goole Hospital 2.2m

Info- *Minor Injuries Unit.*
Dir'n- *Signposted on the A614 to Goole.*
Tel- *01405 720720*

Car Dealers

Info- *Peugeot/Vauxhall/Ford.*
Dir'n- *Ford near Total garage, Peugeot & Vauxhall next to McDonald's.*

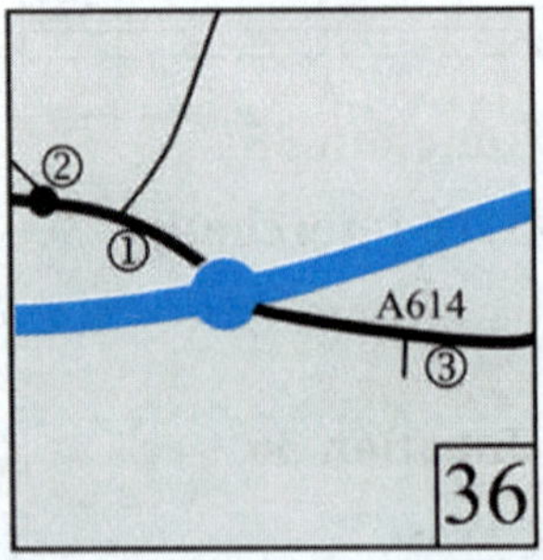

M62 Junction 37
Howden

FUEL

Keyfuels **SAVE** £ 0.5m ①

Open- *M-F 0700-2200, Sat 0800-2200, Sun 0900-1700*
Info- *WC, HGV fuelling.*
Tel- *01430 430388*

BP **SAVE** £ 1.0m ②

Open- *Daily 24 hours*
Info- *WC, carwash, HGV fuelling.*
Tel- *01430 430717*

FOOD

Ferry Boat Inn £5.00 1.2m ③

Open- *M-F 1200-1400, 1800-2200, Sat/Sun 1200-2200*
Info- *Varied hot & cold food. Bridge views & river walk from car park.*
Tel- *01430 430300*

Redbeck Cafe £4.00 1.3m ④

Open- *M-F 0530-2200, Sat/Sun 0700-1600*
Info- *Transport cafe. HGV parking.*
Tel- *01430 430409*

ACCOMMODATION

Redbeck Cafe £11 1.3m ④

Info- *B&B at the transport cafe.*
Tel- *01430 430409*

ESSENTIALS

Nissan Dealer 0.9m ⑤

THINGS TO DO

Howden 1.2m

Info- *This village is quite pretty, has a few pubs, and is good for a short break.*

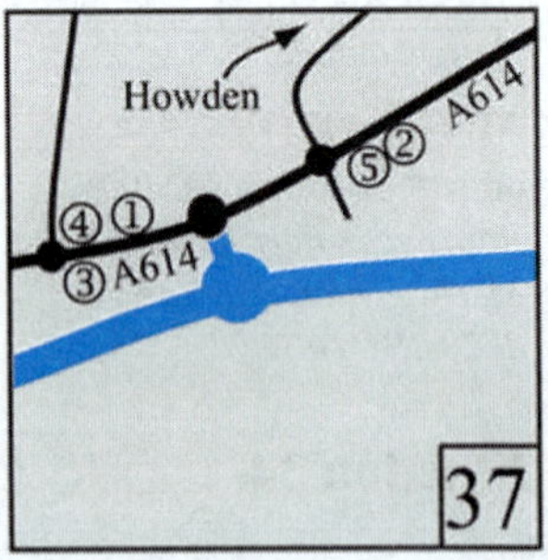

M62 Junction 38
Motorway merges with A63

ACCOMMODATION

Travelodge £45 0.5m ①

Info- *Hull South Cave location.*
Tel- *0870 191 1647*

ESSENTIALS

Hull Royal Infirmary 16m

Dir'n- *Follow signs to Hull, and the hospital is signposted close to the centre.*
Tel- *01482 328541*

Hull Tourist Information Centre

Tel- *01482 223559*

Beverley Tourist Information Centre

Tel- *01482 867430*

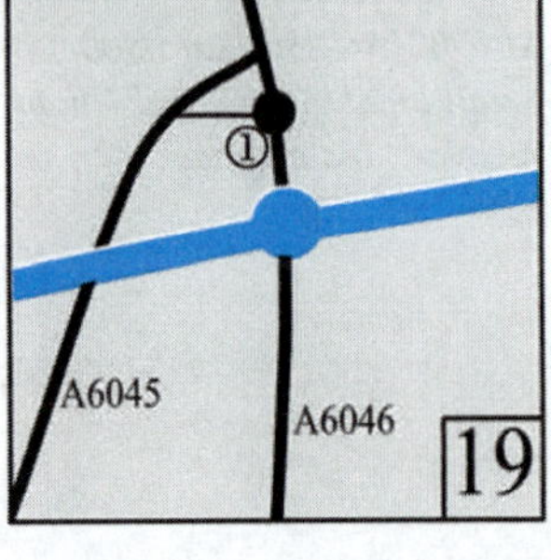

M74-Glasgow to Carlisle

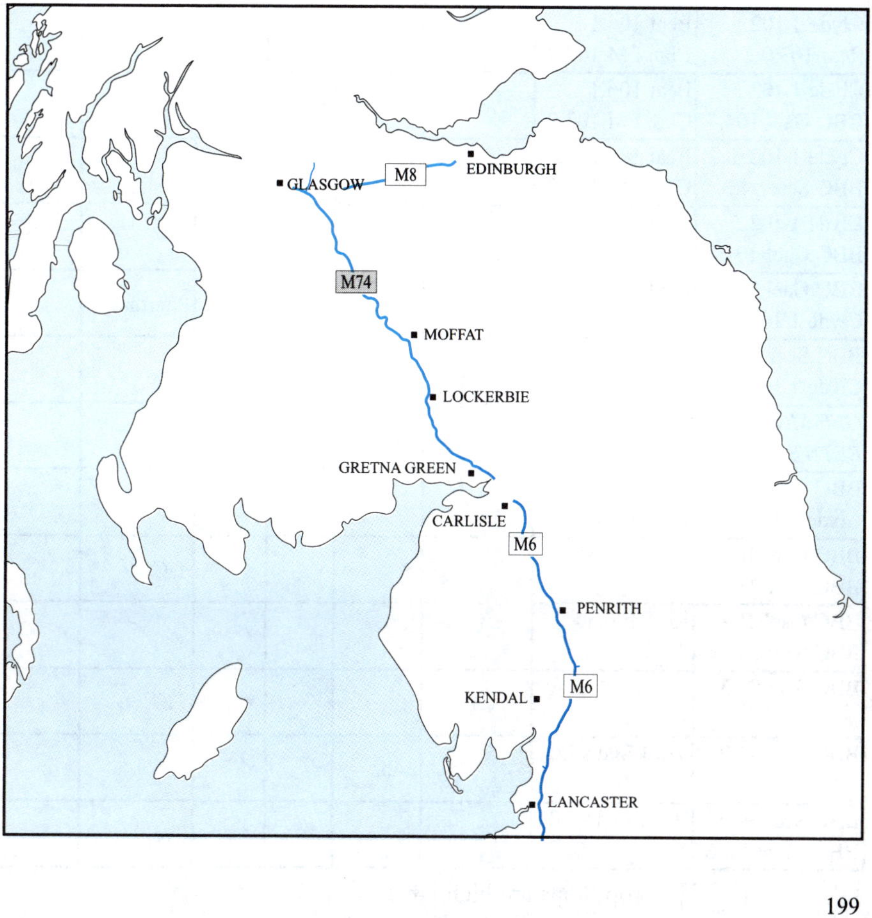

M74 Summary of Junctions

Radio stations & frequencies		Junction	Fuel	Food	Hotels	Essentials	Things to do
Beat 106.1 Clan FM 17.9	QFM 96.3 BBC Scot 94.3	1	24hr	✓		A&E, Svc TIC	
Beat 106.1 Clan FM 17.9	QFM 96.3 BBC Scot 94.3	2					
Beat 106.1 Clan FM 17.9	QFM 96.3 Clyde 11.2,5	3					
Beat 106.1 Clan FM 17.9	QFM 96.3 BBC Scot 94.3	4					
Beat 106.1 Clan FM 17.9	QFM 96.3 BBC Scot 94.3	S	24hr	✓			
Beat 106.1 Clan FM 17.9	QFM 96.3 Clyde 11.2,5	5		✓			
Clyde 1 102.5 Real 103.0	Beat 106.1 Clan FM 107.9	S	24hr	✓	✓	TIC	
Clyde 1 102.5 BBC Gael 104.7	Beat 106.1 Clan FM 107.9	6	24hr	✓		A&E, Svc	✓
Clyde 1 102.5 BBC Scot 94.3	Beat 106.1 Clan FM 107.9	7				A&E	
Clyde 1 102.5 BBC Gael 104.7	Beat 106.1 Clan FM 107.9	8		✓	✓		
BBC Gael 104.7 Clyde 1 102.5	Real 100.3 BBC Scot 94.3	10	24hr	✓	✓	Pharmacy	
BBC Scot 94.3 Clyde 1 102.5	Beat 106.0 Real 100.3	11					
OFF MOTORWAY SERVICES BETWEEN JUNCTIONS 11-12		S	24hr	✓			
BBC Gael 104.7 Clyde 1 102.5	Real 100.3 BBC Scot 94.3	12					
BBC Gael 104.7 BBC Scot 94.3	Real 100.3	13 S	✓	✓	✓	TIC	
BBC Gael 104.7 BBC Scot 94.3	Real 100.3	14		✓	✓	Svc	
BBC Scot 94.3		15	✓	✓	✓	TIC	✓
BBC Scot 94.7	West Snd 97.0	16 S	24hr	✓	✓		
BBC Scot 94.7 BBC Cmbr 95.6	West Snd 97.0	17	✓		✓	Svc	

Top Stops are highlighted

Radio stations & frequencies		Junction	Fuel	Food	Hotels	Essentials	Things to do
BBC Scot 94.7 BBC Cmbr 95.6		18				A&E	
BBC Scot 94.7 BBC Cmbr 95.6		19					
CFM 96.4 BBC Cmbr 95.6	BBC Scot 94.7	20					
CFM 96.4 BBC Cmbr 95.6	BBC Scot 94.7	21	✓	✓	✓	Svc	
CFM 96.4 BBC Cmbr 95.6	BBC Scot 94.7	S	24hr	✓	✓		
CFM 96.4 BBC Cmbr 95.6	BBC Scot 94.7	22	✓	✓	✓	A&E TIC	✓

M74 Junction Details

M74 Junction 1
Motorway starts

FUEL

Shell SAVE ££ 0.4 ①
Open- *Daily 24 hours*
Info- *LPG, HGV fuelling, WC, cash machine, jetwash.*
Tel- *0141 764 2340*

FOOD

McDonald's☞ £3.50 0.3m ②
Open- *Daily 0800-2300*
Tel- *0141 778 8879*

Brewsters☞ £6.50 0.3m ②
Open- *M-Sat 1130-2200, Sun 1230-2200*
Tel- *0141 764 2655*

ESSENTIALS

Victoria Royal Infirmary 5.2m
Dir'n- *At the exit follow signs to the A74 west, and then turn left on the A77 just after passing the River Clyde. Next turn left on the B762, and the hospital is on the left.*
Tel- *0141 201 6000*

Glasgow Tourist Information Centre
Tel- *0141 204 4400*

Arnolds Motorstore 0.3m ③
Open- *M-F 0800-1645, Sat 0800-1200*
Info- *Tyres, exhausts, brakes etc.*
Tel- *0141 764 2200*

Ford Dealer 0.3m ③

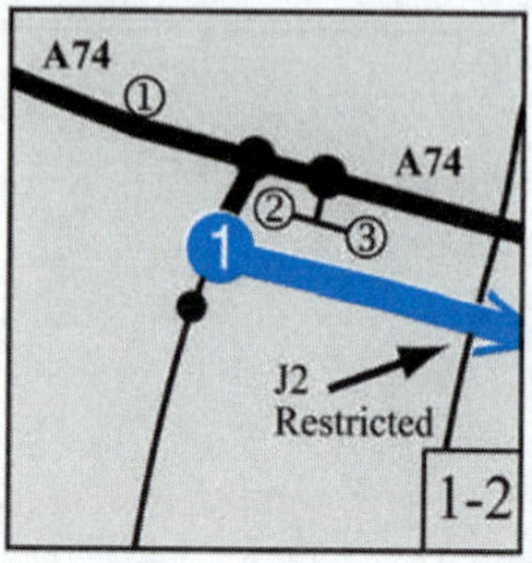

M74 Junction 2
Restricted

Junction 2 allows exit northbound, and entry southbound.

M74 Junction 3 -4
Complex junctions

Junction 3-4 are complex junctions, and it is advisable to exit here only if it is on your route.

Bothwell Services

Southbound access only.

FUEL BP
HGV fuelling & parking. Free parking for 2 hours then £6 per day.

FOOD ROADCHEF
onroute, Costa Coffee
Open- *Daily 0700-2300*
Info- *Cash machines.*

M74 Junction 5
Bothwell

FOOD

Cricklewood Hotel £8.50 0.7m ①
Open- *M-F 1200-2200, Sa-Sun 1000-2200*
Info- *Extensive menu at local pub.*
Tel- *01698 853172*

Da Luciano £11 0.8m ②
Open- *M-F 1200-1430, 1730-2300, Sat 1200-1400, 1730-2200, Sun 1100-2230*
Info- *Extensive menu at independent Italian restaurant.*
Tel- *01698 852722*

China Cottage £12 0.8m ③
Open- *M-Th 1200-1400, 1700-2330, F-Sa 1700-2330*

Info- *Chinese restaurant with takeaway.*
Tel- *01698 852217*

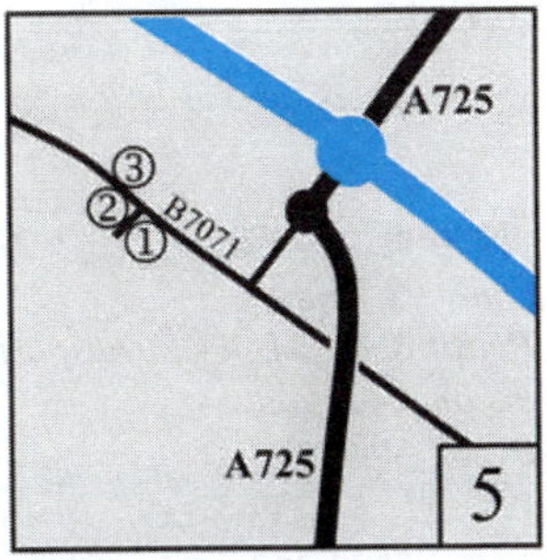

Hamilton Services

Northbound access only from motorway.

FUEL BP

HGV fuelling & parking. Free parking for 2 hours then £6 per day.

FOOD ROADCHEF

onroute, Costa Coffee
Open- *Daily 0700-0200*

ACCOMMODATION

Travel Inn☞ £45
Info- *Hamilton location.*
Tel- *0870 197 7124*

ESSENTIALS

Hamilton Tourist Information Centre
Tel- *01698 285590*
Info- *Cash machines.*

M74 Junction 6
Motherwell

Dir'n- *For food facilities mentioned below follow signs to Hamilton, & then Retail Park.*

FUEL

Jet SAVE £££ 0.7 ①
Open- *Daily 24 hours*
Info- *WC, carwash.*
Tel- *01698 264162*

FOOD

Asda Cafe☞ £3.50 0.6m ②
Open- *Daily 0800-2100*
Info- *Cash machines at store.*
Tel- *01698 456700*

Spaghetti's £8.0 0.6m ②
Open- *Daily 1200-2200*
Info- *Italian restaurant & bar.*
Dir'n- *Between the SBC building & Asda.*
Tel- *01698 540131*

McDonald's☞ £3.50 0.6m ③
Open- *Daily 0800-2100*
Info- *Cash machines nearby.*
Tel- *01698 200131*

Other 0.7m ④
Info- *Hamilton has a good range of restaurants & pubs in its pedestrianised zone. As you approach Hamilton turn off the roundabout just before the 'SBC' to park.*

ESSENTIALS

Wishaw Hospital 4.5m
Dir'n- *Take the A723 east, and turn south on the A721, and then right on to the B764. The hospital is signposted on this road.*
Tel- *01698 361100*

Halfords 0.7m ③
Open- *M-F 0900-2000, Sat 0900-1800, Sun 1000-1700*
Tel- *01698 283323*

Vauxhall Dealer ①

THINGS TO DO

Hamilton Heritage Pk £nil 0.8m ⑤
Info- *Large counry park, lake & watersports.*

M74 Junction 7
Restricted

This junction only allows northbound entry and southbound exit.

ESSENTIALS

Wishaw Hospital 4.5m

Dir'n- *Take the A72 south and turn left onto the A71. Next turn left onto the B764 where the hospital is signposted.*

Tel- *01698 361100*

M74 Junction 8
Stonehouse

FOOD

Shawlands Hotel £6.50 0.3m ①

Info- *Extensive menu at the hotel bar & restaurant.*

Tel- *01698 791111*

ACCOMMODATION

Shawlands Hotel £40 0.3m ①

Info- *Bar and restaurant. Independent hotel.*

Tel- *01698 791111*

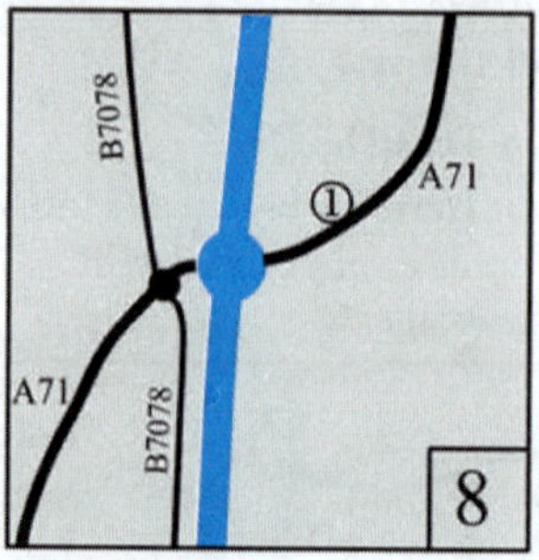

M74 Junction 9
Non-existent

M74 Junction 10
Restricted

There is no southbound exit at this junction.

FUEL

Star Truckstop SAVE £ 0.1 ①

Open- *Daily 24 hours*

Info- *Petrol & diesel, WC, transport cafe, accommodation.*

Tel- *01555 894889*

Thames SAVE ££ 0.1 ②

Open- *M-Sat 0700-2200, Sun 0800-2200*

Info- *Jetwash.*

Tel- *01555 892875*

FOOD

Star Truckstop £4.50 0.3m ①

Open- *M-Th 0500-2300, Fr 0530-2130, Sat 0600-1600, Sun 0900-2100*

Info- *Transport cafe.*

Tel- *01555 894889*

Fountain Cafe £6 0.8m ③

Open- *M-Th 0900-1630, Fr-Sa 0930-2100, Sun 1200-1530*

Info- *Varied menu in the heritage centre. Internet facilities available, cash machine nearby.*

Tel- *01555 893237*

Azurro Bistro £12 0.8m ④

Open- *W-Sat 1700-2200, Sun 1200-1330, 1700-2100*

Info- *Refined dining at this independent Italian restaurant.*

Tel- *01555 895921*

ACCOMMODATION

Star Truckstop £15 0.3m ①

Info- *Shared bathroom. Price is for a single room.*

Tel- *01555 894889*

ESSENTIALS

Moss Pharmacy 0.9m ①

Open- *M/Tu/Th/F 0900-1300, 1400-1730, Wed 0900-1300, Sat 0900-1300, 1400-1700*

Tel- *01555 893393*

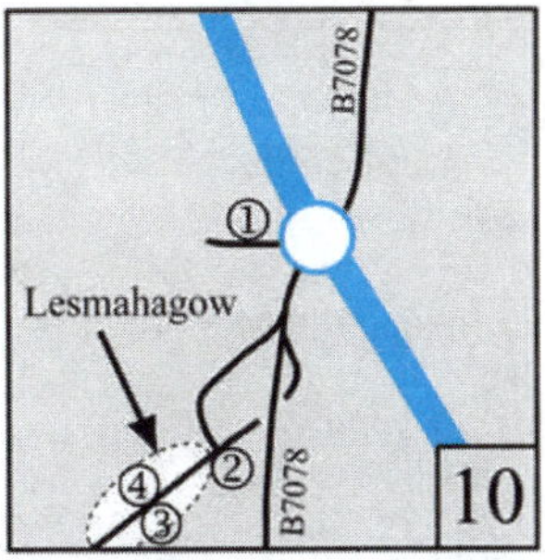

M74 Junction 11
Restricted

No northbound exit or southbound entry, but these are provided by Junction 12 about 2 miles away. The only facilities nearby are the Happendon Services below.

Junction 11-12 Services Happendon

These are located on the B7078, between Junctions 11 and 12. They are easily accessible and well signposted from the motorway.

FUEL SHELL

HGV fuelling & parking. Free parking for 2 hours then £6 per day.

FOOD

'The Lodge' Restaurant
Open- Daily 0630-2230
Info- Cash machines.

M74 Junction 12
Restricted

No southbound exit or northbound entry, but these are provided by Junction 11 about 2 miles away. The only facilities nearby are the Happendon Services above.

J13 Abington Services

These are located just off the motorway at Junction 13.

FUEL SHELL

HGV fuelling & parking. Free parking for 2 hours then £6 per day.

FOOD WELCOME BREAK

Red Hen, Burger King, foodconnection
Info- Cash machines.

ACCOMMODATION

Days Inn☞ £45
Info- Abington location. Dogs by arrangement.
Tel- 01864 502782

ESSENTIALS

Abington Tourist Information Centre
Tel- 01864 502436

M74 Junction 13
Abington

FOOD

Abington Hotel £7.00 0.8m ①
Open- Daily 1200-2300
Info- Varied menu at the hotel in this pleasant village.
Tel- 01864 502467

ACCOMMODATION

Abington Hotel £78 0.8m ①
Info- Bar & restaurant. Independent hotel.
Tel- 01864 502467

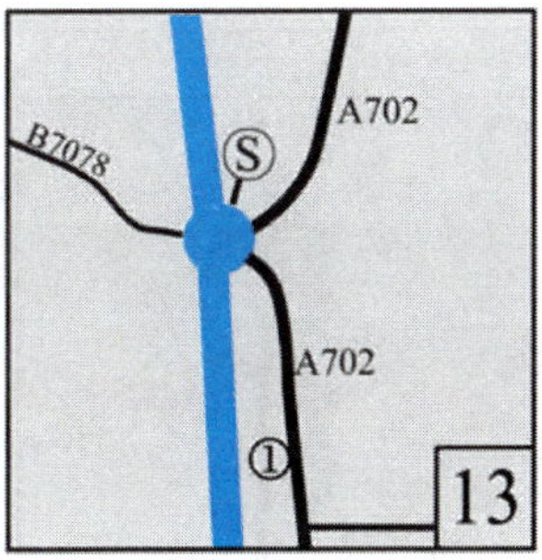

M74 Junction 14
Crawford

The northbound and southbound junctions are about 2 miles apart at this junction. Return to your starting point to re-enter the motorway.

FOOD

Hungry Trucker Cafe £3.75 0.1m ①
Open- *Tu-F 0600-2130, Sun 1200-2000*
M & Sat 0700-2130
Info- *Small & basic transport cafe.*
Tel- *01864 502227*

Crawford Arms Hotel £5.00 1m ②
Open- *M-F 0600-2100, Sat 0700-2100, Sun 1200-2100*
Info- *Pub meals.*
Tel- *01864 502267*

ACCOMMODATION

Holmlands B&B £50 0.2m ③
Info- *Private B&B in Crawford village, gardens for residents.*
Tel- *01864 502753*

Crawford Arms Hotel £53 1m ②
Info- *Village pub with B&B. Single £27. HGV pkg. Pets welcome.*
Tel- *01864 502267*

ESSENTIALS

SSC Recovery 0.3m ④
Info- *24 hour HGV & car recovery & repair.*
Tel- *01864 502236*

Westons Recovery 1.5m ⑤
Info- *24 hour recovery*
Tel- *01864 502451*

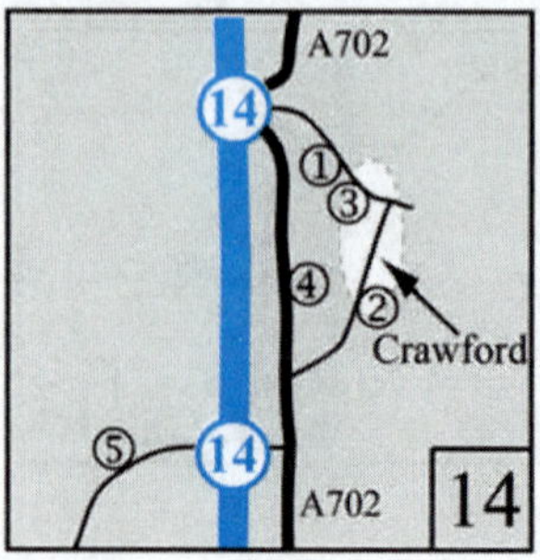

M74 Junction 15
Moffat

FUEL

Esso SAVE ££ 1.4m ①
Open- *Daily 0600-2000*
Info- *WC*
Tel- *01683 220010*

FOOD

The Old Brig Inn £6 0.1m ②
Open- *Daily 1200-2100*
Info- *Varied meals at village pub.*
Tel- *01683 300401*

Other 1.7m ②
Info- *Many pubs & restaurants in Moffat.*

ACCOMMODATION

The Old Brig Inn £30 0.1m ③
Info- *B&B at local inn.*
Tel- *01683 300401*

Annandale House B&B £35 1m ③
Info- *Private B&B. Pets by arrangement.*
Tel- *01683 221460*

Beechwood Ctry Hs Htl £85 2m
Info- *Bar & restaurant*
Dir'n- *Just outside Moffat. Phone for directions.*
Tel- *01683 220210*

Moffat House Hotel £80 2m
Info- *Bar & restaurant.*
Dir'n- *In central Moffat. Phone for directions.*
Tel- *01683 220039*

Others 2m
Info- *There are many other hotels, guest houses, etc in Moffat. Phone Tourist Information for details.*

ESSENTIALS

Moffat Tourist Information Centre
Tel- *01683 220620*

THINGS TO DO

Moffat 1.7m
Info- *Moffat has a pretty town centre, with many places to eat and stay. Moffat park, as you enter the town, is good for a stroll and picnicking.*

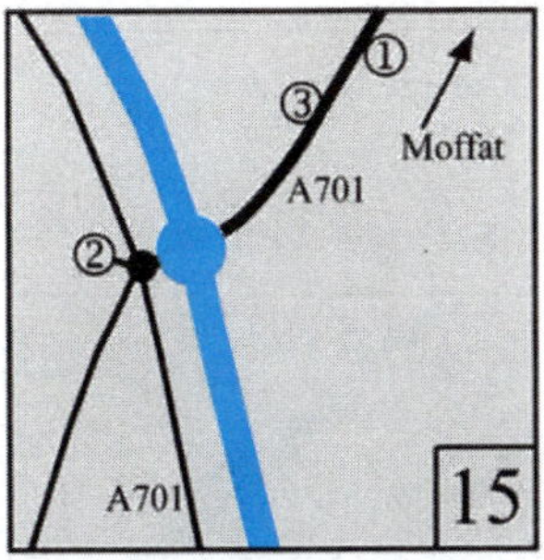

Junction 16 Services

This services is located off the motorway at Junction 16.

FUEL TEXACO

HGV fuelling & parking. Free parking for 2 hours then £6 per day.

FOOD ROADCHEF

onroute, Costa Coffee, Wimpy

Info- Cash machine.

ACCOMMODATION

Travel Inn☞ £45

Info- Lockerbie (Annandale) location.

Tel- 0870 197 7163

THINGS TO DO

Lakeside picnic area & views.

M74 Junction 16 Johnstonebridge

FOOD

Dinwoodie Lodge Rest. £7 1.5m ①

Open- W-Su 1200-1400, M-Sa 1800-2100
Sun 1630-2100

Info- Varied menu at the hotel.

Tel- 01576 470289

ACCOMMODATION

Dinwoodie Lodge Hotel £70 1.5m ①

Info- Bar & restaurant.

Tel- 01576 470289

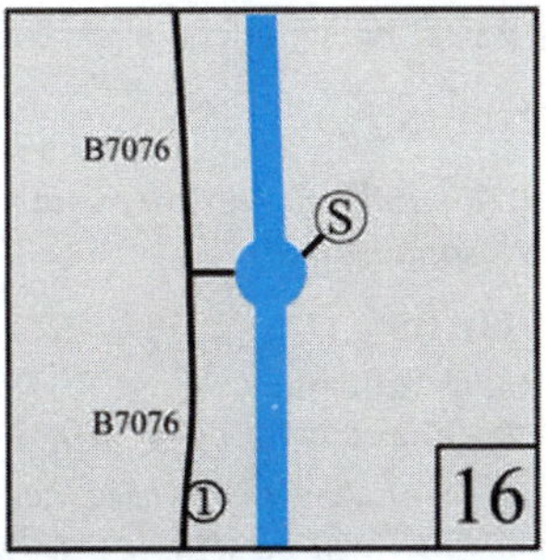

M74 Junction 17 Lockerbie

FUEL

Texaco **SAVE** ££ 1.4 ①

Open- M-F 0700-1900, Sat 0800-1900,
Sun 0930-1630

Info- WC

Tel- 01576 204280

ACCOMMODATION

Lockerbie Manor Hotel £74 0.8m ②

Info- Bar & restaurant.

Tel- 01576 202610

ESSENTIALS

SSC Car & Truck 0.5m ③

Info- 24 hour recovery.

Tel- 01576 204424

McConnechy's Tyres 1.1m ④

Info- Tyres, exhausts, repairs.

Tel- 01576 202648

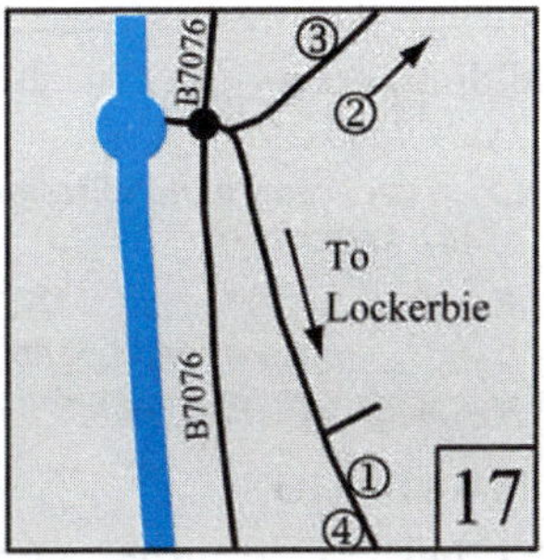

M74 Junction 18
Restricted

This junction only allows exit northbound and entry southbound.

ESSENTIALS

D&G Royal Infirmary 12m

Dir'n- *Take the B7076 north, then the A709 to Dumfries, where the hospital will be signposted. (D & G is 'Dumfries & Galloway').*

Tel- *01387 246246*

M74 Junction 19
Ecclefechan

There are no facilities near to this junction.

M74 Junction 20
Eaglesfield

There are no facilities at this junction.

M74 Junction 21
Kirkpatrick Fleming

FUEL

WCF SAVE £ 1m ①

Open- *M-Sat 0630-1800, Sun 0830-1200*

Info- *Small independent garage.*

Tel- *01461 800233*

FOOD

The Mill Restaurant £7.00 0.5m ②

Open- *Daily 1800-2100*

Info- *Extensive menu at hotel restaurant..*

Tel- *01461 800344*

The Station Inn £5 1.1m ③

Open- *Daily 1200-1400, 1800-2100*

Info- *Bar meals at village pub.*

ACCOMMODATION

The Mill Hotel £68 0.5m ②

Open- *Daily 1800-2100*

Info- *Bar & restaurant at private hotel.*

Tel- *01461 800344*

ESSENTIALS

Moffat Garage Services £68 1.1m ①

Open- *M-F 0830-1700*

Info- *Village garage for small repairs.*

Tel- *01461 800233*

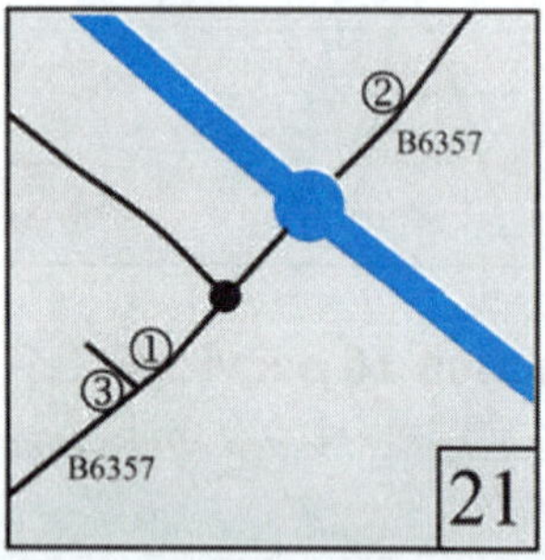

Gretna Green Services

There is a roadbridge between carriage-ways.

FUEL BP

LPG, HGV fuelling & parking. Free parking for 2 hours then £6 per day.

FOOD WELCOME BREAK

Burger King, foodconnection, Coffee Primo

Info- *Cash machine.*

ACCOMMODATION

Welcome Lodge £45

Info- *Gretna Green location.*

Tel- *01461 337566*

M74 Junction 22
Gretna Green/M6 link

Joins the M6 via the A74.

FUEL

Texaco SAVE £ 0.5m ①

Open- *M-F 0700-1900, Sat 0800-1800, Sun 0800-1800*

Info- *WC*

Tel- *01461 337554*

FOOD

Hazeldene Hotel £7.00 0.5m ②

Open- *Daily 1200-1400, 1800-2100*

Info- *Extensive menu at this village pub.*
Tel- *01461 338292*

Crossways Inn £6.50 0.5m ③
Open- *M-F 1200-1500, 1800-2000, Sa/Sun 1200-2000*
Info- *Varied menu at village pub.*
Tel- *01461 337465*

Gretna Chase rest. £8.50 0.5m ④
Open- *M-Sat 1200-1430, 1900-2030, Sun 1200-1430, 1800-2130*
Info- *Extensive menu at the Gretna Chase Hotel.*
Tel- *01461 337517*

ACCOMMODATION

Gretna Chase Hotel £90 0.4m ④
Info- *Bar & restaurant. Price is B&B.*
Tel- *01461 337766*

Crossways Inn £50 0.5m ③
Info- *B&B at village pub.*
Tel- *01461 337465*

Garden House Hotel £90 0.4m ⑤
Info- *Bar, restaurant & leisure club. Price is B&B.*
Tel- *01461 337621*

Travelodge☞ £50 4.5m ⑧
Info- *Carlisle North location.*
Dir'n- *Take the A74 south towards Carlisle and the hotel is on the left. Be sure not to miss the turn off!*
Tel- *0870 191 1627*

Others £50 4.5m ⑧
Info- *Numerous small hotels, guest houses & B&Bs. Phone Tourist Information for more details.*

ESSENTIALS

Cumberland Infirmary 10m
Dir'n- *Take the A74 south, and then the A7 to Carlisle. After crossing the river turn right on Castle Way, then right again on Newtown Road, where the hospital is on the right.*
Tel- *01228 523444*

Gretna Tourist Information Centre
Tel- *01461 337834*

Dumfries Tourist Information Centre
Tel- *01387 253862*

THINGS TO DO

The Old Toll Bar 0.2m ②
Info- *Famous location for 'runaway' marriages.*

Old Blacksmith's Shop £2.50 0.2m ⑦
Open- *Daily 0900-1700*
Info- *Exhibition about Gretna history.*
Tel- *01461 338441*

Gretna Outlet Centre 0.2m ⑧
Open- *Daily 1000-1800*
Info- *The Gretna Gateway Outlet Village. About 30 stores, and 2 cafes.*
Tel- *01461 339028*

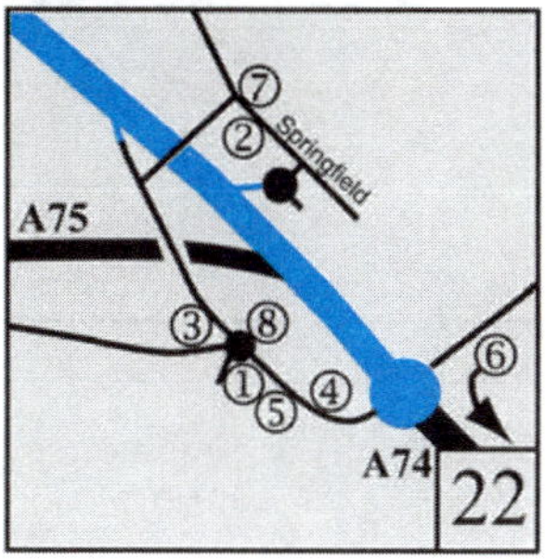

A1(M)-Potters Bar to Letchworth

A1(M) Summary of Junctions

Radio stations & frequencies		Junction	Fuel	Food	Hotels	Essentials	Things to do
Virgin 105.8 Jazz FM 102.2	BBC 3CR 94.9 LGR 103.3	1 S	24hr	✓	✓	Svc A&E	
BBC 3CR 103.8 Virgin 105.8	Mercury 96.6 LDN 94.9	2		✓	✓		✓
BBC 3CR 103.8 Virgin 105.8	Chiltern 97.6 LDN 94.9	3	✓	✓	✓		✓
Chilt FM 96.9 Chiltern 97.6	Magic 105.4 LBC 97.3	4	24hr	✓	✓	A&E TIC	✓
Chilt FM 96.9 Chiltern 97.6	Magic 105.4 Virgin 105.8	5					
3CR 103.8 Hertbeat 106.7	LDN 94.9 Capital 95.8	6	✓	✓	✓	A&E	✓
BBC 3CR 95.5 Hertbeat 106.7	Chiltern 97.6 XFM 104.9	7		✓	✓	Svc	✓
BBC 3CR 95.5 Hertbeat 106.7	Chiltern 97.6 XFM 104.9	8	✓	✓	✓	A&E	
Chilt FM 96.9 BBC 3CR 103.8	Camb 96.0 Magic 105.4	9	✓				
Chilt FM 96.9 BBC 3CR 103.8	Camb 96.0	10 S	24hr	✓	✓		

Highlighting denotes a 'Top Stop'

A1(M) Junction Details

South Mimms Services

This services is located just off the motorway at Junction 1.

FUEL **BP**

Cash machine, HGV fuelling & parking. Free parking for 2 hours then £6 per day.

FOOD WELCOME BREAK

Red Hen, KFC, Burger King, Coffee Primo, The Granary Restaurant

Info- *Cash machines.*

ACCOMMODATION

Days Inn☞ £45

Info- *South Mimms location.*

Tel- *01707 665440*

A1(M) Junction 1

M25 interchange

FUEL

Murco **SAVE** £ 0.7m ①

Open- *M-Sat 0600-2300, Sun 0800-2200*

Info- *WC, jetwash.*

Tel- *01707 654610*

FOOD

The Green Dragon £5.00 1.2m ②

Open- *M-Sat 1200-2200, Sun 1200-2130*

Info- *Bar & restaurant.*

Tel- *01208 4492972*

The White Hart £6.00 0.7m ③

Open- *M-Sat 1200-1430, 1830-2100, Sun 1200-1800*

Info- *Extensive hot & cold menu.*

Tel- *01707 642122*

ACCOMMODATION

Holiday Inn☞ £96 0.2m ④

Info- *On-site restaurant. South Mimms location.*

Tel- *01870 4009072*

ESSENTIALS

Barnet Hospital 8m

Dir'n- *From exit follow A1 south, then A411 east. The hospital is signposted on the right in Wellhouse Lane.*

Tel- *0208 2164000*

Lantern Recovery 0.3m ⑤

Open- *Daily 24 hours*

Dir'n- *Just beyond the Holiday Inn.*

Tel- *01707 644691*

Lantern Car Hire 0.3m ⑤

Dir'n- *Just beyond the Holiday Inn.*

Tel- *01707 654465*

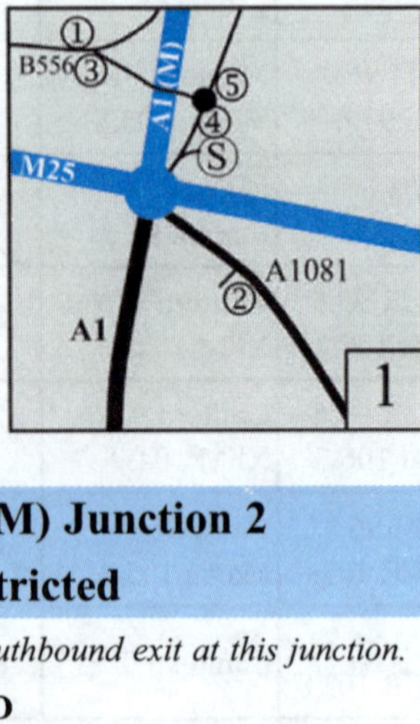

A1(M) Junction 2

Restricted

No southbound exit at this junction.

FOOD

Quality Hotel restaurant £12 0.5m ①

Info- *Extensive menu at the Quality Hotel restaurant.*

Tel- *01707 275701*

ACCOMMODATION

Quality Hotel☞ £115 0.5m ①

Info- *Bar & restaurant. Hatfield location.*

Tel- *01707 275701*

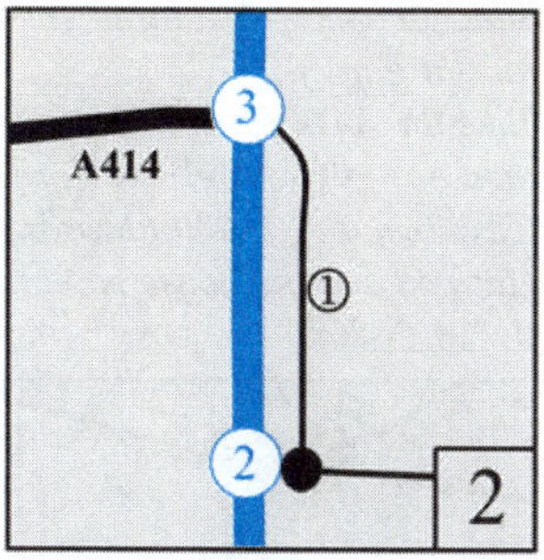

A1(M) Junction 3 Restricted

Entry to the motorway southbound is via Junction 2.

FUEL

Jet SAVE £££ 1.1m ①
Open- *M-F 0630-2200, Sat 0730-2230, Sun 0830-2230*
Info- *WC*
Tel- *01707 264521*

FOOD

Ramada Htl restaurant £13 0.7m ②
Open- *M-F 0700-1000, Sat/Sun 0700-1130 Sun-F 1230-1400, M-Sat 1900-2200*
Info- *Extensive menu.*
Tel- *01707 265411*

Quality Hotel rest. £12 0.5m ③
Info- *Extensive menu at the Quality Hotel restaurant.*
Tel- *01707 275701*

Pavilion Restaurant☞ £4.00 1.1m ④
Open- *Daily 0700-0900, 1200-1430, 1900-2130*
Info- *Extensive menu at the Hatfield Lodge Hotel.*
Tel- *01707 288500*

Burger King☞ £4.00 1.1m ⑤
Open- *Sun-Th 0930-2130, F/Sa 0930-2200*
Tel- *01707 270448*

Deep Pan Pizza £7.00 1.1m ⑤
Open- *Su-Th 1200-2200, F/Sa 1200-2300*
Info- *Pizzas & pasta.*
Tel- *01707 265517*

McDonald's☞ £3.40 1.1m ⑤
Open- *Daily 0700-2300*
Tel- *01707 268440*

ACCOMMODATION

Hatfield Lodge £3.50 0.2m ④
Info- *Bar & restaurant. A Beales hotel.*
Tel- *01707 288500*

Quality Hotel☞ £115 0.5m ③
Info- *Bar & restaurant. Hatfield location.*
Tel- *01707 275701*

Ramada Jarvis☞ £114 0.7m ②
Info- *Bar & restaurant. Hatfield location.*
Tel- *01707 265411*

THINGS TO DO

Galleria Shopping Mall 0.8m
Open- *M-F 1000-2000, Sat 1000-1800, Sun 1100-1700*
Info- *Outlet centre with over 60 shops.*
Tel- *01707 278301*

A1(M) Junction 4 Hatfield North/Welwyn

FUEL

Tesco SAVE ££ 0.2m ①
Open- *Daily 24 hours*
Info- *LPG, WC, cafe at store.*
Tel- *0845 677 9344*

FOOD

Tesco Cafe☞ £3.50 0.2m ①
Open- *M-F 0700-1800, Sat 0700-1800, Sun 0930-1600*
Tel- *0845 677 9344*

The Bull £7.50 0.6m ②
Open- *Daily 1200-2200*
Info- *Extensive hot & cold menu.*
Tel- *01707 262530*

Brewers Fayre☞ £7.00 0.8m ③
Open- *Daily 1200-2200*
Tel- *01707 268990*

Kipling's Restaurant £10.50 0.9m ④
Open- *M-F 1200-1400, M-Sat 1900-2130 Sun 1200-1400, 1930-2130*
Info- *Refined dining at the Bush Hall Hotel.*
Tel- *01707 271251*

ACCOMMODATION

Travel Inn☞ £45 0.8m ③
Info- *Hatfield location.*
Tel- *0870 197 7129*

Bush Hall Hotel £99 0.9m ④
Info- *Independent hotel with restaurant & bar.*
Tel- *01707 271251*

ESSENTIALS

QE2 Hospital 2.7m
Dir'n- *Take the A414 east towards Hertford, and then the A1000 towards Welwyn Garden City. The hospital is signposted as you drive into Welwyn Garden City.*
Tel- *01707 328111*

Hertford Tourist Information Centre
Tel- *01992 584322*

Car Dealers 0.3m ⑥
Info- Porsche, Lexus, Chrysler & Jeep.

Car Dealers 0.6m ②
Info- Jaguar & Aston Martin.

THINGS TO DO

Stanboro' Pk & Lakes £nil 0.7m ⑤
Info- *Park, boating lakes, nature trail, fishing, boating, open air pool & cafe. Parking charge at peak times.*

Hatfield House & Gdn £7.50 1.1m ⑤
Open- *Daily Easter to end September. House 1200-1600 Park & Garden 1100-1730*
Info- *Stately home with a large park and formal gardens.*
Dir'n- *Take the A414 towards Hertford, then turn off for Welwyn Garden City. Take the A1000 towards Hatfield and the house is on the left.*
Tel- *01707 287010*

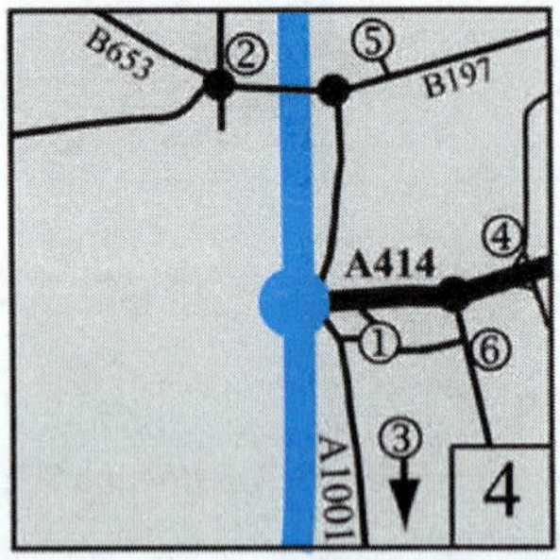

A1(M) Junction 5 Restricted

This junction only allows access on to the northbound carriageway, and has no exits.

A1(M) Junction 6 Welwyn North

FUEL

BP SAVE ££ 0.1m ①
Open- *Daily 0600-2200*
Info- *WC & carwash.*
Tel- *01438 714258*

FOOD

Quality Hotel rest. £12 0.2m ②
Info- *Extensive menu at the Quality Hotel.*
Tel- *01438 716911*

ACCOMMODATION

Quality Hotel☞ £99 0.2m ②
Info- *Bar & restaurant. Welwyn location.*
Tel- *01438 716911*

ESSENTIALS

QE2 Hospital 3m
Dir'n- *Take the A1000 towards Welwyn Garden City & the hospital is signposted.*
Tel- *01707 328111*

THINGS TO DO

Roman Baths £1.00 0.3m ③
Info- *Jan-Nov, Sats/Suns & bank holidays. Open 1400-1700.*
Tel- *01707 271362*

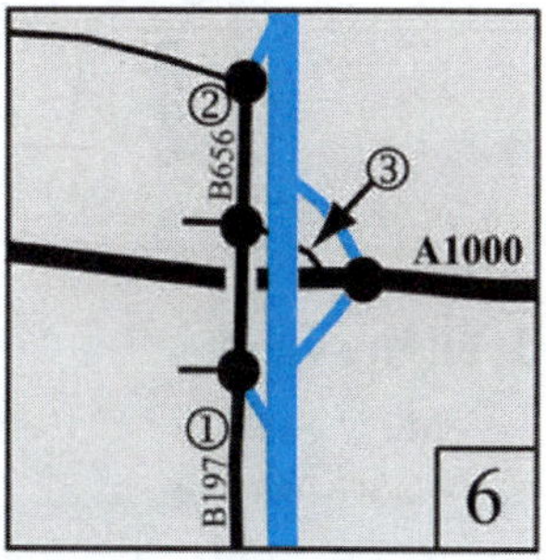

A1(M) Junction 7
Stevenage South

FOOD

Pizza Hut☞ £6.00 0.5m ①
Open- *M-Sat 1130-2300, Sun 1200-2300*
Tel- *01707 740924*

Burger King☞ £4.00 0.5m ①
Open- *Daily 0800-2300*
Tel- *01707 740924*

Brewsters☞ £6.00 1.2m ②
Open- *Daily1130-2200*
Info- *With a children's 'fun factory'.*
Tel- *01438 316654*

Roebuck Inn £6.00 1.3m ③
Open- *M-F 0630-0930. Sat/Sun 0730-1030*
M-Sa 1230-1430, Sun 1200-1500
M-Sa 1830-2230, Sun 1900-2200
Info- *Bar & restaurant at this Best Western Hotel.*
Tel- *0700 474474*

ACCOMMODATION

Novotel☞ £116 0.2m ④
Info- *Bar & restaurant. Outdoor pool. Hatfield location.*
Tel- *01438 346100*

Roebuck Inn☞ £99 1.3m ③
Info- *Bar & restaurant. A Best Western Hotel.*☞
Tel- *0700 474474*

ESSENTIALS

Halfords 1.1m ⑤
Info- *Car parts & accessories.*
Tel- *01438 741414*

BMW Dealer ⑥

Ford Dealer ⑦

THINGS TO DO

Knebworth Hs & Gdns £5.50 0.3m ⑧
Open- *Mid April to end August 1200-1730*
Info- *Stately home & formal gardens. About 250 acres of park.*
Tel- *01438 812661*

Stevenage Borough FC 0.3m ⑨
Info- *Live football just off the motorway!*

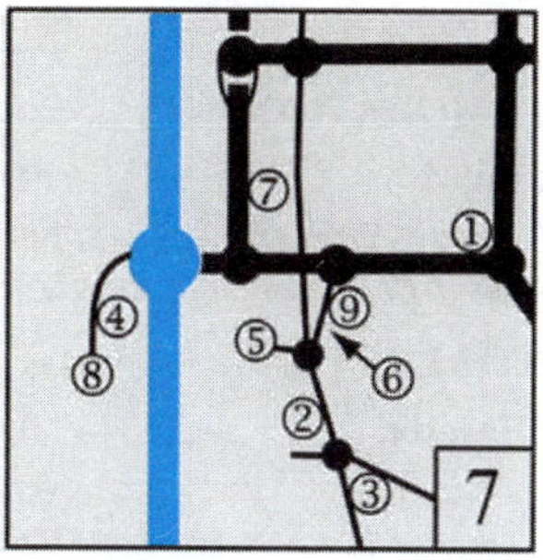

A1(M) Junction 8
Stevenage North

FUEL

Sainsbury SAVE £££ 0.2m ①
Open- *M-F 0600-2400, Sat 0600-2330, Sun 0730-2000*
Info- *WC & cash machines at store.*
Tel- *01438 759602*

FOOD

The Bucks Head £7.00 0.6m ②
Open- *Daily 1200-2130*
Info- *Varied menu in village pub. Carvery Sundays. Real ales.*
Tel- *01438 353320*

Plume of Feathers £6.00 0.6m ③
Open- *M-F 1200-1400, 1800-2100*
Sat 1200-1430, 1830-2100,
Sun 1200-1545
Info- *Extensive menu & real ales.*
Tel- *01438 729503*

Beefeater☞ £7.00 0.6m ④

Open- *Sun-Th 1200-2200, F/Sa 1200-2300*

Tel- *0870 1977263*

Waggon & Horses £7.50 0.8m ⑤

Open- *M-Sat 1200-1430, 1800-2100, Sun 1200-1700*

Info- *Extensive menu in village pub. Real ales. Satellite TV.*

Tel- *01438 367658*

George & Dragon £7.00 0.8m ⑤

Open- *M-F 1200-1400, 1900-2100, Sat 1200-1400, 1830-2130, Sun 1200-2130*

Info- *Varied menu in village pub. Real ales.*

Tel- *01438 351362*

ACCOMMODATION

Travel Inn☞ £45 0.6m ④

Info- *Welwyn Garden City location.*

Tel- *0870 197 7263*

ESSENTIALS

Lister Hospital 0.6m ⑥

Dir'n- *Take the A602 towards Stevenage and the hospital is signposted off to the left near to the Beefeater restaurant.*

Tel- *01438 314333*

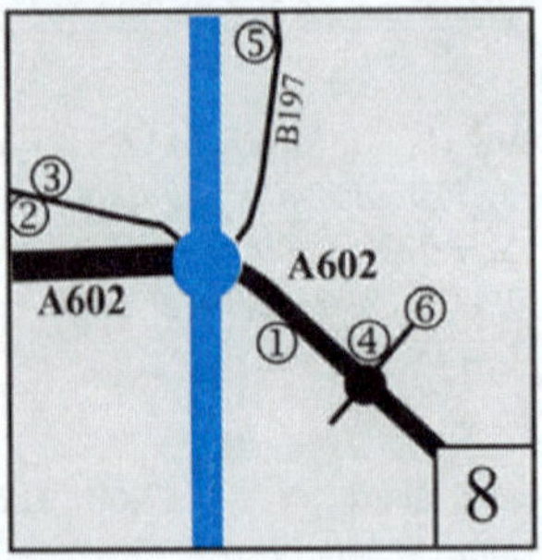

A1(M) Junction 9
Letchworth

FUEL

Shell SAVE ££ 0.6m ①

Open- *Daily 0630-2230*

Info- *WC, carwash & cash machine.*

Tel- *01462 473000*

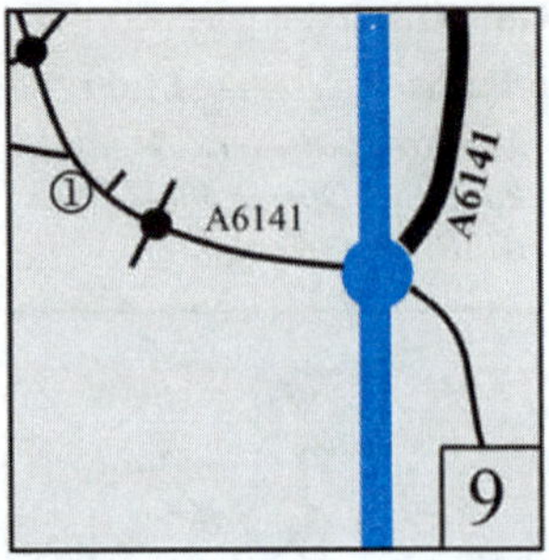

Baldock Services

This services is located just off the motorway at Junction 10.

FUEL TEXACO

HGV fuelling & parking. Free parking for 2 hours then £6 per day.

FOOD

McDonald's, Malongo Cafe, Buffet Rapide, deli france (Food is available 0700-2300).

Info- *Cash machines.*

ACCOMMODATION

Sleep Inn☞ £52

Info- *Baldock location.*

Tel- *01462 832900*

A1(M) Junction 10
Baldock/A1 interchange

FOOD

Baldock town centre 1.2m

Info- *Baldock has a good range of restaurants and pubs in the town centre, and makes for a pleasant short break.*

Restaurant Groups, Hotel Groups & Meeting Facility Directory

This section gives information about many of the hotel and restaurant groups that appear in this guide. Any facility in the main part of the guide marked with a '☞' is part of a group that is described in this section.

This section also gives details of groups who provide meeting rooms.

Restaurant Groups

ASDA CAFE

These are cafes within the stores of this supermarket chain. They are designed for shoppers and offer a limited range of snacks and light meals at very competitive prices. Many stores have filling stations attached. Some or all of these may become converted into McDonald's in the future.

Speed- Quick

BEEFEATER

There are over 200 Beefeaters in the UK, many of these located next to Travel Inns. Beefeater restaurants try to create a friendly pub-like atmosphere, which suits both adult and family diners. The menu leans heavily towards steaks, though other meat and fish dishes are available. There are typically 3 main course options for vegetarians.

Speed- Medium

BELLA PASTA

Bella Pasta has 63 restaurants around the UK, often situated in leisure parks alongside other facilities. The restaurants are generally large but provide a relaxing atmosphere that is especially popular with younger adults. The menu is predominantly pasta and pizzas, though other types of food are available. There are usually about 4 main course vegetarian options and vegans have a good chance of finding something to eat. There is also a special children's menu.

Speed- Medium

BIG STEAK PUB/ SPIRIT FOOD PUBS

There are over a 100 Big Steak Pubs. These were recently acquired by the Spirit Group, and are expected to be rebranded over the next year.

Speed- Medium

BREWER'S FAYRE

There are over 250 of these pub/restaurants which are designed to appeal to adult diners of all ages and families. There is a wide range of meat and fish options on the menu. The menu also includes a number of steak and grills, pasta dishes, and at least 2 vegetarian options can be expected.

Speed- Medium

Tel- 0845 222 8000 (locator)

BREWSTERS

Restaurant chain which tries to create a relaxing pub-like atmosphere, and also be well suited to families with young children. Many Brewsters restaurants have a 'Fun Factory' where children can play safely while parents dine. The menu has a wide range of options and provides a number of options for vegetarians, and a children's menu.

Speed- Medium

BURGER KING

This is a well known burger chain with hundreds of restaurants at popular locations. Many of these are adjacent to Little Chefs. Vegetarian burgers available.

Speed- Quick

CHEF & BREWER

This is a chain of over 100 restaurants with a relaxing pub-like atmosphere. The menu offers a wide range of meat and fish dishes, and typically offers 3 vegetarian main course options.

Speed- Medium

CHIQUITO

Mexican style restaurant & bar with a lively atmosphere. The menu offers traditional Mexican food, as well as salad and burgers.

There are around 3 main course options for vegetarians, and special meals for children.
Speed- Medium-Slow

DOMINO'S PIZZA

Takeaway pizza chain with the emphasis on home delivery. Most are located in residential areas and town centres, and tend to stay open until around midnight. Typically 3 vegetarian pizza options are available.
Speed- Quick

EMBER INNS

Dining in a pleasant pub-like atmosphere. The menu generally offers about 15 main course items to choose from, and a special Sunday roast. There are typically 3 vegetarian main course options.
Speed- Medium

FRANKIE & BENNY'S

These provide the atmosphere and menu of a 'New York Italian' restaurant. Often they are located in leisure parks or shopping malls. The menu inclines towards a wide range of sandwiches, pastas, salads,pizzas and steaks.There are typically 3 main course vegetarian options, and special meals for children.
Speed- Medium-Slow

HARRY RAMSDEN'S

Well-known fish and chip shop chain. Most of these are restaurants, but there are also a few that are only takeaway. The menu is mainly fish but there are other alternatives, and generally at least one vegetarian option. There are also children's specials on offer.
Speed- Medium

HARVESTER

A pub-restaurant that provides a relaxing atmosphere, and a wide range of flame-grilled meat dishes. There are also some pasta and fish dishes, and about 3 main course dishes for vegetarians. There is also a special children's menu. Many of these restaurants are adjacent to hotels, and they are often located near to major roads.
Speed- Medium

HENRY'S TABLE

Informal pub-restaurants which cater well for customers who want food or just drinks. The menu has a wide range of meat and fish dishes, and typically has about 3 vegetarian options. They are often located next to hotels such as Premier Lodges.
Speed- Medium

HUNGRY HORSE

These pub-restaurants cater equally for customers who require drinks or food. The menu is extensive and offers a wide range of steaks, burgers and other meals. Typically, expect 3 main course vegetarian options and a children's menu.
Speed- Medium

LITTLE CHEF

A very widespread restaurant chain, often located on major roads or next to hotels. These offer food from breakfast-time to supper, in an cafe-like environment. Often they have a Burger King attached, and provide meals from Harry Ramsden's, Upper Crust or other well known brands. Designed to appeal to all, as well as offering baby food and baby-changing facilities. The menu offers a wide range of popular favourites, and usually has at least 3 main course options for vegetarians. There is also a children's menu available.
Speed- Medium

KFC

A widespread fast food restaurant, which offers meals which are almost all chicken-based. KFC also offers a chicken-based children's menu.
Speed- Quick

McDONALD'S

This is a well-known and widespread burger chain. Most tend to open between 7am to about 11pm.
Speed- Quick

MILLHOUSE INNS

These offer a friendly pub-like atmosphere, that is aimed at adults of all ages. The menu offers a wide variety of food, and there is a special 'Pirate Pete's' menu for children. Typically there are around 3 options for

vegetarians. Some Millhouse Inns have accommodation adjacent.
Speed- Medium

MILLERS KITCHEN

These are pub-restaurants that are sometimes located next to Premier Lodges. They offer a wide variety of hot & cold meals, and usually have about 3 vegetarian main course options as well as a special children's selection.
Speed- Medium

MORRISONS CAFE

These are cafes within the stores of this supermarket chain. They are designed for shoppers and offer a limited range of snacks and light meals at very competitive prices. Many stores have filling stations attached.
Speed- Quick

OUT & OUT PUB

Smart pub-restaurants with a light and airy feel and a relaxing atmosphere. They have an extensive menu which has traditional meals as well as curries, risottos and pasta. There are children's specials, and an above average range of vegetarian meals that is likely to include a meal suitable for vegans.
Speed- Medium

PIZZA HUT

Widespread and well known pizza chain which mainly offers pizza and pasta.
Speed- Medium

SAFEWAYS CAFE

These are cafes within the stores of this supermarket chain. They are designed for shoppers and offer a limited range of snacks and light meals at very competitive prices. Many stores have filling stations attached.
Speed- Quick

SAINSBURY CAFES

These are cafes within the stores of this supermarket chain. They are designed for shoppers and offer a limited range of snacks and light meals at very competitive prices. Many stores have filling stations attached.
Speed- Quick

STARBUCKS

This is a well-known chain of coffee shops, offering a wide range of teas and coffees, incluidng herbal teas. There is also a good range of sandwiches and cakes. Some stores are located within supermarkets or bookshops.
Speed- Quick

TESCO CAFES

These are cafes within the stores of this supermarket chain. They are designed for shoppers and offer a limited range of snacks and light meals at very competitive prices. Many stores have filling stations attached.
Speed- Quick

TGIF

TGIF are American style restaurants which try to create a lively party-like atmosphere. The menu leans heavily towards burgers and fish, and features styles such as Cajun and Mexican. Typically there will be about 3 vegetarian main course options, and there are special meals for children. They also provide free 'Organix' baby food.
Speed- Medium-Slow

TOBY INN

These pub/restaurants have a relaxing atmosphere that will appeal to a wide range of adults. They offer a wide-ranging menu that includes a 'carvery' with 3 choices of meat, but also other popular dishes including fish. There are typically 3 vegetarian options. Many Inns are adjacent to a hotel (Innkeeper's Lodge or Express by Holiday Inn).
Speed- Medium

TOM COBLEIGH

This is a large pub/restaurant chain aimed at family and adult diners. The menu includes a wide range of grills, burgers, pasta, seafood, sandwiches, etc. There is a range of children's meals, and typically about 5 vegetarian main course options.
Speed- Medium

WAITROSE CAFE

These are cafes within the stores of this supermarket chain. They are designed for shoppers and offer a limited range of snacks and light meals at very competitive prices.
Speed- Quick

Hotel Groups

BEST WESTERN

Best Western is a grouping of about 400 independent hotels, and therefore guests are likely to see some variety between locations. Many of the hotels are situated in city and town centres, often being handy for other facilities. Hotels are generally well equipped with bars and restaurants, and may have facilities such as health clubs and swimming pools. Many also have gardens or are situated in pleasant parts of the town. Most of these hotels are rated 3 star for facilities, and some have restaurants that have been awarded AA rosettes. Generally, these hotels have good support for business people, offering meeting facilities. Prices vary from location to location and depending on availability.

Info- www.bestwestern.co.uk
Tel- 0845 773 7373

CAMPANILE

There are about 10 Campaniles in the UK. Rooms are well equipped, and an 'all you can eat' buffet breakfast is available. All have a Cafe-Bistro, and a meeting room. Dogs are accepted at some locations.

Info- www.envergure.fr/campanilefr
Tel- No central booking number

CHOICE HOTELS

There are about 110 Choice hotels in the UK (17 in London), which are branded as either Comfort Hotels, Sleep Inns, Quality Inns or Clarion Hotels. In general, the facilites improve as you progress through the selection above, and the room rates increase. Comfort Inns are the bottom of the range, providing budget accommodation, but having bars and restaurants. Quality Inns may offer swimming pools and fitness clubs, whilst Choice Hotels are generally rated 4 star.

Info- www.choicehotelseurope.com
Tel- 0800 444444

CLARION HOTELS

See the entry for Choice Hotels.

COMFORT HOTELS

See the entry for Choice Hotels.

COPTHORNE/MILLENNIUM HOTELS

There are about 13 of these hotels in the UK, generally situated in prime city and town centre locations. All have gyms and many have other leisure facilities, such as saunas and swimming pools. All feature bars and fine restaurants, many of which have AA rosettes. Rooms are very well equipped and all hotels cater for business meetings. Special packages are generally available, such as packages for accommodation, breakfast and dinner. Prices vary depending on location and availability.

Info- www.millenniumhotels.com
Tel- 0845 302 0001

CORUS/REGAL

Corus has about 70 hotels in the UK, most of which are situated close to major road intersections though some are located in town centres. These are bright & stylish and provide good value accommodation for business, leisure & frequent travellers. In all cases meals & drinks are available in restaurant, pub or lounge areas. Some have swimming pools or other leisure facilites. Special family rooms are available. Rates are generally per room and vary between location and depending on availability. Special breaks are often available. Prices generally include breakfast. Most of these hotels will allow dogs on request, and at a £5 charge.

Info- www.corushotels.co.uk
Tel- 0845 300 2000

COURTYARD BY MARRIOTT

There are 11 of these hotels in the UK, all located in popular business destinations. They all have restaurants & bars, and tend to have leisure centres and swimming pools. Some hotels allow dogs on request and special packages are often available. All rooms and hotels are well equipped for business travellers.

Info- www.courtyard.com
Tel- 0800 221 222

CROWNE PLAZA

There are around 10 Crowne Plaza Hotels in the UK, mainly located in major cities. This is a premium brand hotel chain and tends to offer luxury accommodation and facilities. All have good leisure facilities such as swimming pools and health clubs. They also feature bars and fine restaurants. All provide meeting facilities and have rooms well equipped for business people.

Info- *www.crowneplaza.com*
Tel- *00 800 8222 8222*

DAYS INN/HOTEL

There are about 30 Days Inns in the UK, and these are often situated at motorway service areas or in major cities. They are designed to offer good value to business people, and all offer continental breakfast. Rates are per room, which can accommodate up to 2 adults and 2 children. Days Hotels offer more facilities, for example offering a full cooked breakfast, a supper menu and a bar. Days Inns generally offer some business and meeting facilities at each location.

Info- *www.daysinn.com*
Tel- *0800 028 0400*

HILTON HOTELS

Hilton have about 60 hotels in the UK, generally located in town and city centre locations. These hotels tend to be relatively large and well equipped. It is usual for these hotels to have some form of leisure facility, such as a swimming pool, fitness centre or spa. All hotels offer bars and restaurants. Most hotels have good meeting facilities. Prices can vary substantially depending on location and availability, and Hilton often offers special rates for 'holiday breaks'.

Info- *www.hilton.co.uk*
Tel- *0870 590 9090*

HOLIDAY INN

Holiday Inns are a long established brand in the UK, and there are about 100, often situated in cities and towns. They tend to be well equipped hotels, offering a range of leisure facilities such as fitness centres. All offer bars and restaurants and facilities for business meetings. A full breakfast is available at all locations, and rooms are generally well eqipped for business people. Some locations may accept pets.

Info- *www.holiday-inn.com*
Tel- *0800 405 060*

EXPRESS BY HOLIDAY INN

This is a rapidly growing chain in the UK, currently with around 90 hotels. Generally, these are situated close to major roads or business centres. In general, these hotels offer a pleasant environment, but they have few of the leisure facilities that one would expect at, for instance, a Holiday Inn hotel. Rooms, however, are well equipped for business people and continental breakfast is always included in the price. All locations offer a bar and meeting rooms. Some locations may accept pets.

Info- *www.hiexpress.co.uk*
Tel- *0800 434 040*

IBIS HOTELS

Ibis have over 40 hotels in the UK, usually sited towards the centre of larger cities. All have bars and many have restaurants and meeting rooms. Snacks are available at any time of day (at reception or bar) and breakfast is available at all hotels. Bedrooms generally offer plenty of space to work. Dogs are allowed at most hotels at the manager's discretion, but there may be a charge.

Info- *www.ibishotel.co.uk*
Tel- *0870 609 0963*

INNKEEPER'S LODGE

A chain of about 65 hotels which tend to be located in, or close to, town centres. These hotels are aimed at frequent business and leisure travellers, and rooms provide space to work if needed. The rooms tend to be large and well equipped, but the hotels dispense with shared services such as swimming pools. A buffet breakfast is included in the price, while tea and coffee making facilities are provided in all rooms. Prices tend to be relatively fixed and not open to negotiation. As a rule they are quoted as being 'from...' rather than quoting a rack rate which can be discounted. These hotels are normally situated next to a pub-restaurant such as a Toby

Carvery or Harvester. Prices are quoted per room.

Info- *www.innkeeperslodge.com*
Tel- *0870 243 0500*

MACDONALD HOTELS

There are around 100 Macdonald hotels in the UK, often located in market towns or tourist destinations. Many also have good views and gardens. Each hotel has a distinctive appearance, and many offer good leisure facilities such as health clubs or swimming pools. Each has a bar and restaurant, and rooms are generally well equipped for business people. Rates vary depending on location and availability, but special rates are often available (for dinner B&B, romantic breaks, leisure breaks, etc).

Info- *www.macdonaldhotels.co.uk*
Tel- *0870 400 9090*

MARRIOTT

There are over 60 Marriott hotels in the UK, usually on prime sites in town and city centres. These tend to be well equipped hotels, many of which have swimming pools and fitness centres. All are equipped well for business travellers and business meetings. All have bars and restaurants offering refined evening dining. Some hotels allow dogs on request. Rates vary between hotels depending on location and availability, and special packages are often available.

Info- *www.marriott.co.uk*
Tel- *0800 221 222*

MARSTON

There are about 15 Marston Hotels in the UK, often situated in towns popular with tourists, such as York and Chester. Each hotel offers its own unique appeal, though the majority have swimming pools and leisure clubs, and some offer golf courses or tennis courts. All have bars and restaurants, some of which have AA rosettes. These hotels will appeal equally to business and leisure guests, and are well equipped to host business meetings. Rates vary between location, but discounted packages are often available for special breaks (including bridge breaks, fitness breaks, beauty breaks, etc).

Info- *www.marstonhotels.com*
Tel- *0845 130 0700*

MILLENNIUM HOTELS

See entry for Copthorne Hotels.

MILLHOUSE MOTELS

This is a chain of about 15 hotels, each of which is different and relatively small. They are generally located in smaller towns in England. Often they are alongside a Millhouse Inn, and they may be set in a garden or an attractive location.

Info- *www.millhouseinns.co.uk*
Tel- *0800 0838 8123*

MOAT HOUSE

There are over 40 Moat House Hotels in the UK, usually situated in or close to a major city. These tend to be large and well equipped hotels. Each has good meeting facilities and has at least 1 bar and a restaurant. All have some form of leisure facility, such as a swimming pool or fitness centre, and many have saunas or solariums. Rooms are generally provided with tea and coffee making facilities, and a complimentary newspaper is available to guests.

Info- *www.moathousehotels.com*
Tel- *01708 730 522*

NOVOTEL

This group has about 30 hotels in the UK, generally situated towards the centre of larger towns and cities. Many hotels have leisure facilities such as a swimming pool, and most have a brasserie-restaurant which is usually open from 0600-2400 every day, and a bar. The rooms are well equipped for business travellers, and generally have tea and coffee facilities in the rooms. All offer meeting rooms and facilities. Weekend breaks are often available.

Info- *www.novotel.com*
Tel- *0870 609 0961*

PREMIER LODGE

A chain of about 150 hotels which tend to be located in town centre or edge of town locations. These hotels have a consistent feel and are primarily aimed at frequent business and holiday travellers. The rooms tend to be large and well equipped, but the hotels have little by way of shared services such as swimming pools and fitness clubs. Tea and coffee making facilities are provided in all rooms. Prices tend not to be open to negotiation. As a rule prices are quoted as being 'from...' rather than quoting a rack rate which can be discounted. These hotels tend to be situated next to a bar-restaurant such as a 'Millers Kitchen', or a 'Chef and Brewer', where breakfast is available. Some Premier Lodges allow you to order food at the bar and then take it to your room to eat. Prices are quoted per room. A few hotels offer meeting facilities.

Info- www.premierlodge.com
Tel- 0870 201 0203

QUALITY INNS

See the entry for Choice Hotels.

RAMADA INNS

Ramada Jarvis offer about 70 hotels in the UK, which are often situated towards the centre of towns and cities. These tend to be well equipped and to be situated in long-established buildings with individual character. Many hotels have leisure clubs, swimming pools or gardens. All have bars and restaurants, and provide meeting facilities. These hotels will tend to appeal equally to business or leisure travellers. Rates vary depending on location and availability, and special rates are available for leisure breaks, etc.

Info- www.ramadajarvis.co.uk
Tel- 0845 730 3040

REGAL HOTELS

See the entry for Corus Hotels.

SHIRE HOTELS

Shire Hotels have 8 hotels in the UK. They are all individual and have a high standard of decor and facilities. Most have swimming pools and a health club. All have bars and a fine restaurant, some of which have AA Rosettes. These hotels are equally suited to business or leisure travellers, and all have good meeting facilities.

Info- www.shirehotels.co.uk
Tel- 0800 854290

ROOM AT THE INN

These are generally characterful inns located in popular market towns. All are located in England, southwest of a line drawn between Birmingham and London. Accommodation varies between locations, but generally is within a traditional inn, and there is always a bar and restaurant on the premises. Each location offers full breakfast facilities, and tea and coffee making facilities are generally available in rooms. Many hotels have meeting facilities, and dogs are welcome at some locations by arrangement.

Info- www.roomattheinn.co.uk
Tel- No central number

SLEEP INNS

See the entry for Choice Hotels.

THISTLE HOTELS

There are around 60 Thistle Hotels in the UK. Often, these are siutated in the heart of cities or near airports, and they tend to be large and well equipped. They are likely to appeal equally to people on business or pleasure. Many have swimming pools and some have leisure clubs. All have a bar and restaurant and offer a cooked breakfast. Rates vary depending on location, and several discounted package types tend to be available.

Info- www.thistlehotels.com
Tel- 0870 414 4141

TRAVEL INN

A chain of over 300 hotels which tend to be located near to major roads or the edges of towns. These hotels have a consistent feel, and are primarily aimed at frequent business travellers who need a room where they can work if needed. The rooms tend to be large and well equipped, but the hotels have few luxury shared services such as swimming pools and fitness clubs. Tea and coffee making facilities are provided in all rooms. Prices tend not to be open to negotiation. As a rule prices are quoted as being 'from...' rather than quoting a rack rate which can be discounted. These hotels are normally situated next to a pub-restaurant where breakfast is available. Prices are quoted per room, and many of these hotels offer meeting facilities.

Info- *www.travelinn.co.uk*
Tel- *0870 242 8000*

TRAVELODGE

A chain of over 200 hotels which tend to be located near to or at motorway service stations or on major roads. These hotels have a consistent feel and are primarily aimed at frequent business travellers who need a room where they can work if needed. The rooms tend to be large and well equipped, but the hotels dispense with shared services such as swimming pools. Tea and coffee-making facilities are provided in all rooms. Prices tend not to be open to negotiation. As a rule prices are quoted as being 'from...' rather than quoting a rack rate which can be discounted. These hotels are normally situated in motorway service areas where meals are available, or next to a Little Chef restaurant. Breakfast can be brought to your room door on request. Where these hotels are located on motorways, they can be found with the maximum of ease, but it can be difficult to go out for the evening. Prices are quoted per room, and some of these hotels offer meeting facilities. Dogs are usually allowed at these hotels but there is a charge per pet.

Info- *www.travelodge.co.uk*
Tel- *0870 0850 950*

VILLAGE HOTELS

Village Hotels is a brand of the De Vere hotel group who have over 40 hotels in the UK, often located in handsome buildings or with a peaceful setting. These hotels are generally well equipped with leisure facilities such as health clubs and swimming pools and many are sited near to golf courses and other attractions. They all have bars and restaurants, which offer a relaxing environment. Rooms are well equipped for business guests, but these hotels will appeal equally to people on business or pleasure. Prices vary depending on location and availability, and leisure breaks are available.

Info- *www.villagehotelsonline.co.uk*
Tel- *0870 606 3606*

WELCOME LODGE

There are only about 8 Welcome Lodges and these are sited at Welcome Break motorway service areas. They are well suited to business travellers who need to make a quick overnight stop, and who want to make use of the facilities offered by the service area. Rates are quoted per room, and these can accommodate 2 adults and 2 children. Prices tend not to be open to negotiation. As a rule prices are quoted as being 'from...' rather than quoting a rack rate which can be discounted. A complimentary newspaper is also provided for each room, and breakfast is available at the service area.

Info- *www.welcomebreak.co.uk*
Tel- *0800 731 4466*

Business Meeting Facilities

DAYS INN MEETING PLACE

These business meeting places are located at selected Welcome Break Service Stations; there are about 17 currently in operation. Meeting facilities for up to about 10 people are available. Services provided include fax, copying and AV facilities. Lunches are available whilst you work or at the nearby service station.

Tel- *0800 028 0400*

MOTO BUSINESS CENTRES

Moto business centres are available at selected Moto Service areas. At time of press there were about 5 of these, located at Cherwell Valley (M40), Reading, Heston and Leigh Delamere (all M4), and Birch (M62). These offer meeting rooms, catering, a lounge, washroom and showers, internet access and other services such as photocopying. If required, meeting rooms can be rented by the hour.

Info- *www.moto-way.com*
Tel- *0208 571 5721*

OTHERS

Most of the hotels listed on the preceding pages will offer good facilities for business meetings.

RESTAURANT MEETING CENTRES

Meeting facilities are avalable at some of the following restaurants - Beefeater, Brewer's Fayre, Brewsters, Out & Out, and TGIF. Many of these meeting centres have Travel Inns nearby and all can provide catering and special facilities to support your meeting. There are over 100 of these meeting centres available and a directory can be obtained at some of the above restaurants.

TOUCHBASE MEETING CENTRES

These are situated at a few selected Travel Inns and are open between 7am-7pm Monday to Friday. By mid 2003, there were meeting centres at Swindon, Mansfield and Hemel Hempstead, but it seems likely more will be added soon. They offer meeting rooms with good support and equipment such as projectors. They also offer hot desking capability with modem and ISDN connectivity, and a business lounge for informal meetings. There is a clear pricing system available on the website.

Info- *www.letstouchbase.co.uk*
Tel- *0870 243 3113*

Useful Numbers Nationwide

This section lists telephone numbers that drivers on the motorway might find useful.

AIRLINE FLIGHT BOOKING

Aer Lingus	0845 084 4444
Aeroflot	0207 355 2233
Air France	0845 359 1000
Air India	0207 495 7950
Air New Zealand	0800 028149
Alitalia	0870 544 8259
Austrian Airlines	0207 766 0300
American Airlines	0845 7789789
British Airways	0845 7733377
Cathay Pacific	0208 834 8800
Delta	0800 4144767
Easyjet	0870 6000000
Egyptair	0207 7342395
El Al	0207 957 4100
Emirates	0870 243 222
Iberia	0845 850 9000
Lufthansa	0208 750 3500
Malaysia Airlines	0207 3412000
Northwest	0870 074074
PIA Pakistan Airlines	0207 290 3600
Quantas	0208 846 0466
Royal Jordanian	0207 878 6400
Ryanair	0871 2460000
Singapore	0208 563 6767
United	0845 844477
USAirways	0207 484 2100
Virgin Atlantic	01293 747747

AIRPORTS ENQUIRIES

Aberdeen	023 80620021
Birmingham	0121 7677798
Cardiff	01446 711111
East Midlands	01332 852852
Edinburgh	0131 333 1000
Gatwick	0870 0002468
Glasgow	0141 8871111
Heathrow	0870 0000123
Inverness	01667 464 000
Leeds-Bradford	0113 250 9696
Liverpool	0870 750 8484
London City	020 7646 0088
Luton	01582 405100
Manchester	0161 489 3000
Newcastle	0191 286 0966
Southampton	023 80620021
Stansted	0870 0000303

ANIMAL RESCUE ORGANISATIONS

RSPCA	0870 5555999

CAR RENTAL COMPANIES

AVIS	0870 6060100
Budget	0870 01565656
Eurodrive	0800 0852524
Europcar	0870 6075000
Hertz	08708 448844
Sixt Kenning	0870 1555900
Thrifty	01494 751600

CAR RESCUE ORGANISATIONS

THE AA & RAC will offer help to non-members on the motorway for the price of membership plus an additional fee, otherwise the Police can arrange rescue from the motorway at your cost.

AA	0800 085 2721
Autonational	08459 500 999
Britannia Rescue	0800 591563
Green Flag	0800 3288772
Direct Line Rescue	0845 2461012
National Breakdown	0870 9024700
RAC	0800 0922222

COACH TRANSPORT

National Express	08705 808080

DIRECTORY ENQUIRIES

All calls charged at a premium rate apart from Talking Pages which is a business services directory.

Talking Pages	0800 600 900
118 888	118 888
Agent 119	118 119
BT	118 500
British Gas	118 411, 118 511
Orange	118 000
One Tel	118 111, 118 211
Opal Telecom	118 114
Share	118 499
Telegate	118 866
The Number	118 118

Welsh Speaking Svc	118 404
Yellow Pages	118 247
Yell	80248

Info- *Yell is a text message number. Text a query such as 'Vet Newcastle' to the above number for a response.*

EMERGENCIES

Ambulance	999
Coastguard	999
Fire Service	999
Police	999

FERRY COMPANIES

Brittany Ferries	08703 665 333
Caledonian MacBrayne	01475 650100
Color Line	+47 810 00 811
Condor	0845 345 2000
Hover travel	01983 811000
Hoverspeed	0870 240 8070
Irish ferries	08705 17 17 17
P&O European	0870 5202020
Red Funnel Isle of Wight	0870 4448898
DFDS Seaways	08705 333 000
SeaFrance	08705 711 711
Stena	08704 00 67 98
Swansea Cork	01792 456116
Wightlink	0870 582 7744

HOTEL BOOKING SERVICES

AA Booking Service	0870 505 0505
RAC Hotels	0870 603 9109
London Tourist Board	020 7604 2890

MEDICAL ADVICE

NHS Direct 0845 4647

Info- *Free online medical advice*

ROAD MAINTENANCE

Autolink 0845 796666

Info- *Maintains the M74*

Highways Agency 0845 7504030

Info- *Maintains many major roads and motorways in the UK.*

TRAVEL INFORMATION

AA Roadwatch 09003 401 100

Info- *About 60p per minute. From most mobiles dial 401100 instead of number above.*

RAC 0906 470 1740

Info- *About 60p per minute.*

TOURIST INFORMATION

CADW 029 20500200

Info- *Manages Welsh historic monuments.*

English Tourist Board 0308 8469000

Info- *Tourist advice, accommodation advice & booking service.*

English Heritage 0 870 333 1181

Info- *Manages many historic and protected sites in England.*

Historic Scotland 0131 6688600

Info- *Manages Scottish monuments.*

National Trust 0870 609 5380

Info- *Manages historic and protected sites in Britain.*

Scottish Tourist Board 0845 2255121

Info- *Tourist advice, accommodation advice & booking service.*

Welsh Tourist Board 0293 0499909

Info- *Tourist advice, accommodation advice & booking service.*

TRAIN ENQUIRIES & BOOKING

National Rail Enquiries 0845 748 4950

WINDSCREEN REPLACEMENT

Autoglass	0800 363636
RAC Auto Windscreens	0800 919700
Silver Shield	0800 880800

Driver's Reference Section

Personal Records

Insurance company		**Phone**
Name	....	....
Policy Number	....	
Car rescue company		
Name	....	....
Policy Number	....	

Regular garages used

....	....
....	....
....	....

Other useful numbers

....	....
....	....
....	....
....	....
....	....
....	....

Tyre pressures	**Low Load**	**Full Load**
Front	....	....
Rear	....	....

Motorway Breakdown Advice

1) PREVENT MORE DANGER

- Put on hazard warning lights and display a warning triangle if available.
- Move people away from the car if there is somewhere safer.
- Move the car to the left of the carriageway, or to the hard shoulder if there is one. This is to minimise the chance of a collision, but you should only do this if it does not put anyone in danger.

2) CALL FOR HELP

- The next step is to call for help. If the car is in a very dangerous position or likely to cause major disruption, it may be appropriate to call the local Police for help. You can do this by phoning directory enquiries and asking for the number of the Police at the nearest town. Otherwise call a rescue organisation. The numbers in this guide may help.

3) LONE DRIVERS/WOMEN DRIVERS

- If you feel in danger you should stay in the car as much as possible and wait for help to arrive.
- Drivers should only open their car door if they feel safe.
- Women drivers are advised to carry a mobile telephone and advise any rescue agency they are alone.

What to do after an Accident

1) PREVENT MORE DANGER

- Put on hazard warning lights, and use any warning triangles.
- Move people away from danger if you will not make their injuries worse. In some instances people may be safer remaining in the car.
- Make sure no-one smokes near the scene, and be aware of the risk of fire from cars that have been damaged.
- Beware of hazardous materials that may have spilled from lorries.

2) ORGANISE THE HELPERS AVAILABLE

- If there are several people around make sure who is doing what. You may need people to 1) Call emergency services 2) Look after the injured 3) Prevent further accidents and manage traffic.

3) CALL THE EMERGENCY SERVICES IF NEEDED

- You must know your location first. There are roadside markers every 100 metres on the motorway to help you.

4) DEAL WITH THE INJURED

- If you are not confident in first aid, see if anyone else is!
- Remember- Quick and effective help may save lives!
- If people are trapped or appear to have neck or back injuries, they should not be moved unless they are in great danger. Likewise do not try to remove the helmets of motorbike riders unless it is absolutely essential.
- If people are likely to need surgery make sure they don't eat or drink anything before medical help arrives.

5) ARE PEOPLE UNCONSCIOUS?

- First check their airways to see they are not blocked by food etc. Next check to see if they are breathing. If not, you should attempt the ' Kiss of Life', but be careful of possible neck injuries. Next check circulation. Is their heart beating?. If not you should attempt heart massage (firm pressure in the centre of the chest about once every 3 seconds).

ARE PEOPLE BLEEDING?.

- Put light pressure on wounds to prevent bleeding, but try to keep wounds clean. Where possible, raise limbs that are bleeding, to reduce the blood loss. Apply bandages if available.

BURNS

- Try to cool the burn with a clean & harmless liquid, and then try to keep the burn clean.

SHOCK

- People at accidents are often in shock. Make sure people are warm and comfortable. Try to get them to sit and relax if appropriate. Reassure them and keep a watchful eye on them, in case it should get worse.

6) IF THERE ARE NO INJURIES, OR THEY HAVE BEEN DEALT WITH

- If there are no injuries you should first consider whether you want the police to attend (but they are not obliged to do so).
- Next you need to decide if you wish to move the the vehicles involved so traffic can pass. You may not want to do this if the Police are due soon, or you want to take a few photographs first. Make sure you are safe if moving vehicles by hand.

6) RECORD WHAT HAPPENED

- Once any injuries have been dealt with, you will want to gather witnesses and record what happened. If the police are on scene they will co-ordinate most of this but you may be able to help.
- The accident record pages that follow will prompt you for the questions you need to answer.

7) DRIVING ON

- Before driving on be aware you may have some degree of shock. You may wish to find somewhere calm to sit and relax for a while. Consider getting a non-alcoholic drink somewhere, and avoid another accident!

Accident Record

Date of accident		Time	
Road conditions & visibility		Your speed	
Lighting conditions		Speed limit	
Location of accident			
Details of others involved (1)			
Car registration number			
Car type and colour			
Driver's name, address & tel. no.			
Names or number of others in car			
Insurance company name & tel. no.			
Policyholder name & policy number			
Details of others involved (2)			
Car registration number			
Car type and colour			
Driver's name, address & tel. no.			
Names or number of others in car			
Insurance company name & tel. no.			
Policyholder name & policy number			

Witness names and addresses

Sketch of accident & road layout

Accident Record

Date of accident		Time	
Road conditions & visibility		Your speed	
Lighting conditions		Speed limit	
Location of accident			

Details of others involved (1)	
Car registration number	
Car type and colour	
Driver's name, address & tel. no.	
Names or number of others in car	
Insurance company name & tel. no.	
Policyholder name & policy number	
Details of others involved (2)	
Car registration number	
Car type and colour	
Driver's name, address & tel. no.	
Names or number of others in car	
Insurance company name & tel. no.	
Policyholder name & policy number	

Witness names and addresses

Sketch of accident & road layout

Your Notes

Your Notes